Wallace-Homestead

❖ PRICE GUIDE TO ❖

Pattern & Glass

ELEVENTH EDITION

Edited by Dori Miles
Robert W. Miller

Contents

———

The editors wish to thank the Houston Antique Museum in Chattanooga, Tennessee, for their invaluable assistance.

Cover photographs by Perry L. Struse, Jr. Items pictured appear through the courtesy of Kenilworth Antiques and Valley Antiques, West Des Moines, Iowa
Cover design: Geri Wolfe Boesen
Interior layout: Anthony Jacobson

Other photography: Tom Needham, Panama City Beach, Florida; Marshall Thurman, Knoxville, Tennessee; and John Shuman III, Pottsdown, Pennsylvania

ISBN 0-87069-442-1
Library of Congress Catalog Card Number 84-050515

Copyright © 1986
Wallace-Homestead Book Company
10 9 8 7 6 5 4

Published by

Wallace-Homestead Book Company
201 King of Prussia Road
Radnor, Pennsylvania 19089

One of the ABC PUBLISHING 🔵 Companies

Introduction

Although pressed glass was seen in Egypt during the Eighteenth Dynasty (1412-1375 B. C.) in the form of small, press-molded cups and amulets, and the same techniques used by the Egyptians were generally followed down through the ages, most historians credit the Americans for developing the art of pressing glass.

Deming Jarves's founding of the Boston and Sandwich Glass Company at Sandwich, Massachusetts, in 1825 and the invention of a mechanical means for producing press-molded glass articles in the 1820 s were probably the most significant events in the development of the American glass industry in the nineteenth century. However, an unfortunate fire on December 17, 1836, which destroyed much of the United States Patent Office and its records, left the patent records for the first half of the nineteenth century somewhat incomplete; therefore, the controversy of who was first in pattern glass, and with what, still rages.

On December 6, 1845, Joseph Magoun of the New England Glass Company, Cambridge, Massachusetts, patented the first real improvement in a manually operated glass press. In layman's language, his innovation embodied a sliding frame capable of receiving the cap plate of molds of various sizes and design.

The O'Hara Glass Company's William O. Davis registered a patent on January 31, 1854, for the improvement of a glass press that arranged various parts so that little or no pressure would be placed on the framework of the press. This assured that the pressure from the various parts was always central and vertical.

Ten years later, on March 29, 1864, Charles Ballinger and Frederick McKee patented a steam-operated glass press, and, on May 9, 1871, William C. King of Pittsburgh patented his idea for a revolving, block-type press, a refinement of a similar revolving mold patented on June 8, 1869, by Robert D. Haines of Boston.

King's improvement allowed production to be stepped up considerably.

Henry J. Leasure's air-cooled glass press, patented on March 5, 1872, was considered one of the milestones in the industry. This Wheeling, West Virginia, gentleman filed a joint patent with James S. Gill on December 4, 1866, that covered a means of water-cooling the plunger of a glass press.

There are three methods of pressing glass: block molding, the simplest; split molding, where the mold is made up of two or more parts; and font molding, whereby each article is made absolutely identical in form and dimension.

For those who could not afford expensive, hand-cut pieces, pressed glass, which gave way to pattern glass with a clear, rather than a stippled background, conferred a great benefit of beauty and utility. This inexpensive glass for everybody revolutionized the glass industry in America.

Pattern glass reproductions first caused problems in the 1920s when the Turkey jam jar was reproduced in clear as well as colored glass. It was imported from Czechoslovakia. Later, in 1933 or 1934, a tumbler was reproduced in the Horn of Plenty pattern. Since then literally millions of pieces of pattern glass have been reproduced in such popular patterns as U. S. Coin, Daisy and Button, Lion, Ruby Thumbprint, Three Face, and Westward Ho, to mention just a few. For an in-depth look at all types of reproductions, read Dorothy Hammond's book, *Confusing Collectibles*.

It's easy to say, "Anyone can tell the difference!" But that is not true if you're a beginning collector or someone who refuses to read about pattern glass and study the various patterns.

Expert collectors are not born that way. They develop their expertise by reading, actually handling the "old" and the "new," and buying from reputable and knowledgeable dealers. Study this edition of the *Wallace-Homestead Price Guide to Pattern Glass*. Notice that wherever possible we've indicated which patterns and which particular pieces are being reproduced. Be alert! Reproductions are worth only a fraction of the value of the real thing.

Many rare and superb examples of pattern glass can be seen at various museums throughout the country. The Houston Antique Museum, Chattanooga, Tennessee, houses a fine collection. We highly recommend the enriching experience of a museum visit to the beginner and the expert collector, alike.

How To Use This Guide

Here's the new Eleventh Edition of the *Wallace-Homestead Price Guide to Pattern Glass!* We've added **117 new patterns, thousands of new items,** and **computed all of the prices** to bring them in line with those being paid in the pattern glass field as we go to press. The ever-popular "Guide to Pattern Glass with Duplicate Names" section is larger than ever, with **more than 500 new listings!** We continue to list duplicate names whether they are in "favor" or not, because many have told us how helpful it is. We feel that every documented name we can list is bound to help someone trace a particular pattern back to its beginnings.

We strive to make all of the information in this guide as accurate as possible, but always appreciate the "updates" furnished by knowledgeable readers over the years. Research is an ongoing job for each edition, and we are extremely grateful to those who help make our task easier and the book more factual.

The *Wallace-Homestead Price Guide to Pattern Glass* is based on what can be confirmed, not on conjecture or guesswork. We have not given names to particular pieces of glass, nor will we ever do so.

From the very first edition of this book, we established two important features:

clear photographs and the **two-price system.** We feel that inexpensive line drawings don't show enough detail and are virtually worthless for determining the identity of patterns of great similarity. We give you a two-price listing because many factors determine value. It's not just a question of adding or subtracting 20 to 25 percent from a single posted price. You must also consider geographical area and the scarcity, demand, and condition of the item. The majority of private collectors, qualified dealers, auction houses, and show operators agree with the principles behind our two-price system. They find such pricing soundly versatile and practical.

Remember that all editions of the *Wallace-Homestead Price Guide to Pattern Glass* are meant to be used as buyers' guides. Purchasing pattern glass on the open market is one thing; buying it from a dealer is quite another. Use the information in this book as a *guide* to evaluating and combine it with good common sense when making a purchase.

Thank you for buying what we believe is the best and most informative price guide to pattern glass on the market! While every effort has been made to avoid them, the editors and publishers cannot be held responsible for errors in typography or in judgment as applied to prices.

Guide to Pattern Glass with Duplicate Names

Acme—see Butterfly with Spray;
  also see Panelled Cable
Acorn—see Willow Oak
Adonis—see Washboard
Akron Block—see Richmond
Alaska—see Polar Bear
Albany—see Anthemion
Aldine—see Beaded Ellipse
Alexis—see Priscilla
Alfa—see Rexford
Alhambra—see Wigwam
Amberette—see Klondike
America—see Swirl and Diamond
Andes—see Beaded Tulip
Arcadia—see Thistleblow
Archaic Gothic—see Beaded Arch
Arctic—see Polar Bear
Argent—see Rope Bands
Ashland—see Snowdrop
Atlanta—see Square Lion Head;
  also see Royal Crystal
Austrian—see Fine Cut Medallion

Bagware—see Heavy Finecut
Ball—see Notched Bar
Ball and Claw—see Crossed Fern
Ball and Swirl—see Ray; also see Lutz
Ball and Swirl Band—see Ball and
  Swirl; Tiffin
Bamboo—see Bamboo Edge;
  also see Pioneer's No. 15
Banded Buckle—see Buckle
Banded Paling—see Paling
Banner—see Floral Oval
Bar—see Richmond
Bars and Buttons—see Richmond
Bead and Bar Medallion—see Aegis
Beaded Arch Panels—see Beaded Arch
Beaded Bull's Eye and Drape—see Alabama
Beaded Jewel—see Lacy Dewdrop
Beaded Star—see Shimmering Star
Bean—see Egg in Sand
Bearded Man—see Queen Anne
Bearded Prophet—see Bearded Head
Beatty Rib—see Ribbed Opal
Beaumont Buzz Star—see Buzz Star
Bedford Line No. 1000—see The Bedford
Berkeley—see Blocked Arches
Berry Spray—see Grape Bunch
Bevelled Diamond and Star—see Diamond
  Prisms

Big Block—see Henrietta
Blackberry and Grape—see Loganberry
  and Grape
Blazing Pinwheels—see Shoshone
Block and Palm—see Eighteen-Ninety
Block and Pleat—see Pentagon,
Block and Ring—see Regal Block
Block with Stars—see Hanover
Blockade—see Diamond Block with Fans
Blockhouse—see Hanover
Bluebird—see Bird and Strawberry
Bone Stem—see King's 500
Boswell—see Seashell
Bosworth—see Star Band
Boylan—see Rexford
Bradford Blackberry—see Bradford Grape
Brazil—see Panelled Daisy
Brazillian—see Brazilian
Breton—see Cat's Eye
Bright Star—see Bethlehem Star
Brilliant—see Double Spear;
  also see Stars and Stripes
Broughton—see Pattee Cross
Bryce—see Banded Buckle
Buckle and Diamond—see Buckle with
  Diamond Band
Bull's Eye and Loop—see Loop and Moose Eye
Button and Star Panel—see Rainbow
Button Arches—see Cane Insert
Buttressed Loop—see Buttressed Arch

Caledonia—see Cannonball Pinwheel
California—see Beaded Grape
Cameo—see Ceres; also see Classic Medallion
Canadian "Crown"—see Notched Bar
Canadian Flange—see Beaded Flange
Candlewick—see Banded Raindrops
Candy Ribbon—see Ribbon Candy
Cane and Star Medallion—see The States
Cane Column—see Panelled Cane
Centennial—see Liberty Bell
Centennial Shield—see American Shield
Chain Lightning—see Lightning
Challinor No. 313—see Challinor Tree of Life
Challinor Thumbprint—see Barrelled
  Thumbprint
Cherry Thumbprints—see Panelled Cherry
Cherry with Cable—see Panelled Cherry
Chimo—see Oneata
Chippendale—see Starlyte

Cincinnati—see Honeycomb
Clear Lion Head—see Square Lion Head
Clear Panels with Cord Bands—see Rope Bands
Cobb—see Zipper
Colonial—see Starlyte
Colonial with Garland—see Fern Garland
Colorado—see Lacy Medallion
Colossus—see Lacy Spiral
Columbia—see Church Windows;
  also see Heart with Thumbprint
Column Block—see Panel and Star
Comet—see Draped Fan
Compact—see Snail
Concave—see Mirror
Concaved Almond—see Arched Ovals
Co-op's No. 190—see Regal Block
Coral—see Fishscale
Corona—see Sunk Honeycomb
Crescent and Fan—see Starred Scroll
Crosby—see Buckingham
Crossbar—see Bevelled Diagonal Block
Crossroads—see Ashman
Crow-Foot—see Yale
Crown Jewels—see Chandelier
Crystal—see Madison
Crystal Anniversary—see Crystal Wedding
Crystal Ball—see Eye-Winker
Crystal Jewel, Daisy—see Lacy Daisy,
  Westmoreland's
Cube with Double Fan—see Divided Block
  with Sunburst, Variant
Cube with Fan—see Pineapple and Fan
Cut Log—see Cat's-Eye and Block

D and M 30—see Duncan No. 30
Daisy—see Thousand Eye
Daisy and Button, Almond Band—see Clio
Daisy and Cube—see Stars and Bars
Daisy in Oval Panels—see Bull's Eye and Fan
Daisy in Panel—see Two Panel
Darling Grape—see Late Panelled Grape
Delta—see Panelled Thistle
Derby—see Pleat and Panel
Dewdrop—see Hobnail
Dewdrop and Fan—see Beaded Fan
Dewdrops with Flowers—see Nova Scotia
  Starflower
Dewey—see Spanish-American
Diagonal Bead Bands—see Fancy Diamonds
Diamond Bar—see Lattice
Diamond Concave—see Diamond Thumbprint
Diamond, Fan and Leaf—see Eighteen-Ninety
Diamond Flute—see Flamboyant
Diamond Horseshoe—see Aurora
Diamond Medallion—see Grand
Diamond with Diamond Point—see English

Diamonds with Double Fan—see Hobbs
  Diamond and Sunburst
Divided Star—see Orante Star
Dixie—see Northwood's Near-Cut
Dog and Pail—see Bulldog with Hat
Dog with Hat—see Bulldog with Hat
Dogwood—see Art Novo
Doll's Eye—see Memphis
Dolly Madison—see Jefferson's No. 271
Doric—see Feather; also see Indiana
Dot—see Beaded Oval and Scroll;
  also see Stippled Forget-Me-Not
Double Arch—see Interlocking Crescents
Double Icicle—see Smooth Diamond
Double Loop—see Ribbon Candy
Double Prism—see Heck
Double Wedding Lamp—see Wedding Lamp
Doyle No. 76—see Triple Triangle
Draped Red Top—see Victoria, Riverside
Draped Top—see Victoria
Dunkirk's—see Starlyte
Dynast—see Radiant
D and M 30—see Duncan No. 30
Daisy—see Thousand Eye
Daisy and Button, Almond Band—see Clio
Daisy and Cube—see Stars and Bars
Daisy in Oval Panels—see Bull's Eye and Fan
Daisy in Panel—see Two Panel
Darling Grape—see Late Panelled Grape
Delta—see Panelled Thistle
Derby—see Pleat and Panel
Dewdrop—see Hobnail
Dewdrop and Fan—see Beaded Fan
Dewdrops with Flowers—see Nova Scotia
  Starflower
Dewey—see Spanish-American
Diagonal Bead Bands—see Fancy Diamonds
Diamond Bar—see Lattice
Diamond Concave—see Diamond Thumbprint
Diamond, Fan and Leaf—see Eighteen-Ninety
Diamond Flute—see Flamboyant
Diamond Horseshoe—see Aurora
Diamond Medallion—see Grand
Diamond with Diamond Point—see English
Diamonds with Double Fan—see Hobbs
  Diamond and Sunburst
Divided Star—see Orante Star
Dixie—see Northwood's Near-Cut
Dog and Pail—see Bulldog with Hat
Dog with Hat—see Bulldog with Hat
Dogwood—see Art Novo
Doll's Eye—see Memphis
Dolly Madison—see Jefferson's No. 271
Doric—see Feather, also see Indiana
Dot—see Beaded Oval and Scroll;
  also see Stippled Forget-Me-Not

Double Arch—see Interlocking Crescents
Double Icicle—see Smooth Diamond
Double Loop—see Ribbon Candy
Double Prism—see Heck
Double Wedding Lamp—see Wedding Lamp
Doyle No. 76—see Triple Triangle
Draped Red Top—see Victoria, Riverside
Draped Top—see Victoria
Dunkirk's—see Starlyte
Dynast—see Radiant

Early Diamond—see Smooth Diamond
Early Heart—see Heart
Eclipse—see Panelled Cosmos
Eighteen-Ninety—see Block and Palm
Elite—see Pillow and Sunburst
English Hobnail Cross—see Klondike
Enigma—see Wyoming
Esther—see Zanesville
Etruria—see Halley's Comet
Euclid—see Rexford
Excelsior—see Giant Bull's-Eye

Fairfax Strawberry—see Strawberry
Fan and Flute—see Millard
Fancy Diamonds—see Three-in-One
Feather and Block—see Plume and Block
Feathered Medallion—see Georgia Belle
Fernland—see Snowflake
Figure Eight—see Ribbon Candy
Finecut Four Panel—see Heavy Finecut
Finger Print—see Almond Thumbprint
Fisheye—see Torpedo
Flamingo—see Frosted Stork
Flat Panel—see Pleating
Fleur-de-Lis and Tassel—see Fleur-de-Lis
  and Drape
Flora—see Opposing Pyramids
Floradora—see Bohemian
Florida—see Emerald Green Herringbone,
  also see Sunken Primrose
Floradora—see Bohemian
Flower and Panel—see Stylized Flower
Flower Flange—see Dewey
Flower Medallion—see Panelled Cosmos
Flower Panelled Cane—see Cane Column
Flowered Scroll—see Duncan 2000
Flute and Cane—see Huckabee
Fluted Diamond Point—see Panelled Sawtooth
Flying Robin—see Hummingbird
Forest Ware—see Ivy-in-Snow
45 Colonis—see Colonis
Four Petal Flower—see Delaware
Fringed Drape—see Crescent
Frost Flower—see Twinkle Star
Frosted—see Stippled Band
Frosted Fleur-de-Lis—see Stippled Fleur de Lis

Frosted Leaf and Basketweave—see Basket
  Leaf with Leaf
Frosted Lion—see Lion
Frosted Magnolia—see Water Lily
Frosted Waffle—see Hidalgo

Garter Band—see Hobnail Band
Gem—see Nailhead
Geneva—see Massachusetts
Georgia—see Peacock Feather
Gillinder's Westmoreland—see Westmoreland
Gloria—see Pattee Cross
Goddess of Liberty—see Actress; also see Ceres
Gold Rose—see American Beauty
Golden Agate—see Holly Amber
Golden Jewel—see Blazing Cornucopia
Gothic—see Spearpoint Band
Grape Jug—see Late Panelled Grape
Grated Ribbon—see Beaded Panels
Grecian—see Diamond Mirror
Greek Key and Wedding Ring—see Double
  Greek Key
Greensburg Pillows—see Greensburg's 130
Gridley—see Spanish-American
Guardian Angel—see Cupid and Venus

Haley's Comet—see Halley's Comet
Heart Plume—see Marlboro
Hearts and Spades—see Medallion
Hearts of Loch Haven—see Shuttle
Heavy Panelled Finecut—see Heavy Finecut
Heavy Panelled Grape—see Panelled Grape
Herringbone Rib—see Cactus
Hexagon Block—see Henrietta;
  also see Hexagonal Bull's Eye
Hinoto—see Diamond Point with Panels
Historic American—see Capitol Building
Hobnail with Bars—see Hobnail in
  Big Diamonds
Hobstar and Feather—see Fern Burst
Holbrook—see Pineapple and Fan
Hops Band—see Maple
Horseshoe—see Good Luck
Huckabee—see Flute and Cane
Huckel—see Feather Duster

Iceberg—see Polar Bear
Ida—see Sheraton
Idaho—see Snail
Idyll—see Jefferson's 251
Imitation-Cut Atlanta—see Atlanta, Late
Imperial—see Jewelled Moon and Star
Indian Tree—see Barley
Indiana—see Cord Drapery;
  also see Eight-O-Eight
Inverted Diamond Point—see Umbilicated
  Sawtooth
Inverted Prism—see Masonic

7

Inverted Sawtooth—see Umbilicated Sawtooth
Inverted Thistle—see Late Thistle
Inverted Thumbprint with Daisy Band—see
  Honeycomb with Flower Rim
Iris—see Wild Bouquet
Irish Column—see Broken Column
Isis—see Jubilee

Japanese—see Grace
Jeanette—see Flamboyant
Jenkins No. 809—see Grape Jug
Jersey Swirl—see Swirl
Jewel—see Lacy Medallion
Jewel and Crescent—see Tennessee
Jewel Band—see Scalloped Tape
Jewelled Diamond and Fan—see Tacoma
Jewelled Vermont—see Honeycomb with
  Flower Rim
Job's Tears—see Art
Joyce—see Capital

Kamoni—see Balder
Kansas—see Jewel and Dewdrop
King's Comet—see King's 500
Kirkland—see Sunk Daisy
Klondyke—see Fluted Scrolls
Knobby Bull's Eye—see Cromwell

La France—see American Beauty
Lacy Daisy—see U. S. Daisy
Lacy Medallion—see Colorado
Ladders—see Panelled Pleat
Ladders and Diamond with Star—
  see Ornate Star
Ladies Medallion—see "Wild Rose and
  Ladies" Lamp
Large Stippled Chain—see Stippled Chain
Late Panelled Grape—see Grape Jug
Late Westmoreland—see Westmoreland,
  Westmoreland's
Laverne—see Star in Honeycomb
Lawrence—see Bull's Eye
Leaf—see Maple Leaf
Leaf and Fan—see Murano
Leaf and Star—see Tobin
Leaf Medallion—see The Regent
Lily—see Sunflower
Lincoln Sweetheart—see Heart
Lion's Leg—see Alaska
Little Ladders—see Paris
Locket—see Northwood's Near-Cut
Locust—see Grasshopper with Insect
London—see Picket
Long Spear—see Grasshopper with Insect
Loop and Jewel—see Jewel and Festoon
Loop and Pillar—see Michigan
Loop with Stippled Panels—see Texas
Looped Cord—see Beaded Chain
Lotus Serpent—see Garden of Eden

Lucerne—see Lucere
McKee's Gaines—see Hairpin
Magic—see Rosette
Magnolia—see Water Lily
Maiden Blush—see Banded Portland
Majestic—see Divided Block with
  Sunburst, Variant
Maltese—see Jacob's Ladder
Maple—see Hop's Band
Marriage Lamp—see Wedding Lamp
Medallion—see Ceres, also see Gibson girl
Mellor—see Block and Circle
Menagerie—see Little Owl
Midway—see Pillow Encircled
Millard's Atlanta—see Atlanta, Late
Millard's Pathfinder—see Pathfinder, Late
Mirror—see Galloway
Mitered Diamond—see Sunken Buttons
Mitred Diamond Points—see Mitred Bars
Muchness—see Minnesota

No. 11—see Thousand Eye
No. 103—see Thousand Eye
No. 261—see Imperial
No. 321—see Klondike
No. 339—see Continental
Nautilus—see Argonaut Shell
Nebraska—see Mismarc Star
Neptune—see Queen Anne
Nettle Apple Blossom—see Apple Blossom
New Century—see Delaware
New Jersey—see Loops and Drops
New Westmoreland—see Westmoreland,
  Westmoreland's
Notched Rib—see Broken Column
North Pole—see Polar Bear
Northwood No. 12—see Northwood's Near-Cut
N. P. L.—see Pressed Leaf
Nova Scotia Starflower—see Dewdrop
  and Flower
Nursery Rhyme—see Nursery Tales

Oak Leaf—see Willow Oak
Oaken Bucket—see Wooden Pail
O'Hara—see Loop
Old Acorn—see Chestnut Oak
Old Man—see Queen Anne
Old Man of the Woods—see Queen Anne
Omnibus—see Pathfinder, Late
101—see One-Hundred-and-One
Open Basketweave—see Open Plaid
Oregon—see Beaded Loop
Orient—see Buckle with Star
Oriental—see Palm Leaf
Orion—see Cathedral
Orion Inverted Thumbprint—see Orion
  Thumbprint
Outdoor—see Drinking Scene on Mug
Owl in Fan—see Parrot

Paisley—see Blazing Cornucopia
Palm and Scroll—see Missouri
Panelled Agave—see Cactus
Panelled Cane—see Cane Column
Panelled Daisy and Button—see Queen
Panelled Diamond and Fine Cut—see Carmen
Panelled Dogwood—see Art Novo
Panelled Flowers—see Stylized Flowers
Panelled Iris—see Thistleblow
Panelled Stippled Bowl—see Late Diamond
  Point Band
Paris—see Star and Pillar
Parrot—see King's 500
Parthenon—see Egyptian
Peerless—see Lady Hamilton
Pennsylvania—see Balder; also see Hand
Persian—see Regal Block
Pert—see Ribbed Forget-Me-Not
Picket Fence—see Picket
Pilgrim—see Divided Block with Sunburst,
  Variant
Pillar—see Flat Diamond
Pimlico—see King's Breastplate
Pineapple Stem—see Pavonia
Pins and Bells—see Nova Scotia Tassel
  and Crest
Pinwheel—see Cannonball Pinwheel
Pittsburgh—Tree of Life—see Tree of
  Life with Hand
Plaid—see Open Plaid
Plain Smocking—see Smocking
Plain Tulip—see Tulip
Pleat and Tuck—see Washboard
Pointed Panel Daisy and Button—see Queen
Pointed Thumbprint—see Almond Thumbprint
Potted Plant—see Flower Pot
Prayer Rug—see Good Luck
Pressed Leaf Band—see Hops Band
Pretty Band—see Flower and Quill
Pride—see Leaf and Dart
Prism and Block Band—see Regal Block
Prism and Finecut—see Huckabee
Prism Arc—see X-Log
Prism with Double Block—see Masonic
Prison Windows—see Indiana
Prosperity—see Ferris Wheel
Puffed Bands—see Snow Band
Pygmy—see Torpedo

Quantico—see Dewdrop and Flowers;
  also see Nova Scotia Starflower
Question Mark—see Oval Loop
Quihote—see Harvard
Quixote—see Harvard

Radiant Daisy—see Slewed Horseshoe
Radiant Daisy and Button—see Jubilee
Radiant Union Stopper's—see Sawtooth
  Honeycomb

Ramsey Grape—see Nova Scotia Grape
  and Vine
Raspberry and Grape—see Loganberry
  and Grape
Rayed Divided Diamond Heart—see Marlboro
Rayed Pineapple—see Marlboro
Regal—see Panelled Forget-Me-Not
Reardon—see Chain Thumbprint
Rib—see U.S. Rib
Ribbed Ellipse—see Admiral
Ribbed Pineapple—see Prism and Flattened
  Sawtooth
Ribbed Sawtooth—see File
Ripple Band—see Ripple
Riverside Ladies—see "Wild Rose and
  Ladies" Lamp
Rochelle—see Princess Feather
Roman Cross—see Crossed Block
Rose and Sunbursts—see American Beauty
Rose Garland—see Garland of Roses
Rosetta—see Circular Saw
Rosette Medallion—see Feather Duster
Roughneck—see Paris
Royal Lady—see Royal
Ruby Star—see O'Hara Diamond
Russian—see Fine Cut and Panel

Sampson—see Teardrop and Tassel
Sanborn—see Iron Kettle
Sandwich Loop—see Hairpin
Santa Claus—see Queen Anne
Sawtooth and Star—see O'Hara Diamond
Sawtooth Band—see Amazon
Scalloped Daisy, Red Top—see Button Arches
Scalloped Diamond Point—see Diamond
  Point Band
Scalloped Flower Band—see Fan Band
Scalloped Loop—see Yoked Loop
Scalloped Six-Point—see Duncan No. 30
Sedan—see Panelled Star and Button
Seneca Loop—see Loop
Serenade Mug—see Troubadour Mug
Sequoia—see Heavy Finecut
Serrated Block and Loop—see Sawtooth
  Honeycomb
Shell—see Fan with Diamond
Shell and Scroll—see Geneva
Shell and Spike—see Shell and Tassel
Shield—see Bullet Emblem
Shields—see Tape Measure
Skilton—see Oregon
Smocking Bands—see Double Beetle Band
Solar—see Feather Swirl
Spades—see Medallion
Spanish-American—see Gridley Pitcher
Sparton—see Barred Star
Spearhead—see Squared Star

9

Spector Block—see Westmoreland
Sprig—see Barley; also see Ribbed Palm
Square and Diamond Bands—see Home
Square and Dot—see Spirea Band
Squared Dot—see Spirea Band
Squared Sunburst—see Sunburst
Star and Oval—see Lens and Star
Star Burst—see Bethlehem Star
Star Flower Band—see Stippled Star
  Flower
Star Galaxy—see Effulgent Star
Star Medallion—see Amelia
Star of David—see King's Breastplate
Starlight—see Twinkle Star
Starred Jewel—see Louise
Stars and Bars—see Star and Pillar
Stemless Daisy—see Cosmos
Stippled—see Maine
Stippled Diamond—see Stippled
  Forget-Me-Knot
Stippled Fuchsia—see Fuchsia
Stippled Leaf and Flower with Moth—see
  Stippled Leaf and Flower
Stippled Panelled Flowers—see Maine
Stippled Scroll—see Scroll
Stippled Star Flower, Banded—see
  Stippled Star Flower
Stippled Star Variant—see Stippled Sandbur
Strawberry—see Fairfax Strawberry
Striped Dewdrop—see Panelled Dewdrop
Sultan—see Curtain; also see Wild Rose
  with Scrolling
Sun and Star—see Priscilla
Sunburst—see Duncan No. 40; also see
  Flattened Diamond and Sunburst
Sunburst Medallion—see Daisy Medallion
Sunburst Rosette—see Frosted Medallion
Sunflower and Leaf—see Fern Burst
Swan with Mesh—see Swan
Swirl—see Jersey Swirl
Swirl and Ball, Ray—see Ball and Swirl
Swirl and Diamond—see America
Swirl with Beaded Band—see Nova Scotia
  Buttons and Bows
Swiss—see Aegis

Teardrop and Thumbprint—see Teardrop
Teardrops and Diamond Block—see Art
Teepee—see Wigwam
Theatrical—see Actress
The Kitchen Stove—see Jersey
The Mosaic—see Daisy and Bluebell
Thistle—see Willow Oak
Thousand Eye—see Ancestral
Threaded—see Threading
Three Graces—see Three Face

Three Sisters—see Three Face
Three Stories—see Pentagon
Thumbprint with Spearhead—see Cat's Eye
Tiffany—see Medallion Sunburst
Togo—see Bismarc Star
Tong—see Excelsior Variant
Tooth and Claw—see Esther
Trilby—see Valentine
Triple Bar—see Scalloped Prism
Triple X—see Tacoma
Trump—see Mitered Prisms
Tulip—see Tulips with Sawtooth
Tulip Petals—see Church Windows

U. S. A.—see Minnesota
U. S. Columbia—see Interlocking Crescents
U. S. Optic—see Optic
U. S. Peacock—see Slewed Horseshoe
U. S. Whirligig—see Buzz Star
Utah—see Twinkle Star

Valencia Waffle—see Block and Star
Venus—see Jewel and Festoon
Vera—see Fagot
Vermont—see Honeycomb with Flower Rim
Vernon—see Honeycomb
Victor—see Shell and Tassel; also see Shoshone
Victory—see Paris
Viking—see Bearded Head
Vine—see Falling Leaves
Virginia—see Banded Portland

Water Lily—see Frosted Magnolia;
  also see Rose Point Band
Western Star—see Georgia Belle
Westmoreland No. 920—see Sharp Sunburst
  and File
Wheat—see Panelled Wheat
Whitton—see Heavy Gothic
Wild Rose—see Single Rose
Winona—see Barred Hobnail
Wisconsin—see Beaded Dewdrop
Wish Bone—see Interlocked Hearts
With Stippled Leaf—see Stars and Bars
With the Band, called Star Flower—
  see Stippled Star Flower
Wycliff—see Scroll with Star

X-Bull's Eye—see The Summit

Yale—see Fan Band

Zenith Block—see Plaid
Zephyr—see Pressed Diamond
Zipper Cross—see Paris
Zippered Spearpoint—see Helene

Pattern Glass from A to Z

Aberdeen

Aberdeen

Maker unknown, c. early 1870s. Clear, nonflint.

Butter dish, covered	$ 37-46
Compote, open	20-25
Creamer, applied handle.	37-43
Egg cup	23-31
Goblet (ill.)	18-24
Pitcher, water, applied handle	48-56
Sauce, flat.	9-14
Sugar bowl, open, ...	25-30

Acanthus Scroll

U. S. Glass Company #15030 (Ripley), c. 1896. Clear, nonflint

Butter dish, covered	$ 37-43
Cake stand	27-36
Creamer.	36-44
Pitcher	38-45
Salt/pepper, pr. (scarce)	56-64
Spoonholder.	23-33
Sugar bowl, covered	25-35

Acorn

Maker unknown, c. 1870. Clear, nonflint.

Butter dish, covered, acorn finial. . . .	$ 37-45
Celery, tall	33-42
Compote	
Covered, acorn finial	59-69
Open	37-42
Creamer.	48-57
Egg cup	29-37
Goblet.	33-39
Pitcher	47-55
Sugar bowl	
Covered, acorn finial	46-55
Open	29-35

Goblet reproduced.

Actress

Actress

(Theatrical; Goddess of Liberty): La-Belle Glass Company, Bridgeport, Ohio, c. 1872; probably Crystal Glass Company, same town, 1879. Clear; clear and frosted prices given, 30 percent less for clear. Nonflint.

11

(continued)

Butter dish, covered	$ 97-113
Cake stand, 7″ high	136-145
Celery "Pinafore"	165-175
Cheese dish, covered, scene from	
"The Lone Fisherman"	210-220
Compote	
Covered, 8″ high, standard	165-175
Covered, low standard	130-140
Creamer.	72-82
Goblet, ...	99-109
Marmalade jar, w/cover	124-34
Pickle dish, "Love's Request"	50-56
Pitcher	
Milk (ill.)	230-245
Water	235-250
Platter	
Scene from "Pinafore".	95-110
"Miss Nielson"	93-115
Salt/Pepper, pr.	74-84
Sauce	
Flat	14-18
Footed.	18-24
Spoonholder, ...	62-74
Sugar bowl	92-110
Tray, bread, "Give Us This Day" . .	98-118

Admiral

(Ribbed Ellipse): J. C. Higbee, c. 1905. Clear, nonflint.

Bowl	
7″ cupped to 6″, 3⅞″ high.	$ 19-24
10″ shallow.	14-19
Butter.	28-34
Creamer, applied handle.	30-37
Cake stand	22-30
Compote, open, high.	17-27
Cruet	22-29
Goblet.	18-26
Mug.	13-18
Pitcher	32-40
Plate	
8″ round	12-17
9″ square.	15-22
Sugar, covered.	25-35
Spoonholder.	15-21
Tumbler.	12-19
Wine	16-22

Aegis

(Bead and Bar Medallion; Swiss, original name): McKee, c. 1880. Clear, nonflint.

Butter, covered, flat or footed	$ 34-42
Compote	
6″ dia., covered, high ("sweetmeat") .	39-47
7″, 8″ dia., flat rim, open,	
high or low	19-29
7″, 8″ dia., covered	34-42
Creamer, pressed handle.	28-33
Dish, oval, 7″, 8″, 9″.	15-24
Egg cup	22-28
Goblet.	25-33
Pitcher, ½ gal., applied handle	52-65
Salt, master on pedestal	24-30
Sauce	
Flat, 4″.	7-10
Footed, 3½″, 4″	9-12
Spoonholder.	18-22
Sugar, covered.	30-35
Wine	25-32

McKee also made "Swiss" lamps, not part of this pattern.

Alabama

Alabama

(Beaded Bull's Eye and Drape): U.S. Glass Company, Pittsburgh, c. 1890. First of the extensive "States" series made by this company. Clear, green, ruby stain (scarce).

Butter dish, covered	$ 44-54
Cake stand	46-54

Celery, tall	46-53
Compote	
Covered	47-55
Open, 5″	31-37
Creamer	42-52
Honey dish, covered (rare)	57-65
Nappie, handled	25-33
Pitcher	
Milk (ill.)	57-65
Syrup	71-80
Water	57-65
Relish dish, oblong, 3 sizes, ea.	17-24
Spoonholder	29-37
Sugar bowl, covered	46-53
Tumbler	25-35

Creamer	23-28
Cup	8-12
Goblet	16-22
Salt dip	
Flat, master	14-19
Footed, individual	12-16
Footed, individual, heavy sterling rim (ill.)	27-32
Spoonholder	14-19
Sugar, covered	25-31
Toothpick	25-35
Wine	12-16

Pattern name should be prefixed with Fostoria name because Dalzell also made an Alexis pattern.

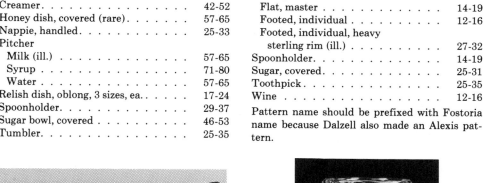

Alaska

Alaska

(Lion's Leg): Northwood Glass Company, 1897. Clear, green, opalescent blue, yellow.

Berry set	
Bowl, berry, opal blue	$ 80-87
Sauce	28-34
Butter dish, covered, opal blue	230-245
Creamer, blue (ill.)	55-67
Creamer, sugar, square, opal blue, set	220-230
Cruet, blue (decorated)	275-325
Jewel tray (celery)	120-130
Pitcher, water, decorated, vaseline	365-385
Spoonholder, clear, green	41-47

Alexis, Fostoria's

Fostoria Glass Co., c. 1900; wine reissued by D. C. Jenkins Glass Co., Kokomo, Indiana, (1906-1932). Clear, nonflint.

Butter, covered	$ 29-36

Alligator Scales

Alligator Scales

Maker unknown, c. 1870s. Nonflint.

Goblet (ill.)	$ 31-35

If you have information concerning *any* pattern, please let us hear from you. If you don't agree with the prices quoted, please let us hear from you. If you think the piece illustrated is a spoonholder rather than a celery (etc.), please let us hear from you. Constructive criticism is *always* welcome.

13

Almond

Almond

U.S. Glass Co., No. 5601, c. 1890s to 1915. Clear, probably emerald green.

Wine set
Decanter.	$ 38-44
Tray, ruffled edge	30-37
Wine (ill.)	13-18

Almond Thumbprint

Almond Thumbprint

(Pointed Thumbprint; Fingerprint): Bakewell, Pears, (1860s, flint) and Bryce Bros., Pittsburgh, 1890. Clear, nonflint.

Butter dish, covered, cable edge	$86-108
Celery vase	53-62
Creamer (ill.)	48-55
Compote, covered High standard 4¾″, 7″, 10″	66-73

Low standard	62-72
Egg cup	30-36
Goblet.	30-35
Pitcher, water	90-95
Sugar bowl, covered	64-72
Tumbler.	45-55

Prices are for flint. Nonflint, 50 percent less.

Amazon

Amazon

(Sawtooth Band): Bryce Bros., Pittsburgh, c. 1890. Crystal, plain and engraved. Reissued by U.S. Glass Company after 1891. Uncommon in vaseline and blue. Nonflint.

Bowl, oval, covered, 6½″, 7½″ lion handles and finials	$ 31-46
Butter dish, covered	56-63
Cake stand, large	57-64
Compote, open, 8″ dia.	31-38
Cordial	29-34
Creamer.	37-46
Goblet (ill.)	32-38
Pitcher, water, milk	55-65
Salt/Pepper, pr.	45-54
Sugar bowl, open, covered	42-49
Wine	30-36

More than 65 pieces made. Color, 80 percent more; engraving, 20 percent more.

Amelia

(Star Medallion): Imperial Glass Co., c. 1925. Clear, orange iridescent, nonflint.

14

Bowl
  Lily, 5″. . . . . $ 7-12
  Salad, 7½″. 10-13
Butter. 28-35
Candlestick, 7″
  Star in panel. 23-29
  Without star 17-21
Celery
  Tall 16-20
  Tray, 8″ handled 10-13
Compote, flared, open
  (orange irid.). 28-35
Creamer. 17-24
Cup, custard. 6-10
Goblet, 8 oz.. 15-24
Ice cream, tall, 6 oz. 8-13
Pickle, oval, 6¼″. 7-11
Pitcher, milk (large pint) 25-32
Plate, 6″. 6-10
Spoonholder. 14-18
Sugar
  Covered, lid does not have star 23-30
  Uncovered. 12-16
Tumbler, iced tea, 12 oz.. 13-17
Vase, "Bouquet", 6″ 12-18

Orange iridescent add 20 percent to clear prices listed.

America

America

(Swirl and Diamond): American Glass Co. and Riverside Glass Works, 1890. Clear, nonflint. Included in many "States" collections.

Bowl, berry, 8½″. . . . . $ 16-20
Butter on pedestal, covered 32-39
Carafe. 28-32
Celery vase 19-24
Compote, flat rim, 8″ dia. x 8″ high . . . 31-38
Creamer, tankard, applied handle . . . 25-31
Goblet. 18-25
Pitcher, tankard, applied
  handle, ½ gal. 36-42
Relish 11-16
Sauce, flat, 4½″ 5-9
Spoonholder. 15-20
Sugar, covered
  Individual 17-23
  Large 28-34
Tumbler. 13-17

Confusing pattern is Zippered Swirl and Diamond.

American Beauty

(La France, original name; erroneously Gold Rose; Rose & Sunbursts): Co-operative, c. 1910, formerly attributed to Northwood. Clear, clear with gold trim, clear with painted red roses, green leaves and gold; solid rose color, with gold trim. Nonflint.

Bowl, berry, 8″. . . . . $ 23-34
Butter, covered 52-65
Creamer, flat 30-37
Pitcher, ½ gal. 44-56
Sauce, flat, 4″ 10-14
Spoonholder, two handles 24-30
Sugar, covered, two handles 39-45
Tumbler. 19-25

Prices are for clear with good gold, less 20 percent for no gold. Painted decoration add 30 percent. Solid rose color with good gold, add 100 percent. No goblet.

American Shield

(Centennial Shield): Maker unknown, probably made for 1876 Centennial. Clear, nonflint.

Butter dish, covered $165-175
Creamer. 125-133
Spoonholder. 125-134
Sugar bowl, covered 158-167

Only known pieces. Don't confuse with Bullet Emblem, or with Banner butter dish.

Ancestral

(Erroneously Thousand Eye): New Martinsville No. 14 pattern, c. 1920s. Reissued in early 1940s from original molds, in crystal. Reissued by Viking in late 1950s in colors. Earliest production in clear only, nonflint.

Bonbon	
5″, 3-crimp	$ 9-12
7″, 6-crimp	12-16
Bowl, ivy, 3½″	10-14
Champagne, saucer	9-13
Cocktail	11-15
Compote	
Crimped rim, 5″ (3¼″ high), 6″	13-17
Plain rim, open, 5½″ dia. x 3″ high	12-15
Cordial	8-11
Dresser set (puff box, 2 perfumes)	42-56
Goblet	12-16
Hat, 2″, 4″	14-19
Sherbet, single knob	8-12
Tumblers	
2 oz. whiskey	5-7
5 oz., 7 oz. old fashioned	9-12
10 oz., 12 oz., 14 oz. water, iced tea	11-14
Vase, 3″, 3-crimp	10-12
Wine	12-15

Although this is later glass, it is included here because it is collectible, and to differentiate it from the true Thousand Eye pattern.

Angel Head

Angel Head

Maker unknown, 1870s. Blue or opaque white, nonflint.

Plate, blue, 7½″, 8½″, 9″ (ill.)	$ 49-53

Angora

Maker unknown, c. late 1880s. Clear, nonflint.

Goblet	$ 26-35

Anheuser Busch

"A" ale glass possibly LaBelle Glass Company, Bridgeport, Ohio, c. 1880. Clear, nonflint.

Ale glass	$ 30-38

Anthemion

Anthemion

(Original name, Albany): Albany Glass Company and Model Flint Glass Company, Findlay, Ohio, 1890. Clear, amber, cobalt.

Bowl, 7″	$ 23-32
Butter dish, covered	58-67
Cake stand, high standard, 9¼″ high	37-46
Celery, tall	27-36
Creamer	27-36
Marmalade jar	32-40
Pitcher	
Milk (ill.)	40-47
Water	39-47
Plate, 9″	18-27
Relish dish	10-15
Sauce, flat, square	10-13
Spoonholder	24-31

Sugar bowl, covered	43-52
Tumbler.	32-40

Color, 60 percent more. No goblet.

Anvil

Toothpick (or match holder, anvil-shaped), Windsor Glass Company, Pittsburgh, c. 1887.

Amber.	$ 43-51
Blue.	47-56
Canary	50-59
Clear	35-42

Apollo

Apollo

Adams & Company, Pittsburgh, 1875. Clear, frosted, engraved. Prices are for frosted; clear, 30 percent less.

Bowl, 8″ dia.	$ 34-42
Butter dish, covered	49-54
Cake stand, 10″ (scarce)	64-74
Celery, frosted (ill.)	24-32
Cheese dish (scarce)	49-54
Compote	
Covered, high standard, 5″	55-63
Open, low standard, 8″	37-46
Creamer.	39-44
Egg cup	23-30
Goblet.	37-44
Pickle	21-28
Pitcher	
Syrup	62-76
Water	55-65
Sauce	
Flat	8-10
Footed.	12-16
Spoonholder.	28-36
Sugar bowl, covered	44-50
Sugar shaker	42-50
Tray, water	38-42

Tumbler.	29-36
Wine	32-38

McKee's Apollo is different pattern.

Apple Blossom

(Netted Apple Blossom): Northwood Glass Company, Indiana, Pennsylvania, c. 1896, decorated milk glass.

Berry set	
Bowl, large.	$ 62-74
Sauce	23-28
Butter dish, covered	70-78
Cake stand	62-72
Compote	60-68
Creamer.	38-42
Pitcher	
Syrup	107-111
Water	126-144
Salt/Pepper, pr.	70-80
Spoonholder.	40-46
Sugar bowl, covered	88-94
Sugar shaker	82-92
Tumbler.	48-55

Aquarium

Aquarium

U.S. Glass Company, c. 1890s. Clear, amber, green, nonflint. Only piece known.

Water pitcher (ill.).	$152-166

Color, 100 percent more.

17

Arabesque

Arabesque

Bakewell, Pears & Company, Pittsburgh, 1860s. Clear, nonflint.

Butter dish	$ 50-60
Celery.	38-44
Compote	
Covered, 10″ high standard.	63-76
Open, low standard	32-39
Creamer, applied handle (ill.)	51-57
Goblet.	35-39
Pitcher, water	63-78
Sauce, flat.	12-16
Spoonholder.	28-33
Sugar bowl, covered	41-45

**Arch and Fern
with Snake Medallion**

Arch and Fern with Snake Medallion

Sandwich glass, mid-1800s. This is a quart decanter, stopper not original. "Rum" is marked on central medallion. NOT pressed glass. It is blown into a three-part mold, not plunger-pressed. Flint.

Arch and Forget-Me-Not Bands

Arch and Forget-Me-Not Bands

Maker unknown, 1880s. Clear, nonflint.

Berry bowl	$ 22-29
Butter dish, covered	36-42
Creamer.	30-35
Pitcher, water (ill.)	42-48
Saucedish	8-11
Spoonholder.	23-28
Sugar bowl, covered, cross	
finial	31-37
Tumbler.	18-24

18

Arched Grape

Arched Grape

Sandwich glass, 1880s. Clear glass, non-flint.

Butter dish, covered	$ 45-54
Celery vase	42-51
Compote	
Covered, high standard	54-63
Covered, low standard	51-60
Cordial	27-37
Creamer (ill.)	39-45
Goblet.	28-33
Pitcher, water	64-72
Sauce, 4″.	9-14
Spoonholder.	27-36
Sugar bowl	
Covered	42-48
Open	24-29

Arched Leaf

Arched Leaf

Maker unknown, c. 1870s. Clear, flint, nonflint. Rare in color.

Goblet.	$ 24-32
Plate, 7″, 9″, 10″	24-34
Salt, footed	18-24
Sugar bowl, covered (base ill.)	42-52

Flint, 150 percent higher than nonflint prices listed.

Arched Ovals

Arched Ovals

(Concaved Almond): U.S. Glass Company, c. 1900. Clear, cobalt, emerald green, rose-flashed, ruby, nonflint. Some with gold trim.

Berry set, belled, deep	
Bowl, 8″	$ 14-19
Sauce, 4½″.	6-9
Butter dish	34-40
Cake stand, 10″	28-34
Compote	
9″ high, open	26-35
Jelly	30-36
Creamer.	24-29
Cruet	29-35
Cup, 2 types	12-17
Goblet.	21-27
Lamp, tall	67-95
Spoonholder.	18-23
Sugar bowl, covered	32-38
Syrup	30-36
Toothpick holder	19-24
Tumbler.	12-18
Wine	14-19

Color, 35 percent higher.

If you have information concerning *any* pattern, please let us hear from you. If you don't agree with the prices quoted, please let us hear from you. If you think the piece illustrated is a spoonholder rather than a celery (etc.), please let us hear from you. Constructive criticism is *always* welcome.

Argonaut Shell

Argonaut Shell

(Nautilus) Northwood Glass Company, c. 1900. Clear, blue, canary, carnival, custard (decorated green, gold), opalescent.

	Custard	Color
Berry set		
Large bowl.	$225-260	$144-152
Sauce	58-65	58-64
Butter dish, covered . .	265-280	250-262
Compote, jelly	120-142	270-288
Pitcher, water	332-342	170-188
Salt/Pepper, pr.	310-340	112-123
Sugar bowl, covered . .	229-242	226-242
Tumbler.	261-271	135-145

Berry set, jelly, salt/pepper, toothpick, tumbler reproduced in custard.

Arrowhead in Oval

Arrowhead in Oval

(Original name, Madora): Higbee Glass Company, c. 1890. Clear, nonflint. Some pieces embossed with "bee" trademark; add 25 percent

Basket, 7″ long	$ 48-56
Cake stand.	33-39
Celery, handled	31-37
Cup, punch	14-20
Goblet (ill.)	25-32
Plate, 7″ square	20-26
Play set	
Butter	30-38
Creamer	23-29
Spoonholder	21-27
Sugar, covered	28-35
Rose bowl, high stem.	30-37
Salt dip, individual.	12-16
Salt/Pepper, pr.	42-49
Sherbet, stemmed	19-24
Sugar, covered	28-35

Art

Art

(Job's Tears, Teardrops and Diamond Block): Adams & Company, Pittsburgh, 1870s and U. S. Glass Company, 1891. Clear, ruby, nonflint.

Basket, fruit, 10″.	$ 56-65
Bowl, berry, 8″.	46-52
Butter dish, covered	56-62
Cake stand, 10″	59-69
Compote	
Covered, footed, 7″.	64-72
Open, footed, 8″, 9″, 10″.	46-56

20

Cracker jar	49-59
Creamer, 2 types (ill.)	38-47
Cruet	48-57
Dish, banana (flat)	42-44
Goblet	34-42
Mug	33-39
Pitcher, water, ½ gal.	54-62
Relish	25-32
Sauce, flat, 4″ shallow	15-19
Spoonholder	29-35
Sugar bowl, covered	45-52
Tumbler	28-37
Wine	28-37

Artichoke

Bowl, 8″	29-32
Butter dish	58-64
Cake stand	46-53
Compotes	
Covered, high standard	62-74
Open, low standard, 8″ dia.	50-58
Creamer (ill.)	35-42
Cruet	30-40
Goblet	
Lamp, miniature, with shade	210-240
Pitcher, water (bulbous)	95-115
Sauce, flat	11-14
Spoonholder	26-34
Sugar bowl, covered, handled	45-55

Goblet not part of original production. All clear, 30 percent less than clear with frosted prices given.

Art Novo

Art Novo

(Dogwood, Panelled Dogwood): Co-Operative Flint Glass Company, Beaver Falls, Pennsylvania, 1905. Clear, rose-flashed, ruby, frosted milk glass. Some with decoration. Nonflint.

Berry set	
Bowl	$ 33-37
Sauce	10-14
Butter dish	28-34
Creamer	24-32
Goblet	29-35
Lamp (ill)	32-40
Salt/Pepper, pr.	50-60
Spoonholder	23-32
Sugar bowl	28-34
Toothpick	35-40

Add 40 percent frosted, decorated, and milk glass; 100 percent for color with good gold.

Artichoke

(Original name, Valencia): Fostoria Glass Company, c. 1890. Frosted clear, nonflint.

Bobeche	$ 36-42

Ashburton

(Large Thumbprint): New England Glass Company, Sandwich, McKee and others, 1840 to 1880. Clear, colors, flint and nonflint.

Ale glass, 5″ high, flint	$ 58-64
Bitters bottle	62-70
Butter dish	130-150
Celery	
Plain top	82-91
Scalloped top	88-98
Cordial, 4½″ high	54-64
Creamer, (rare)	170-182
Decanters, 7 types	70-96
Egg cup	75-90
Goblet	
Flared, flint, barrel	35-40
Straight sides, lady's	31-40

21

(continued)

Mug.	10-14
Sauce, 2 sizes	12-14
Spoonholder.	36-43
Sugar bowl, covered	89-98
Toddy jar, covered, (rare)	335-375

Tumbler

Footed.	75-85
Water	60-70
Whiskey, handled	63-72
Wine	33-36

Creamer, goblet, sugar, wine reproduced.

Ashman

(Crossroads) Maker unknown, c. mid-1880s. Clear, amber, blue, nonflint.

Butter dish, covered	$ 49-53
Cake stand, 9″	49-53
Celery.	28-37

Compote

Covered, high standard, 8″	45-55
Open, 12″	32-45
Creamer.	35-41
Goblet.	30-34
Pitcher, water	65-75
Spoonholder.	28-34
Sugar bowl, covered	43-51

Add 40 percent for color.

Assassination Mug

Assassination Mug

(Also called "The Martyrs' Mug"): Garfield on one side, Lincoln on other. Made after 1881, the year Garfield was assassinated. By whom this mug was made is not known. Clear, cobalt, nonflint.

Mug, 2¼″ high (ill.) . . . . $ 77-97
Cobalt 100 percent higher.

Atlanta, Late

(Imitation-Cut Atlanta, Millard's Atlanta): Westmoreland No. 228, c. 1905. Clear, nonflint.

Butter, covered	$ 31-36
Celery.	19-25
Compote, jelly.	13-18
Creamer.	24-30
Goblet.	20-25
Lampshade, electric or gas, uncommon.	24-32
Salt shaker, single	16-21
Sauce, flat.	4-9
Spoonholder.	16-22
Sugar, covered.	27-34
Syrup	30-37
Toothpick, scarce	32-42
Wine	12-16

Atlas

Atlas

(Crystal Ball): Bryce Bros., Mount Pleasant, Pennsylvania. 1889. Clear, ruby engraved. Nonflint. Made in flat and footed forms.

Bowls, covered, flat	$ 23-34
Butter dish covered	46-54
Cake stand, 10″ high, clear	32-40
Champagne	28-34
Cordial	29-35
Creamer (ill.)	32-40
Goblet (scarce)	31-40
Pitcher, water, 2 types	46-52
Salt dip, individual	13-17
Sauce, footed	13-16

Spoonholder, flat or footed base 28-33
Sugar bowl, covered 34-45
Wine, clear 26-32

Pieces known, 84, including hotel table set with raindrop base. Ruby, 100 percent higher.

Aurora

(Diamond Horseshoe): The Brilliant Glass Works, Brilliant, Ohio, c. 1888 and Greensburg Glass Company, 1889. Clear, ruby, nonflint. Sometimes engraved.

Butter dish, covered . . . . $ 45-52
Cake stand 42-46
Compote
    Covered 42-51
    Open 27-31
Creamer 35-42
Decanter, original patterned
    stopper 47-54
Goblet 34-41
Pitcher, water 45-52
Salt/Pepper, pr. 22-31
Spoonholder 24-32
Sugar bowl, open 37-45
Wine 21-25

Add 30 percent for engraving; 100 percent for ruby stain.

Bakewell Block

Bakewell, Pears & Company, Pittsburgh, c. early 1850s. Clear, flint.

Celery . . . . $ 90-108
Champagne 87-96
Creamer 150-160
Decanter, ovoid 125-140
Goblet 130-140
Spoonholder 50-57
Sugar bowl, covered 89-102
Tumbler, bar, whiskey 89-104
Wine, applied handle 110-122

Balder

(Kamoni; Pennsylvania): U.S. Glass Company, Pittsburgh, through early 1900s. Clear, emerald green, ruby. Some pieces gold trimmed.

Berry set
    Bowl, 8" . . . . $ 20-26
    Sauce, 4", deep 9-13
Butter dish, covered 50-59

Balder

Creamer
    Individual 19-25
    Large 33-40
Carafe 37-50
Compote, ruffled, jelly 44-54
Cup 10-15
Goblet 26-33
Pitcher, syrup (ill.) 45-56
Plate, 8" 33-38
Sauces, shallow
    Good quality 8-11
    Poor quality (no gold) 4-6
Spoonholder 25-31
Sugar bowl
    Covered, large 41-50
    Open, small, handled 17-23
Tumbler, water 25-33
Wine 19-23

Clear 30 percent less than prices listed. Play set (toothpick is toy spoonholder).

If you have information concerning *any* pattern, please let us hear from you. If you don't agree with the prices quoted, please let us hear from you. If you think the piece illustrated is a spoonholder rather than a celery (etc.), please let us hear from you. Constructive criticism is *always* welcome.

23

Ball and Bar

Ball and Bar

Westmoreland Glass Company, Grapeville, Pennsylvania, 1896. Clear.

Creamer, 4″ (ill.) . . . . $ 37-42
Other pieces?

Ball and Swirl

(Swirl and Ball; original name, Ray): McKee Brothers, 1894. Clear, ruby stained; engraved or frosted.

Butter, covered, flanged . . . . $	28-36
Cake stand	30-37
Candlestick	31-40
Compote	
Jelly.	15-22
Open, flat rim, 9″ dia., 7½″ high . . .	19-28
Creamer on swirled pedestal,	
rope handle	18-25
Goblet.	16-21
Mug.	13-18
Pickle dish	15-20
Pitcher, tankard: qt., 2 qts.	35-45
Sauce, footed,	
3 11/16″ dia. x 2 3/8″ high.	7-10
Spoonholder.	15-20
Sugar, covered.	25-32
Syrup	32-42
Tumbler, underbase has button center,	
swirls go out to ball edge	16-22

Wine	19-25

Thirty-five pieces are listed in the original advertisement.

Ball and Swirl, Tiffin

(Ball and Swirl Band): Tiffin Glass Co., c. 1888. Attribution by this writer on the basis of water tray described below. Decorated with frosted bands or engraved ferns.

Butter, covered, on pedestal . . . . . . $	25-35
Creamer.	20-26
Goblet.	19-28
Relish, scoop shaped.	12-17
Sauce, footed	9-12
Spoonholder.	16-22
Sugar, covered.	24-34
Tray, 10⅞″ dia., embossed picture of	
factory, captioned "The Tiffin Glass	
Co., Incorporated Apr 24th, 1888". . .	100+
Tray, 11″ dia., swirled ray center	33-40
Wine	16-23

Balloon

Balloon

Made in lower Ohio Valley in early 1850s. Clear, flint.

Creamer (ill.)	$140-160
Goblet.	75-87
Pitcher	294-299
Sugar bowl	199-220

Bamboo Edge

(Bamboo erroneously): LaBelle Glass Company, Bridgeport, Ohio, 1883. Clear, nonflint. Also engraved.

Bamboo Edge

Butter dish	$ 33-40
Celery	24-29
Compotes, 7″, 8″, 9″, covered	45-60
Creamer (ill.)	32-36
Dish, 7″, 8″, 9″, oblong	20-24
Pitcher, water	43-52
Salt/Pepper, pr.	34-42
Sauce, 4″.	11-13
Spoonholder.	19-23
Sugar bowl, covered	32-39

Banded Buckle

Banded Buckle

Sandwich Glass Company, mid-1850s; other factories, Pittsburgh, 1870s. Clear, flint and nonflint. (Also see Buckle.)

Bowls, open, flat rim.	$ 27-33
Butter dish	47-52
Compote	
Open, low standard	37-43
Covered, low standard	39-52
Cordial	35-42
Creamer.	50-59
Egg cup	31-35
Goblet (ill.)	32-42
Pitcher, water	210-235
Salt, footed	14-20
Spoonholder.	27-33
Sugar bowl, covered	38-50
Tumbler.	52-62

Banded Fleur-de-Lis

Banded Fleur-de-Lis

Imperial Glass Company, Bellaire, Ohio, 1890s. Clear, nonflint.

Butter dish	$ 31-39
Creamer (ill.)	27-36
Goblet.	19-26
Pitcher, water	44-52
Salt/pepper, pr.	33-43
Spoonholder.	27-31
Sugar bowl, covered	29-40

Flint prices given. 30 percent less for nonflint.

Banded Icicle

Banded Icicle

Bakewell, Pears & Company, 1870s. Clear, nonflint and flint.

Butter dish	$ 44-52
Compote	
Covered, 6″, 8″, high standard	61-67
Open, 8″, low standard	35-41

(continued)

Creamer.	40-48
Goblet.	29-38
Pitcher (ill.)	72-81
Sauce	12-15
Spoonholder.	29-34
Sugar bowl	42-51

Flint prices given; 30 percent less for nonflint.

Banded Raindrops

Banded Raindrops

(Candlewick): Clear, rare in amber, opalescent blue. These pieces, 100 percent more. Milk glass 40 percent more than clear prices listed.

Butter dish	$ 37-45
Celery.	28-35
Compote, 7″, covered	34-43
Creamer.	32-41
Cup and saucer	28-35
Goblet.	29-35
Pitcher, water (ill.)	52-60
Plates, 7½″ and 8¾″.	27-37
Relish, squared	17-24
Sauce, flat.	8-13
Spoonholder.	27-35
Sugar bowl, covered	38-45
Wine	31-36

Banded Portland

Banded Portland

(Virginia; frequently called Maiden Blush): U.S. Glass Company, 1901. Clear and flashed with blue, green, ruby, and yellow.

Bottle, water	$ 42-50
Butter dish, covered	49-56
Celery.	39-46
Compote	
Covered	81-90
Covered, jelly	80-88
Cup.	18-23
Cruet.	47-56
Dish, sardine	18-27
Goblet.	37-43
Pitcher, syrup (ill.)	32-41
Relish.	23-28
Salt/Pepper, pr.	55-62
Sugar	
Bowl, covered, large	38-45
Shaker.	39-44
Toothpick holder	28-38
Tumbler.	35-39
Wine	40-45

Probably other pieces. 50 percent higher for colors than for clear prices listed.

Banner Butter Dish

Banner Butter Dish

Probably Bryce Brothers, made for Centennial, 1876. Clear, blue, and amber. Uncommon.

Butter dish (ill.)
Clear $136-144
Blue, amber 182-192

Barley

Barley

(Sprig; Indian Tree): Campbell-Jones Company, late 1870s. Clear, any piece in color, rare; 100 percent more than clear. Nonflint.

Butter dish, covered	$ 35-44
Cake stand, 9″, 9¼″, 9½″, 9⅝″	27-34
Celery.	21-30
Compote, covered	39-48
Cordial	18-27
Creamer.	32-40
Dish, oval	16-23
Goblet.	25-33
Jam jar, (scarce with lid).	54-62
Pickle	18-27
Pitcher, water, 2 types	46-57
Plate, 6″ (scarce).	33-39
Platter, oval, 6″ (scarce)	25-31
Relish, wheelbarrow, dated 1882	56-63
Sauces, footed, 4″ 5″	10-13
Spoonholder.	15-25
Sugar bowl, covered and open	35-42
Wine	23-33

Barberry

Barberry

(Original name, Berry): Boston & Sandwich Glass Company, Sandwich, Massachusetts, 1860s. McKee, 1880. Clear, amber, blue, and pale green, 50 percent and 70 percent more.

Bowl, covered, 8″	$ 53-63
Butter dish	46-58
Cake stand	146-155
Celery.	46-55
Compote, covered, high and low standard.	52-62
Cordial	42-52
Creamer (ill.)	40-46
Egg cup, oval berries.	30-37
Goblet, oval berries	29-33
Pickle	19-27
Pitcher, water, applied handle.	94-107
Plate, 6″.	24-30
Salt, footed, ...	29-36
Sauce, flat and footed	21-30
Spoonholder.	33-40
Sugar bowl, covered	47-58
Syrup jug, pewter top	100-117
Wine	28-35

Came with round or oval berries. Number of berries varies on goblets.

Barred Forget-Me-Not

(continued)

Barred Forget-Me-Not

Canton Glass Company, Canton, Ohio, 1883. Clear, amber, blue, apple green, yellow, nonflint

Butter dish	$ 39-47
Cake plates	
Closed handles, 9″	32-45
Extra large, on stand	47-56
Compote	
Covered, on high foot, 8″	47-56
Covered, low foot, 8″	40-50
Open, jelly, on high foot	31-39
Cordial	19-27
Creamer (ill.)	32-40
Goblet, 2 sizes	35-42
Pickle dish, square handles	17-26
Pitcher, water	42-52
Spoonholder	27-37
Sugar bowl, square handles,	
covered	34-43
Wine	23-30

Probably other pieces. Yellow, 30 percent; blue, 60 percent; apple green, 100 percent higher than clear prices listed.

Barred Hobnail

Barred Hobnail

(Winona): Brilliant Glass Works, Brilliant, Ohio, 1888. Clear, frosted, nonflint.

Bowls	$ 18-28
Butter dish, covered	36-45
Creamer	31-37
Goblet, patterned stem	29-37
Pitcher, water, ½ gallon (ill.)	47-52
Salt shaker	17-21
Sauce, flat	21-26
Spoonholder	21-24
Sugar bowl, covered	35-42

Original ad states "Satin finish and opalescent colors."

Barred Oval

Barred Oval

George Duncan & Sons, Pittsburgh, c. 1890, clear, frosted or ruby flashed. Reissued after 1891 by U.S. Glass Company. Nonflint.

Bottle, water	$ 38-44
Butter dish, covered	35-46
Celery	32-46
Compote, open	32-39
Creamer	32-41
Cruet, original faceted stopper	41-53
Goblet	32-44
Pitcher, water	57-66
Plate, small	31-40
Sauce	13-16
Spoonholder	25-33
Sugar bowl, covered (ill.)	49-59
Tumbler	19-24

Frosted 50 percent higher, ruby 200 percent higher.

Barred Star

(Spartan): Gillinder & Company, Pittsburgh, c. early 1880s. Clear, nonflint.

Butter dish, covered	$ 40-48
Cake stand	35-42
Celery	34-43
Compote, covered	36-41
Creamer	44-49
Pitcher	45-52
Salt/Pepper, pr.	23-30
Spoonholder	28-34
Sugar bowl, covered	45-52

Barrel Excelsior

Barrel Excelsior

Sandwich, early; later, McKee Bros., Pittsburgh, 1850s and 1860s. Clear.

Ale glass.	$ 48-56
Butter dish, covered, early	89-107
Celery	
Plain top	56-62
Scalloped top	86-93
Decanter, pint, quart, 3 pints,	
early	90-107
Goblets, flaring and	
straight sides	42-52
Lamp, early	160-170
Mug.	54-63
Spoonholder (ill.)	52-61
Sugar bowl, covered, early	172-181
Tumbler, water, whiskey.	46-52
Wine bottle, with tumble-up,	
early.	160-169

Barrelled Thumbprint

Barrelled Thumbprint

(Challinor's Thumbprint): Challinor, Taylor, Ltd., Tarentum, Pennsylvania, 1880s.

Bowl, 7″, 9″	$ 48-54
Butter dish, covered	52-60
Celery.	42-52
Creamer.	49-51
Goblet.	49-60
Nappy, 4″, 4½″, 6″, 8″	47-53
Pickle	38-44
Pitcher (ill.)	67-72
Salt/Pepper, pr.	45-52
Spoonholder.	43-46
Sugar bowl	48-58
Tumbler.	24-32
Water bottle.	65-73
Wine	37-52

Bartholdi

O'Hara Glass Co., c. 1885. Clear and stained in iridescent colors—topaz (light amber) and rainbow, a pale green. Also comes with engraved leaf, fern, and berry combination.

Bowl, 7″, 8″	
Covered	$ 24-30
Open	16-21
Butter, flanged	29-36
Celery.	23-29
Compote, covered, high, 7″, 8″	32-40
Creamer, applied rope handle	24-28
Cruet, rope handle (pattern is	
atypical).	26-33
Lamp, tall	
Base patterned, clear font	40-46
Font and base patterned	55-62
Font patterned, clear base	46-54
Pitcher, quart, applied	
rope handle	40-53
Spoonholder.	16-20
Sugar, covered.	26-32

Possible attribution of lamps is from comparison with lamp stem and compote stem that appear to be identical, although the fonts are also made with a dewdrop base typical of Campbell, Jones. Prices are for clear. Add 20 percent for engraving or color stain.

Basket Weave

Basket Weave

Mid-1880s. Clear, amber, blue, canary, apple green, nonflint.

Bowl
Berry	$ 19-27
Covered, flat	21-29
Large, finger or waste	24-33
Butter dish	35-42
Cake plate	29-37
Compote, covered	36-44
Cordial	25-32
Creamer	28-34
Cup and saucer	29-36
Egg cup, double	17-27
Goblet	28-32
Lamp	29-37
Mug	22-31
Pitcher	42-52
Syrup, metal top, clear	32-41
Water (ill.)	44-52
Plate, 8¾″; 10¼″ with	
handles	15-20
Salt	9-12
Salt/Pepper, pr.	28-34
Sauce, round, flat	18-26
Spoonholder	22-31
Sugar bowl	34-43
Tray, round, 12″ dia., water,	
scenic	34-42

Goblet, water pitcher and tumbler being reproduced. Color pieces 25 to 75 percent higher than clear pieces listed.

Basketweave with Leaf

Basketweave with Leaf

(Frosted Leaf and Basketweave): A design of the early 1900s, possibly Northwood. Clear, possibly clear with frosted leaf; clear, blue, yellow, all with opalescence.

Butter dish, covered	$ 69-78
Creamer (ill.)	47-55
Spoonholder	42-50
Sugar, covered	60-67

Prices are for clear. Yellow, 40 percent more; blue, 100 percent more.

Bead and Scroll

Bead and Scroll

Probably U. S. Glass Company, c. 1890. Clear, blue, frosted, ruby, cobalt, emerald, amber, nonflint. Prices are for good gold.

Berry bowl, 8″	$ 24-32
Butter dish, covered	47-54
Compote, jelly	25-32
Creamer (ill.)	35-40
Goblet	22-29
Mug	17-23
Pitcher, water	33-40
Play set	
Butter dish	122-140
Creamer	64-72
Spoonholder	60-66
Sugar bowl	110-124
Saucedish, flat	16-21
Spoonholder	29-37
Sugar bowl, covered	36-42
Tumbler	17-25

Frosted 20 percent more; emerald, amber 80 percent more; blue, ruby 120 percent more. Transfer-etched mugs are souvenirs of Pan-American Exposition.

Bead Column

Bead Column

Maker unknown, c. 1910.

Butter dish, covered	$ 22-29
Creamer (ill.)	18-23
Pitcher	39-45
Spoonholder	15-18
Sugar bowl	20-26

Beaded Acorn Medallion

(Same as Beaded Grape Medallion but with Acorns and Leaves in medallion): The Boston Silver-Glass Company, East Cambridge, Massachusetts, c. 1869. Clear, nonflint.

Butter dish, covered	$ 52-62
Champagne	46-55
Creamer, applied handle	48-55
Goblet	35-45
Pitcher	72-86
Plate, 6″	28-35
Spoonholder	34-42
Sugar bowl, covered	44-50

Sugar bowl lid has small eagle in beaded medallion.

Beaded Arch

Beaded Arch

(Beaded Arch Panels; Archaic Gothic): attributed to Burlington Glass Works, Canada, c. 1890. Clear, cobalt, nonflint.

Goblet	$ 32-42
Mug, handled, 2⅝″ (ill.)	34-41
Table set	
Butter dish	38-46
Creamer	35-43
Spoonholder	25-32
Sugar bowl	39-47

Beaded Band

Attributed to Burlington, c., 1884. Clear, color (rare), nonflint.

Butter dish, covered	$ 38-46
Compote, covered	46-52
Creamer	27-34
Goblet	32-37
Jug, syrup	22-31
Pitcher	
Syrup (Pat. June 29, '84)	59-70
Water	44-56

31

(continued)

Beaded Band

Beaded Dart Band

Relish, lobed	15-18
Spoonholder.	27-36
Sugar bowl, open, (base ill.)	30-37
Wine	34-40

If color, 100 percent higher than clear prices listed.

Beaded Chain

(Looped Cord): Maker unknown, c. 1870s. Clear, nonflint.

Butter dish, covered	$ 39-46
Celery.	41-44
Creamer, applied handle.	36-44
Goblet.	34-42
Pitcher, water, applied	
handle.	55-62
Plate, 6″.	38-42
Relish	13-17
Sauce, flat.	22-28
Spoonholder.	26-33
Sugar bowl, covered	38-44

Beaded Dart Band

Geo. Duncan & Sons, c. 1894. Pittsburgh. Clear, ruby, nonflint.

Butter dish	$ 36-45
Celery, tall	27-34
Compote	32-40
Creamer.	31-40
Goblet.	23-30
Pickle caster with fork (ill.)	66-70
Spoonholder.	18-21
Sugar bowl, covered	32-41

Ruby 100 percent more.

Beaded Dewdrop

Beaded Dewdrop

(Original name, Wisconsin): U.S. Glass Company, Gas City, Indiana, 1898. Clear, nonflint.

Bottles, oil, vinegar	$ 35-42
Bowl, open, round, 7″, 8″	32-40
Butter dish, covered	66-77
Celery tray	27-36
Celery vase	34-42
Compote	
Covered, 6″, 7″, 8″, high	57-66
Open, ...	35-41

Condiment set, 4-piece in holder . . . 122-145
Creamer, individual and large 34-42
Cruet 42-50
Dish
  Candy 22-31
  Oval, handled, covered, 6″ 49-53
  Oval, handled, open, 6″ 22-29
  Sweetmeat 26-29
Goblet 43-47
Mug, large 35-39
Pitcher
  3 pints 43-48
  1 quart (ill.) 52-58
Salt/Pepper, short, tall, pr. 37-48
Sauce, flat, 4″ 12-19
Spoonholder 34-38
Sugar bowl, large and small,
  covered 33-50
Syrup jug, with cover 59-72
Toothpick holder, kettle, tripod
  base 34-39
Tumbler 41-52
Wine 42-51

Handled toothpick reproduced in colors.

Beaded Ellipse

Beaded Ellipse

(Original name, Aldine): McKee, c. 1900. Cambridge Glass Company, probably limited production.

Butter dish . . . . $ 40-50
Celery 19-27
Creamer 27-32
Compote, open 26-32
Cruet 28-34
Pitcher
  Milk 42-47
  Water (ill.) 44-52

Salt/Pepper, pr 38-49
Spoonholder 17-22
Sugar bowl 31-37
Syrup, spring tin top 38-44

Beaded Fan

Beaded Fan

(Dewdrop and Fan): Maker unknown, c. 1880. Clear, nonflint.

Butter dish . . . . $ 29-36
Celery vase 24-30
Compote 26-34
Creamer (ill.) 21-26
Pitcher 32-42
Spoonholder 18-22
Sugar bowl
  Covered 30-35
  Open 20-26

Opalescent Beaded Fan is a different pattern..

Beaded Fine-Cut

Beaded Fine-Cut

Dalzell, Gilmore and Leighton, c. 1885. Clear, nonflint.

33

(continued)

Butter dish	$ 29-36
Creamer (ill.)	21-29
Goblet	31-40
Pitcher	35-44
Spoonholder	28-31
Sugar bowl	29-36

Beaded Flange

Beaded Flange

(Canadian Flange): Fostoria Glass Company, 1891. Also Burlington. Clear, colors, nonflint.

Butter dish	$ 41-49
Candlestick	40-48
Creamer	39-40
Goblet	31-34
Pickle dish	19-27
Spoonholder	24-27
Sugar bowl	27-34

Colors, 50 percent higher than clear prices listed.

Beaded Grape

Beaded Grape

(California): U.S. Glass Company, Pittsburgh, 1880s. Clear, emerald green, nonflint. Gold trim on some pieces.

Bowl, square	$ 22-30
Butter dish, covered	48-55
Cake stand, large	54-62
Celery tray, oblong	26-34
Compote, covered	
High foot, 7″, 8″, 9″	47-52
Shallow, on standard	37-39
Small, 4″ high (jelly)	42-50
Cordial	47-52
Creamer	42-48
Cruet, original swirl stopper	68-77
Goblet, green (ill.)	48-55
Pickle	25-32
Pitcher, water	
Round, several sizes	67-80
Square, several sizes	72-88
Plate, square, 8½″	24-33
Platter, oblong (rare),	
10¼″ x 7¼″	47-54
Salt/Pepper, metal tops, pr.	57-66
Sauce, 3½″, 4″, 4½″	11-15
Spoonholder	26-34
Sugar bowl, covered	46-56
Toothpick holder	41-49
Tumbler, water	32-39
Vase, 6″	24-31
Wine	36-41

Green pieces, 50 percent higher than clear prices listed. Reproduced without gold.

Beaded Grape Medallion

Boston Silver Glass Company, East Cambridge, Massachusetts, late 1860s. Clear, nonflint. Pattern also made in England. Comes banded with plain or patterned foot.

Butter dish, acorn finial	$ 55-62
Celery vase	38-47
Champagne	55-66
Compote, covered, high, low,	
oval	66-82
Creamer, applied handle	49-52
Egg cup	22-31
Goblet, various sizes	27-36
Pitcher, water (ill.)	107-118
Salt, footed, round, flat	32-39
Spoonholder	32-39

Beaded Grape Medallion

Sugar bowl, acorn finial,
 covered 56-63
Goblet with pink flash reproduced after World
War II.

Bowl, berry, covered, 6″, 7″, 8″	$ 18-28
Butter dish, 2 types	48-54
Cake stand, 6″, 9½″	36-42
Celery	32-41
Compote	
Large, covered	42-47
Open, jelly	38-48
Cordial	23-34
Creamer	29-37
Dish, oval, 7½″, 9½″, 10½″	20-30
Goblet	38-44
Mug, handled	32-41
Pickle dish, boat shape	21-29
Pitcher	
Milk (ill.)	42-51
Syrup	52-70
Water, ½ gallon	54-62
Saucedishes, 2 types	12-19
Shakers	
Salt/Pepper, pr.	38-45
Sugar	31-42
Spoonholder, footed and flat	49-56
Sugar bowl	
Covered	38-45
Open	22-29
Toothpick holder (rare)	68-79
Tray, bread	43-49
Tumbler	32-46
Vase or individual decanter	32-37
Wine	
Flat	44-54
Pedestaled	55-65

Beaded Medallion

Dalzell, Leighton and Gilmore, c. 1890s.
Clear, nonflint.

Butter dish	$ 28-36
Compote, open, scalloped edge	
8½″ dia.	29-35
Creamer	23-30
Spoonholder	21-28
Sugar bowl, covered	27-34

Beaded Mirror

Sandwich glass, late 1860s, or early
1870s. Clear only.

Butter dish, covered	$ 40-49
Compote, covered	55-62
Creamer (ill.)	35-42
Egg cup	30-37
Goblet (?)	28-36
Pitcher	92-107
Relish dish	37-42
Salt dish, footed	35-43
Sauce, flat and footed	10-15

Beaded Loop

Beaded Loop

(Oregon): U.S. Glass Company, 1906-08.
Clear, rare in emerald green. Rose flashed
pieces not of the period.

35

(continued)

Beaded Mirror

Spoonholder.   26-32
Sugar bowl, covered   44-49

Like Beaded Acorn Medallion and Beaded Grape Medallion but medallion is clear.

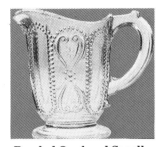

Beaded Oval and Scroll

Beaded Oval and Scroll

(Dot): Bryce Bros., Pittsburgh, late 1870s. Clear, nonflint.

Bowl, 8″ . . . . $ 20-25
Butter dish, covered   34-40
Cake stand   33-37
Compote
  High standard, covered   39-46
  High standard, open   29-35
Creamer (ill.)   25-30
Goblet.   26-31
Pickle dish   16-19
Pitcher, water   36-44
Salt/Pepper, pr.   32-42
Sauce, flat   9-11
Spoonholder.   19-26
Sugar bowl
  Covered   32-37
  Open   19-24
Wine   23-29

Beaded Panel

Beaded Panel

Indiana Tumbler and Goblet Company, Greentown, Indiana, c. 1900. Limited production (syrup known) by Dunkirk Glass Company after 1907. Clear, nonflint.

Butter dish, 7¼″, flanged . . . . . . $ 42-56
Compote, jelly, covered, 5½″.   42-50
Creamer (ill.)   34-42
Honey dish   17-21
Pitcher   82-95
Salt shaker.   33-39
Sauce, 4⅛″, 4¾″ dia..   16-22
Spoonholder.   30-35
Sugar bowl, covered   45-55
Toothpick holder with inner
  "ledge" (rare)   115-128
Tumbler.   32-41
Wine   22-29

Twenty-one pieces made.

Beaded Panels

Beaded Panels

(Grated Ribbon): Crystal Glass Company, Pittsburgh, c. 1877. Clear, nonflint.

Butter dish, covered	$ 31-37
Celery (ill.)	30-36
Compote	25-35
Creamer.	25-32
Goblet.	22-28
Jam jar	28-35
Spoonholder.	22-29
Sugar bowl, covered	28-35

Beaded Swirl and Disc

Beaded Swirl and Disc

(Beaded Swirl with Disc Band): U. S. Glass Company (Bryce), c. 1904. Clear, blue, green; yellow, rose stains, sometimes combined. Nonflint.

Butter dish, covered	$ 34-40
Cake stand	32-39
Celery.	26-32
Compote, covered	38-44
Creamer (ill.)	25-32
Cruet	28-33
Goblet.	28-34
Pitcher	
Milk	33-39
Syrup, tin spring top	41-46
Water	40-46
Salt/Pepper, pr.	28-32
Spoonholder.	18-25
Sugar bowl, covered	30-39
Toothpick (scarce).	43-49

Colors, color-stained 50 percent more than clear prices listed. Salt shaker recorded with embossed advertising on base.

Beaded Tulip

(Andes): McKee Bros., Pittsburgh, c. 1894. Clear, nonflint. Colors scarce.

Beaded Tulip

Bowl, oblong	$ 19-27
Butter dish, covered	45-51
Cake stand, 9″ high	55-62
Creamer.	34-39
Goblet (ill.)	27-34
Pickle, oval	21-28
Pitcher, water,.	57-64
Spoonholder.	34-39
Sugar bowl, covered	48-54
Tray, water	60-66
Wine	29-36

Blue water tray 100 percent higher than clear water tray.

Bearded Head

(Viking; Bearded Prophet; Old Man of the Mountain): Hobbs, Brockunier & Company, Wheeling, West Virginia, 1876. Clear. The head is that of a Roman warrior.

Bowl, covered, large	$ 63-68
Butter dish, covered	65-70
Celery.	38-42
Compote, covered, 7″, 8″	72-82
Creamer, 3 heads	47-53
Egg cup	35-40
Mug, made from egg cup, reed	
applied handle.	58-70
Pickle dish	31-36
Pitcher, water (ill.)	60-69
Platter	62-70
Relish, footed	41-48
Salt, master	44-53
Sauce	19-24
Spoonholder.	36-44
Sugar bowl, covered	59-63

Goblets and tumblers were not made.

37

(continued)

Bearded Head

The Bedford

The Bedford

(Bedford Line No. 1000): Fostoria Glass Company, Moundsville, West Virginia, 1901-1905. Clear, nonflint. Over 60 pieces made.

Bonbon, 5″, 6″, one handle . . . . . . $	17-22
Butter dish	41-45
Celery vase	23-30
Claret	29-37
Creamer (ill.)	26-32
Goblet	26-36
Horseradish, orig. patterned	
hollow stopper	30-34
Pitcher ("jug")	40-49
Spoonholder	28-37
Sugar bowl	41-47
Toothpick	32-39

Tray, ice cream, rectangular	37-42
Tumbler	
Water	16-22
Whiskey (shot)	10-14

Fifty-four pieces known. Number and shape of "tiers" varies with size of piece.

Bellflower

Bellflower

(Ribbed Leaf): Boston and Sandwich Glass Company, 1840s. McKee Brothers, 1868, called it Ribbed Leaf. Clear, cobalt, amber, opaque. Amber considered rarest; blue next. Its many qualities and types must be taken into consideration when giving a price on a particular piece.

Bowl	
Berry, flat, scalloped	$125-135
Deep, oval, 5″ x 7″,	
6″ x 9″	43-53
Flat, scallop and point edge	140-149
Round, 6″, 8″ edge	130-138
Butter dish, covered	
Beaded edge	100-118
Rayed edge, etc.	105-120
Cake stand (rare)	1,800+
Caster sets, 5 bottles (rare)	280-300
Celery vase (rare)	175-190
Champagne	115-130
Compotes, open, 6 types,	
low, high	118-132
Creamer, double or single vine	132-145
Decanter, patterned stopper,	
3 types (rare)	172-235
Egg cup	36-42
Goblets, 6 types	36-45
Honey dish, 3¼″ x 2½″	13-18
Lamp	
Bracket	315-345
Tall, marble base	105-125
Mug, handled, small (rare)	240-250

Pitcher
Milk, double vine (rare) . . . . . .   600+
Syrup, 10-sided (rare) . . . .   700+
Water, 2 sizes (ill.)   200-250
Plate, 6″ (rare).   125-135
Salt
Covered, footed (rare)   175-185
Open, footed.   42-50
Sauce   13-17
Spoonholder, double or single vine . .   35-43
Sugar bowl
Double vine, covered.   125-135
Octagonal (rare) . . . .   355+
Single vine, covered   112-122
Tumbler
Footed, fine rib   235-250
Water   80-92
Whiskey, small tumbler (rare)   175-185
Wine, single vine   95-108

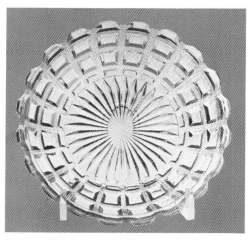

Berlin

Belted Worchester

Belted Worchester

Maker unknown, c. 1850s. Clear, flint.

Champagne . . . . $ 43-51
Cordial   34-41
Goblet (ill.)   35-41
Sugar bowl, covered   48-55
Whiskey, handled   33-41
Wine   31-40

Berlin

Adams & Company, Pittsburgh, 1874. Clear, nonflint.

Bowl, deep, 7″ (ill.). . . . . $ 25-35
Butter dish   34-42

Compote
Covered   52-60
Open   41-50
Creamer.   32-42
Dish, oval   21-30
Egg cup   25-34
Honey dish   22-31
Pickle dish   22-29
Pitcher
Milk.   35-41
Water   38-46
Plate, 7″ deep   19-23
Salt/Pepper, pr.   29-34
Sauce   8-11
Spoonholder.   17-22
Sugar bowl   32-40
Tumbler.   19-26

Berry Cluster

39

(continued)

Berry Cluster

Maker unknown, 1880s. Clear, nonflint.

Butter dish	$ 48-57
Creamer (ill.)	42-46
Spoonholder.	27-34
Sugar bowl	
Covered	44-53
Open	23-31

Bevelled Diagonal Block

Pitcher, water	35-42
Plate	22-29
Spoonholder.	16-22
Sugar bowl	30-36
Tumbler.	15-20
Wine	17-23

Bethlehem Star

Bethlehem Star

(Bright Star; Star Burst): Indiana Glass Company, Dunkirk, Indiana, 1910-1920. Clear, nonflint.

Butter dish	$ 32-40
Celery, handled	19-28
Compote, covered jelly,	
4⅝″ x 7⅝″	34-40
Creamer (ill.)	22-27
Cruet, original stopper.	35-42
Goblet.	22-27
Pitcher	39-42

Bevelled Diagonal Block

(Crossbar): Challinor, Taylor & Company, 1880s. Also by Bryce Bros., 1888. Ruby, nonflint.

Bowl, finger	$ 12-16
Butter dish	42-47
Cake stand	30-36
Celery vase (ill.)	26-31
Compote	24-32
Cordial	22-29
Creamer.	24-30
Goblet.	17-23

Bevelled Star

Bevelled Star

(Original name, Pride): Model Flint Glass Company, c. 1900. Clear, emerald green, cobalt, amber, nonflint.

Bowl, 9″	$ 22-29
Butter dish, covered	43-50
Celery tray, 5″ x 10½″	29-33
Compote, covered, high standard . . .	54-61
Creamer.	37-47
Pitcher, water (ill.)	53-61
Salt/Pepper, pr.	32-42
Sauce, 4″.	20-22
Spoonholder.	31-36

40

Sugar bowl 39-43

Twenty-six pieces made. Appears in Sears 1900 catalog. Emerald green, cobalt, 50 percent higher, amber, 100 percent higher than clear prices listed.

Cordial	49-57
Decanter, bar type.	80-90
Goblet, various heights, types	30-40
Mug, handled	68-77
Tumblers	56-64
Wine	38-44

Bicycle Girl

Bicycle Girl

Dalzell, Gilmore and Leighton, Findlay, Ohio, 1880s; later by National Glass Company, Greentown, Indiana.

Pitcher, water, clear (ill.) $325-375

Birch Leaf

Birch Leaf

Maker unknown, c. 1870s. Clear, milk glass, flint, nonflint.

Butter dish, covered, on pedestal (ill.)	$ 64-72
Creamer.	35-42
Egg cup	24-29
Goblet.	28-34
Salt, master, footed	22-27
Spoonholder.	25-32
Sugar bowl, covered	50-55

Milk glass, 100 percent higher than clear prices listed. Pattern not same as birch leaf shaped bowls, sauces.

Bird and Strawberry

(Bluebird): Indiana Glass Company, c. 1918. Clear or painted with bluebirds and pink strawberries and green leaves. Nonflint.

Bowl, footed, berry, round, 9″	$ 25-33
Butter dish, covered	89-96
Cake stand, 9″ diameter	62-72
Compote	
Covered, 6½″ dia., 9½″ high	82-96
Open, ruffled, high.	70-75
Creamer, w/color	53-63

Bigler

Bigler

Boston & Sandwich Glass Company, Sandwich, Massachusetts, c. 1850s. Clear, flint.

Bowls	$ 38-46
Champagne	61-76

41

(continued)

Bird and Strawberry

Goblet.	50-66
Pitcher (ill.)	135-150
Relish, heart-shaped.	29-39
Sauce, clear, footed, 5″	27-32
Spoonholder.	49-52
Sugar bowl, covered	60-70
Tumbler.	44-53
Wine	36-44

Bird Napkin Ring

Bird Napkin Ring

With salt (in bird's back) and pepper. Thought to be Sandwich glass; considered scarce. There is a pair of these at the Houston Museum, Chattanooga, Tennessee.

Bird napkin ring w/Salt/Pepper, (ill.)	$ 350+

Bird on Nest Mug

Bird on Nest Mug

(Bird and Harp): Challinor & Taylor, Ltd., Tarentum, Pennsylvania, 1880s. Clear, purple slag, nonflint.

Mug (ill.)	$ 30-37

(Harp on reverse side). Purple slag 50 percent more.

Birds at Fountain

Birds at Fountain

Early 1880s. Clear, milk glass, nonflint.

Bowl, shallow	$ 20-27
Butter dish	48-54
Cake stand	49-55
Compote, covered, 8″	67-73
Creamer.	39-42
Goblet.	38-48
Mug, toy (ill.)	32-42
Sauce	11-16

Bismarc Star

(Nebraska; original, name Togo): Indiana Glass Co., Dunkirk, 1908, and erroneously to U. S. Glass Co. Clear, nonflint. Goblet does not have characteristic feather detail.

Bonbon, 5″ square, flat	$ 15-21

Bowl
    Berry, flat, 6″, 7″   16-20
    Low foot, 6″, 7″   18-24
Butter, covered   32-39
Compote, high footed jelly, 5″ dia. . . .   17-25
Creamer
    Large   25-33
    Medium (berry)   20-25
Cruet, orig. paneled banded
    stopper   32-39
Goblet.   22-32
Olive, 6″ flat, lobed, tab handle.   13-18
Spoonholder, straight, no handles . . .   16-21
Sugar
    Large, covered, straight,
      no handles   30-36
    Medium, two handles (berry)   20-25
Tumbler, iced tea   14-19
Wine   25-35

Blackberry

Blackberry

Patented by William Leighton, Jr., Hobbs Brockunier, Wheeling, West Virginia, 1870. Clear, milk glass, nonflint.

Butter dish, covered . . . . $ 42-50
Celery vase (scarce, especially in
    milk glass)   60-68
Champagne   42-51
Compote
    Covered, high foot   79-88
    Covered, low foot 7″, 8″   64-71
Creamer.   57-67
Dish, oval, 8¼″ × 5½″   18-27
Egg cup, double and single   37-49
Goblet (rare)   35-43
Honey dish   7-11
Lamp, tall, clear with unpatterned
    milk glass base.   115-141
Pitcher, water, rare (ill.)   162-172
Salt, footed, 2 styles   25-36

Sauce, flat, 4⅜″ high.   8-12
Spoonholder, berry handles   31-38
Sugar bowl, open   60-67
Syrup, (rare) 6⅞″ high.   125-150
Tumbler.   29-37

Milk glass, 80 percent higher than clear prices listed. Some milk glass goblets, spoonholders, creamers dated. Add 20 percent to milk glass prices. Reissued by Cooperative Glass Company and Phoenix Glass Company until World War II.

Blaze

New England Glass Company, East Cambridge, Massachusetts, c. 1869. Clear, flint.

Butter dish, covered . . . . $ 65-75
Celery.   80-89
Champagne   59-70
Compote, covered, low standard
    7″, 8″   80-87
Cordial   48-55
Creamer, pressed handle.   53-63
Goblet.   50-58
Plate, 6″, 7″   36-44
Sauce, 4″, 5″   13-19
Spoonholder.   33-40
Sugar bowl, covered   70-76
Tumbler.   51-60
Wine   64-72

Blazing Cornucopia

(Golden Jewel, Paisley): U. S. Glass, c. 1913. Clear, nonflint. Also painted purple, pink, olive green, and with gold trim.

Bonbon, 6¼″ flared . . . . $ 13-20
Bowl, deep, 7″, 8″, 8½″   19-28
Butter, covered   33-40
Celery tray, 9¼″ x 5½″.   17-25
Compote, jelly, 5½″ dia.   17-24
Creamer.   28-35
Cruet.   31-43
Cup, sherbet, one handle.   10-14
Dish, oblong, 7½″ x 4″   16-21
Goblet.   18-25
Olive, 5″, one handle   15-22
Pitcher, ½ gal   36-45
Relish   14-19
Sauce, flat, 4½″, 5″.   9-13
Spoonholder.   20-26
Sugar, covered.   30-37
Toothpick, handled   32-39

43

(continued)

Tumbler. 16-21
Wine 20-30

Also made without the star and punty in the divided, heart-shaped panel and has been named Blazing Heart, the scarcer of the two patterns.

Bleeding Heart

Bleeding Heart

(Original name, Floral):Sandwich Glass Company, 1860-1875, then King, Son and Company, c. 1870s, made two types. Clear, milk glass.

Bowl, waste	$ 36-45
Butter dish	60-70
Cake plate on stand, 9½″ high	64-73
Compote	
Covered, high foot	77-92
Covered, low foot	75-90
Covered, Oval	98-104
Creamer, applied handle.	59-66
Dish, oval, large	31-39
Egg cups	
Barrel shape.	38-42
Straight side.	31-40
Goblet	
Knob stem, 6 types (ill.)	28-44
Mug, handled	46-52
Pickle dish, oval	26-32
Pitcher, water (ill.)	132-142
Plates (rare)	75-85
Platter, oval	66-77
Salt	
Oval (rare).	21-28
Round, footed	21-28
Sauces, 3 types	13-19
Spoonholder.	32-42
Sugar bowl	73-80
Tumbler	
Footed.	46-51
Water	63-80
Wine	92-118

Milk glass 30 percent higher.

Block and Circle

Block and Circle

(Original name, Mellor): Gillinder, c. 1880.

Butter dish	$ 37-50
Celery vase	31-36
Compote	
Covered, 6″ (sweetmeat)	40-50
Open, high, 7″, 8″, 9″	34-40
Creamer.	29-37
Dish, oval, 7″, 8″, 9″.	18-24
Goblet.	24-31
Lamp, miniature	31-40
Mug, beer	33-41
Pitcher, water (ill.)	47-52
Tumblers to match	21-25

Block and Fan

Block and Fan

Richards & Hartley Glass Company, Tarentum, Pennsylvania, 1880s. Clear, ruby, nonflint.

Bowl, berry, 8″ dia., flat	$ 31-39
Butter dish, covered	45-55
Cake stand, 10″ dia.	41-50
Celery tray	23-28
Compote, open, high.	39-46
Creamer.	41-47
Cruet, no stopper (ill.)	25-32

Goblet.	58-68
Pitcher, water, pedestal base.	43-50
Plate, 10½".	28-37
Salt/Pepper, pr.	46-51
Sauce	
Flat, square	13-19
Footed, round, 4".	15-20
Spoonholder.	30-39
Sugar, covered and open.	44-52
Tumbler.	36-43
Wine	47-53

Ruby 120 percent higher than clear prices given.

Block and Honeycomb

Block and Honeycomb

McKee & Bros., Pittsburgh, 1868. Clear, nonflint.

Butter dish, pedestal	$ 31-41
Creamer (ill.)	37-47
Goblet.	23-27
Spoonholder.	23-28
Sugar bowl	33-37

Block and Palm

(Eighteen-Ninety): Beaver Falls Co-Operative Glass Company, Beaver Falls, Pennsylvania, c. 1890. Clear, milk glass, nonflint.

Butter dish, covered	$ 28-35
Cake stand	31-37
Celery.	20-27
Creamer.	20-26
Goblet.	20-25
Pitcher, water	41-45

Salt/Pepper, pr.	39-45
Sauce, flat.	20-26
Spoonholder.	17-28
Sugar bowl, covered	24-29

Milk glass, 25 percent higher than clear prices listed.

Block and Rib

Block and Rib

Maker unknown, c. 1880. Clear, milk glass, nonflint.

Butter dish, covered	$ 28-34
Celery holder	18-25
Creamer (ill.)	19-25
Pitcher, water	24-31
Spoonholder.	15-20
Sugar bowl, covered	25-32

Milk glass 30 percent more than clear prices listed.

Block and Star

(Valencia Waffle): U. S. Glass Company (Adams). Clear, blue, amber, apple green, nonflint.

Butter dish, covered	$ 33-43
Celery.	26-32
Compote	
Covered	39-45
Open	24-32
Creamer.	30-37
Goblet (ill.)	24-30
Relish.	20-25

45

(continued)

Block and Star

Salt dip, oblong master	18-26
Sauce	
Flat, square	13-19
Footed.	15-18
Spoonholder.	24-29
Sugar	
Covered	33-43
Open	22-32
Wine	30-34

Probably other pieces. Color, 60 percent more than clear prices listed.

Block and Thumbprint

Block and Thumbprint

Gillinder, Philadelphia, c. 1850 and possibly Union Glass Company, Somerville, Massachusetts, c. 1860. Clear, flint and nonflint.

Butter dish, covered	$ 43-52
Celery (ill.)	33-43
Compote, covered	48-56

Creamer.	45-53
Goblet, knob stem	40-47
Spoonholder.	33-39
Sugar bowl, covered	45-55
Tumbler, footed	38-43

Nonflint, 40 percent less than flint prices listed.

Blockade

Blockade

(Diamond Block with Fans; Challinor No. 309): Challinor, Taylor, Ltd., Tarentum, Pennsylvania, 1885. Clear.

Bowl	
Finger	$ 16-23
Butter dish, covered	36-46
Celery	33-40
Compote	
Covered, high stem, 6″, 7″, 8″	36-44
Open, 4″, 6″, 7″, 8″	28-41
Creamer.	25-33
Dish, square, 7″, 8″, 9″	20-32
Goblet (ill.)	25-31
Nappy, flat bottom, 4½″, 6″	18-22
Pitcher, water, qt. ½ gal.	50-58
Spoonholder.	17-23
Sugar bowl, covered	38-45
Tumbler.	19-24

Thirty pieces made. Lower half of stem is hollow.

Blocked Arches

(Berkeley); U.S. Glass Company, c. 1893. Clear, clear with frosted ruby, nonflint. Also came engraved.

Bowl, finger	$ 20-26

Blocked Arches

Butter dish, covered	41-47
Creamer.	34-39
Cup/saucer	27-33
Goblet.	30-38
Shaker, salt	20-24
Spoonholder.	21-31
Sugar bowl (base ill.)	40-47
Syrup	49-57
Tumbler.	28-36
Wine	32-40

Prices are frosted ruby. Clear 30 percent less.

Bohemian

(Floradora, or correct spelling Florodora that refers to the rose-flashed decoration rather than the pattern name): U. S. Glass No.15063, c. 1899. Clear, clear with rose flash; frosted allover with rose and yellow flashing; rose-flashed, emerald green. Usually with gold. Nonflint.

Butter.	$145-162
Celery vase (clear with paint)	64-72
Creamer.	93-110
Mug, 3½″ high (clear with paint and gold)	68-79
Spoonholder.	72-85
Straw jar, covered (frosted with paint).	142-159
Sugar, covered.	105-119
Toothpick.	110-125

No goblet or cruet known. Prices listed are for allover rose flashing unless stated. Green, 20 percent less; clear with rose decoration, 40 percent less; frosted with paint, 25 percent less.

Bosc Pear

Indiana Glass Co., Dunkirk, Indiana 1913. Clear, with or without gold, nonflint. Also with pink pears, green leaves and gold trim.

Bowl, 8½″ berry	$ 14-18
Butter, covered	23-30
Creamer.	15-21
Pitcher, ½ gal.	31-36
Spoonholder, two handles	13-19
Sugar, covered, two handles	21-27
Tumbler.	12-16

For painted pieces in good condition, add 40 percent to clear prices given.

Bow Tie

The Thompson Glass Company, Uniontown, Pennsylvania, c. 1889. Clear, nonflint.

Bowl, fruit, 10″ deep	$ 34-38
Butter dish, covered	54-61
Cake stand	53-63
Creamer.	40-45
Goblet.	38-47
Pitcher, water	77-85
Salt dip, individual	17-23
Spoonholder.	31-38
Sugar bowl, covered	50-55

Firm only in business for three years.

Boxed Star

Boxed Star

Jenkins Glass Company, c. 1900. Clear, nonflint.

Butter dish	$ 27-33
Creamer (ill.)	18-24

47

(continued)

Pitcher, water	28-35
Spoonholder.	17-21
Sugar bowl	23-30
Tumbler, 9 oz..	13-17

Bradford Grape

Bradford Grape

(Bradford Blackberry): Sandwich attribution, c. 1860. Clear, flint.

Butter dish, covered	$109-118
Champagne	80-90
Creamer.	110-125
Goblet (ill.)	69-85
Pitcher, water	205-216
Spoonholder.	60-68
Sugar bowl, covered	115-130
Tumbler (rare)	123-131
Wine	91-98

Branched Tree

Branched Tree

Dalzell, Gilmore and Leighton, c. 1890s. Nonflint.

Butter dish	$ 58-63
Celery.	33-41
Compote, covered, high	53-63
Creamer.	36-42
Pitcher, water (ill.)	81-89
Spoonholder.	31-36
Sugar bowl	46-55

Brazilian

(Brazillian erroneously, Cane Shield): Fostoria, c. 1898. Clear, emerald green

Bowl	
Berry 7", 8", 10".	$ 17-30
Finger, 4½" dia.	16-22
Butter, covered, flat	32-40
Carafe.	30-38
Celery tray	19-23
Celery vase	26-31
Compote, low open 8" footed	22-32
Cracker jar, covered	48-59
Creamer, applied handle.	30-39
Cruet, original faceted stopper. . . .	42-55
Jar, canned milk, advertising "Red	
Cross" milk, flat, patterned lid	40-50
Olive, handled	18-25
Pickle jar, covered	33-42
Pitcher, tankard, jug shape	40-50
Relish, advertisement embossed	17-23
Rose bowl	24-31
Salt dip, individual	12-18
Salt shaker	20-30
Sauce, 4½"	10-14
Sherbet	12-18
Spooner	22-33
Sugar, covered.	35-42
Syrup "molasses can"	49-60
Toothpick.	32-37
Tumbler.	17-25
Vase, 7", 9", 11"	16-30

No goblet. Emerald green add 80 percent to clear prices listed.

Brickwork

Brickwork

Maker unknown, c. 1900. Clear and caramel slag, nonflint.

Creamer (ill.) . . . . $ 31-40
Caramel slag, 70 percent higher than clear price listed.

Brilliant

Brilliant

McKee Bros., Pittsburgh, c. 1860. Clear, flint.

Bowl, 6″	$ 31-37
Butter dish, covered	49-60
Champagne	63-72
Compote, open, 8″	
High.	46-58
Low	41-47
Creamer, applied handle.	50-60
Egg cup	30-36
Goblet.	44-54
Spoonholder.	34-43
Sugar bowl, covered	46-55
Sweetmeat, covered, 6″.	45-53

Bringing Home the Cows

Bringing Home the Cows

Dalzell, Gilmore and Leighton Company, 1870s. Clear.

Butter dish, covered	$205-220
Creamer.	147-161
Pitcher, milk, 10¼″ (ill.)	325-345
Spoonholder.	110-120
Sugar bowl, covered	178-195

Britannic

Britannic

McKee Bros., Pittsburgh, 1893. Clear, amber, green, ruby. Popular after Columbian Exposition of 1893.

Butter dish, covered	$ 35-42
Cake stand, small, large	47-56
Caster bottle (mustard)	18-25
Compote	
Covered	33-45
Open, 7½″	30-34
Creamer.	31-38
Cruet	37-46
Cup, custard.	25-33
Goblet.	29-35
Honey dish, square, covered	42-53
Pitcher (ill.)	49-58
Rose bowl	30-34
Salt/Pepper, pr.	35-45
Spoonholder.	35-44
Sugar bowl, covered	55-65
Tumbler.	40-49
Wine	26-33

Ruby, 65 percent higher; amber, green 45 percent higher than clear prices listed.

Broken Column

Broken Column

(Irish Column, Notched Rib): U.S. Glass Company, 1892, before that by Columbia Glass Company, Findlay, Ohio, 1891. Portland Glass Company by tradition. Clear with ruby notches. Cobalt cup known. Nonflint. Occasionally found with gold trim.

Banana dish, flat	$ 41-46
Basket, handled, 13½" long	88-92
Bowl	
8½" diameter	33-43
Covered, various sizes	40-50
Butter dish, covered	50-60
Cake stand, large	59-67
Celery	40-50
Celery tray	30-38
Compote	
Covered, high standard	60-70
Open, high standard	40-50
Creamer (ill.)	40-50
Cruet, patterned stopper	48-58
Custard cup	20-27
Finger bowl	20-27
Goblet, lady's	40-50
Pickle caster, complete	90-112
Pitcher, water	50-58
Plate, 7¾"	35-43
Salt/Pepper, pr.	32-40
Sauce, flat	13-17
Spoonholder	30-40
Sugar	
Bowl, open	30-38
Shaker	59-66
Syrup jug	61-71
Tumbler, plain	30-38
Water bottle	52-62
Wine	50-60

Goblet, covered square compote reproduced. Ruby pieces 150 percent higher than clear prices listed.

Brooklyn

Brooklyn

Maker unknown, c. late 1860s, early 1870s. Clear, flint.

Compote	
Covered	$ 72-81
Open	42-48
Creamer, pressed handle	60-65
Decanter	60-70
Goblet (ill.)	45-53
Pitcher, water	105-135
Sugar bowl, covered	75-83

Buck and Doe

Maker unknown. Transfer-etched pattern on pressed blank, c. 1870s.

Goblet	$127-140

Buckingham

(Crosby): U.S. Glass Company, 1906. Clear, iridescent-flashed souvenirs, combined rose and green flashed, nonflint. Some with gold.

Basket	$ 47-54
Butter dish, covered	33-43
Celery	27-31
Compote	
Covered	33-41
Open	24-30
Creamer	24-30
Goblet	24-33
Pitcher, water	35-41
Spoonholder	19-23
Sugar bowl, covered	31-37
Toothpick, 3 handles	31-37

Tumbler. 15-19

Color, 25 percent higher than clear prices listed. Confusion with "Diamond" pattern originating from Kamm-Wood Encyclopedia (pg. 226) grouping.

Buckle

Buckle

Sandwich Glass, early 1870s; also Gillinder & Sons, Philadelphia, same period. Clear, sapphire blue (rare); flint and nonflint. (Also see Banded Buckle.)

Bowl, rolled rim	$ 65-72
Butter dish, covered, flat	59-64
Champagne	52-63
Compote, open, low standard	39-48
Creamer, applied handles,	
pedestal foot.	47-59
Egg cup	27-31
Goblets	30-34
Pickle dish, large, oval	19-26
Pitcher, water, applied handle	
(very rare)	650+
Salt dip	
Footed.	19-27
Oval, flat, pattern in base	24-32
Saucedish, flat, 4″	7-10
Spoonholder, scalloped rim (ill.) . . .	33-42
Sugar bowl, covered	50-58
Tumbler.	30-38
Wine	57-67

Color, 80 percent more than clear prices listed. Flint, 50 percent higher than nonflint prices listed.

Buckle with Diamond Band

(Buckle and Diamond): McKee, c. 1880s. Clear, nonflint.

Butter dish, covered	$ 35-42
Creamer.	28-35

Goblet.	23-30
Pitcher, water	46-54
Spoonholder.	19-26
Sugar bowl, covered	32-39

Buckle with Star

Buckle with Star

(Original name, Orient): Bryce, Walker & Company, Pittsburgh, c. 1875. Clear, nonflint.

Bowls, oval, round	$ 23-28
Butter dish, covered	36-45
Celery	31-37
Compote, covered	60-66
Creamer (ill.)	41-49
Goblet.	34-43
Pitcher	55-65
Relish, oval	15-23
Sauce, flat	11-18
Spoonholder.	23-32
Sugar bowl, covered	37-49
Wine	33-40

Bulldog with Hat Toothpick or Match

(Dog with Hat; Dog and Pail): Belmont Glass Company, Bellaire, Ohio, c. 1885. Reproduced in all colors.

Amber.	$ 59-69
Blue.	68-81
Clear	40-47

(continued)

Bulldog with Hat Toothpick or Match

Bullet Emblem

Bullet Emblem

(Shield): Clear, originally red, white, and blue paint with silver bullet finial. Spanish-American War commemorative, made in 1898.

Butter, covered (ill.)	$300-339
Creamer.	187-198
Spoonholder.	152-163
Sugar bowl, covered	270-325

Clear 20 percent less than painted prices listed.

Bull's Eye

(Lawrence): New England Glass Company; also Sandwich, c. 1850s. Clear, milk-white, colors (rare), flint.

Bitters bottle	$ 49-56
Butter dish, covered	131-147

Bull's Eye

Caster bottle	38-47
Celery vase (ill.)	76-85
Champagne	91-109
Cologne bottle.	82-90
Compote	
Open, large, high, standard.	62-72
Open, low standard	47-53
Creamer.	134-139
Decanter	
Bar lip, pint and quart	93-117
Pint and quart, stoppered	129-140
Egg cup	
Covered (rare)	172-180
Regular	43-55
Goblet, knob and plain stem	66-79
Jar, covered, small.	77-85
Lamp	89-96
Pickle dish, oval	38-45
Salt	
Footed.	31-40
Footed, oblong, covered (rare)	112-116
Spoonholder.	39-47
Sugar bowl, covered	122-131
Tumbler, water	89-100
Water bottle with tumble-up	129-150

Colored pieces, 150 percent higher than clear prices listed. Prices are for good quality. Non-flint or poor tone, 50 percent less.

Bull's Eye and Daisy

Bull's Eye and Daisy

(Original name, Newport): U. S. Glass Company (Glassport), c. 1909. Clear, emerald green; clear with bull's eye in rose, red, purple; gilt rims; nonflint.

Butter dish, covered	$ 31-37
Creamer	25-30
Goblet	19-25
Pitcher, water	35-42
Salt shaker	18-22
Spoonholder	17-21
Sugar bowl, handled, open*, (ill.)	24-29
Tumbler	16-22
Wine	21-28

Colors, 60-80 percent higher than clear prices listed.
* Sugar lid has plain convex panel and no bull's eye.

Bull's Eye and Fan

Bull's Eye and Fan

(Daisy in Oval Panels): U. S. Glass Company, c. 1905. Clear, clear with colored bull's eyes; blue, green, nonflint. Sometimes with gold.

Bowl	$ 17-23
Butter dish, covered	32-41
Creamer	24-31
Goblet	20-24
Pitcher, water (ill.)	34-42
Sauce, flat	5-10
Spoonholder	18-22
Sugar	
Covered	31-36
Open	20-25
Tumbler	14-20

Pieces with colored bull's eyes, 20 percent higher than clear prices listed. Solid colors 50 percent higher.

Bull's Eye and Prism

Bull's Eye and Prism

Probably English, c. late 1840s, early 1850s. Clear, flint.

Goblet (ill.)	$ 69-78

Bull's Eye and Spear Head

Bull's Eye and Spear Head

Dalzell, Gilmore & Leighton, Findlay, Ohio, c. late 1870s. Also U. S. Glass (Bellaire) and Model Flint (Findlay and Albany plants). Clear, nonflint.

Butter dish, covered, flanged	$ 45-53
Compote	
Covered	67-75
Open, scallop and point rim	33-41
Creamer	36-45
Decanter (ill.)	47-64
Goblet	31-38

(continued)

Lamp, night, ("Remington"),
  tall domed shade.   155-180
Spoonholder.   27-32
Sugar bowl, covered   43-50
Tankard, 7" claret 38-43
Tray, 7" round   28-33
Wine (ill.) 27-32

Stemware illustrated also known as Bull's Eye, by Bellaire.

Bull's Eye with Fleur-de-Lis

Bull's Eye with Fleur-de-Lis

Boston & Sandwich Glass Company, mid-1800s; probably Union Glass Company, Somerville, Massachusetts, 1860s. Clear and amber, flint only.

Ale glass (rare) $170-185
Butter dish, covered   125-145
Celery   95-105
Compote
  Open, high standard   128-135
  Open, low standard   115-122
Creamer (rare)   265-275
Decanter, original stopper
  Pint   114-130
  Quart 139-155
Goblet.   99-116
Lamp
  Glass only   113-137
  Glass bowl, brass stem
    marble base   170-200
Pitcher, water, rare (ill.) 292-322
Salt, footed   65-73
Sugar bowl, covered   146-155

Amber, 60 percent higher than clear prices listed.

Butterfly

Butterfly

U.S. Glass Company. Clear, nonflint.

Pitcher, water,
  8", ½ gal. (ill.) $117-129
Only piece known.

Butterfly and Berry

Butterfly and Berry

Fenton Art Glass Company, Williamstown, West Virginia, c. 1911. Marigold, blue, and purple carnival. Rare bowl in chocolate and also in white carnival.

Bowl
  Berry . . . . $ 55-60
  Sauce   25-32
Butter dish, covered   74-89
Creamer.   61-72
Pitcher, water, jug, not footed 73-90
Spoonholder.   44-49
Sugar bowl, covered, footed 74-86
Tumbler.   37-41

Prices are for marigold.

Butterfly with Spray

Butterfly with Spray

(Acme): Bryce, Higbee and Company, Pittsburgh, c. 1885. Clear, nonflint.

Butter dish, covered	$ 60-68
Celery	30-36
Compote, covered, high, low	
standard	43-53
Creamer	31-37
Mugs, 2 sizes (ill.)	35-40
Pitcher, water	56-62
Spoonholder	32-39
Sugar bowl, covered	48-55
Tumbler	23-31

Butterfly handles and finials make covered pieces difficult to find in perfect condition. "Butterfly with Fan" is not this pattern, but is the name given to the goblet that goes with "Japanese" or "Grace."

Button Arches

(Scalloped Daisy, Red Top): Duncan & Miller Glass Company, Washington, Pennsylvania, 1897. Clear, clear with ruby. Engraved, decorated and souvenir pieces and with frosted band. Also in clam broth with red transfer souvenir.

Bowl, 8″	$ 32-37
Cake stand	52-65
Compote, jelly	24-33
Creamer	29-37
Cruet	42-45
Cup	20-25
Goblet	36-46
Mug	28-37
Pitcher, water (ill.)	51-61
Salt/Pepper, pr.	29-37
Spoonholder	25-31
Sugar bowl, covered	43-53
Syrup	125-142
Toothpick holder	39-44
Tumbler	25-32

Wine	30-39

Prices listed are for Ruby. Clear 50 percent less. Reproduced table set, toothpick, goblet, and wine. Frosted band not reproduced.

Button Arches

Button Band

Button Band

(Umbilicated Hobnail. Original name, Wyandotte): U. S. Glass Company (Ripley), c. 1891. Clear, nonflint. Sometimes engraved.

Bowl	$ 22-28
Butter dish, covered	39-45
Cake stand, 10″	50-55
Caster set, 5 bottles, patterned	
stoppers, pedestal or flat	
holder	114-135
Compote, open, small	52-61
Creamer	31-38
Goblet	29-34
Pitcher, water (ill.)	49-56
Spoonholder	23-30
Sugar bowl, covered	34-42
Tumbler	24-27
Wine (rare)	42-51

Buttressed Arch

(Buttressed Loop): Possibly Adams Glass Company, Pittsburgh, mid-1880s. Clear, probably colors, nonflint.

(continued)

Buttressed Arch

Butter dish, covered	$ 27-35
Celery vase	16-22
Creamer (ill.)	22-27
Pitcher, water	32-40
Sauce	6-9
Spoonholder.	14-19
Sugar bowl, covered	25-34

Buttressed Loop

Adams No. 16, c. 1874. Clear, amber, vaseline known. Light yellow, medium blue, and green also listed.

Butter, covered (base lacks	
characteristic "bullets")	$ 24-30
Creamer.	20-27
Spoonholder.	15-20
Sugar, covered.	22-29

Information welcomed regarding other pieces and colors other than amber and vaseline. Color add 50 percent to clear prices listed.

Buttressed Sunburst

Tarentum Glass Co., 1909-1911. Clear, nonflint.

Bowl, berry, flared, 8½"	$ 17-23
Butter, covered	31-40
Celery.	20-29
Creamer.	23-30
Cruet	27-35
Goblet.	24-31
Olive	15-21
Pitcher	
Milk.	25-34
Water	34-42
Plate, dinner	18-25
Relish	10-14
Rose bowl, miniature	19-27
Sauce	7-12

Spoonholder, two handles	16-22
Sugar, covered, two handles	30-38
Tumbler.	14-19
Vase, 11¾" high	18-26
Wine	20-30

Buzz Star

(U. S. Whirligig, erroneously Beaumont Buzz Star): U. S. Glass (Bryce), c. 1907. Clear, nonflint. Some with gold trim. Very rare in emerald green.

Butter, covered	
Large	$ 28-35
Toy	25-32
Creamer	
Large	20-27
Toy	20-25
Cup, toy punch	9-14
Goblet.	20-26
Pitcher, tankard	36-42
Punch bowl, toy	28-36
Salt dip, individual	11-16
Spoonholder	
Large	16-21
Toy (is toothpick)	18-24
Sugar, (lid swirled, buzz star finial)	
Large, covered	24-32
Toy, covered.	22-30
Toothpick (is toy spoonholder)	18-24
Tumbler.	14-19
Wine	22-27

Toy punch bowl reproduced. Toothpick (toy spoonholder) known in emerald green.

Cabbage Leaf

Cabbage Leaf

Maker unknown, c. 1880s. Clear, amber leaves, heavily stippled or frosted, opalescent.

Butter dish, covered	$109-126
Celery	70-80
Creamer (ill.)	83-97
Pickle dish, large leaf shape	38-43
Pitcher, water	142-168
Plate, rabbit head in center	62-70
Spoonholder	44-53
Sugar bowl, covered	94-102

Goblet not originally made. New goblets in many colors. Prices for frosted, stippled 20 percent less.

Cabbage Rose

Cabbage Rose

Central Glass Company, Wheeling, West Virginia, 1880s; possibly at Sandwich earlier. Clear, nonflint.

Butter dish, covered	$ 50-57
Cake stand, 11″, 12½″	69-75
Celery vase	49-54
Compotes, covered, high	
6″, 7″, 8″, 9″	52-74
Creamer, applied handle	47-55
Egg cup	34-39
Goblet	32-40
Pickle dish	19-27
Pitcher	
Quart (ill.)	110-118
Three pints (rare)	135+
Salt, footed, master (beaded rim)	29-35
Saucedish, 6 sizes	12-24
Spoonholder	29-39
Sugar bowl	
Open	33-40
With lid	52-62
Tumbler, water	44-53

Wine	48-55

Goblet reproduced.

Cable

Cable

Sandwich glass of the 1850s. Clear, flint; rare in opaque, blue opaque, green opaque, amber panels. Made to commemorate laying of Atlantic cable.

Butter dish, covered	$ 90-112
Compote, open,	
11″ dia. x 5¾″ high	84-97
Creamer (rare)	365-425
Egg cup	40-48
Goblet	66-74
Lamp, marble base	94-103
Pitcher, water (rare)	425+
Plate, 6″	115-125
Salt dip, flat, individual	20-26
Spoonholder (ill.)	39-47
Sugar bowl, covered	92-102
Tumbler, footed	165-185

Colors, 120-140 percent higher than clear prices listed.

Cable with Ring

57

(continued)

Cable with Ring

Sandwich Glass Company, 1860s. Clear only, flint.

Creamer (ill.)	$110-127
Honey dish	12-16
Lamp	91-106
Sauce, flat	18-28
Sugar bowl, covered	94-112

No goblet or tumbler known. Sugar bowls lacking lids are common.

Cactus

Cactus

(Panelled Agave, Herringbone Rib): Indiana Tumbler & Goblet (National) Company, 1903. Crystal, chocolate (caramel slag), nonflint.

Bowl, berry	$ 64-72
Butter dish	
Flat	120-140
Stemmed (cheese)	240-260
Compote	
Large, 9"	170-191
Medium, 7"	152-162
Small, 5"	109-118
Cracker jar, covered	140-150
Creamer, large	132-142
Cruet	118-127
Mug, 3½", 4¾"	77-84
Pitcher, water (ill.)	205-215
Plate	68-78
Salt/Pepper, pr.	77-87
Smoker's set	
Ashtray (4" sauce)	24-32
Cigar holder (4" tumbler)	50-59
Match holder (toothpick)	67-75
Tray, 7½" round	68-78
Spoonholder	49-56
Sugar bowl, flat	87-97
Syrup metal lid	110-125
Toothpick	67-75

Tumbler	
Water, lemonade, and iced tea . . .	50-59

Prices listed are for chocolate. Reproduced in chocolate. Modern production in vaseline opalescent, not made originally.

Cadmus

Beaumont, 1902-1908; reissued by Wellington Glass Co. (formerly Cumberland Glass Co.) of Cumberland, Md., that became Dugan and then Lonaconing Glass Co., both at Maryland; c. 1915. Clear, may have gold trim.

Basket, 6½" handled	$ 29-37
Bowl	
Berry, crimped	16-22
Fruit, round, deep or shallow 7¾" . .	14-25
Butter, covered	25-34
Compote, jelly	16-22
Creamer	17-25
Cruet, 6 oz., original faceted	
stopper	28-36
Goblet	16-23
Pitcher, ½ gal. tankard	31-39
Sauce, crimped, flat, 4"	8-11
Spoonholder	13-19
Sugar, covered	25-34
Toothpick	33-40
Wine, 2½ oz.	15-21

California

California

Shown in New England Glass Company and Curling catalogs, c. 1850. Attributed to Sandwich by early authors. Blue, amethyst, flint.

Creamer (shown with sugar
in New England Glass catalog but
is not exact match). . . . . $300+
Sugar bowl with lid . . . . 300+

Canadian

Canadian

Burlington Glass Works, Canada, 1870s. Clear.

Butter dish, covered . . . . $ 56-64
Celery. 42-52
Compote
  Covered, 6″, 7″, 8″, 10″ 71-118
  Open, high and low standard 47-52
Cordial 18-24
Creamer (ill.) 59-66
Goblet. 53-64
Jam jar, 6½″,
  Covered, ribbed lid. 48-56
Pitcher
  Water, ½ gal. 69-79
  Medium (milk) 63-71
Plate, including handles 34-47
Sauce, flat and footed, 4″. 13-18
Spoonholder. 34-41
Sugar bowl, covered 57-66
Wine 40-47

Forms similar to Cape Cod. Both patterns have different scenes on the various pieces, but the frames on Canadian form an arch and on Cape Cod, an oval.

Cane

Cane

Sandwich Glass Company attribution by early authors, c. 1880. Also Gillinder Glass Company and McKee Glass Company, 1894 called "Hobnail." Clear, amber, apple green, blue, yellow, nonflint.

Bowl, berry, 3-panel, footed . . . . . . $ 22-27
Bowl, finger, waste. 18-25
Butter dish, covered 39-46
Creamer. 25-35
Goblet. 22-27
Jam jar 22-31
Pickle dish, oval 14-18
Pitcher, water ½ gal.(ill.) 40-47
Salt/Pepper, pr. 32-40
Sauce, flat. 9-12
Spoonholder, flat rim 22-28
Sugar bowl, covered 54-63
Toddy plate 14-20
Tray, water 35-42
Tumbler, water 22-31

Apple green and yellow, 60 percent more; amber and blue, 80 percent more than clear prices listed. Comes with raised or inverted "buttons." The Cane salt shaker listed in Peterson is not this pattern, nor is the Kettle toothpick with Cane rim.

Cane Column

(Panelled Cane, Flower Panelled Cane): Portland Glass Company attribution, late 1870s, called "Jewel." Clear, canary, amber, blue, nonflint.

Butter dish, covered . . . . $ 35-42
Celery 30-36

59

(continued)

Cane Column

Champagne	30-39
Compote, open (scalloped rim)	19-26
Creamer (ill.)	40-50
Goblet	35-42
Jam jar	33-39
Pitcher	45-55
Sauce, footed	9-11
Spoonholder	25-29
Sugar bowl	
Covered	35-45
Open	19-24
Wine	24-34

Colored pieces, 80 to 100 percent higher than clear prices listed. Also comes with rosette in panels and is called Cane and Rosette.

Cane Insert

Cane Insert

(Erroneously Button Arches): Tarentum Glass Company, Tarentum, Pennsylvania, 1898-1906. Clear, emerald green, pink, custard, green custard; nonflint. Gold decorated.

Bowl, berry	$ 24-33
Butter dish, covered	48-54
Creamer (ill.)	38-42
Dish, folded, 6″	14-19
Goblet	40-47
Hair receiver, metal lid with hole	29-37
Mug	24-30
Pitcher, water	49-61
Spoonholder	29-35
Sugar bowl, covered	40-47

Yellow custard 75 percent higher, green custard 100 percent more than clear prices listed.

Cannonball Pinwheel

(Pinwheel; Caledonia original U. S. Glass name): U. S. Glass No. 15094, c. 1906, and Federal Glass, c. 1915. Clear or trimmed with gold. Nonflint.

Bowl	
Deep, 6¼″, 7¼″, 8″ round	$ 13-18
Shallow, 9″ round	12-16
Butter, covered, flat, flanged	24-30
Celery tray, 10″ long	12-17
Celery vase	15-21
Compote, jelly, 5″ dia.	9-14
Creamer	18-24
Cup	5-10
Goblet	17-25
Jelly, flat, one handle	10-15
Olive, 5″ square, no handles	9-13
Pickle, 7″ long	8-12
Pitcher, 3-pint jug	22-32
Plate, 6″ square	11-18
Sauce	
Flat, shallow, 4¼″, 4¾″	4-8
Footed, 4″	6-10
Salt shaker	18-25
Spoonholder	13-19
Sugar, covered	
Handled	21-28
Plain	18-25
Tumbler	11-16
Wine	12-19

Cape Cod

Sandwich attribution by early authors; possibly Canadian. Clear, nonflint.

Bowl, handled	$ 23-28
Butter dish, covered	59-64
Celery	33-40
Compote	
Covered, 6″, 7″, 8″	52-60
Open, 6″, 7″, 8″	28-34

Creamer.	41-46
Goblet.	34-42
Jar, jam,.	44-52
Pitcher, water	64-70
Spoonholder.	33-39
Sugar bowl, covered	48-56
Wine	43-51

Capital

(Joyce): Westmoreland, c. 1910. Clear, clear with gold or silver; pale orange iridescent.

Cracker jar	$ 32-39
Hair receiver, 3½″ x 3¼″.	19-24
Perfume, 2½″ high	
Stopper missing	9-13
Complete	18-26
Puff box 3½″ x 3¼″	15-22
Toilet bottle 7½″ high, original	
stopper	24-30
Toothpick.	22-31
Tray	
Comb and brush, 11¾″ x 8½″,	
scrolled edge	27-34
Pin, 5″ x 3¼″.	13-19

Prices are for gold or silver trim. Iridescent add 20 percent. No goblet.

Capitol Building

Capitol Building

(Original name, Historic America): Fenton Glass Company, c. 1937. Clear, nonflint. Pieces have different scenes.

Bowl, finger, 4″ dia., 2⅛″ high	
"The Rockies".	$ 20-27
Butter pat,	
"Mt. Vernon" (scarce)	19-24
Goblet,	
"Capitol Building" (ill.)	30-35
Plate, dessert, 7¾″,	
"Niagara Falls"	17-24
Sherbet, 4½″,	
"Independence Hall"	17-24
Tumbler, 5½″	
"Broadway, New York"	20-27
Wine/cocktail, 2¾″ dia. x 4¼″ high,	
"Fort Dearborn".	23-29

The sherbet can be used as a champagne.

Caprice

Cambridge Glass Company, Cambridge, Ohio, 1936. It is known to have been produced in clear, pink, blue, and satin.

Candleholder, 2⅝″ high	$ 9-12
Dish, candy (bridge set)	21-28
Pitcher, blue, 80 oz.	88-95
Sherbet, footed, low, 7 oz.	11-16
Sherbet, tall, blue	20-30
Sugar, blue	15-19
Sugar	8-11
Tumbler, footed, 12 oz.	12-15

Caramel Strigil

Caramel Strigil

Indiana Tumbler and Goblet Company, before 1903, when the factory burned. McKee Bros. used the same design in clear glass in 1897, calling it Nelly. In 1900, both firms joined National Glass Company, so either firm could have made this pattern.

Tankard, cream (ill.).	$130-152

61

Cardinal

Cardinal

Probably Ohio Flint Glass Company, Lancaster, late 1870s. This company was the ancestor of the Anchor-Hocking Glass Company. Clear.

Butter dish, covered	$ 45-53
Creamer.	39-46
Goblet.	33-39
Pitcher, water (scarce)	118-130
Sauce	
Flat, round	10-14
Footed, 4", ...	13-17
Spoonholder (ill.)	28-33
Sugar bowl, covered	42-50

Goblet reproduced.

Carmen

(Panelled Diamond and Fine Cut): Fostoria Glass Company, Moundsville, West Virginia, c. 1896. Clear, clear flashed with yellow, nonflint.

Bowls, berry, 7", 8".	$ 22-27
Butter dish, covered	32-39
Cake stand	37-45
Celery.	24-32
Compote	
High standard, covered, 7", 8"	37-46
Low standard, open	25-33
Creamer.	24-33
Cruet, oil	24-32
Cup	10-14
Decanter, patterned stopper	38-46
Goblet.	27-36
Pitcher, water, tankard	35-42

Relish, 7"	13-19
Salt/Pepper, pr.	30-36
Sauce, flat, 4⅞"	6-10
Spoonholder.	19-25
Sugar bowl, open	16-21
Wine	25-37

Yellow flashing, 20 percent higher than clear prices listed.

Carnation

New Martinsville, after 1901. Clear, ruby stain, both usually with gold, nonflint.

Bowl	
Deep, 8½" dia.	$ 22-29
Punch, 14" dia. on pedestal	67-75
Butter, covered	33-39
Creamer.	25-34
Cup, custard.	10-15
Pitcher, ½ gal. jug	39-47
Sauce, flat	9-12
Spoonholder.	19-26
Sugar bowl, covered	31-37
Toothpick	39-49
Tumbler.	21-27

Pattern name should be preceded by maker's name, because Lancaster made a different carnation pattern. Ruby stain add 200 percent to clear prices listed, for good gold.

Cat on a Hamper

Cat on a Hamper

Indiana Tumbler & Goblet (National) Company, Greentown, Indiana, before 1903. Chocolate, amber, blue, green, clear. Two types made, short and tall. Prices listed, same for both.

Amber.	$ 170+
Blue.	198-220
Chocolate	220+
Clear	120-135
Green	170-190

Extremely rare when top of hamper is in so-called red agate. The Houston has this type hamper.

Catawba Grape

Catawba Grape

Imperial Glass Company's No. 473, 1910-1929 in "Nuruby-Peacock-Sapphire" was iridescent (carnival); after that, in clear iridescent frosted called "Niagara." Milk glass also made.

Basket, tall, handled.	$ 30-38
Bowl	
Finger, 4¼"	10-14
Lily, 6" (cupped)	13-19
Shallow, 8½", 12"	14-20
Compote, 5½" dia., ruffled.	27-34
Cup/Saucer	17-22
Decanter, ribbed stopper	38-43
Goblet, 10 oz.	21-27
Pitcher, water	35-41
Plate, 9½", 12½"	8-14
Tray	
Fruit, 9" round, central handle	25-29
Lunch, 10" round, central handle . . .	25-29
Tumbler, 10 oz.	20-25
Vase, 8" (carafe)	27-33
Wine, 2 oz. (ill.)	22-27

Cathedral

(Orion): Bryce Bros., Pittsburgh, late 1880s. Crystal, amber, vaseline, blue amethyst.

Cathedral

Bowl, berry, 5", 6", 7", 8"	$ 21-32
Butter dish, covered	59-66
Cake plate on stand	43-52
Compote	
Covered, large, high	
standard	56-64
Open, low standard	29-38
Creamer, tall	44-52
Dish, round, footed	19-26
Egg cup	29-34
Goblet.	39-46
Pitcher, water, 3 quart.	59-66
Saucedish	
Flat, 4".	12-15
Footed, 4", 4½"	17-22
Spoonholder.	29-38
Sugar bowl, covered	35-43
Tumbler, water	29-34
Wine glass.	33-42

Vaseline and amber, 30 percent; blue, 40 percent; amethyst, 100 percent higher than clear.

Cat's Eye

(Original name, Breton. A salt shaker in the literature is called Thumbprint with Spearhead.) Early authors set the date as 1880s, but we now know this is Paden City's Breton pattern, c. 1930. The factory closed in 1951 and the molds were bought by Canton Glass Company, Marion, Indiana. Cat's Eye appears in a 1954 Canton catalog. Clear, amber, possibly blue.

Bowl, flared or cupped, 8"	$ 7-11
Champagne, saucer type	5-8
Claret	7-9

(continued)

Cocktail, low	5-8
Cordial	6-9
Creamer	5-9
Decanter, square; also comes round	19-28
Goblet	10-12
Jug, 44 oz., ice lip	17-23
Plate	
6″, 8″	3-6
11″	8-13
Sauce, flat, 4½″	2-4
Sherbet, low footed, 3″ dia.,	
4 oz., 4½ oz.	4-6
Sugar, handled, open	5-9
Tumbler	
Juice, 5 oz.	4-7
Iced tea, 12 oz.	8-10
Water, 9 oz., 12 oz.	6-9
Whiskey, 2 oz	5-8
Wine	7-10

Centennial Beer Mug

Cat's Eye and Block

(Cut Log): Westmoreland Specialty Company, c. 1896. Clear, sometimes in camphor glass, nonflint.

Butter dish, covered	$ 66-73
Cake stand	66-71
Celery	60-68
Creamer, 3″, 5″	24-32
Goblet	33-41
Pitcher, water	52-62
Sugar bowl, covered	59-69
Tumbler	32-42
Wine	41-50

Camphor, 50 percent higher than clear prices listed.

Centennial Beer Mug

Designed by M. Daniel Connolly.

Beer mug	$ 43-50

If you have information concerning *any* pattern, please let us hear from you. If you don't agree with the prices quoted, please let us hear from you. If you think the piece illustrated is a spoonholder rather than a celery (etc.), please let us hear from you. Constructive criticism is *always* welcome.

Centennial Beer Mug

Centennial Beer Mug

Hobbs, Brockunier & Company, designed for Philadelphia Centennial, 1876.

Centennial mug (ill.)	$ 56-70

Ceres

(Cameo; Goddess of Liberty; original name, Medallion): Atterbury, c. 1880s. Clear, opaque white, opaque turquoise, purple-black opaque.

Butter dish	$ 54-62
Creamer	37-49
Mug, handled	29-35

Ceres

Spoonholder (ill.) 35-42
Sugar bowl, covered 52-62
Colored and opaque pieces, 100 percent higher than clear prices listed.

Chain

Chain

Attributed to Portland Glass Company, c. early 1880s. Clear, nonflint.

Butter dish, covered . . . . $ 33-40
Compote, covered, high 36-43
Creamer 19-24
Goblet 19-27
Plate
  7″ 16-20
  11″ 26-32
Spoonholder 22-29

Sugar bowl, open (ill.) 37-44
Wine 17-25
Probably other pieces.

Chain

Chain

Possibly Sandwich, c. 1840. The creamer shown here is almost identical with one made by R. B. Curling & Sons, Fort Pitt. This glassworks was located in Pittsburgh.

Creamer (ill.) $110-145

Chain and Shield

Chain and Shield

Attributed to Portland Glass Company. Clear, nonflint.

65

(continued)

Butter, covered	$ 39-47
Creamer	29-37
Goblet	30-37
Pitcher (ill.)	38-44
Platter, oval	27-35
Sauce, flat	7-10
Spoonholder	20-25
Sugar, covered	35-42

Chain Thumbprints

(Reardon): Maker unknown, c. 1880. Clear, or transfer-etched, nonflint.

Butter on low pedestal	$ 24-30
Creamer	19-24
Goblet	16-21
Pitcher	25-35
Sauce, footed	4-8
Spoonholder	13-17
Sugar	22-29

Add 20 percent for etching.

Chain with Star

Chain with Star

Attributed to Portland Glass Company, 1800s. Clear.

Bowl, footed, small and large	$ 18-23
Butter dish, covered	39-44
Cake stand, 10½″	34-40
Compote, covered, high and low standard	49-54
Creamer	28-37
Goblet	22-31
Pickle dish	12-17
Pitcher, water (ill.)	45-52
Plate, bread, handled	29-34
Salt/Pepper, pr.	30-40
Sauce, flat and footed	9-14
Spoonholder	19-24
Sugar bowl, open	16-22
Wine	22-27

Challinor Tree of Life

Challinor Tree of Life

(Challinor No. 313): Challinor, Taylor, Ltd., Tarentum, Pennsylvania, 1885-1893. Opaque white, olive green, blue, butterscotch. Pieces were plain or hand decorated in colors. Nonflint.

Bowl	$ 33-39
Butter dish, covered	52-60
Creamer	34-42
Dish, diamond-shaped	18-24
Jar, cracker (ill.)	59-68
Salt/Pepper, pr.	46-57
Spoonholder	32-40
Sugar bowl, covered	51-60
Syrup, (blue)	98-115

Chandelier

Chandelier

(Original name, Crown Jewels): O'Hara Glass Company, Ltd., 1880s. U. S. Glass Company after 1891. Also made in Canada. Clear, nonflint.

Bowl, finger	$ 18-27
Butter dish	54-69

Celery	30-39
Compote	
Covered, 8″	57-62
Open, 6″	34-42
Creamer, clear or etched	39-46
Goblet	57-69
Pitcher, water (ill.)	56-66
Sauce, flat	14-19
Spoonholder	32-37
Sugar	
Covered	45-52
Open	30-37
Shaker	62-78

Cherry

Milk glass 80 percent higher than clear prices listed. Goblet reproduced in clear and milk glass.

Checkerboard

(Bridle Rosettes): Westmoreland Glass Company, Grapeville, Pennsylvania, c. 1900. Clear, nonflint.

Bowls	
Large, shallow, 9″	$ 20-27
Small, sauce	6-11
Butter dish, covered	33-38
Celery	27-37
Compote, low, 7¾″ dia.	15-21
Creamer	22-28
Cruet, original tall notched	
stopper	32-41
Goblet	22-29
Pitcher, milk	24-31
Plate, 7″, 10″	18-29
Salt/Pepper, pr.	23-32
Spoonholder	14-19
Sugar bowl, covered	30-36
Tumbler, iced tea, water	19-25
Wine	16-24

Some pieces in milk glass reproduced by Kemple Glass Company. Cambridge "Ribbon" is similar but forms are attenuated, pattern is more compact, and pieces usually trademarked "Nearcut."

Cherry

Bakewell, Pears & Company, Pittsburgh, c. 1870. Clear, milk glass, nonflint.

Butter dish, covered	$ 48-62
Compote	
Covered, high standard	52-66
Open, high and low standard	38-48
Creamer, applied handle	45-55
Goblet (ill.)	27-35
Sauce, flat	8-12
Spoonholder	29-34
Sugar bowl, covered	50-60

Cherry Lattice

Cherry Lattice

Northwood Glass Company, 1890s. Clear with pink/gold decoration.

Berry set	
Large bowl	$ 51-60
Sauce	18-22
Butter dish, covered	57-66
Compote	47-56
Creamer (ill.)	45-52
Spoonholder	40-49
Sugar bowl, covered	56-64

Chestnut Oak

(Old Acorn): Maker unknown, c. 1870s-1890s. Clear.

Butter, covered, flat	$ 50-59

(continued)

Chestnut Oak

Celery, flat	25-32
Compote	
Covered, high	47-56
Open, low	25-32
Creamer	
Flat, pressed handle	32-39
Pedestal, applied handle	35-47
Egg cup	19-25
Goblet	24-31
Pitcher, water, applied handle (ill.)	51-70
Sauce, flat	7-12
Spoonholder	23-28
Sugar	
Covered	42-49
Open	21-31

Distinguished from Acorn (Cable Band) by bracketed banding, Chestnut Oak comes in an early form with applied handles and pedestaled bases and a later form with pressed handles and flat bases.

Chrysanthemum Sprig

Chrysanthemum Sprig

Northwood Glass Company, 1890s. Custard, gold and color decorated, nonflint.

Berry set
Large bowl	$166-175
Sauce	59-69
Butter dish, covered (ill.)	190-220
Compote, jelly	45-55
Creamer	90-110
Pitcher, water	310-335
Salt/Pepper, pr.	135-146
Spoonholder	82-92
Sugar bowl, covered	125-145
Tumbler, water (rare in blue)	55-67

Rare in blue, 100 percent higher than custard prices listed. Prices are for good paint.

Church Windows

Church Windows

(Original name, Columbia; Tulip Petals): U.S. Glass Company (King, Richards and Hartley), c. 1903. Clear, rose/green flash with gold. Nonflint.

Butter dish, covered	$ 56-64
Cake stand	32-40
Celery	27-36
Compote, jelly, covered	46-50
Creamer	32-42
Dish, sardine	24-30
Goblet	27-33
Pitcher, ½ gal.	47-56
Spoonholder	26-36
Sugar bowl	
Covered	64-72
Open	47-57

Many other pieces.

Circled Scroll

Northwood attribution, c. 1900. Clear, green, blue, opalescent; some carnival, nonflint.

Circled Scroll

Bowl set
Large	$ 41-49
Sauce	15-21
Butter dish	82-99
Creamer.	45-52
Cruet	124-143
Pitcher, water (ill.)	71-80
Salt/Pepper, pr.	61-73
Spoonholder.	38-48
Sugar	
Covered	56-62
Open	30-38
Tumbler.	33-38

Colored pieces, 65 percent higher than clear prices listed.

Circular Saw

Circular Saw

(Rosetta): Beaumont Glass Company, c. 1904. Clear, some with gilt trim, nonflint.

Bowl
Berry	$ 20-25
Punch	52-62
Butter dish, covered	26-35
Cracker jar	22-30
Creamer (ill.)	21-26
Saucedish	6-9
Spoonholder.	16-21
Sugar bowl, covered	23-31

Tumber 15-22
No goblet or toothpick known.

Classic

Classic

Gillinder & Sons, c. 1880s. Clear, frosted.

Bowl, log feet, ...	$105-132
Butter dish, covered, log feet.	220-235
Celery vase, 6 log feet	115-135
Compote, covered	162-172
Creamer.	110-120
Goblet.	195-220
Pitcher	
Collared base	210-228
Log feet (ill.).	280-290
Plate	
Blaine, Hendricks, Logan	182-228
President Cleveland	172-182
Warrior	162-170
Sauce, log feet. 3¾″ dia.	31-39
Spoonholder, open, log feet	108-120
Sugar bowl, covered, very	
large.	161-170

Footed type brings 25 percent more than collared base type.

Classic Medallion

(Cameo): Maker unknown, c. 1880s.

Butter dish, covered	$ 33-39
Celery vase	25-30
Compote	
Covered, 9″	39-49
Open, low	20-27
Creamer (ill.)	22-31
Pitcher, water	35-42
Spoonholder.	15-19

(continued)

Classic Medallion

Sugar bowl
   Covered, no medallion on lid,
   curved finial 38-47
   Open 21-27

Clear Diagonal Band

Clear Diagonal Band

Ripley and Canadian attribution. Appears in Wm. Rogers catalog, Toronto, c. 1880s. Clear, nonflint.

Butter dish . . . . $ 35-46
Celery vase 23-29
Compote
   Covered, high standard 36-47
   Covered, low standard 29-35
Creamer. 27-32
Goblet. 18-28
Marmalade jar, covered 32-42
Pitcher, water (ill.) 38-46
Platter, "Eureka" 28-39
Salt/Pepper, pr. 33-42
Sauces, flat and footed. 5-11
Spoonholder. 16-22
Sugar bowl
   Covered 34-43
   Open 17-24

Clear Stork

Clear Stork

Possibly Mosaic Glass Company, Fostoria, Ohio, 1890-91. Clear, frost, nonflint.

Butter dish . . . . $ 52-60
Creamer (ill.) 40-50
Goblet. 45-54
Pitcher, water 82-92
Spoonholder. 29-34
Sugar bowl, covered
   (stork finial) 60-68
Tumbler. 25-35

Goblet, spooner reproduced. Frosted, add 20 percent to clear prices listed.

Clematis

Maker unknown, c. 1876. Clear, nonflint.

Butter bowl, covered. . . . . $ 33-39
Creamer, applied handle. 30-40
Goblet. 24-31
Pitcher, applied handle 52-65
Sauce, flat. 6-10
Spoonholder on pedestal,
   scalloped rim 22-28
Sugar, covered. 32-40

A 12″ lamp with picture of pink cat in stem is described by Kamm. Thuro (*Oil Lamps: The Kerosene Era in North America*, p. 218.) shows a pattern similar to Clematis, with a stem for such pictures. This lamp is 12¼″ high and may be the one Kamm refers to, but if so, it is not part of this pattern, and no true Clematis lamp is in the literature.

Clio

Coarse Cut and Block

Clio

(Daisy and Button, Almond Band): Challinor, Taylor, Ltd., Tarentum, Pennsylvania, 1885-1891. Clear, green, canary, blue, nonflint.

Butter dish, covered	
large, small	$ 40-46
Celery	25-29
Compote, covered, 7″, 8″ (ill.)	34-42
Goblet	24-32
Pitcher, qt., ½ gal.	45-54
Plate, 7″, 10″	19-29
Spoonholder	22-29
Sugar bowl, covered	46-54

Plate has no panels or thumbprints. Colors, add 80 percent. Illustration is low compote as described in original catalog. No reproductions. One of the safe D & B types.

Coach Bowl

Coach Bowl

McKee & Bros., 1886. Crystal, amber, canary, blue (draft tongue in photo broken off). Reproduced in milk glass, amber, purple, blue, other colors.

Coach bowl (ill.)	$150+

In colors, 100 percent higher.

Coarse Cut and Block

Model Flint Glass Company, Findlay, Ohio, 1880s. Clear, nonflint.

Creamer, 5¾″ (ill.)	$ 19-25

Coin

Coin

(Original name, Silver Age): U. S. Glass Company (Central) and Hobbs, Brockunier, c. 1891. Dollar used in tumbler base dated 1878. Because real coins were used, the Treasury Department made the company stop after only a few months' production. Very scarce today: 5¢, 10¢, 25¢, 50¢ pieces and the silver dollar. Clear, frosted, sometimes silvered or gilded. Prices given for indicative pieces. Skillfully reproduced.

Bowl, berry	
25¢	$255-270
$1.00	295-320
Bread platter, frosted coins	540-552
Butter dish	
50¢	470-480
$1.00	500-525

(continued)

Cake stand
50¢	425-432
$1.00, frosted	400-425

Celery
25¢	230-242
50¢	300-340

Compote, covered
25¢ (ill.).	460-470
50¢, 8″ dia..	500-525
$1.00, frosted, finial	620-632

Creamer, 25¢ 325-345

Goblet
10¢	310-332
$1.00.	320-340

Mug, $1.00 220-240

Pitcher
Milk, 50¢	400-452
Water, $1.00	525-562

Sugar bowl, covered
25¢	485-520
50¢	450-520

Toothpick holder, $1.00 158-170

Tumbler
10¢	230-240
$1.00 on base (rare)	258-275
Wine, one-half dime (rare).	322-342

The toothpick holder was reproduced in Indiana several years ago, before the government stopped it. A few reached the market. Bread tray (50¢), tumbler ($1.00 on base), toothpick being reproduced.

Coin

Coin, Columbian

(Spanish Coin): U. S. Glass Company, c. 1891. When government intervened, Spanish coins were substituted for U. S. coins. Clear, ruby, frosted, bronze painted. Nonflint.

Bowl
Berry, 10″	$ 49-56
Finger	70-78

Butter dish, covered (ill.) 125-145
Cake stand 60-64

Compote
Covered, 6″, 7″, 8″.	95-120
Open, 7″, 8″, 10″	69-79

Creamer. 82-92
Goblet. 70-80
Pitcher, water 115-130
Salt/Pepper, pr.. 66-74
Spoonholder. 35-49
Sugar bowl, covered 75-84
Toothpick holder 48-55
Tumbler. 44-52

Goblet, toothpick, tumbler reproduced.

Colonial

Colonial

Sandwich glass, 1850-1860. Clear, opalescent or other colors, rare. Flint.

Ale glass, tall, footed.	$ 46-55
Celery glass	68-76
Champagne	58-68
Creamer (ill.)	110-135
Egg cup	22-32
Goblet, knob stem	55-63
Pitcher	148-169
Spill holder	38-45
Sugar bowl	81-95

Prices for belltone flint. Inferior quality, 50 percent less. Colors, 150 percent higher than clear prices listed.

Colonis

(45 Colonis): U.S. Glass Company, No. 15145, c. 1913. Clear, nonflint. Decorated gold, liege, rose bud or blue flower.

Bowl, berry, 8″. . . . . $ 14-19

Colonis

Butter dish 23-32
Celery tray, 10″ 27-35
Creamer. 17-23
Pickle, oval, 7″. 9-14
Pitcher
   Milk "squat jug"(ill.). 28-35
   Water, tankard 30-40
Sauce, flat, 4″, 4½″. 5-8
Spoonholder. 42-52
Sugar bowl, 2 handles, covered. 19-25
Tumbler. 11-15

Only large pitchers have horizontal raised band. Decorated pieces, add 30 percent.

Colorado

Colorado

U.S. Glass Company, 1897, another of their "States" series. Clear glass, both plain and engraved, and clear with ruby or amethyst stain (rare); green and cobalt blue with or without decorations. Occasional piece in clam broth. (Also see Lacy Medallion.)

Bowl, triangular . . . . $ 15-19
Butter dish, covered 43-49

Cheese dish, low, footed 21-30
Creamer, large (ill.) 25-37
Cup, engraved stars 12-16
Dish
   Crimped edge, 4″, 8″ 17-26
   Flared edge, 4″, 8″ 14-24
Pitcher, water 32-39
Salt/Pepper, pr., 3 feet. 38-45
Spoonholder. 25-32
Sugar bowl
   Individual, open handles 20-25
   Large, covered 41-48
Toothpick holder 25-35
Tumbler (only unfooted piece
   in pattern). 19-27
Vase, 12″ (trumpet) 24-30

Ruby, 20 percent; blue, 55 percent; green, 75 percent; amethyst, 200 percent higher than clear prices listed.

Columbia, Co-op's

Co-operative, c. 1899. Clear, apple green, cobalt blue (rare). Gold and various shades of bronzes. Nonflint.

Bowl
   Berry, 8″. . . . . $ 21-27
   Salad (flared), 8″. 23-30
Butter, flat 32-42
Celery. 28-34
Compote, high, open, with ruffled edge. 29-37
Creamer. 30-36
Cruet 31-40
Pitcher, ½ gallon 34-42
Salt shaker 19-25
Sauce 9-13
Spoonholder. 22-29
Sugar, lid lacks "eyes". 30-39
Syrup 37-45
Toothpick. 31-39
Tumbler. 20-28
Vase. 16-22

Toothpick reproduced in clear, blue, and other colors. Thirty-nine pieces were advertised in 1900 for $3.40.

Columbian Exposition

Maker unknown, c. 1892. Clear, emerald green, usually nonflint, although a tumbler is known in flint.

Goblet
   Plain stem, regular medallion . . . . $ 25-32
   Ring stem, fleur-de-lis in medallion . 29-35

(continued)

Tumbler, regular medallion 22-32

No other pieces known. Emerald green or flint glass, add 50 percent to clear prices listed.

Columned Thumbprints

Westmoreland No. 185, c. 1905. Clear, amber; clear with blue, green, red, and yellow thumbprints.

Butter. . . . . $ 24-34
Creamer. 17-23
Cup 6-12
Spoonholder. 13-19
Sugar, covered. 23-30
Toothpick (scarce). 32-39

For amber or painted pieces, add 50 percent to clear prices listed.

Comet

Comet

Sandwich glass, c. late 1840s. Clear, flint. Comet pattern by McKee Bros. is Horn of Plenty.

Goblet (ill.) . . . . $ 92-103
Pitcher, water 420-450
Tumbler, whiskey, water. 150-162

Connecticut

U.S. Glass Company, c. 1898. Clear, ruby stained (scarce), engraved and transfer etched. Nonflint.

Bowls, 5½", 8", flared . . . . $ 15-26
Butter dish, covered 38-49
Cake stand, 10" 42-52
Celery
  Tray. 19-24
  Vase 30-38

Creamer. 29-34
Dish, olive, reeded applied
  handle 19-26
Goblet. 30-40
Pitcher, tankard, 3 types. 37-46
Salt/Pepper, pr. 36-48
Spoonholder. 25-31
Sugar bowl, covered 35-45
Sugar shaker 36-42
Toothpick
  Cup, transfer-etched 59-66
  Flared 65-75
Tumbler. 15-27
Wine 27-35

Not as common as many of the "States" patterns. Ruby, add 200 percent to clear prices listed.

Continental

Continental

(No. 339): A. H. Heisey Company, Newark, Ohio, 1903-1910. Not all pieces marked with "Diamond H."

Butter dish
  Covered . . . . $ 45-55
  Covered, footed 52-60
Creamer
  Flat 29-35
  Footed (ill.) 32-39
Goblet. 23-30
Pitcher, water, ½ gal. 48-55
Spoonholder
  Flat 21-26
  Footed. 24-30
Sugar bowl
  Covered 38-46
  Covered, footed 40-50

Prices are for trademarked pieces. No. 339 is without bases on the stemmed items. No. 339½, the companion pattern, has stems of medium height. Thirty-nine pieces made.

Continental Bread Tray

Continental Bread Tray

Another in the series of historical plates sold at the Philadelphia Exposition in 1876. Atterbury and Company, Pittsburgh. Clear, nonflint.

Plate, 13″ by 9″ (ill.) . . . . $ 80-95

Coolidge Drape

Coolidge Drape

(Original name, Bellevue): Clear, pale amber, blue. Several sizes. The tall lamp is famous because this was the lamp used when Coolidge took presidential oath after Harding's sudden death.

Any size in clear . . . . $ 65-118
Any size in transparent colors 124-182

Coral Gables

Maker unknown. Clear, nonflint of the 1890s.

Cruet . . . . $ 39-46
Goblet. 20-25
Wine, 4½″ high 16-21

Please write if you know of other pieces in this elusive pattern.

Cord and Tassel

Cord and Tassel

Central Glass Company, 1872. Clear.

Bowl, oval	$ 27-32
Butter dish, covered	45-52
Cake stand	34-42
Caster bottle, cruet	30-37
Celery	38-45
Compote, high standard	56-62
Cordial	18-22
Creamer	
Applied handle	38-47
Pressed handle.	30-36
Egg cup	28-37
Goblet.	31-40
Lamp, applied handle,	
low pedestal	65-73
Mug, applied handle.	39-44
Pitcher, water, applied	
handle (ill.)	69-80
Sauce, flat.	8-12
Spoonholder.	22-29
Sugar bowl, covered	41-49
Wine	29-37

Handles can be applied or pressed..

Cord Drapery

Cord Drapery

(Indiana): Indiana Tumbler & Goblet (National) Company, Greentown, Indiana,

75

(continued)

c. 1900. Clear, amber, emerald green, cobalt blue, canary; opaque (Nile) green, white, chocolate, nonflint.

Berry bowl	$ 24-29
Butter dish, clear	52-68
Cake stand	49-58
Compote	
Fluted, open	74-79
Jelly, covered	43-53
Large, covered	74-79
Creamer (ill.)	47-56
Cruet, amber, original Dewey	
stopper	230-295
Goblet.	41-49
Pitcher, water	52-60
Salt/Pepper, pr.	41-52
Spoonholder.	34-40
Sugar bowl	40-50
Tumbler.	29-36
Wine	30-39

Not all forms made in all colors. Chocolate, 300 percent more; other colors, 50 percent more.

Cordova

Cordova

O'Hara Glass Company, Pittsburgh, 1890. Clear, ruby, green, nonflint.

Bowl	
Covered	$ 29-36
Finger/waste.	19-28
Open	15-22
Butter dish, covered	39-47
Cake stand	36-42
Celery.	30-37
Cologne, orig. stopper	25-30
Compote, covered,	
high standard, 7″, 8″	44-52
Creamer, regular.	31-38
Cruet	44-53
Inkwell (scarce)	92-101

Pitcher	
Syrup (ill.)	40-44
Water, ½ gal.	37-44
Salt/Pepper, pr.	22-28
Spoonholder.	24-32
Sugar bowl, covered	34-42
Toothpick.	16-21
Tumbler.	25-31
Vase, bud	13-19

Coreopsis

Possibly Consolidated Glass Company, c. 1902. White opaque, decorated. Glossy and satin finish. Nonflint. Red satin with white decoration, rare.

Berry set	
Bowl.	$ 42-55
Sauce	18-23
Butter dish, covered, metal base . . .	98-108
Cracker jar	127-139
Creamer.	78-83
Spoonholder.	58-67
Sugar bowl, covered	92-103
Water set	
Pitcher	33-38
Tumbler.	16-23

Not reproduced. Prices are for white with decoration.

Cornell

Tarentum Glass Co., 1898-1912. Clear, emerald green, with or without gold trim.

Butter.	$ 33-40
Cake stand	36-43
Canned milk jar, flat glass lid	32-38
Celery.	27-34
Cordial	22-32
Creamer	
Berry or breakfast	18-23
Regular	24-31
Cruet	33-40
Cup	10-14
Cup and saucer	18-25
Goblet.	20-30
Hair receiver	17-26
Jam jar, patterned lid	35-42
Perfume.	23-34
Pickle caster, metal lid and frame . . .	69-81
Plate, small or large	14-29
Punch bowl with separate base.	110+
Rose bowl	19-25
Salt shaker	17-23
Spoonholder.	16-22

Sugar

Berry or breakfast, scalloped rim. . .		16-22
Regular, covered		32-39
Syrup		31-40
Tobacco jar		40-52
Tumbler		
Water		15-21
Whiskey (shot glass)		10-15
Wine		19-26

Emerald green with good gold, add 75 percent to clear prices listed.

Cosmos

Butter dish, open and covered (ill.)	$190-225
Condiment set; salt/pepper, mustard	251-262
Creamer.	140-150
Lamps	
Large, round with shade	190-198
Miniature, base only	72-98
Miniature with shade	147-168
Lemonade pitcher with 6 mugs. . . .	340-360
Pitcher, water, 8¾" high	165-182
Salt/Pepper, pr.	118-127
Spoonholder.	116-122
Sugar bowl, covered	177-190
Syrup	165-179
Tumbler.	100-110

Probably other pieces.

Cornucopia

Cornucopia

Dalzell, Gilmore and Leighton, c. 1885. Clear, fine fruit group on reverse side.

Butter dish, covered	$ 37-42
Cake stand, 11"	42-52
Celery	24-33
Compote, covered	48-58
Creamer.	27-36
Goblet.	28-33
Mug.	29-35
Pitcher, water (ill.)	52-62
Spoonholder.	19-28
Sugar bowl, covered	37-45

This pattern is a grouping of assorted fruit designs using the same blank molds. Cherry and fig, strawberry and currant, and blackberry and grape are among the combinations on individual pieces. Strawberry and currant goblets reproduced in clear as well as new colors including opalescent. Clear and blue miniature lamps may be later production.

Cosmos

(Stemless Daisy): Consolidated, c. 1900. Clear, milk glass and cased glass. Decorated pink, yellow, blue, nonflint.

Cottage

Cottage

(Dinner Bell; Fine Cut Band): Adams & Company, Pittsburgh, 1874. Clear, dark green, amber, ruby, blue, nonflint.

Bowl, waste	$ 22-31
Butter dish	
Flat	33-43
Regular, footed	39-49
Dinner Bell lid (scarce)	105-132

(continued)

Cake stand, 9″ high	36-45
Celery vase	24-29
Compote, covered and open, high standard, 6″, 7″, 8″.	42-52
Cup/saucer	30-37
Creamer.	22-29
Cruet, w/stopper	43-51
Goblet.	27-35
Pitcher, water, half gal.	38-54
Plate, 6″, 7″, 8″, 9″, 10″	14-29
Salt/Pepper, pr.	39-47
Spoonholder.	23-32
Sugar bowl, covered	34-40
Syrup	49-60
Tray, water (lacks pattern characteristics)	29-30
Tumbler.	20-27
Wine	26-31

Colors, 100-150 percent higher than clear prices listed.

Cradled Prisms

Challinor, Taylor, Ltd., c. late 1880s. Clear, nonflint.

Butter dish, covered	$ 30-36
Creamer, footed	25-32
Goblet.	19-26
Spoonholder.	16-22
Sugar bowl, covered	29-34

Crescent

(Fringed Drape): McKee, c. 1901, National Glass Co., up to c. 1920. Clear, ruby stain, nonflint.

Bowl

Boat shaped, deep, with ledge, 5½″ long	$ 13-19
Oval, graduated sizes 5″-11″	12-25
Salad 9″, flat rim, deep, with peg for mounting on silverplated base, complete	42-55
Round, flared, 6″, 8″, 9½″.	14-30
Round, straight, 7″, 8″, 9″	17-29
Shallow, 5½″ (plate)	15-19
Butter, covered	
Bowl type, so-called "English"	23-31
Flat, flanged.	33-40
Celery tray	17-22
Celery vase, flat base, straight sides	19-26
Compote, footed jelly, 4½″.	15-20

Cordial	21-30
Cruet, orig. faceted stopper	30-41
Creamer	
"English" (medium)	21-27
Individual	13-19
Large	23-33
Cup	10-15
Handle for salad fork, unique	29-33
Pickle jar, covered	35-45
Pickle tray	13-17
Salt shaker	15-22
Sauce, with ledge, flared, 4½″, 5″ (ruby stained, in silverplated holder), price for clear	10-14
Sugar	
"English" (shallow footed jelly compote)	18-25
Individual, open	15-20
Large, covered	30-40
Syrup	32-41
Tumbler.	14-19
Vase	
Flat, swung, 10″, 14″	16-22
Footed, 6″, 8″, 9″, flared top.	14-25

Ruby stain add 100 percent to clear prices listed. No goblet.

Crochet Band

New Martinsville, c. 1901, and others. Made in thin crystal (usually flint) and heavier pressed glass, usually nonflint. Clear, needle etched on various clear blanks.

Butter, base is not etched	$ 19-25
Creamer.	15-20
Cruet, orig. faceted stopper, 8 oz.	22-32
Goblet.	14-19
Pitcher, 9 oz.	22-31
Spoonholder.	13-17
Sugar	17-23
Tumbler.	9-14
Water bottle.	21-30
Wine	10-15

Crochet band etching is distinguished from other types by looping that forms a fleur-de-lis like design equidistant above and below a central band within which there are continuous loops.

Croesus

Riverside Glass Works, Wellsburgh, West Virginia, 1897. Clear, decorated with gold. Nonflint.

Croesus

Berry set
Bowl, scalloped rim . . . . $ 32-39
Covered, 7″ 34-40
Sauce 12-19
Butter dish, covered 109-119
Celery . . . . 69-79 .
Creamer
Berry 33-43
Individual 19-24
Regular (ill.) 51-62
Cruet, 2 sizes 69-82
Pickle dish (condiment tray) 31-37
Pitcher, water 85-98
Salt/Pepper, pr. 52-64
Spoonholder 41-49
Sugar bowl, covered 81-92
Toothpick holder 39-44
Tumbler 24-34

Emerald green, 100 percent; amethyst, 250 percent higher than clear prices listed. 4 piece table set reproduced in Japan. Toothpick and tumbler reproduced domestically.

Cromwell

(Knobby Bull's Eye): U. S. Glass, c. 1918. Clear, emerald green (rare); also with gold, and with amethyst or green painted eyes.

Bonbon . . . . $ 10-14
Bowl
Orange bowl, 10½″ 19-27
Punch, flared,
12½″ dia. x 5⅝″ high 47-58
Salad, 9″ 15-21
Butter, flat, covered 28-36
Celery
Tray 14-20
Vase 18-24

Creamer
Individual, oval 13-18
Medium 16-20
Regular 21-27
Cup, custard, lemonade 9-13
Goblet 16-22
Jelly, 6½″, two handles 12-16
Nappy, 4″, 4½″, 5″, 6″, 7″ 5-15
Pitcher
Large 30-37
Medium 25-30
Oval, 7½″ high 27-35
Plate, 8″ butter 16-21
Salt shaker
Medium (bulbous base),
s.p. top 14-20
Ordinary (straight), Brittania
top, glass insert 16-21
Saucer, 5″ 10-13
Spoon tray 13-17
Sugar
Individual, open, oval 12-17
Medium, open, two handles 15-21
Regular, covered 24-31
Toothpick, "Sanitary" flat,
rectangular (scarce) 39-45
Tumbler 13-19
Wine, flared or straight 14-20

Similar pattern, Millard's Bull's Eye and Fan. Add 25 percent for painted decoration, 100 percent for solid color.

Crossed Block

Crossed Block

(Roman Cross): Maker unknown, c. 1890. Clear, nonflint.

Butter dish, covered . . . . $ 30-37
Creamer, 3⅝″ (ill.) 23-29
Goblet 17-23
Spoonholder 16-20
Sugar bowl, covered 27-32

Crossed Fern

(Ball and Claw): Atterbury & Company, Pittsburgh, c. 1876. Clear, milk glass, opaque green, blue, nonflint.

Bowl, collared, 7″	$ 30-37
Butter dish, covered,	
patterned drain	67-78
Creamer.	50-61
Sauce	16-22
Spoonholder.	34-43
Sugar bowl, covered	63-75
Tumbler.	21-30

Opaque green, blue, 40 percent higher than milk glass prices listed.

Crossed Shields

Crossed Shields

Fostoria Glass Company's No. 1303, late 1890s. Clear, nonflint.

Butter dish, covered	$ 33-39
Compotes, several sizes	32-46
Creamer (ill.)	24-36
Pitcher, water	36-42
Spoonholder.	16-21
Sugar bowl, covered	29-34
Tumbler.	14-19

Crystal

McKee Bros. Pittsburgh, c. 1859, and other manufacturers. Clear, flint and later in nonflint. Colors (scarce); also came engraved.

Ale glass.	$ 26-39
Bowl, covered	42-50
Butter, covered	49-56
Celery.	31-39
Compote, covered, high standard . . .	49-59
Creamer.	45-49
Decanter, qt.	54-66
Egg cup	16-25

Goblet.	19-28
Pitcher, water	92-107
Spoonholder.	29-34
Sugar bowl, covered	49-54
Tumbler	
Bar	21-30
Footed.	25-33

Prices are for flint. Nonflint, 50 percent less than flint prices listed.

Crystalina

U. S. Glass (Hobbs), c. 1891. Clear, ruby stain, amber stain; emerald green and cobalt. Nonflint. A coaster in a pattern called Scalloped Plume was made by New Martinsville after 1901, appears to be identical to Crystalina, and may be the 4″ plate described below.

Bowl, oval	$ 19-25
Butter, flat, unpatterned lid	
(finial is patterned)	30-40
Butter pat.	10-14
Celery tray	17-22
Cheese plate, 7″, tab handle	
(cover is patterned, finial is	
stepped cone)	38-45
Creamer	
Individual, oval, tab handle	18-23
Regular, applied handle	25-32
Nappy, 4½″, tab handle	13-18
Olive, oval, tab handle	14-19
Pickle, 9″, leaf	15-21
Plate	
4″ for sherbet	11-15
Oval bread, 12″.	30-39
Round, 9″, 10″	22-32
Sherbet (cup), tab handle	12-17
Spoonholder.	17-22
Sugar	
Berry, open, shaped like	
spooner but lower and wider	15-20
Regular, covered	30-40

Prices are for amber stain. Ruby stain 30 percent more, all clear 30 percent less.

Crystal Queen

Northwood, 1897-1900, unmarked. Clear, nonflint. Also selected pieces by Cambridge Glass Co., early 1900s.

Basket, handled (scarce).	$ 67-78
Butter, covered	35-45
Creamer.	29-34

Spoonholder.	23-30
Sugar, covered.	35-45
Vase, low, hat-shaped, crimped . . .	20-26

Pattern similar to Fancy Loop. Although Northwood advertised 125 pieces, very little is seen of this pattern.

Crystal Wedding

Crystal Wedding

(Crystal Anniversary, Collins): Adams Glass Company, early 1880s. Clear, amber, canary, blue, nonflint. Banded, frosted and engraved.

Banana stand (fruit basket),	
varies from pattern	$108-118
Butter dish, covered	52-61
Cake stand, high standard	61-70
Celery.	40-47
Claret	36-45
Compote	
Covered, high standard (ill.)	77-89
Covered, low standard	72-81
Open, low standard	74-83
Creamer, clear.	59-68
Cruet (square stopper,	
divided blocks)	51-60
Goblet.	33-42
Pickle dish (slash-type base),	
oblong	40-45
Pitcher, water, square	154-164
Salt dip, master (slash-type base) . .	34-43
Salt/Pepper, pr.	52-61
Spoonholder.	31-36
Sugar bowl, covered	52-63
Tumbler.	31-39
Vase, "bouquet." Pattern	
swirled with "slashes".	49-59

Goblet, compote, other pieces reproduced. Colors, 100 percent more than clear prices listed.

Cube with Fan

U.S. Glass Company, c. 1900. Clear, ruby, green, nonflint.

Bowl, finger	$15-20
Butter dish	30-36
Candlestick (scarce)	43-50
Celery, flat base	18-24
Cup	
Collared base ("mug")	8-10
Flat base (custard)	6-9
Dish, jelly	20-24
Goblet.	19-25
Plates, 5″, 7½″.	14-19
Salt dip, individual	8-11
Spoonholder, flat base	16-19
Sugar bowl, covered	28-34
Tumbler.	15-19
Water bottle.	31-37

Cupid and Venus

Cupid and Venus

(Guardian Angel): Richards & Hartley Glass Company, Pittsburgh (Birmingham), 1875-1884. Clear, vaseline, amber, nonflint.

Butter dish, covered	$ 52-69
Cake plate, 11″.	36-44
Celery	45-52
Champagne (scarce)	108-116
Compote	
Covered, high and low	
standard	57-74
Open, high standard	39-49
Creamer, ...	37-42
Goblet.	60-70
Jam jar with glass lid (ill.)	94-115

(continued)

Mug, 2″, 2½″, 3½″ 26-36
Pickle caster. 18-22
Pickle caster in frame,
   metal lid 146-170
Pitcher, water (large),
   milk (medium). 60-72
Plate, bread, 10½″, round 38-46
Plate, bread, handles, 10½″ round . . . 32-40
Sauce
   Flat, round 7-11
   Footed, 3½″, 4″, 5″ 10-13
Spoonholder. 33-39
Sugar bowl, covered 64-72
Wine (scarce) 88-99

Color, 135 percent higher than clear prices listed.

Currant

Currant

Sandwich glass, 1870s. Later, Campbell, Jones & Company, Pittsburgh, 1870s. Clear, nonflint, with an occasional piece in flint.

Butter dish . . . . $ 50-59
Cake stand, 2 types 52-64
Celery vase 47-52
Compote, covered
   8″ high foot 60-69
   8″, 9″, low foot 49-58
Cordial 35-43
Creamer, applied handle (ill.) 36-42
Dish, oval, 6″ × 9″, 5″ × 7″ 17-27
Egg cup 25-34
Goblet, 5½″, 6″ 34-44
Jelly, poor quality 15-21
Pitcher, water 70-83
Spoonholder. 26-32
Sugar bowl, covered 49-58
Tumbler, footed 32-41
Wine 34-42

Currier and Ives

Currier and Ives

Bellaire Goblet Company, Findlay, Ohio, 1880s. Clear, scarce in colors—amber, blue, nonflint.

Butter dish,
   covered (scarce) . . . . $ 63-75
Cordial 28-37
Creamer. 34-42
Cup and saucer 36-47
Decanter, orig. stopper. 49-60
Goblet, knob stem 29-38
Lamp, No. 2, complete w/ burner
   and chimney 37-46
Pitcher
   Milk 42-49
   Water (ill.). 50-60
Salt/Pepper, pr. 50-60
Spoonholder. 25-34
Sugar bowl, covered 47-53
Tray
   "Balky Mule on RR Tracks" 64-72
   Water, 12″ 38-45
   Wine, 9⅜ 40-49
Wine 24-32

Color, 300 percent higher than clear prices listed.

Curtain

Curtain

(Sultan): Bryce Bros., Pittsburgh, 1875-1885. Clear, nonflint.

Bowl, covered, 6″, 7″, 8″.	$ 24-33
Bowl, open, 6″, 7″, 8″	15-20
Butter dish	35-45
Cake plate on stand	34-42
Celery boat	19-24
Compote	
Covered, high standard, 6″, 7″, 8″	51-60
Open, high standard 7″, 8″, 10″	31-45
Creamer	30-37
Goblet	24-31
Mug, large	27-34
Pitcher, quart, half gallon	51-61
Salt/Pepper, pr.	34-39
Spoonholder (ill.)	20-29
Sugar bowl	37-47
Tumbler	21-26

Curtain Tieback

Maker unknown, c. 1880s. Clear, non-flint. Two types of bases. Nonflint.

Bowl, berry, 7″ square	$ 18-24
Butter dish, covered	33-38
Celery tray	17-21
Creamer	22-31
Goblet	
Flat base	24-30
Fancy base	29-35
Pitcher, water	40-50
Spoonholder	23-32
Sugar bowl, open	21-31
Tumbler	19-27
Wine	27-36

Cut Log

Cut Log

(Original name, Ethol; Cat's Eye and Block): Greensburg Glass Company, c. 1885. Clear, nonflint.

Bowls	
7″, 10″	$ 13-16
10″ deep, footed, scalloped	53-61
Butter dish, covered	55-63
Cake stand	
Large	88-95
Small	43-51
Celery	42-50
Compote	
Covered	
5½″	42-50
7¼″	58-64
Open	
7″, low standard	22-29
8″, high standard	38-44
10″, high standard	50-59
Creamer	
3″	14-18
5″	44-51
Goblet (ill.)	37-44
Mug	22-28
Nappy, handled	14-19
Pitcher, water, applied handle	87-96
Sauce	
Flat	8-12
Footed	26-32
Salt/Pepper, pr.	63-72
Spoonholder	26-31
Sugar bowl, covered	52-60
Tumbler	26-31
Vase, 16¼″	41-50
Wine	26-32

Dahlia

Dahlia

Canton Glass Company, Canton, Ohio, 1880s. Portland Glass and Canadian attribution. Clear, amber, vaseline, blue, green.

83

(continued)

Bowl, oval, 8¾" x 6"	$ 16-22
Butter dish, covered	40-47
Cake plate on stand, 10"	35-43
Champagne	40-48
Compote, large, covered, high standard	57-62
Cordial	42-52
Creamer	22-30
Egg cup, double (rare)	52-60
Goblet, ...	38-44
Mug, handled, 2 sizes	23-31
Pickle/Relish	19-27
Pitcher	
Milk	39-47
Water, bulbous, applied handle (ill.)	125-145
Plate, round, handled	22-30
Platter, grape handles, oval	32-41
Sauce	7-11
Spoonholder	24-32
Sugar bowl, covered	44-53
Wine	39-46

Colors, 50 percent higher than clear prices listed. Blue, 100 percent higher. There is also a Dahlia pattern transfer–etched on various clear blanks.

Daisy and Bluebell

(Original name, The Mosaic): Mosaic Glass Co. No. 51, c. 1891. Clear, nonflint.

Creamer . . . . $ 20-25
There should be other pieces. If you know of any, please write.

Daisy and Button

Daisy and Button

Gillinder and Sons, Philadelphia, 1876, in time for the Centennial; also, Hobbs, Brockunier and Company, Wheeling, West Virginia. Souvenir items were extremely popular at the Fair. Wheelbarrow with metal wheel is rare today. It can be seen at the Houston Museum.

This pattern with its many variants has been in continuous production from its original issue until present. Buying from a pattern glass specialist is the best protection against buying reproductions. There are many "safe" types listed here. Brilliance and factory polished bases are evidence but not guarantees of authentic pieces.

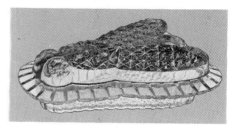

Daisy and Button

Daisy and Button Fly

(Bee): U.S. Glass Company (Bryce Brothers), c. 1890s. Clear, amber, yellow, blue, nonflint. Original factory illustration shows lid separate and inverted as "fly pickle" and base separate as "fly dish." Illustration shows that the 2 pieces make a covered dish.

Clear (ill.) . . . . $ 78-93
Colors 115-147
Not reproduced.

Daisy and Button Helmet

Daisy and Button Helmet

Duncan, c. 1880s. One of rarest pieces in the pattern is this "Helmet" covered butter dish. Can be seen at the Houston Museum in Chattanooga.

Clear as shown . . . . $180+
Not reproduced.

**Daisy and Button,
Oval Medallion**

Daisy and Button, Oval Medallion

(Daisy and Button with Rimmed Oval Panel)

Butter dish, covered . . . . $ 37-46
Celery (ill.) 26-34
Creamer. 32-37
Goblet. 29-36
Pitcher, water, milk 39-50
Sauce 12-15
Spoonholder. 23-30
Sugar bowl, covered 34-42
Not reproduced.

Daisy and Button, Panelled

Daisy and Button, Panelled

(Original name, Ellrose): George Duncan & Sons, c. 1884. Clear, amber, blue, vaseline, apple green; clear with blue or amber panels (amberette), nonflint.

Berry set
Bowl, 7″, 8″. . . . . $ 30-40
Sauce, flat, footed, 4½″ 18-24
Bowl, covered, 7½″, 8½″. 46-57
Butter dish, 6″. 74-89
Compote, open, high standard, 8″ . . 63-78
Creamer (ill.) 49-57
Cruet, original square
D & B stopper 93-125
Pitcher, water 126-145
Plate, oval, bread 64-79
Tumbler. 36-40

Prices are for amber stripe. Solid color, 25 percent less; clear 50 percent less. Not reproduced.

Daisy and Button Triangle

Daisy and Button Triangle

(Daisy and Button, thin Bars)This is an unusual blue creamer with clear handle. Possibly Hobbs, Brockunier and Company.

Creamer (ill.), blue with
clear handle . . . . $ 40-46
Goblet. 31-38
Salt dip, individual 11-14
Sauce, triangular 10-15

Not reproduced. Prices are for clear unless stated. Color, add 80 percent.

Daisy and Button with Crossbar

(Original name, Mikado): U. S. Glass Company (Richards and Hartley, c. 1890). Clear, yellow, amber, light and dark blue; nonflint.

Bowl, finger . . . . $ 17-22
Butter dish, flat, footed 37-43

85

(continued)

Daisy and Button with Crossbar

Compote
Covered, 7", 8".	40-46
Open, 7", 8"	20-30
Creamer, small (ill.)	16-20
Cruet	26-34
Goblet.	25-29
Lamps, tall, 4 sizes.	49-69
Mugs, 2 sizes	14-22
Pitcher, quart, ½ gal.	36-41
Plate, bread	24-30
Salt/Pepper, pr.	30-40
Spoonholder.	24-28
Sugar bowl, covered	32-40
Syrup	40-50
Tray, water	30-35
Tumbler.	16-22
Wine	22-27

Amber, yellow, 40 percent higher; blue, 100 percent higher than clear prices listed.

Daisy and Button with Narcissus

Daisy and Button with Narcissus

(Clear Lily): Dunkirk Glass Company, c. 1907-1930. Clear, rose, flowers, green leaves.

Butter dish	$ 39-47
Celery, tall	24-31
Compote, open	39-48
Creamer.	29-34
Decanter, w/stopper.	56-62
Goblet.	27-35
Pitcher, water (ill.)	42-50
Salt/Pepper, pr.	45-52
Sauce, 4"	10-16
Spoonholder.	24-30
Sugar bowl, covered	34-42
Tray	
Celery, oval	26-31
Water, round	32-37
Tumbler.	19-27
Wine	19-27

Prices are for brilliant quality with good paint. Wine reproduced in clear and muddy green.

Daisy and Button with Prisms

Daisy and Button with Prisms

Maker unknown, c.1880s. Clear, possibly colors, nonflint.

Creamer, 4½" (ill.) . . . . $ 18-24
Other pieces? Not reproduced.

Daisy and Button with V Ornament

A. J. Beatty & Company, 1886-1887. Clear, amber, yellow, blue.

Butter dish, covered	$ 35-40
Bowl, waste (ill.).	20-25
Celery.	23-29

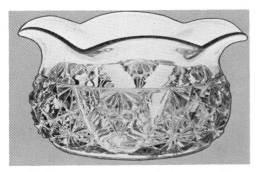

Daisy and Button with V Ornament

Creamer. 30-36
Cup 13-16
Dish, oblong. 16-19
Pickle caster in frame 59-69
Spoonholder. 21-27
Sugar bowl, covered 35-40
Toothpick. 20-24
Tumbler. 15-20

No goblet, but there is a fine cut goblet with a V-like design that goes well with pattern. Daisy and Button with Crossbar confusing in some pieces, but has plain buttons. V-ornament has rayed buttons.

Daisy in Diamond

Daisy in Diamond

O'Hara Glass Company, Pittsburgh, 1886. Clear, amber, rose, blue, nonflint.

Butter dish, covered . . . . $ 32-42
Celery. 23-32
Compote, 8" (convex ovals
  separate the "stars" 42-49

Creamer (ill.) 27-37
Egg cup 18-22
Mug. 16-21
Pitcher, water 35-42
Salt/Pepper, pr.
  Half size, bulbous 34-40
  Regular size, straight. 32-38
Spoonholder. 24-33
Sugar bowl, covered 29-38
Tumbler. 22-31

Colors, 110-130 percent higher than clear prices listed. Bulbous salt shaker lacking prism, called Star and Bar by Peterson.

Daisy Medallion

Daisy Medallion

(Sunburst Medallion): Maker unknown, 1880s. Clear, nonflint.

Butter dish, covered . . . . $ 28-33
Compote, high, open. 23-27
Creamer. 19-24
Goblet. 15-19
Pitcher 30-37
Spoonholder. 14-17
Sugar bowl, uncovered (ill.) 12-16

Daisy Whorl

87

(continued)

Daisy Whorl

(Couchman; Daisy Whorl with Diamond Band): Maker unknown, 1870s. Clear, also in colors. Nonflint.

Butter dish, covered	$ 31-38
Compote	
Covered	32-41
Open	21-26
Creamer (ill.)	22-27
Goblet.	17-24
Pitcher, water	35-44
Spoonholder.	15-21
Sugar bowl	
Covered	29-34
Open	16-22

Colors, 50-75 percent higher than clear prices listed.

Dakota

Dakota

(Baby Thumbprint; Thumbprint Band): U. S. Glass Company (Doyle), Pittsburgh, 1890s. Clear, ruby-flashed, nonflint. Transfer, etched or engraved. A few scarce pieces in cobalt.

Bowl, berry, 8".	$ 32-41
Butter dish, covered, etched	54-64
Cake stand, 10"	48-57
Celery, flat base	22-27
Compote, covered, 5", 6", 7", 8"	44-62
Creamer, pedestal base (ill.)	59-67
Goblet, etched.	36-44
Pitcher, water, etched	32-42
Salt/Pepper, pr.	62-72
Spoonholder, pedestal	24-29
Sugar bowl, covered, etched	52-68
Tray, water, 13", ruffled	
edge (scarce).	66-75
Tumbler.	42-50

Wine	
10½"	72-85
Etched.	40-46

Ruby-flashed, 60 percent higher than clear. Cobalt, 200 percent +.

Dalton

Tarentum, c. 1904. Clear, nonflint.

Celery vase	$ 14-19
Creamer	
Breakfast	11-16
Regular	20-26
Cup	5-9
Goblet.	16-21
Pitcher, 1 qt., 8" high	25-32
Plate, 10½"	14-20
Rose bowl, miniature, 2" dia. x 2" high .	22-32
Spoonholder.	12-18
Sugar	
Breakfast, open, scalloped	
rim, 2⅞" high	10-15
Regular, covered	24-30
Toothpick.	28-34

Dancing Goat

Possibly LaBelle Glass Company, Bridgeport, Ohio, c. 1878. Clear, nonflint.

Ale glass.	$ 75+

Dart

Maker unknown, c. 1880. Clear, nonflint.

Butter dish, covered	$ 32-40
Compote, 5⅞" dia., 8" high	
with lid	32-38
Creamer.	23-31
Goblet.	22-30
Sauce, footed	10-12
Spoonholder.	18-24
Sugar bowl, covered	31-39

Deer and Oak Tree

Dalzell, Gilmore & Leighton, Findlay, Ohio, c. 1888. Also, Indiana Tumbler & Goblet (National) Company, Greentown, Indiana. National took over both factories in 1889.

Mug, chocolate	$ 200+
Pitcher, water (ill.)	285-310

Deer and Oak Tree

Deer and Pine Tree

Deer and Pine Tree

(Deer and Doe): Sandwich glass by early authors, c. 1860s. McKee, 1880s and probably Belmont. Clear, blue, amber, green, yellow, nonflint.

Butter dish, covered	$ 66-74
Cake stand	78-84
Celery.	49-54
Compote, covered, oblong, large	44-56
Creamer (ill.)	42-52
Goblet.	39-46
Jam jar, covered	49-54
Mug, 3 sizes	32-48
Pickle dish, oblong, deep.	24-32
Pitcher, large	70-82
Platter, 13¼″ × 8″	47-57
Sauce, flat and footed	18-24
Spoonholder.	35-45
Sugar bowl, covered	56-64
Tray, large, 11″ × 15″, handled	79-86

Colors, 40-60 percent higher than clear prices listed. Reproduced.

Delaware

Delaware

(New Century, Four Petal Flower): U.S. Glass Company, (Bryce Bros. and King Glass Company) c. 1899. Clear with rose stain and gold; clear with gold; rose, green; milk glass, opaque green. Nonflint.

Bowl, round, fluted, boat-shaped, banana	$ 37-45
Butter dish	49-55
Celery.	35-44
Creamer.	33-39
Cruet	60-69
Cup	16-22
Pitcher, "jug" (ill.).	40-50
Spoonholder.	25-34
Sugar bowl, covered	41-47
Toothpick holder	24-32
Tumbler.	24-29

Colors, 100 to 150 percent higher than clear prices listed. Not reproduced.

Dew and Raindrop

Dew and Raindrop

Kokomo Glass Manufacturing Company, Kokomo, Indiana, c. 1900-1905. Jenkins Glass Company after 1906. Clear, clear/gilded, clear/ruby, nonflint.

Bowl, berry	$ 44-55
Butter dish	49-59

(continued)

Cordial, plain stem	19-29
Creamer.	41-45
Cup, jelly quality	10-12
Goblet	
Dewdrop stem, good quality	36-44
Jelly, poor quality	14-19
Pitcher, water (ill.)	70-80
Sauce	13-17
Salt/Pepper, square, pr.	50-68
Spoonholder.	31-37
Sugar bowl	41-44
Tumbler.	17-26
Wine, plain stem	13-17

Poor quality goblet and cup (jelly containers), straight-stem cordial, wine made at Kokomo-Jenkins factory. Brilliant quality is earlier production, maker unknown.

Dewberry

Maker unknown, c. 1890. Clear, gold trim, blue; ruby stain (scarce) known in souvenir champagne. Nonflint.

Butter.	$ 30-36
Champagne, price for clear.	22-30
Creamer.	21-26
Goblet.	17-25
Spoonholder.	16-20
Sugar	23-39

Kemple called their reproduction milk glass creamer in this pattern "Blackberry." Ruby stained champagne valued at $30-35.

Dewdrop and Flowers

Dewdrop and Flowers

(Quantico; Nova Scotia Starflower): Made in Nova Scotia, c. 1890. Clear, nonflint.

Butter dish, covered	$ 35-42
Cake stand	30-37

Compote	
Covered	45-52
Open	31-40
Creamer.	27-32
Goblet.	29-37
Pitcher, water (ill.)	37-45
Spoonholder.	14-22
Sugar bowl	
Covered	32-39
Open	19-28

Dewdrop in Points

Dewdrop in Points

Greensburg Glass Company, Greensburg, Pennsylvania, c. 1875-1885. Clear, nonflint.

Butter dish, covered	$ 35-42
Cake stand, large	39-44
Compote	
Covered, high	42-51
Open, low	22-27
Creamer (ill.)	30-38
Goblet.	23-29
Pickle dish, oval	16-19
Pitcher	39-43
Plate, bread	27-32
Sauce, footed	6-9
Spoonholder.	16-20
Sugar bowl, covered	32-39

Dewdrop with Star

Campbell, Jones & Company, Pittsburgh, c. 1877. Clear, nonflint.

Butter dish, covered, star base	$ 41-49
Cake plate on standard	64-72
Cheese dish	81-105
Compote, covered	
Footed, 6″, 7″, star base.	49-66
High and low standard	79-84

Dewdrop with Star

Creamer (ill.)	39-44
Pickle dish	14-20
Pitcher, water (ill.)	92-107
Plates, 4½″ through 11″	19-36
Sauce, flat and footed	9-14
Spoonholder.	31-37
Sugar bowl, covered, star base	48-58

No goblet. 7″, 11″ plate, footed salt, footed sauce reproduced in clear and in color.

Dewey

Dewey

(Flower Flange): Indiana Tumbler & Goblet Company, 1898. Clear, canary, green, amber, blue; opaque white, Nile green, chocolate. Golden agate (amber opalescent) in serpentine tray only. Nonflint.

Bowl, berry	$ 20-29
Butter dish, covered, (ill.), 4″, 5″	35-42
Creamer, 4″, 5″.	29-36
Cruet	42-50
Mug.	31-36
Parfait (vase-shaped), 6″.	30-36
Pitcher, water, 9½″ high	48-57
Salt/Pepper, pr.	34-41
Spoonholder.	25-32
Sugar bowl, covered	35-42

Tray, serpentine.	22-28
Tumbler.	29-37

Chocolate, 300 percent higher; other colors, 70 percent higher than clear prices listed. Not all forms made in all colors.

Diagonal Band

Diagonal Band

Maker unknown, c. 1880s. Clear. Apple green. Probably other colors.

Butter dish, covered	$ 32-40
Compote, covered	30-37
Creamer (ill.)	29-33
Goblet.	19-27
Plate, bread	23-31
Relish	14-17
Sauce, flat.	7-10
Spoonholder.	18-24
Sugar bowl, covered	30-40
Wine	24-29

Diagonal Band with Fan

(Manufacturer's original name, Greek): U.S. Glass Co. (Ripley), c. 1891. Clear, nonflint.

Butter dish, covered	$ 34-39
Celery vase	24-29
Compote, high, open, 8″ dia.	24-36
Creamer (ill.)	26-32
Goblets	22-30
Pitcher, milk, 8″	33-40
Plate, 6″, 7″, 8″	14-18
Salt/Pepper, pr.	49-57
Sauce, footed, 4″, 4½″	6-9

(continued)

Diagonal Band with Fan

Spoonholder. 19-24
Sugar bowl, covered 32-36
Wine, 4½" high 21-27

Diamond and Sunburst

Diamond and Sunburst

Maker unknown, late 1860s. Clear, nonflint.

Butter dish, covered . . . . $ 29-35
Cake stand 34-43
Celery vase 24-32
Compote
　Covered, 17" 35-44
　Open 24-32
Creamer, applied handle. 34-39
Decanter 28-34
Egg cup 18-22
Goblet. 19-23
Pitcher, water (ill.) 39-49
Salt dip, master 17-25
Spoonholder. 19-26
Sugar bowl, covered 30-38
Tumbler. 22-31

Diamond Band

Diamond Band

(Scalloped Diamond Point; Panel with Diamond Point): Central Glass Company, Wheeling, West Virginia, c. 1870. Clear, "electric blue" (turquoise), cobalt blue, nonflint.

Butter dish, covered . . . . $ 38-46
Celery. 24-35
Compote
　Cobalt blue on clear
　　pedestal, 8½" dia. 90-115
　Open, 7½" dia.. 33-39
Creamer. 31-36
Dish, shallow, oval, 6" 12-18
Goblet. 24-32
Pitcher, water (ill.) 37-44
Spoonholder. 19-27
Sugar bowl, covered 34-41
Wine 21-27

Colored pieces worth 200 percent more than clear.

Diamond Block with Fans

(Blockade): Challinor, Taylor, Ltd., c. 1880. Clear, nonflint. It was their No. 309. U.S. Glass Company after 1891.

Bowl, waste . . . . $ 18-24
Butter dish, covered 34-45
Celery. 24-33
Creamer. 29-38
Goblet. 19-26
Pitcher, water 49-57
Spoonholder. 20-24
Sugar bowl, covered 32-39
Tray, water 30-36

Diamond Mirror

Diamond Mirror

(Grecian): Maker unknown, late 1880s. Clear, nonflint. Diamonds may be engraved.

Butter dish, covered	$ 29-34
Celery	19-25
Creamer	21-28
Goblet	24-31
Jam jar/pickle caster base (ill.)	19-27
Spoonholder	18-21
Sugar bowl	
Covered	27-33
Open	15-22

Add 25 percent for engraving.

Diamond Point

Diamond Point

Sandwich glass, 1830. Bryce, Richards & Co., Pittsburgh, c. 1854; others, c. 1880s. Clear, rare in colors, flint.

Ale glass	$ 45-53
Butter dish, covered	105-115
Celery	62-72
Champagne	62-72

Compote		
Covered, 6", 7", 8", high and low standard	105-129
Open, 6", 7", 8", high (ill.) and low standard	59-67
Creamer, footed, scalloped	118-136
Egg cup (rare in color)	27-36
Goblet, knob stem	42-48
Pitcher	70-80
Plates, 3" through 8"	32-55
Spoonholder	39-49
Sugar bowl, covered	88-99
Tumbler, water, whiskey	64-82

Color, 400 percent higher; opaque, 200 percent higher than clear prices listed.

Diamond Point Discs

Diamond Point Discs

Higbee (some pieces may be trademarked); later in limited production by New Martinsville.

Butter dish, covered	$ 29-37
Cake stand	32-39
Celery	18-27
Compote, covered	
7", 8", high standard	37-47
Creamer	27-36
Goblet	20-27
Pitcher (ill.)	47-56
Plate, 7" sq.	20-27
Relish	13-16
Salt/Pepper, pr.	17-27
Spoonholder	22-31
Sugar bowl, covered	30-34
Wine	22-29

Diamond Point with Panels

(Hinoto): Boston and Sandwich Glass Company, 1850s. Clear, flint.

(continued)

Diamond Point with Panels

Celery.	$ 51-63
Champagne	61-69
Creamer, applied handle.	110-128
Goblet.	56-68
Mug, applied handle.	43-55
Pitcher, applied handle (ill.)	152-161
Salt, footed	39-46
Spoonholder.	42-50
Sugar bowl	80-92
Wine	50-60

Diamond Prisms

(Beveled Diamond and Star): Maker unknown, c. 1895. Clear, nonflint. These ruby pieces known: 7″ open compote, scalloped rim; syrup; wine; decanter 10¾″ high with faceted stopper; tumbler.

Bowl	
Oblong	$ 13-17
Round, 6¾″ 8″	15-21
Butter, covered	28-36
Cake stand	30-38
Cheese, covered, flat base	35-42
Compote	
Covered, 3 sizes	31-49
Open, scalloped rim	19-27
Cracker jar	34-40
Creamer	25-32
Cruet, patterned stopper	26-34
Cup	10-13
Decanter, patterned stopper	
2 sizes	37-46
Egg cup	15-22
Goblet (scarce)	30-35

Pickle.	12-16
Pitcher	
Milk, allover pattern.	21-30
Tankard, applied handle.	34-45
Plate, dinner, 9⅞″.	20-25
Salt shaker	17-22
Sauce, flat or footed	8-13
Spoonholder.	15-21
Sugar, covered.	25-35
Syrup	39-44
Tray, water, 9½″	19-27
Wine	20-25

Pattern usually has plain top with pattern below, but also can be found with allover pattern. Kamm lists a toothpick but no proof found in modern literature. Confusing pattern name: there is another Diamond Prisms. Ruby stain, add 80 percent to clear prices listed.

Diamond Quilted

Diamond Quilted

Maker unknown, c. 1880s. Clear, amber, yellow, blue, 2 shades; amethyst, 2 shades; nonflint.

Butter dish, covered	$ 39-46
Creamer.	29-34
Goblet.	20-26
Pitcher, water	37-42
Sauce, footed (ill.)	9-13
Spoonholder.	19-23
Sugar bowl, covered	38-47
Tray, water	35-44
Tumbler.	21-27

Canary, 100 percent; light blue, 150 percent; light, dark amethyst, 200 percent higher than clear prices listed. Goblet, tumbler reproduced.

Diamond Thumbprint

(Diamond and Concave): Sandwich glass; McKee & Bros., 1850s. Clear, green-tinted, amethyst (due to improper mixing of metal), and yellow (rare), flint.

Diamond Thumbprint

Bowl	$107-129
Butter dish, covered	160-170
Celery.	134-142
Champagne (rare)	240+
Creamer (ill.)	175-195
Decanter, original stopper, qt.	112-118
Goblet (rare)	350+
Pitcher, water, rare	550+
Sauce, flat.	22-29
Spoonholder.	72-82
Sugar bowl, 2 styles, covered	134-144
Wine jug, places for holding	
glasses, set	1,000+

Extremely rare. Goblet reproduced.

Dickinson

Dickinson

Sandwich glass, 1860s. Clear, average quality glass. Flint.

Butter dish, covered	$ 55-62
Compote	
Covered	79-84
Open, sweetmeat (ill.)	52-60
Creamer.	49-60
Goblet.	34-42
Sauce, flat.	12-16
Spoonholder.	33-43
Sugar	
Covered	58-64
Open	35-42
Pitcher, water	98-122
Wine	51-63

Diapered Flower

Diapered Flower

Probably Westmoreland Glass Company, c. 1890s. Opaque blue with white paint. It was a container for mustard or other condiments. Nonflint.

Creamer, covered (ill.)	$ 42-51
Sugar bowl, covered	45-53

Sugar and creamer lids are not interchangeable.

Divided Block with Sunburst

Divided Block with Sunburst, Variant

(Cube with Double Fan; Majestic; Pilgrim): U.S. Glass Company, after 1891. Clear, green, blue, chartreuse, chocolate, and clear with ruby stain. Nonflint.

95

(continued)

Butter dish, covered	$ 35-40
Celery vase	18-24
Compote, covered, high or low	
standard	36-49
Creamer	27-32
Goblet	19-27
Pitcher, water (ill.)	20-26
Salt/Pepper, pr	22-31
Spoonholder	19-24
Sugar bowl, covered	33-39
Tumbler	22-31

The pitcher shown is not as good as those with scalloped rims and applied handles.

Divided Hearts

Boston & Sandwich Glass Company, c. early 1860s. Clear, flint.

Butter dish, covered	$139-152
Compote	
Covered	132-150
Open	78-89
Celery	67-75
Creamer	121-140
Egg cup	79-89
Goblet	92-103
Lamp, marble base	130-144
Salt, master, pedestal base	34-45
Spoonholder	51-59
Sugar bowl, covered	142-152

Dixie Belle

Maker unknown, c. 1910. Clear or trimmed with gold, nonflint.

Compote	
Ruffled jelly	17-23
Straight flared rim, open	15-20
Goblet	22-29
Plate, dinner, 10¾″	20-25

Dog and Child Mug

Indiana Tumbler & Goblet Company (National), Greentown, Indiana, 1902. Clear, chocolate, Nile green, nonflint.

Chocolate	$225+
Nile green (ill.)	250+
Rare!	

Dog and Child Mug

Dog Hunting

Dog Hunting

Maker unknown. Attributed to Greentown by early authors, but no proof.

Pitcher, water (ill.)	$222-231

Dolphin

Maker unknown, c. 1870s. Clear with frosting. Nonflint.

Butter dish, covered,	
dolphin finial	$168-172
Compote, high standard, open	99-107
Creamer, 6¼″ (ill.)	120-130
Goblet	210-235
Pitcher, water	198-226
Salt/Pepper, pr	110-134
Spoonholder	91-101
Sugar bowl, covered,	
dolphin finial	132-154

Dolphin

Double Beetle Band

Creamer (ill.)	20-26
Goblet.	17-24
Pitcher	32-37
Sauce, footed, flat	6-10
Spoonholder.	14-19
Sugar bowl	
Covered	25-32
Open	16-20
Wine	15-21

Yellow, 50 percent higher; amber and blue, 100 percent higher than clear prices listed.

Dolphin

Dolphin

Covered dish, Indiana Tumbler & Goblet Company, 1899. Clear, chocolate, blue, amber, emerald green, teal blue, canary, opaque white, Golden Agate, nonflint.

Chocolate
Fantop mouth	$238-275
Smooth mouth (ill.)	194-207

Reproduced, 1974. Not all forms made in all colors.

Double Beetle Band

(Smocking Bands): Columbia Glass Company, Findlay, Ohio, 1880s. Clear, yellow, amber, blue, nonflint.

Butter dish, covered . . . . $ 26-34

Double Dahlia and Lens

Double Dahlia and Lens

Maker unknown, c. 1890. Clear; clear with rose flash and green leaves; emerald green. Gold decorated. Nonflint.

Butter dish, covered	$ 30-37
Creamer, berry (ill.)	22-26
Goblet.	23-33
Spoonholder.	16-21

97

(continued)

Sugar bowl, covered	25-35
Vase.	18-25
Wine	25-31

Color-flashed, 25 percent, emerald green, 80 percent more than clear prices listed.

Double Donut

Double Donut

Maker unknown, c. 1880s. Clear, nonflint.

Creamer, 5½″ (ill.). . . . . $ 26-32
This took a metal lid and could have been a syrup. Other pieces?

Double Greek Key

Double Greek Key

(Greek Key and Wedding Ring, Canadian name): Burlington Glass Works, Hamilton, Ontario, 1880s. Also made by Nickel Plate Glass Company. Clear, green, blue opalescent, nonflint.

Berry set	
Bowl, 8″	$ 32-38
Sauce	16-23
Butter dish, covered	118-132
Celery.	42-51
Compote, covered	85-97
Creamer (ill.)	52-68
Pickle tray	31-40
Pitcher	133-149
Salt/Pepper, blown, pr.	75-92
Spoonholder.	40-50
Sugar bowl, covered	82-95
Toothpick.	92-114
Tumbler.	37-47

Prices are for color. Clear, 50 percent less.

Double Ribbon

Double Ribbon

Bakewell, Pears & Co., c. 1870. Clear, clear with frosted ribbons. Nonflint. Occasionally found in flint.

Butter dish	$ 54-63
Compote	
Covered, high foot	58-65
Open, high foot	43-52
Creamer, pressed handle.	32-42
Egg cup	27-36
Goblet.	30-39
Pickle dish	19-27
Pitcher, applied handle (ill.)	58-70
Platter, bread, 9″ x 13½″, oval	38-47
Sauce, footed, 4½″.	12-17
Spoonholder.	24-34
Sugar bowl, covered	36-47

Double Spear

(Brilliant): McKee & Brothers, 1880s. Clear, nonflint.

Butter dish, covered . . . . $ 33-39

Double Spear

Celery.	19-26
Compote, covered, high standard	
(sweetmeat), 6″	30-40
Creamer.	25-31
Dish, oval, deep, 7″, 8″, 9″.	18-24
Goblet.	25-34
Pickle dish, scoop shaped	13-19
Pitcher, water, ½ gal. (ill.)	32-40
Sauce, 4″, 5″, flat	6-11
Spoonholder.	17-22
Sugar bowl, covered	27-34

Douglass

Co-operative, c. 1903. Clear, ruby stain, engraved.

Bowl	
Berry	$ 14-20
Finger, square	12-16
Punch	89-115
Butter	
Flat	28-33
Pedestaled.	31-38
Creamer.	23-30
Cup	6-9
Pitcher	34-44
Salt shaker	13-18
Sauce, flat.	5-9
Spoonholder.	16-21
Sugar	30-35
Toothpick	24-29
Tumbler.	12-16
Water bottle, 2 shapes	30-37

No cruet, goblet, or jelly compote known. Ruby stain add 100 percent to clear prices listed.

Draped Fan

(Original name, Comet): Doyle and Company, Pittsburgh, c. 1880s. Pattern reissued by U.S. Glass Company in 1890s. Clear, amber, vaseline, nonflint.

Butter dish, covered	$ 31-38
Cake stand	29-39
Celery.	22-29
Compote	
Covered	33-39
Open	19-22
Creamer.	22-29
Goblet.	24-29
Pitcher, water	25-37
Spoonholder.	16-20
Sugar bowl, covered	30-36

Amber, vaseline, 50 percent higher than clear prices listed.

Drapery

Drapery

(Lace): Sandwich, c. 1870. Doyle & Company, Pittsburgh, 1870. Clear, nonflint.

Butter dish, covered	$ 39-49
Compote, covered, 7″, low	37-42
Creamer, applied handle (ill.)	35-43
Dish, oval	18-27
Egg cup	30-36
Goblet.	27-36
Pitcher	49-54
Plate, 6″.	18-26
Saucedish, flat, 4″	9-12
Spoonholder.	23-29
Sugar bowl, covered	29-38

Early issue had fine stippling, applied handles; later version with coarse stippling, pressed handles, 20 percent less.

Drapery

Drapery

Northwood & Company, c. 1905. Clear and blue opalescent. Gold trim.

Berry Set
Bowl.	$ 70-80
Sauce	31-36
Butter dish	136-149
Creamer.	53-67
Pitcher (ill.).	146-155
Spoonholder.	52-63
Sugar bowl	89-99
Tumbler.	43-51

Not reproduced.

Drinking Scene on Mug

Drinking Scene on Mug

Outdoor version by Indiana Tumbler & Goblet (National) Company, late 1890s. Nonflint.

Chocolate	$100-130
Clear (rare)	118-129
Cobalt (rare)	200+
Nile green (ill.)	92-115

Drum

Drum

Bryce, Higbee & Company, Pittsburgh, 1880s. Clear, nonflint. Finials are tiny cannon. This is a play set.

Butter dish, covered,	
2¼" high (ill.)	$94-125
Creamer, 2¾" high (ill.)	66-75
Mug	
Large, 2½" high	40-50
Small, 2" high	45-55
Mustard jar, covered,	
adult size	96-117
Spoonholder, 2⅝" (ill.)	67-77
Sugar bowl, covered,	
3½" high (ill.)	84-100

Spoonholder collectible as toothpick.

Duncan No. 30

(Scalloped Six-Point, D & M 30): Duncan and Miller, c. 1893. Clear, some with gold trim; rare in ruby-stain and amberstain. Nonflint. At least 133 pieces made.

Bowl, round or square	$ 14-22
Butter.	32-42
Celery vase, flat	23-30
Champagne	
Saucer, stemmed.	19-25
Tumbler (juice)	13-17
Claret, cupped or straight	22-29
Cocktail, flared, small and large	21-28
Cordial, cupped or straight	25-35
Creamer.	24-30
Goblet, cupped or straight	29-35
Pickle jar, covered (similar to but	
smaller than sugar)	32-40
Pitcher, tankard.	39-49
Rose bowl, toy.	45-52
Salt dip, indivudual	11-16
Sherry (flute), plain or flared top	17-23
Spoonholder.	17-23
Sugar	30-37
Toothpick	
Cuspidor.	35-42
Regular	29-36

Tumbler
  Bar (shot)   12-16
  Water   14-19
Wine, cupped or straight.   18-25

Toothpick known in amber stain and ruby stain; individual salt dip known in ruby stain.

Duncan No. 40

(Sunburst): Duncan & Miller, c. 1891. Clear, nonflint.

Bowl
  Finger, round or square . . . . $ 12-17
  Punch   95-128
Butter.   30-40
Celery tray, 8″, 9″, 10″   14-19
Compote, open (10 sizes).   18-35
Creamer
  Individual, flat.   16-21
  Regular, low pedestal   19-24
Cup   6-10
Nappy
  Round or square   11-15
  Handled   14-19
Pitcher
  Jug, ½ gal..   34-42
  Jug, with silver-plated top   42-55
Plate, 8″   14-24
Salt shaker   15-21
Shade, gas, 6 sizes   19-35
Spoonholder.   17-22
Sugar
  Individual, handled, open   15-20
  Regular   29-38
Tankard, ½ gal..   33-40
Tray, punch   41-53
Tumbler.   12-17
Vase (6 sizes)   13-30

Duncan 2000

(Flowered Scroll): George Duncan's Sons & Company, Washington, Pennsylvania, c. 1893. Clear, clear with amber stain. Nonflint.

Butter dish, covered . . . . $ 36-42
Cheese, covered, 8½″ plate base   42-48
Compote, low, triangular.   30-35
Creamer.   29-35
Pitcher, milk   32-39
Spoonholder.   20-28
Sugar bowl, covered   32-40
Tumbler.   18-24

Amber stain, 70 percent higher than clear prices listed.

E Pluribus Unum

E Pluribus Unum

Gillinder & Sons, Philadelphia, Pennsylvania, mid-1800s. Clear, nonflint.

Platter, 5¾″ x 10″ (ill.). . . . . $ 69-75
The center has two cucumbers, and the handles, eagles.

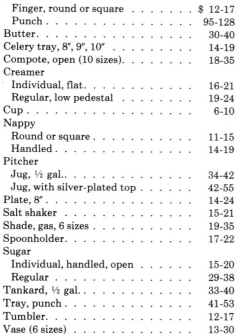

Ear of Corn

Ear of Corn

Vase
  Blue/opal (ill.) . . . . $ 90-105
  Green/opal   139-155

Early Moon and Star

Sandwich, 1850s. Clear, canary, flint.

Creamer. $139-156
Lamp, small handled, (3 sizes)   82-97
Lilac water bottle   80-95
Pomade jar   125-135
Salt dip   27-34

(continued)

Early Moon and Star

Spoonholder or spill	62-74
Sugar bowl, open (ill.)	47-54
Tumbler, bar	68-78

Rare.

Early Panelled Grape Band

Early Panelled Grape Band

Attributed to Sandwich, 1870s. Clear, nonflint.

Butter bowl, covered.	$ 35-42
Celery	28-38
Creamer, applied handle	38-48
Egg cup	28-34
Goblet.	32-38
Pitcher, water, applied handle	69-85
Spoonholder.	24-31
Sugar bowl, (base ill.)	24-33

Effulgent Star

Effulgent Star

(Star Galaxy): Central Glass Company, Wheeling, West Virginia, 1880. Clear, nonflint.

Butter dish, covered	$ 58-69
Cake stand, top, base	
joined by wafer	65-73
Celery	32-41
Creamer (ill.)	35-42
Goblet.	33-40
Pitcher, water	75-85
Salt dip, individual	13-19
Spoonholder.	30-36
Sugar bowl, covered	54-62
Tumbler.	27-36

Probably other pieces.

Egg in Sand

Egg in Sand

(Bean): Maker unknown, 1880s. Clear, blue, amber, nonflint.

Butter dish	$ 40-45
Compote, covered	49-56
Creamer.	25-30
Goblet.	25-32

Pickle dish, swan and
   flower center. 31-38
Pitcher, water (ill.) 40-47
Salt/Pepper, pr. 49-56
Sauce 9-14
Spoonholder. 19-24
Sugar bowl 36-44
Tray, bread 25-33
Tumbler. 22-29
Wine 27-35

Amber, blue, 60-80 percent higher than clear prices listed.

Egyptian

(Parthenon): Sandwich glass attribution by early authors. Clear, flint.

Butter dish, covered . . . . $ 58-68
Celery. 47-52
Compote
   Covered, high, low standard 129-165
   Open, high, low standard. 39-44
Creamer. 40-49
Goblet. 47-52
Pitcher, water 112-134
Plate, 10″ + handles,
   Pyramid and Camel 48-56
Platter
   Figure of a woman (Cleopatra)
     8½″ x 13″, motto 63-70
   "Salt Lake Temple",
     8½″ x 13″, motto . . . . 350+
Spoonholder. 34-39
Sugar bowl, covered 50-60

Eighteen-Ninety

(Block and Palm; Diamond, Fan and Leaf, in milk glass): Beaver Falls Glass Co., 1890. Clear, milk glass, nonflint.

Bowl . . . . $ 15-19
Butter, covered 31-41
Celery. 24-30
Creamer. 25-32
Goblet. 22-29
Pitcher 36-44
Salt shaker 19-23
Sauce, flat. 6-11
Spoonholder. 17-22
Sugar, covered. 28-35
Sugar shaker 29-35

Milk glass add 30 percent to clear prices listed. Confusing pattern name Diamond Point and Leaf.

Eight-O-Eight

(Original name, Indiana): Albany Glass Co. Clear, amber, cobalt, nonflint.

Bowl
   Flared, 6½″, 7½″, 8½″ 16-24
   Regular, 6″, 7″, 8″. 13-20
Butter. 30-40
Cake stand 10″. 31-42
Celery vase 23-32
Compote
   Covered, tall, 6″, 7″, 8″ 32-45
   Open, tall, crimped rim, 6″, 7″, 8″ . . . 25-34
Creamer. 22-30
Dish, oblong, 7″, 8″. 14-18
Nappy, round, one handle, 4½″, 6″. . . 15-19
Olive, triangular, one handle 4½″, 6″. . 18-22
Pitcher 34-41
Plate, 5½″ (ill.), 9″. 13-23
Rose bowl 20-27
Spoonholder. 17-22
Sugar, covered. 31-39
Tumbler. 16-21
Wine 20-26

Elk Medallion

Elk Medallion

Maker and date unknown. The elk is shown in three different panels, and a the frosted raised design was done by a process called "plate etching" or die etching or engraving.

Goblet (ill.) . . . . $125+

Emerald Green Herringbone

(Florida): U.S. Glass Company, 1880s. Clear, emerald green, nonflint.

Bowl, berry, large, deep . . . . $ 32-40
Butter dish 38-42

(continued)

Emerald Green Herringbone

Creamer (ill.)	28-37
Goblet	29-42
Pitcher, water	52-61
Plates, square, 7¼", 9¼"	17-27
Salt/Pepper, pr.	58-70
Spoonholder	34-45
Syrup (rare)	250+
Tumbler, water	24-32
Wine	50-57

Clear, 50 percent less than green prices listed. Goblet reproduced in green.

English

English

(Original name, Diamond with Diamond Point): Westmoreland Glass Company, 1896. Clear, emerald green milk glass, nonflint.

Butter dish	$ 24-29
Celery	32-41
Compote	35-43
Creamer, 3½" (ill.)	13-18
Goblet	24-32
Pitcher, water	26-35
Puff box	17-23
Salt/Pepper, pr.	28-39
Spoonholder	12-15
Sugar bowl, covered	20-25

Tumbler	10-14

Milk glass 40 percent higher than clear prices listed. Dr. Peterson lists the salt shaker as "Diamond Side."

Esther

(Tooth and Claw): Riverside Glass Company, Wellsburgh, West Virginia, c. 1896. Clear, emerald green, ruby and amber stained. Gold trimmed. Nonflint.

Berry set	
Bowl	$ 30-37
Sauce	24-29
Butter dish, covered	100-125
Celery	89-124
Compote	
Covered, high	81-99
Open, jelly	42-50
Creamer	103-124
Cruet	185-218
Goblet	72-89
Relish	30-36
Salt/Pepper, pr.	95-115
Spoonholder	47-60
Sugar bowl	
Covered	68-90
Open	37-42
Syrup (rare)	300+
Toothpick holder	62-75

Emerald green prices given; 50 percent less for clear.

Etched Garden Fruits

Transfer-etched pattern on various blanks. Design may be diagonal or horizontal and has been found on other patterns such as Lion. Maker unknown, c. 1880.

Butter, covered	$ 32-40
Champagne	16-22
Compote, open, low	22-29
Creamer	28-35
Goblet	20-30
Pitcher, water, reeded applied handle	45-53
Sauce, footed	7-12
Spoonholder	18-23
Sugar on pedestal, covered	30-37
Wine	21-27

Etched Grape

U.S. Glass Company, c. 1915. Clear, emerald green; with and without etching. Nonflint.

Etched Grape

Pitcher, water, 8″ high (ill.) . . . . . . $ 54-63
Emerald green is 50 percent higher than clear price listed. Other pieces?

Etruscan

Bakewell, Pears & Company, Pittsburgh, c. 1874. Clear, flint.

Bowl, oval, 7″, 8″, 9″	$ 28-39
Butter bowl, covered.	50-60
Compote, low standard, scalloped rim	41-49
Creamer, applied handle.	54-64
Goblet.	52-62
Spoonholder on pedestal.	30-39
Sugar bowl, covered, on pedestal. . . .	50-60
Tumbler.	34-43

Eugenie

McKee & Bros., Pittsburgh, c. 1850s. Clear, flint.

Bowl, 7″, 9″	$ 35-43
Butter dish, covered	82-91
Celery.	79-87
Champagne	70-80
Compote, covered, on standard . . .	109-115
Cordial	48-55
Creamer (rare)	150+
Egg cup	36-42
Goblet.	58-68
Spoonholder.	42-49
Sugar bowl, covered, dolphin finial (rare)	175+
Tumbler, footed, ½ pt.	37-47
Wine	49-52

Excelsior

Excelsior

Sandwich, 1850s; McKee Bros., 1868. C. Ihmsen and Company, 1851; others. Clear, soft green.

Ale glass.	$ 62-70
Bitters bottle	40-50
Butter dish, covered	110-118
Candlesticks, pr..	200-260
Creamer, 2 styles	100-125
Decanter, pint, quart	47-52
Egg cup, double and single.	39-47
Goblet, barrel, Maltese Cross	35-42
Pitcher	
Milk (rare),	225+
Syrup (rare)	250+
Water, McKee, rare (ill.)	300+
Spoonholder.	31-41
Sugar bowl, 2 styles	70-98
Tumbler, bar	48-57
Whale oil lamp w/Maltese Cross, Sandwich	162-180
Wine	47-56

Excelsior Variant

(Tong): Probably McKee & Bros., 1868. Clear, nonflint.

Butter dish	$ 52-62
Celery	
Plain top	40-48
Scalloped top	54-63
Cordial	40-50
Creamer (scarce)	118-127
Goblet.	37-47
Spoonholder.	38-48
Sugar bowl, covered	56-66
Tumbler, footed (ill.)	32-39

105

(continued)

Excelsior Variant

Eye-Winker

(Crystal Ball): Dalzell, Gilmore & Leighton, c. 1889. Clear, nonflint.

Butter dish, covered	$ 70-82
Cake stand, 9½" dia..	62-77
Compote, open, scalloped edge.	42-49
Creamer.	45-53
Dish, banana	106-110
Lamp, kerosene	92-107
Pitcher, syrup	62-70
Plate, scalloped edge, 8½"	24-31
Salt/Pepper, pr.	65-79
Sauce, flat, square	15-18
Spoonholder.	28-37
Sugar bowl	
Covered	59-68
Open	20-26

Reproduced. Toothpick holder not original, but now made in all colors.

Faceted Flower Swirl

Faceted Flower Swirl

Maker unknown, c. 1900. Clear, nonflint.

Pitcher, water (ill.)	$ 48-54

The writers have added "Swirl" to the name because "Faceted Flower" in the early literature had a plain body. Information please!

Fagot

(Vera): Robinson Glass Co., 1893. Clear, clear with frosted; ruby stain tumbler known.

Bowl, berry	$ 18-25
Butter, covered	35-39
Cake stand, large	46-55
Compote, open	24-28
Creamer, flat; applied handle	29-35
Cup	9-14
Sauce, flat.	8-10
Spoonholder.	19-23
Sugar, covered.	30-35
Tumbler.	16-22

Clear prices 20 percent less than frosted prices given. Ruby stain add 180 percent.

Fairfax Strawberry

Fairfax Strawberry

(Strawberry): Late 1860s, some made at Sandwich. Also made at Bryce, Walker and Company, 1870. Clear and milk glass. Nonflint.

Butter dish	$ 45-55
Compote, covered, 8", high, low . . .	45-55
Creamer.	36-42
Egg cup	60-70
Goblet.	79-88
Pitcher	
Syrup	90-100
Water	139-152

Relish   15-23
Sauce   10-14
Spoonholder.   25-34
Sugar bowl, base only (ill.)   28-36

Prices listed are for clear glass. Milk glass 30 percent more. Goblet reproduced both in clear and milk glass.

Falling Leaves

Falling Leaves

(Original name, Vine): Federal Glass Co., c. 1915. Otherwise ordinary glass, this pattern is unusual because the leaves are embossed on the *inside* of the body. The pattern was on the plunger. Nonflint.

Bowl
Covered, 6", 7", 8"
Open, 6", 7", 8", (ill.) . . . . $ 12-17
Butter dish, covered   19-24
Creamer   14-18
Pickle dish, oval shallow   13-17
Pitcher, round bowl
Milk, pt.   19-23
Water, qt.   20-30
Pitcher, straight (jug)
½ gal.   26-31
3 qt.   30-40
Sauce, flat, 4½"   4-8
Spoonholder.   10-14
Sugar bowl, covered   16-22
Tumbler.   10-15

No goblet. Also came with embossed grapes or plain.

Fan

Dugan Glass Company (some pieces trademarked), c. 1904. Possibly Northwood Glass Company. Emerald green and cobalt blue; white, green, and blue opalescent; custard, carnival.

Fan

Berry set, deep
Large bowl. $127-149
Small bowl.   44-52
Butter dish, covered   112-130
Creamer.   74-84
Gravy boat, green with
gold (ill.).   38-46
Ice cream set, shallow
Large bowl.   137-155
Small bowl.   40-50
Spoonholder.   61-70
Sugar bowl, covered   90-118
Water set
Pitcher   195-238
Tumbler.   63-73

Green with gold 20 percent less; green, blue opalescent 30 percent less than custard prices shown.

Fan and Star

Challinor, Taylor, Ltd., c. 1880s. Clear, milk glass, purple slag. Some pieces decorated with enameled flowers in different colors. Nonflint.

Bowl, 8" . . . . $ 16-22
Butter dish, covered, low foot   27-35
Celery   22-31
Compote, open, 8", fan rim   27-36
Creamer.   24-30
Goblet.   19-24
Pitcher, water   34-43
Plate, 7"   20-26
Sauce   11-18
Spoonholder.   19-27
Sugar bowl, covered   32-42

Slag or opaque white, 100 percent higher; amber, blue, canary, 50-60 percent higher than clear prices listed.

Fan Band

(Yale; original name, Scalloped Flower Band): Bryce, c. 1885. Clear, nonflint. May be engraved.

Bowl, waste	$ 12-16
Butter (lid is unpatterned)	20-28
Celery vase	16-21
Compote, 6″, 7″, 8″	
High	
Covered	28-35
Open	16-21
Low	
Covered	22-27
Open	14-19
Creamer	15-20
Goblet	14-19
Pickle dish	11-14
Pitcher	23-30
Plate, bread	14-19
Sauce, footed	4-7
Spoonholder on pedestal, fan top	13-16
Sugar (lid is unpatterned)	18-25
Tray, water	32-39
Wine	15-20

Add 25 percent for engraving. Water tray is the identical piece for Grand (Diamond Medallion), made by the same company.

Fan with Diamond

Fan with Diamond

(Original name, Shell): McKee Brothers, c. 1880s. Clear, nonflint.

Butter dish	$ 39-46
Compote	
Covered, high foot	49-56
Covered, low foot	32-37
Creamer, applied handle	29-40
Dish, oval, 9″ × 6¾″	19-27

Egg cup	25-35
Goblet	24-29
Pickle dish	16-21
Pitcher, water, applied handle	39-47
Sauce, flat, 4″	10-12
Spoonholder	19-24
Sugar, base only (ill.)	21-27
Syrup, applied handle, bird on finial	89-115
Wine	31-39

Fancy Arch

McKee, c. 1905. Clear, ruby stained.

Decanter, one handle, faceted stopper	$ 40-50
Pitcher	33-40
Salt dip, individual	13-18
Salt shaker (scarce)	18-24
Tumbler (ill. in ruby stain)	14-18
Wine	18-23

Ruby stain worth 100 percent more than clear prices listed.

Fancy Diamonds

Fancy Diamonds

(Diagonal Bead Bands): Model Flint Glass Company, Findlay, Ohio, c. 1890. Clear, nonflint.

Bowl	$ 15-19
Butter dish, covered	33-38
Creamer	22-29
Goblet	18-26
Pitcher (ill.)	31-37
Plate, bread	25-32
Sauce, flat	4-7
Spoonholder	19-22
Sugar bowl, covered	30-34
Wine	18-22

Fancy Diamonds is also the name of a different pattern, Three-In-One.

Fashion

Imperial, c. 1915. Clear, carnival, nonflint. Reproduction toothpick heavier than original, in colors not originally made, and most are trademarked.

Basket, bride's, metal holder. 69-75
Bowl
   Fruit, separate standard 87-98
   Punch 69-80
Compote, jelly. 17-22
Creamer
   Breakfast 17-23
   Regular 30-35
Cup, punch 13-18
Pitcher, water 72-87
Sugar
   Breakfast 15-20
   Regular 30-35
Toothpick. 32-39
Tumbler. 20-25

Prices for clear approximate those of marigold carnival.

Feather

Feather

(Original name, Doric. Finecut and Feather; Indiana Swirl): McKee Glass Co., 1890s. Clear, green, amber, ruby stain. Chocolate, pink stain (see footnote). Nonflint.

Bowl, 7½″, 8½″ . . . . $ 22-29
Butter dish, covered 44-54
Cake stand, 8½″, 11″ (scarce) 47-54
Celery vase 29-39
Compote, high standard 62-80
Cordial 75-89
Creamer, scalloped rim 32-42

Cruet, original stopper. 50-60
Goblet. 29-36
Pitcher, water (ill.) 39-46
Plate, 10″ 32-39
Spoonholder, scalloped rim 28-35
Sugar bowl, covered, large 51-60
Toothpick holder 54-62
Tumbler. 39-51
Wine, scalloped band 32-46

Green, 250 percent; amber, ruby, chocolate, 400 percent higher than clear prices listed. Water pitcher made at Greentown in chocolate glass worth $500-600. Wines with pink stain made in early 1950s.

Feather Duster

Feather Duster

(Huckel; Rosette Medallion): U.S. Glass Company, 1880s. Clear and emerald green, nonflint.

Bowl, berry, 8″. . . . . $ 21-27
Butter dish, 2 types 32-38
Compote, covered, high, 6″. 39-47
Creamer. 24-32
Egg cup 23-32
Goblet. 40-50
Pitcher, water, ½ gal. (ill.) 39-43
Plate, bread
   McKinley Gold Standard, 1896,
     rectangular, clear only 210-245
   Rectangular 25-35
Salt/Pepper, pr. 31-39
Spoonholder. 27-32
Sugar bowl, covered 32-39
Tumbler. 19-27
Wine 30-40

Emerald green, 30-40 percent higher than clear prices listed.

Feather Swirl

(Original name, Solar): U. S. Glass (Bryce, Gas City) from c. 1908 and at least as late as 1919. Clear, nonflint.

Butter	$ 20-29
Cake stand	
Raised rim, 9″, 10″	22-30
Rimless, 9½″, 10½″, 12½″	16-30
Celery vase	15-22
Compote	
Covered, 7″, 8″	24-34
Jelly, 4½″, 5½″	10-15
Creamer	14-17
Cruet, paneled mushroom stopper	22-27
Cup, custard	7-10
Goblet	13-18
Pitcher	
Milk	19-25
Water	24-34
Relish, handled	10-13
Salt shaker	10-15
Sauce	3-7
Spoonholder	12-16
Sugar	18-22
Syrup	30-36
Tray, water, 10″	20-30
Tumbler	7-10
Vase, 8″ high	11-14
Wine	10-14

Feather with Quatrefoil Center

Feather with Quatrefoil Center

Sandwich Glass Company, probably c. 1830-1840. Clear, flint.

Shallow bowl, 9¼″ (ill.)	$155-173

Fragments found at Sandwich factory site.

Fern Burst

Westmoreland, c. 1910. Claimed by Millersburg as Palm Wreath. Clear, nonflint.

Bowl, 8″, straight or flared	$ 15-21
Butter	29-35
Celery vase	19-26
Creamer	
Oval	21-27
Regular, round	24-30
Cruet	29-33
Cup	10-12
Goblet	16-22
Sauce, 5¾″ dia.	6-10
Spoonholder	
Oval, double-spout end	15-20
Round	14-19
Sugar	
Oval, double-spout end, covered	25-30
Regular, covered, round	25-32
Tumbler	
Iced Tea	14-19
Water	15-23

Fern Burst

(Hobster and Feather; Sunflower and Leaf): Jefferson Glass Co. No. 358, c. 1910. Also claimed by Millersburg as Hobstar and Feather and appears in the Canadian literature. Clear, or clear with frosted hobstars and fronds. Orange or green iridized (carnival).

Bonbon, approx. 5″ dia.	
Club	$ 12-17
Diamond	11-15
Heart	15-20
Spade	12-17
Bowl	
Berry, 9″	20-26
Oval, 10″ x 7″	21-29
Punch, 15¼″, height with	
separate stand 13″	137-150
Salad, 10″ flared	18-25
Butter, covered	36-44
Celery boat, 10″ long	19-24
Compote, jelly, 5¾″	16-21
Cracker jar, two handles	42-52
Creamer	26-33
Cup	10-15
Pitcher, bulbous, 8″ high, 22½″ girth,	
3½ qts.	55-69
Spoonholder	20-30
Sugar, covered, two handles	31-40

Tumbler, 4″ high, 3¼″ dia   19-25
Vase, 9″ dia., 7″ cupped   30-38

Prices are for frosted. All clear worth 40 percent less.

Fern Garland

(Colonial with Garland): McKee Glass Company, Jeannette, Pennsylvania, c. 1894. Clear, nonflint. Pieces marked "Pres-Cut."

Butter dish, covered	$ 37-42
Celery, tall	22-31
Compote	
High standard	25-35
Low standard	20-27
Creamer, flat	27-36
Goblet	28-34
Pitcher	35-48
Spoonholder	22-31
Sugar bowl, covered	29-36
Tray, celery	14-22
Vase, violets	19-27
Wine, flared	14-19

Fern Sprig

Bellaire Goblet Company, Bellaire, Ohio, and Findlay, Ohio, c. 1800s. Clear; nonflint.

Butter dish, covered	$ 23-30
Creamer	18-25
Goblet	15-21
Spoonholder	14-19
Sugar bowl, covered	20-29

Ferris Wheel

(Original name, Prosperity): Indiana Glass Co., c. 1910. Clear, nonflint.

Bowl	
Berry, 6½″, 8″	$ 13-18
Covered, low pedestal, 7¼″	24-30
Butter, flat	20-28
Compote, jelly, 4¾″, covered, high . . .	10-13
Creamer	
Berry, pedestal	12-14
Regular	13-17
Cruet, pointed paneled stopper	19-23
Goblet	12-16
Pitcher	
Jug, ½ gal., flat	22-29
Water, on pedestal	19-23

Preserve, 7½″, 5-lobed leaf,	
sixth lobe is handle	11-13
Sauce, flat	4-6
Spoonholder, flat, no handles	10-12
Sugar	
Berry, pedestal, handled	12-14
Regular, covered, handled	16-20
Tumbler	8-12
Vase, 6½″ high	8-12
Wine	9-13

Festoon

Festoon

Attributed to Portland Glass Company, Portland, Maine, 1870s. Nonflint.

Bowl, berry, 7″, 9″, 10″, waste	$ 18-32
Butter dish, covered	54-63
Cake stand, 9″, 10″, dia.	44-52
Creamer	24-32
Pickle jar	50-60
Pitcher, water (ill.)	42-52
Plate, 7″, 8″, 9″	36-42
Sauce, flat	8-13
Spoonholder	30-40
Sugar bowl, covered	49-56
Tray, water	30-40
Tumbler	28-32

File

(Ribbed Sawtooth): Columbia Glass Company, Findlay, Ohio, 1890-1907 and U. S. Glass Company. Also Imperial No. 256, c. 1904-1920. Clear, nonflint.

Bowl, 7″, 8″	$ 14-18
Butter dish	34-42
Celery boat, 10″, curled	14-19
Creamer	21-27
Cruet, 1½ oz.	22-32
Goblet	25-34

(continued)

File

Lamp, tall	58-64
Pitcher, water (ill.)	33-45
Plate, 4¾″ x 8¼″	12-21
Salt shaker	15-19
Sauce, 3½″	5-10
Spoonholder	15-22
Sugar bowl	25-33
Tumbler	15-20
Vase, bouquet, 8″ (4 tiers)	17-23

Fine Cut and Block

Fine Cut and Block

King Glass Company, Pittsburgh, 1880s. Also claimed by Portland Glass Co., Maine. Clear, amber, sapphire blue, clear with colored blocks. Nonflint.

Butter dish, covered	$ 47-56
Compote, jelly	21-29
Creamer (ill.)	30-40
Goblet, buttermilk	28-35
Pitcher, water	46-56
Salt dip, individual	13-20
Spoonholder	25-34
Sugar bowl	48-54
Tumbler	19-28

Wine	20-30

Colors, 60 percent higher; colored blocks, 125 percent higher than clear prices listed.

Fine Cut and Panel

Fine Cut and Panel

(Originally called Russian): Bryce Bros., Pittsburgh, 1880s; reissued by U.S. Glass Company in early 1890s. Clear, amber, 2 shades of blue, yellow, nonflint.

Bowl, 7″, 8″, 9″, oblong	$ 15-22
Butter dish, covered,	32-39
Celery	20-25
Compote, open, high standard	39-47
Creamer (ill.)	20-26
Goblet	20-28
Pitcher	39-47
Plate, 7″	10-15
Sauce, footed	7-12
Spoonholder	14-20
Sugar bowl, covered	25-32
Tray, bread	23-27
Tumbler	17-23
Wine	19-26

Amber, yellow, 50 percent; blue, 100 percent higher than clear prices listed.

Fine Cut and Rib

112

Fine Cut and Rib

Doyle and Company, c. 1880s. Clear and colors, nonflint.

Pitcher, water (ill.) . . . . $ 40-49
Colors, 50 percent more than clear prices listed. Other pieces?

Fine Cut Medallion

Fine Cut Medallion

(Austrian): Indiana Tumbler and Goblet Company, Greentown, Indiana, 1897-1898. Clear, light amber, blue, canary, chocolate, emerald green, Nile green, nonflint.

Banana stand	$ 95-115
Bowl	
Berry	26-32
Rectangular	22-29
Butter dish	48-56
Compote, open, 8″	36-41
Creamer, large (ill.)	27-32
Goblet.	35-42
Pitcher, water	57-62
Punch cup.	14-21
Rose bowl	
Large	40-48
Medium	33-39
Small	39-45
Spoonholder, large.	30-35
Toy set, 4 piece,	
chocolate (rare)	450-500
Tumbler.	20-30

Chocolate, 350 to 450 percent higher than clear; other colors are 300 percent higher than clear. Not all pieces in all colors.

Fine Cut, Squared

Jones, Cavitt and Company, c. 1886. Clear, blue, amber, yellow, nonflint.

Pitcher, water (ill.) . . . . $ 46-54

Fine Cut, Squared

Amber, yellow, 35 percent; blue, 70 percent higher than clear prices listed. Could the Hour Glass goblet be this pattern?

Fishscale

Fishscale

(Coral): Bryce Bros., Pittsburgh, 1880s. Slipper on tray known in amber, blue, clear, and yellow..

Ashtray, Daisy & Button Slipper	
attached to Fishscale rectangular tray	$ 39-49
Bowl, 6″, 7″, 8″, open	19-28
Butter dish, Covered, 6″	35-47
Cake stand, 9″, 10″, 11″	29-36
Celery vase	30-34
Compote	
Covered, high standard, 6″,	
7″, 8″	40-62
Open, high standard, 7″, 8″	
9″, 10″	19-33
Creamer.	30-36
Goblet.	33-42
Pickle dish	15-21
Pitcher, qt. and ½ gal. (ill.)	48-52
Plate, round, 7″, 8″, 9″ sq..	26-32
Salt/Pepper, pr.	59-69
Sauce, flared, footed, 4″	10-16
Spoonholder.	24-29
Sugar bowl, covered	46-52

(continued)

Tray, water	39-49
Tumbler.	27-34

Flamboyant

(Diamond Flute; original name, Jeanette): McKee, c. 1885-1901. Clear, sometimes with gold; emerald green, light blue.

Bowl, berry 9″	$ 13-17
Buttered, covered	22-29
Creamer	
Individual, 3″ high	11-15
Regular	17-22
Cruet	18-25
Goblet.	15-20
Sauce, flat 4½″	4-7
Spoonholder.	12-16
Sugar, covered.	20-30
Sugar shaker	22-30

Color uncommon. Light blue goblet known.

Flat Diamond

Flat Diamond

(Lippman; original name, Pillar): Richards & Hartley Glass Company, Tarentum, Pennsylvania, c. 1875. U. S. Glass Company after 1891. Clear, nonflint.

Butter dish, covered	$ 35-42
Celery.	20-29
Cordial	16-22
Creamer, applied handle, pedestal	33-39
Egg cup	17-21
Goblet (ill.)	21-30

Pitcher, bulbous, applied	
handle.	42-52
Spoonholder.	18-23
Sugar bowl, covered	35-45
Tumbler.	22-30
Wine	20-26

Confusing pattern. King No. 204 has dots in center of diamonds and is ring-stemmed.

Flattened Diamond and Sunburst

Flattened Diamond and Sunburst

(Sunburst): Maker unknown, 1870s. Clear, amber, nonflint.

Butter dish, miniature	$ 22-29
Cake stand	23-31
Celery.	17-26
Creamer.	15-21
Egg cup	17-22
Goblet.	19-27
Pitcher (ill.)	44-52
Plate	
Bread, motto	30-35
6″, 7″.	9-15
11″.	21-26
Relish, double	20-26
Saucedish, handled	5-9
Spoonholder.	11-16
Sugar bowl, covered	25-30

Color is 60 percent higher than clear prices listed.

Fleur-de-Lis and Drape

(Fleur-de-Lis and Tassel): U.S. Glass Company (Adams), c. 1892. Clear, green, opal. Nonflint.

Bottle, water	$ 44-52
Butter dish, covered	39-49
Cake stand	34-45

Celery.	27-34
Claret	36-46
Compote, covered	35-42
Cordial	39-45
Creamer.	26-34
Goblet.	29-35
Lamp, tall	89-110
Pitcher, milk	29-39
Pot, mustard, original ribbed lid	27-37
Sauce, flat, 4″, 4½″.	12-16
Spoonholder.	19-24
Sugar bowl, covered	35-42
Syrup	48-57
Tumbler.	26-35
Wine	38-48

Colors, 40 percent higher than clear prices listed.

Floral Oval

Spoonholder.	24-32
Sugar bowl, covered	35-45
Syrup tankard, glass lid	33-44
Tumbler.	19-26
Wine	18-26

Comes with patterned, cane, or plain base. Reproduced in Amberina.

Florida Palm

(Tidal): Greensburg Glass Company, Greensburg, Pennsylvania, c. early 1900s. Clear, nonflint.

Bowls, berry, 7″, 8″, 9″	$ 15-19
Butter dish	33-39
Cake stand	28-33
Celery.	24-32
Compote, 7½″, covered, high.	39-46
Creamer.	20-25
Goblet.	21-27
Spoonholder.	16-22
Sugar bowl, covered	30-34
Wine	22-30

Flickering Flame

Flickering Flame

Westmoreland Glass Company, 1896. Clear, milk glass, nonflint.

Creamer (ill.)	$ 20-29
Sugar, covered.	25-31

Fifty percent more for milk glass.

Floral Oval

(Original name, Banner; Pittsburgh Daisy): Bryce, Higbee Co., c. 1880s. Also Canadian. Clear, nonflint.

Butter dish	$ 38-48
Celery.	27-33
Compote, jelly.	19-29
Creamer (ill.)	30-40
Cup	13-17
Goblet.	33-40
Plate, 7¼″ square, "Bee" mark. . . .	30-35
Pitcher	50-62

Flower and Quill

(Pretty Band): Attributed to Burlington Glass Works, Canada. Clear, pale green, pale yellow, pale blue. Clear, nonflint.

Butter dish, covered	$ 28-34
Celery, footed	25-32
Creamer.	23-33

115

(continued)

Flower and Quill

Nappy, flange handle, 4″	15-19
Pickle caster.	49-56
Pitcher, water (ill.)	37-46
Plate, large, square	27-36
Spoonholder.	18-23
Sugar bowl, covered	30-37

Colors, 50 percent higher than clear prices listed.

Flower Band

Maker unknown, c. 1870s. Clear, clear with frosted band. Nonflint.

Butter dish, covered, lovebird finial	$ 84-99
Celery	43-50
Compote, covered	135-152
Creamer	62-75
Goblet	58-68
Pitcher, milk, water	41-54
Sauce, footed	19-24
Spoonholder	54-63
Sugar bowl	
Open	42-56
Covered	84-93

Similar to Frosted Oak Band with bands of acorns and leaves. Clear floral band, 30 percent less than frosted prices listed. Reproductions in pastel colors not originally made.

Flower Pot

(Potted Plant): Maker unknown, c. 1880s. Clear, nonflint.

Flower Pot

Butter dish, covered	$ 45-55
Cake stand, 10½″ dia.	38-48
Compote, covered	36-49
Creamer.	29-33
Pitcher, milk (ill.)	30-36
Salt/Pepper, pr.	36-44
Sauce, open, footed	10-13
Spoonholder.	21-26
Sugar bowl, covered	34-40
Tray, bread, "We Trust in God"	49-55

Proof of goblet or tumbler would be appreciated.

Flower with Cane

Flower with Cane

U. S. Glass Company (Gasport), c. 1895-1905. Clear with pink, amethyst, or green decoration. Also with gold. Nonflint.

Creamer	
Flat (ill.).	$ 20-27
Individual, footed, 4½″	18-23
Cup	9-14
Goblet.	21-30

Pitcher	30-38
Sugar bowl, covered	33-37
Wine	18-23

Thirty percent less for clear pieces.

Flute

Flute

Many factories made this clear glass, 1850s and 1860s. It went by many names: Bessimer Flute, Sexton Flute, Reed Stem Flute, Sandwich Flute. Clear, flint, and nonflint. Rare in color.

Ale glass.	$ 29-34
Bitters bottle (6 or 8 flute)	32-42
Bowl, scalloped	33-38
Candlesticks, pr. (6 flute)	44-52
Creamer.	29-35
Decanter, quart size	49-54
Goblet.	27-34
Lamp, whale oil	69-75
Mug, applied handle.	35-42
Tumbler, half pint, (ill.), jelly, one gill, half gill (toy), each.	22-39
Wine	14-30

Colors, 200 percent higher than clear prices listed. Nonflint, deduct 40 percent from flint prices listed.

Flute and Cane

(Original name, Huckabee): Imperial Glass Company, 1920s. Clear, nonflint.

Butter dish	$ 23-30
Celery vase	17-24
Creamer.	15-20
Goblet.	14-19
Pitcher, tankard (ill.)	26-35
Spoonholder.	11-16
Sugar bowl, covered	19-26
Tumbler.	10-15
Vase.	13-17

Flute and Cane

Fluted Scrolls

Fluted Scrolls

(Original name, Klondyke): Harry Northwood Glass Co., Indiana, Pennsylvania, c. 1900. Clear; clear, blue, vaseline, green opalescent; custard. Also with enameled daisy band.

Bowl, berry	$ 31-44
Butter dish, covered	64-70
Creamer.	55-64
Jewel (or puff) tray	21-29
Pitcher, water (ill.)	62-72
Saucedish	11-15
Spoonholder.	22-28
Sugar, covered.	54-63

Blue, 125 percent; vaseline, 200 percent higher than clear opalescent prices listed.

Flying Birds

Maker unknown, c. 1870. Clear, nonflint.

Goblet.	$ 68-73

117

Flying Swan

Flying Swan

Attributed to Westmoreland or Challinor, 1890s. Clear, milk glass, caramel slag, various other slags. Prices are for slag.

Butter dish $128-137
Creamer (ill.) 62-75
Spoonholder 45-52
Sugar bowl, covered 105-122

Fostoria's No. 952

Fostoria's No. 952

Fostoria Glass Company, Fostoria, Ohio, c. 1880. Clear, nonflint.

Pitcher, water . . . . $ 29-39
Tumbler 14-19

Four Petal

Four Petal

McKee & Bros., c. 1850s. Clear, blue, flint.

Creamer, applied handle $115-132
Sugar bowl
  Covered
    Pagoda lid 84-92
    Regular lid 70-80
  Open (ill.) 45-57
Blue, 50 percent higher than clear prices listed.

Forget Me Not in Scroll

Forget Me Not in Scroll

Maker unknown, c. 1870s. Clear, nonflint.

Butter dish, covered . . . . $ 31-36
Creamer, applied handle 34-39
Goblet (ill.) 29-34
Pitcher, applied handle 45-54
Sauce, flat 6-9
Spoonholder 19-24
Sugar bowl, covered 29-37

The Fox and the Crow

Maker unknown, c. 1890s. Nonflint.

Pitcher, water, clear (ill.) $155-166

The Fox and the Crow

Framed Blocks

Framed Blocks

A member of the Block and Thumbprint family, c. 1850s. Clear, flint, nonflint.

Goblet. $115-132
Wine (ill.)   54-64

Nonflint, 50 percent less than flint prices listed.

Framed Circles

Framed Circles

Maker unknown, c. 1850s. Clear, flint.

Goblet. $110-129
Wine (ill.)   53-66

Framed Ovals

Framed Ovals

Possibly Sandwich, c. 1840s. Clear, gold-trimmed, flint. Could also be New England Glass Company, same era.

Brandy or pony ale,
  footed (ill.). . . . . $ 48-55
Goblet.   140-160

Frost Crystal

Frost Crystal

Tarentum Glass Company, Tarentum, Pennsylvania, 1906. Clear, ruby, gold-trimmed, nonflint

Butter dish . . . . $ 30-39
Celery.   26-32
Creamer.   25-34
Custard cup   13-19

119

(continued)

Plate, 6″ (ill.)   19-25
Spoonholder.   17-21
Sugar bowl, no lid   14-19

Ruby stain, 60 percent more than clear prices listed.

Frosted Block

Frosted Block

Imperial Glass Company, 1910-1929, unmarked and later made with trademark. Clear, amber, yellow, ice blue, blue, red, green, pink, vaseline, carnival.

Bowl, 7½″, fluted . . . . $ 18-26
Celery tray (bowl), 8½″, oval.   12-21
Compote, jelly, 4½″ dia., high   10-18
Creamer (ill.)   13-23
Olive, 5½″ dia., one handle.   9-15
Pickle, 6″ long, two handles   12-18
Pitcher, pint, 6″ high, flat   24-32
Plate, square, 7¾″.   18-24
Sugar bowl on pedestal,
    handled   13-23
Vase, 6″ high.   11-17

Lily bowl known in red (rare). Milk glass is recent production and trademarked. Opalescent, iridescent worth 100-200 percent more than clear, amber, and pastel prices listed.

Frosted Circle

Bryce Bros., 1870s, U.S. Glass Company, after 1891. Clear and clear with frosted circles. Nonflint.

Bowl, covered and open, 7″, 8″ . . . . $ 28-39
Butter dish, covered   56-66
Cake stand, 8″, 9″, 10″   45-59

Frosted Circle

Celery.   35-42
Claret   81-93
Compote, covered, 7″, 8″, high   77-84
Creamer (ill.)   36-43
Cup   22-30
Goblet.   44-54
Pitcher, water   65-79
Plates
    4″, 5″.   23-30
    7″, 9″.   40-50
Salt/Pepper, pr.   59-62
Sauce, flat   13-17
Spoonholder.   30-35
Sugar bowl   50-57
Syrup (scarce) 149-165
Tumbler, water   28-34
Wine   44-53

Goblet reproduced.

Frosted Fruits

Frosted Fruits

Maker unknown, 1880-1890s. All clear or all frosted. Nonflint.

Bowl, berry . . . . $ 35-42
Butter dish   64-72

Celery. 32-41
Creamer. 44-52
Pitcher, water (ill.) 82-90
Sauce 17-22
Spoonholder. 31-39
Sugar bowl 55-62
Tumbler. 29-37

Clear worth 50 percent less than frosted prices listed.

Frosted Medallion

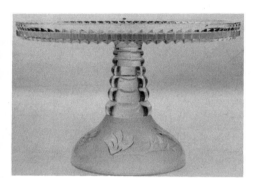

Frosted Magnolia

Frosted Magnolia

(Water Lily): Dalzell, Gilmore & Leighton, West Virginia or Findlay, Ohio, factory, c. 1890. All clear or clear with frosting.

Bowl, 6″, 7″, 8″	$ 38-45
Butter dish, covered	63-73
Cake stand (ill.)	60-75
Celery, tall	34-41
Creamer.	47-56
Goblet.	65-72
Pitcher, tankard, applied handle. . . .	70-83
Salt shaker	13-18
Sauce, flat, deep.	19-24
Sugar bowl, covered	40-50
Syrup jug	57-67

Frosted Medallion

(Sunburst Rosette): Maker unknown, late 1880s. Clear, nonflint.

Bowl, oval	$ 18-27
Butter dish, covered	36-42
Creamer.	31-39
Compote	
Covered	44-51
Open	23-32
Goblet.	27-35

Pitcher, syrup (ill.)	34-42
Relish	14-17
Sauce, flat	5-9
Spoonholder.	24-32
Sugar bowl, covered	33-40
Tumbler.	19-27

The frosting is really very fine stippling.

Frosted Stork

Frosted Stork

(Flamingo): Crystal Glass Company, Bridgeport, Ohio, 1879. Nonflint.

Bowl, waste	$ 39-46
Butter dish	82-91
Creamer.	52-59
Goblet.	51-61
Jam jar, covered	69-74
Pitcher, water (ill.)	120-130
Plate, 9″, round, handled.	49-57
Sauce, flat.	22-27
Spoonholder.	18-22
Sugar bowl, covered	54-68
Tray, large, water	70-82

Probably other pieces. This is a scarce pattern. Goblet and spooner (and possibly other pieces) reproduced.

Fuchsia

Bowl, oval, 9″	$ 25-31
Butter dish	30-37
Creamer.	23-33
Goblet.	25-35
Pitcher, water (ill.)	51-66
Punch cup.	13-18
Relish dish, 7¼″.	15-23
Spoonholder.	16-21
Sugar bowl, covered	25-35
Wine	24-33

Prices are for good paint. Clear, 25 percent less.

Fuchsia

Sandwich, c. 1870. Clear, nonflint.

Butter dish, covered	$ 53-62
Cake stand	59-70
Celery vase	40-48
Compote, covered, low.	48-54
Creamer (ill.)	37-46
Egg cup	32-39
Goblet.	37-43
Pitcher	64-77
Spoonholder.	30-35
Sugar bowl, open, pedestal.	32-38

There is also a Stippled Fuchsia that has clear fuchsia on a stippled background. The forms differ very slightly from the clear Fuchsia list. Comparable values.

Galloway

Galloway

(Original name, Mirror): U.S. Glass Company, 1901, Glassport, Indiana. Clear, ruby stained and rare rose stain; nonflint. Not one of the State series.

Bowl, round, 6″, 9″ rectangular	$ 16-21
Butter dish, covered, large	48-54
Celery.	30-38
Compote	
Covered, 6″, 7″, 8″.	60-92
Open, 7½″, 10¼″.	44-52
Creamer, individual	
Tankard (toy)	29-38
Large, regular	33-36
Cruet	35-40
Cup	8-12
Goblet.	37-44
Jug, ice lip.	78-92
Mug, lemonade	36-43
Pitcher, water (ill.)	55-64
Plate, 6″, 8″	26-35
Salt/Pepper, pr.	
Bulbouse base	70-80
Straight	30-40
Sauce, flared, 4″; straight,	
4″, 4½″, footed sherbet	10-20
Spoonholder.	37-46
Sugar bowl, covered	41-49
Tumbler.	26-32

Gaelic

Gaelic

Indiana Glass Company. The water pitcher is clear and has a gold band at top, painted pink flowers. Nonflint.

122

Vase

10½″, 13½″	20-32
Ruffled, 6¾″ dia. x 6″ high	28-34
Wine	46-58

Ruby stained, 100 percent higher than clear prices listed. An error calling this pattern "Virginia" was acknowledged by Brothers, but not in time to correct it before publication; thus a misnomer has been perpetuated. Canadian name "Woodrow." Unitt pictures a 6″ celery vase that is not this pattern. U. S. Glass Company, Tiffin, Ohio, from 1955-1960 issued a punch bowl, cups, and 20″ tray, calling it "Old Mirror." This set had straight cups and was not gilded.

Garden of Eden

Garden of Eden

(Lotus and Serpent): Maker unknown. Claimed by Portland. Clear, nonflint.

Butter dish, covered	$ 62-69
Cake stand	53-62
Creamer, serpent (ill.)	44-53
Goblet	
Plain	39-46
Serpent head	88-98
Mug, handled, serpent	44-54
Pickle dish, oval	23-30
Pitcher	68-79
Spoonholder	22-30
Sugar bowl, covered	56-63
Tray, bread,	
"Give Us This Day"	39-45

For pieces with serpent, add 50 percent unless serpent price is indicated above.

Garfield Drape

Adams & Company, Pittsburgh, 1880s. Clear. One of the Garfield Memorial plates, not part of this pattern, was produced by Campbell, Jones & Company, in 1881. Clear, nonflint.

Garfield Drape

Bowl	$ 28-36
Butter bowl, covered	61-67
Cake plate on stand	67-74
Celery	41-52
Compote, covered, high standard . .	99-108
Creamer	45-53
Goblet	34-39
Pickle dish, oval	22-26
Pitcher, water, milk	62-71
Plate	
"We Mourn Our Nation's Loss" (ill.)	58-70
Sauce, footed and round	8-11
Spoonholder	26-34
Sugar bowl, covered	53-62

Garland of Roses

Garland of Roses

(Rose Garland): Maker unknown, 1880. Clear, vaseline, blue; chocolate (rare). Nonflint.

Butter dish	$ 34-44
Celery	27-34
Creamer	
Berry (ill.)	19-24
Regular	30-35
Egg cup	29-34

123

(continued)

Pitcher, 7½".	40-50
Salt, open footed	22-33
Spoonholder.	28-32
Sugar bowl, covered	34-42
Toothpick (rare).	40-50

Blue, vaseline, 50 percent higher; chocolate, 300-400 percent higher than clear prices listed. Bowl, creamer, pitcher, sauce, sugar known in chocolate glass. Most pieces have three "legs" connecting the lower bowl to the round base.

Garter Band

Maker unknown, c. late 1880s. Clear, nonflint.

Butter dish, covered	$ 18-23
Celery.	12-17
Goblet.	11-15
Sugar bowl, covered	16-21
Wine	10-13

Gathered Knot

Imperial Glass Co., their No. 3 pattern, c. 1902. Clear, amethyst, nonflint.

Bowl, berry, 7", 8"	$ 14-19
Butter.	30-37
Celery, 6½" high.	20-30
Compote, 7" dia., crimped, open	22-29
Cracker jar, covered	31-44
Creamer.	19-24
Goblet.	20-25
Jam jar (pickle jar), glass lid	30-38
Jelly, low foot, crimped	10-14
Salt shaker	13-19
Sauce, 4½"	4-7
Spoonholder, 4½" high	13-17
Sugar, covered.	25-33
Sugar shaker	32-39
Syrup	37-44
Toothpick (scarce).	33-42

A deep amethyst toothpick is known. Reproductions? Other colors? Add 100 percent for colored pieces.

Geneva

(Shell and Scroll): Northwood National Glass Company, 1900. Clear, emerald green; chocolate; custard, with ruby green paint, nonflint.

Bowls, 3 scroll feet,	
8½" round	$ 75-85
Butter dish, covered	119-140

Geneva

Creamer, covered	53-62
Pitcher, syrup	225-250
Salt/Pepper, pr.	126-144
Spoonholder.	50-60
Sugar bowl, covered	118-130
Tumbler (ill.)	50-58

Clear, 50 percent less than custard prices listed. Deduct 20 percent for unpainted custard. Chocolate, add 200 percent.

Georgia Belle

(Original name, Western Star; Feathered Medallion): U. S. Glass, c. 1906. Clear or with gold, nonflint. Collected as another states pattern, although not part of original U. S. Glass series.

Butter.	$ 23-30
Celery.	16-20
Compote, jelly, ruffled rim.	10-13
Creamer.	15-22
Goblet.	16-21
Salt shaker	13-17
Spoonholder.	12-16
Sugar, covered.	20-25

A different goblet made by Higbee appears in the literature as Feathered Medallion.

Giant Sawtooth

Maker unknown, 1830. Clear, flint.

Goblet.	$ 80-88
Lamp, whale oil (ill.).	215-230
Salt, flat, master.	30-35
Spill holder	55-63
Tumbler.	64-72

Giant Sawtooth

Gladstone "For the Million"

Gibson Girl

Gibson Girl

(Original name, Medallion): National Glass Company (Keystone), c. 1903. Clear, nonflint. Rare.

Butter dish	$129-139
Creamer.	63-72
Pitcher, water (ill.)	162-177
Plate, 10"	84-92
Relish, oval	38-45
Sauce, 4", flat	28-34
Spoonholder.	57-65
Sugar bowl, covered	110-122
Tumbler.	60-69

No goblet.

Gladstone "For the Million"

Wear Glass Works of Henry Greener, Sunderland, England, c. 1869. This pattern honors William Ewart Gladstone, four times prime minister of England (1809-1898).

Bowl, 8½" dia.	$ 39-45
Creamer (ill.)	40-50
Mug, amethyst, 2½" high	84-93
Plate, aqua, 5" dia.	33-43

Goat's Head

Hobbs, Brockunier & Company, Wheeling, West Virginia, c. 1878. Clear and clear with frosting, nonflint. Scarce.

Butter dish, covered	$ 92-110
Creamer.	65-79
Spoonholder.	39-49
Sugar bowl	
Covered	78-90
Open	29-36

Patent drawing of sugar shows knob finial, but goat head finial is also known. Clear, 30 percent less than frosted prices listed.

Gonterman

Maker unknown, c. 1885. Clear, or with frosting; also with amber, and probably blue.

Butter, covered	$ 40-46
Cake stand	47-55
Celery vase, clear (ill.)	30-35

(continued)

Creamer.	29-37
Goblet.	34-41
Pitcher, applied handle	49-54
Spooner.	22-28
Sugar, covered.	32-39
Toothpick (scarce).	33-42
Tumbler.	15-22

Because of the patterned rim band, it is probable that the "goblet" shown in the literature is a spooner, especially since it is a smaller version of the celery vase shown. A goblet is known with a plain rim band, but not pictured. Prices are for clear, add 20 percent for frosted, 100 percent for colored pieces.

Gonterman Swirl

Hobbs or Beatty, c. 1886. Some pieces are embossed with the patent date, August 5, 1876, that probably pertains to the process of the joining of the two types of glass. Translucent solid (not stained) amber or blue tops with frosted or opalescent swirl base.

Bowl, master berry	
Amber/opal	$ 54-66
Blue/frosted	69-75
Butter, amber/opal	161-174
Celery, blue/opal	122-139
Creamer, amber/opal	100-118
Cruet, original stopper (stacked rings), blue/opal	249-272
Finger bowl, blue/frosted	59-70
Pitcher, amber/opal	234-260
Shade, gaslight, blue/opal	52-67
Spoonholder, amber/opal	80-92
Sugar, covered	
Amber/opal	130-140
Blue/opal, complete	159-175
Syrup	
Amber/opal	235-267
Blue/opal	338-366
Toothpick	
Frosted, amber top.	147-152
Frosted, blue top, in silverplated holder.	168-188
Opalescent, amber top	150-160
Tumbler	
Amber/frosted	55-65
Amber/opal	49-59

Similar pattern, Beatty Swirl.

Good Luck

(Horseshoe, Prayer Rug): Adams & Company, c. 1880.

Bowl on pedestal, 8" dia., 4" high.	$ 28-35
Butter, two types: one takes flat lid, the other a collared lid	52-65
Cake stand, 9" dia.	40-48
Celery.	48-59
Cheese, covered; woman churning depicted on base.	184-213
Compote, round, covered, low standard.	64-75
Creamer.	36-42
Dish, deep, 5" x 8".	24-28
Goblet	
Knob stem.	31-36
Plain stem.	25-29
Jam jar, also called marmalade or pickle jar, horseshoe finial	110-129
Pickle dish, 8".	13-17
Pitcher	62-75
Plate	
6", 7"	33-46
8", 10".	33-43
Salt dip	
Individual, horseshoe shape, no pattern	20-28
Master, horseshoe shape, no pattern	30-37
Master, round, deep, patterned (rare)	79-85
Sauce	
4" dia., footed	10-16
3¾" dia., flat	11-14
Spoonholder.	26-32
Sugar, covered.	51-67
Tray, bread	
Double handle.	55-65
Single handle	45-52
Waste bowl	44-55
Wine (scarce)	134-155

Gooseberry

Sandwich Glass, 1870s. Others also made it. Clear, milk glass, nonflint.

Butter bowl, covered.	$ 47-55
Cake stand, 9½" dia.	48-56
Compote	
Covered, high foot, large	56-64
Covered, high foot, 6"	43-52
Creamer (ill.)	28-35
Goblet.	29-37
Honey dish	19-25

Gooseberry

Mug	24-36
Pickle dish	16-22
Pitcher, water	72-80
Saucedish	7-12
Spoonholder	27-34
Sugar bowl	47-56
Tumbler	33-42

Opaque white, 65 percent higher than the clear prices listed. Reproduced in opaque white. Miniature mug with gooseberries is not part of this pattern.

Gothic

Gothic

Sandwich, 1860s. Clear, flint.

Butter dish	$ 69-77
Caster bottle, each	23-29
Champagne (rare)	98-115
Compote	
Covered, on standard	86-105
Open, footed	44-55
Cordial	32-40
Creamer (ill.)	89-105

Egg cup	39-45
Goblets, 2 styles	49-59
Plate (rare)	67-79
Sauce	12-16
Spoonholder	31-37
Sugar bowl, covered	54-69
Wine (rare)	100-150

"Gothic Arch and Panels"

"Gothic Arch and Panels"

Maker, date, and actual name unknown. Information, please!

Grace

Grace

(Japanese): Richards & Hartley Flint Glass Company, Pittsburgh, 1870s. Pattern was discontinued prior to the company's removal to Tarentum in 1884.

Butter dish, covered	$ 54-63
Compote, covered	44-52

127

(continued)

Creamer	37-46
Goblet	37-44
Jam jar (pickle caster insert),	
no lid	28-33
Platter, oval, 9″ x 11″	32-40
Sauce	13-17
Spoonholder	31-38
Sugar bowl, covered	40-47

Scene is different on each individual table piece, though top and bottom horizontal borders are the same.

Grape and Festoon

Grand

Grand

(Diamond Medallion; New Grand): Bryce, Higbee & Company, 1885. Clear, nonflint.

Bowl, waste	$ 25-32
Butter dish, covered, flat	39-46
Cake stand, 8″, 10″	34-39
Celery vase (ill.)	27-32
Compote, open, 7″	20-25
Creamer	23-28
Goblet	24-29
Pitcher, water	35-39
Sauce, footed	9-13
Spoonholder	15-21
Sugar bowl, covered	31-35
Tray, water (fan rim)	39-45
Wine	19-27

Grape and Festoon

Attributed to Sandwich and Portland; Doyle & Company, Pittsburgh, 1870s. Comes with clear, veined or stippled leaf.

Butter bowl, covered	$ 42-46
Celery	30-37
Compote, covered, high standard . . .	52-64
Creamer, applied handle	33-41

Egg cup	24-33
Goblet	22-32
Pickle dish	14-19
Pitcher, water (ill.)	66-74
Plate, 6″	25-34
Salt, footed	28-35
Saucedish, flat, 4″	7-11
Spoonholder	37-46
Sugar bowl, acorn finial	39-46
Wine	35-40

For stippled background, see Stippled Grape and Festoon.

Grape and Festoon with Shield

Grape and Festoon with Shield

Doyle & Company, 1860s. Also attributed to Portland. Clear, blue, nonflint.

Butter bowl	$ 37-42
Celery	30-35
Compote, covered, low standard	39-45
Creamer (ill.)	34-42

Egg cup	24-29
Goblet.	27-34
Mug, miniature	24-30
Pitcher, water	64-70
Saucedish, flat, 4″, 6″.	9-15
Spoonholder.	25-29
Sugar bowl	39-42

Cobalt blue worth 80 percent more. Known in mugs.

Grape Bunch

Grape Band

Grape Band

Bryce, Walker & Company, Pittsburgh, c. 1869. Clear, nonflint.

Butter bowl, covered.	$ 39-43
Compote, covered, high	46-55
Creamer, applied handle.	29-36
Goblet (ill.)	24-27
Pitcher, water	64-79
Plate, 6″.	21-28
Salt, pedestal	24-31
Spoonholder.	25-31
Sugar bowl, covered	39-43
Tumbler.	31-39
Wine	29-38

Made in flint at an earlier date, late 1850s; 50 percent higher than nonflint prices listed. A distinctive feature: tiny leaves under the goblet bowl, with top of stem ending in points.

Grape Bunch

(Berry Spray): Greentown, c. 1900. Clear, nonflint.

Egg cup/wine	$ 12-17
Goblet (ill.)	34-42

Made as jelly containers.

Grape Jug

Grape Jug

(Late Panelled Grape; Jenkins No. 809): Jenkins, after 1900 and into the 1920s. Clear, nonflint. It is possible that an error in the early literature resulted in naming a different pattern Darling Grape. However, because of the embossed "Darling" on the mug, "Darling Grape" would differentiate this pattern from other panelled grape patterns. Jug lids are patterned like jug necks.

129

(continued)

Bowl, 8″
  Covered . . . . $ 25-30
  Open 14-19
Butter (no grapes on base) 30-35
Creamer, 4½″ high, pleated rim,
  no fans 18-23
Goblet 16-25
Mug "Darling" 25-35
Pitcher (jug),
  Half gal.
    Covered 35-45
    Open 27-33
  Pint
    Covered 31-36
    Open (ill.) 19-22
Sauce, 4″, footed 4-6
Spoonholder 13-16
Toothpick (not paneled) 38-45

Grape with Thumbprint

Butter dish . . . . $ 44-47
Creamer 34-42
Goblet 25-32
Pitcher (ill.), ½ gal. jug (took
  glass lid) as shown 30-38
Spoonholder 15-20
Sugar bowl, covered 39-44
Toothpick holder (scarce) 34-40

Prices are for good impression. Poor impression worth 30 percent less.

Grape with Overlapping Foliage

Grape with Overlapping Foliage

Hobbs, patented February 1, 1870. Clear and milk-white, nonflint.

Butter bowl . . . . $ 34-40
Creamer (ill.) 26-30
Goblet 24-28
Spoonholder 21-26
Sugar bowl 32-36

Milk-white, 50 percent higher than clear prices listed. Spoonholder in milk-white confirmed with embossed patent date. One of the scarcer grape patterns.

Grape with Thumbprint

Attributed to Jenkins after 1900 and into the 1920s.

Grape with Vine

Grape with Vine

Maker unknown, probably after 1900. Original pieces, "Goofus" decoration of red paint and gilt. Nonflint.

Butter dish . . . . $ 30-36
Creamer 29-38
Honey dish 23-30
Pitcher, water (ill.) 36-42
Spoonholder 14-18

Sugar bowl 28-34

Original paint would increase value for collectors of "Goofus" glass 20-30 percent above clear prices listed. The beaded handle and distinctive base aid in identification. Is there a goblet?

Grasshopper with Insect

Grasshopper with Insect

(Locust: Long Spear): Maker unknown, c. 1880.

Butter dish	$ 66-74
Celery vase	43-49
Compote, covered	74-82
Creamer.	44-52
Pickle dish, oval	27-34
Pitcher, water (ill.)	77-86
Sauce	19-28
Spoonholder.	35-42
Sugar bowl, covered	55-65

Goblet not part of origional production. Amber, 90 percent higher than clear prices listed.

Grasshopper without Insect

Grasshopper, without Insect

Clear or amber, etched. Nonflint.

Bowl, covered	$ 21-29
Butter, covered	35-42
Compote, covered	39-47
Creamer.	24-30
Pitcher (ill.)	39-47
Plate, footed, 8½".	16-24
Salt dip (scarce)	37-43
Sauce, flat	7-12
Spoonholder.	19-24
Sugar, covered.	31-38

Greek Key with Stars

Sandwich, c. 1880s. Found in the pattern glass literature, but is blown, thin crystal made in the closing days of the Sandwich factory.

Bowl	
Berry	$ 20-30
Finger	18-23
Celery, flat base	30-38
Champagne or juice tumbler.	14-19
Cup plate or butter pat	13-16
Cup	
Flat	10-13
Pedestal	15-18
Decanter, original patterned hollow	
stopper	46-53
Goblet.	21-27
Sherry flute	15-20
Spoonholder.	28-35
Wine	17-23

Greensburg's 130

131

(continued)

Greensburg's 130

(Greensburg Pillows): Greensburg Glass Company, Greensburg, Pennsylvania, late 1880s. Plain and engraved crystal. Nonflint.

Basket, applied handle . . . . $ 39-45
Butter dish, flanged 26-30
Creamer (ill.) 24-28
Pitcher 34-44
Salt, individual, oval. 8-12
Spoonholder. 14-17
Sugar bowl, covered 23-27

Confusing pattern is Westmoreland on which the "pillows" are on the diagonal, rather than vertical. No goblet?

Gridley Pitcher

Gridley Pitcher

Beatty—Brady, c. 1898. Clear, nonflint.

Gridley pitcher (ill.) . . . . $ 77-90

Confirmation of Gridley (not Dewey) tumbler appreciated.

Gyro

National Glass Co., attributed to McKee or Northwood, c. 1900. Clear, ruby stain, milk glass, opalescent. May be gold trimmed.

Puff jar, ruby with gold . . . . $ 38-45
Other pieces?

Hairpin

(Sandwich Loop; McKee's Gaines): Sandwich, c. 1850s. Clear, milk glass, flint or nonflint.

Celery. . . . . $ 42-50
Champagne 50-55
Compote, covered, high standard . . 83-90
Egg cup 23-30
Goblet. 30-35
Mug, whiskey 40-48
Pitcher 138-147
Salt dip on pedestal 24-29
Sauce 10-14
Spoonholder. 31-35
Sugar bowl
   Covered 64-73
   Open 28-33
Tumbler. 42-50

Milk glass, 100-200 percent higher than clear prices listed. Nonflint worth 30 percent less.

Hairpin with Rayed Base

Prices 20 percent more than Hairpin.

(Wm.) Haley's Glass Basket

(Wm.) Haley's Glass Basket

Two dates appear in the bottom: July 21, 1874, and April 5, 1881. Where it was made is not known.

Basket, smoky blue (ill.) . . . . $ 84-92

Halley's Comet

(Erroneously Haley's Comet. Original name, Etruria): Model Flint Glass, Albany, Indiana, c. 1901. Clear, may be engraved. Nonflint.

Bowl, footed	$ 21-26
Butter, covered	35-42
Candy tray, oblong, 8″	20-25
Celery vase	34-41
Creamer	30-36
Dish, oblong, 7″	17-21
Goblet	29-33
Spoonholder, footed	23-27
Sugar, covered	35-42
Syrup	46-55
Tumbler	18-23
Wine	23-30

Engraving worth 20 percent more. Confusing pattern is Snail in which each "snail" is separate, with its own "tail." In Etruria, the loops are connected and continuous. The pattern was named for Sir Edmund Halley, who discovered Halley's Comet. The name is frequently misspelled and mispronounced Haley. The comet, which appears every 76 years, was observed on schedule in late 1985—early 1986.

Hamilton

Hamilton

Sandwich, early 1860s. Clear, flint.

Butter dish, covered	$ 75-82
Caster set, in standard:	
4 bottles	178-195
Celery	45-55
Compote, open, low	49-56
Creamer, handled	51-56
Decanter, w/stopper	139-145
Egg cup	36-42
Goblet	39-47
Pitcher	
Syrup, metal top	200+
Water	166-184
Saucedish, 4″, 5″	10-20
Spoonholder	32-38
Sugar bowl, open (ill.)	32-38
Tumbler, whiskey	105-111
Wine	82-92

Hamilton with Leaf

Hamilton with Leaf

Sandwich, 1870s. Clear or frosted leaf. Other factories, 1890s on.

Butter dish	$ 92-110
Celery vase	50-60
Compote, open, low standard	44-51
Cordial	39-44
Creamer, molded handle (ill.)	61-67
Egg cup	58-69
Goblet	50-58
Lamp, (clear leaf), 7″ high	
all glass (2 types)	112-128
Pitcher (ill.)	139-145
Salt, footed	34-41
Spoonholder	38-43
Sugar bowl, covered	85-93

(continued)

| Tumbler, bar | 79-86 |
| Wine | 84-94 |

Clear leaf worth 20 percent less. Spoonholder is often confused for a low flared goblet.

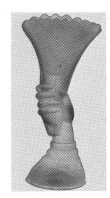

Hand Vase

Hand

Hand

(Pennsylvania): O'Hara Glass Company, Ltd., 1880. Clear, nonflint.

Bowl, 7″, 8″, 9″, 10″	$ 18-36
Butter dish, covered	69-79
Cake plate on stand, 10″	42-52
Celery vase	39-45
Compote	
Covered, high foot	80-97
Open, low	25-30
Creamer (ill.)	45-52
Goblet	40-50
Honey dish	18-25
Jam jar, covered	46-56
Pickle dish	21-27
Pitcher, water	60-67
Platter, 8″ × 10½″	35-43
Saucedish, flat, 4″	10-15
Spoonholder	30-37
Sugar bowl, covered	56-64

No toothpick. Collected as "States" pattern, but not a part of the original series.

Hand Vase

Gillinder and Sons, Philadelphia, for Centennial, 1876. Clear and frosted.

Hand vase (ill.)	$ 69-75

Highly sought by "hand" and historical glass collectors.

Hanging Basket

Hanging Basket

Possibly Mosaic Glass Company, Fostoria, Ohio, 1890s. Clear, nonflint.

Pitcher (ill.)	$125-135

A lamp by this name has similar motif. No goblet listed. Other pieces?

Hanover

(Block with Stars; Blockhouse): Richards & Hartley Glass Company, Tarentum, Pennsylvania, c. 1888. Clear, amber, canary, blue, nonflint.

Butter dish, covered	$ 32-37
Cake stand	34-37
Celery	20-26
Cheese dish, covered	42-48
Compote	
Covered	40-50
Open	18-23
Creamer	25-29

Goblet.	22-29
Pitcher, water	33-41
Spoonholder.	18-22
Sugar bowl, covered	29-35
Tumbler.	20-24
Wine	18-25

Amber, 50 percent more; canary, blue, 80 percent more than clear prices listed.

Harp

Harp

Bryce Bros., Pittsburgh, 1840s or 1850s; McKee, late 1850s. Clear, green, other colors, nonflint.

Butter dish, two sizes	$128-135
Compote, covered, low standard	180-188
Dish, covered, low foot.	
Goblet (rare)	
Flared or straight sides.	500+
Lamp, whale oil, handled, double wick with snuffers	139-146
Larger, on glass standard.	160-168
Nappy, 6½" dia.	
Covered	140-145
Open	88-95
Salt, master	35-40
Spoonholder (or spill) (ill.).	50-58
Sweetmeat on standard, 6½" dia.	
Covered	149-162
Open	95-110

Hartford

Fostoria Glass Company, 1900s. Clear, nonflint.

Basket, spoon	$ 33-42
Berry, one handle, 5½" sq.	15-20
Bowl	
Collared	
5½", 6".	12-27
9" oblong	16-21

Hartford

Flat, 5½", 6", 7", 8", 9"	12-27
Butter dish, covered	31-39
Celery vase	24-28
Creamer (ill.)	22-26
Olive, 5½", folded	10-14
Salt/Pepper, (3 types), pr.,	32-42
Sauce, 4½", (collared base)	6-10
Spoonholder	
Basket.	33-42
Regular	16-19
Sugar bowl, covered, footed, or plain base	30-35
Syrup jug	31-37
Tumbler.	14-18

Hartley

Hartley

(Panelled Diamond Cut and Fan): Richards & Hartley, and U. S. Glass, c. 1890. Clear, amber, blue, canary; nonflint. May be engraved.

Bowl, 6", 8"	$ 18-24

135

(continued)

Butter dish, covered	42-51
Cake stand, 10″	49-56
Celery	27-36
Compote	
Covered	52-61
Open, 7″	25-33
Creamer	30-40
Goblet (ill.)	30-35
Pitcher, qt., ½ gal..	48-57
Sauce, flat, 4″	10-13
Spoonholder.	18-28
Sugar bowl	
Covered	39-44
Open	25-35
Wine	24-32

Colors, 100 percent higher than clear prices listed.

Sauce, 4″, flat	5-8
Spoonholder.	14-19
Sugar bowl, covered	42-51
Wine (ill.)	22-27

Colors, 100 percent higher than clear prices listed.

Heart

Heart

(Early Heart; Lincoln Sweetheart): Sandwich, 1830s. Clear. One of many Sandwich pieces at the Houston Museum, Chattanooga. Clear, opaque blue.

Creamer (ill.) $118-125
Color, add 200 percent.

Harvard

Harvard

(Quihote, erroneously spelled "Quixote"): Tarentum Glass Company, Tarentum, Pennsylvania, 1898-1912. Clear, emerald green; green, yellow, custard; opaque, ruby-stained; nonflint.

Bowl, finger	$ 13-19
Butter dish, covered	30-37
Compote, open	20-26
Creamer.	21-27
Cup, punch	6-11
Goblet.	17-23
Pitcher, water	60-67
Plate	
5″	10-13
7½″	12-15
Salt dip, indivudal	8-12

Heart and Waffle

Heart and Waffle

Probably Sandwich, mid-1850. Clear.

Lamp $168-178

Heart Band

McKee Glass Company, 1897. Clear or with enameled decoration, green; ruby stain; gold trim; nonflint. Souvenirs common.

Heart Band

Heart with Thumbprint

Butter dish	. . . .	$ 36-42
Celery, 2 handles	. . . .	32-38
Compote, covered, 7″ high	. . . . . .	59-67
Creamer, 6″ high (ill.)	. . . .	34-42
Goblet.	. . . .	34-39
Salt shaker (rare)	. . . .	30-35
Spoonholder.	. . . .	31-34
Sugar bowl	. . . .	35-40

Goblet is not shown in the literature.

Creamer

Individual	$ 16-20
Regular (ill.).	30-34
Tankard, ½ pt.	16-20
Cup	13-17
Salt shaker	17-20

Sugar bowl

Individual, open	16-20
Handled, open	19-24

Tumbler

Handled	20-25
Water	18-23

Confusing pattern: Button Arches. No goblet. Souvenir or clear, 30 percent less; green, 100 percent more.

Heart Stem

Heart Stem

Maker unknown, late 1880s or 1890s. Clear, nonflint. May be engraved.

Heart with Thumbprint

Heart with Thumbprint

(Columbia): Sandwich, early; Tarentum Glass Company, 1889-1912. Crystal, sometimes gold rims. Natural and green custard. Ruby stain would be rare.

Bowl, berry, 9″.	$ 25-30
Butter dish, covered	56-64
Celery vase	45-52
Cordial	100-110

Creamer

Individual	19-24
Regular	38-46
Cruet, patterned.	64-74
Goblet.	44-54
Pitcher	64-70
Rose bowl (ill.)	28-34
Salt, master	33-42
Sauce, crimped	14-17
Spoonholder.	32-36

Sugar bowl

Covered	47-55
Individual, open, handled	20-25
Tumbler.	43-50
Vases, 10″, pr.	68-76
Wine	40-45

The cruet came with patterned stopper, but is also shown in an old ad with faceted stopper, worth $50-55. No toothpick (yet!). Green, add 100 percent; custard, add 200 percent.

Heavy Drape

Fostoria Glass Company, 1904. Clear, nonflint.

Bowl, berry, flat and footed finger . . .	$ 25-32
Butter dish, covered	39-47

137

(continued)

Heavy Drape

Celery	32-41
Compote, covered and open	42-51
Creamer	
Individual	27-36
Regular (ill.)	27-36
Tankard	18-21
Egg cup	24-33
Pitcher: milk, water, ½ gal.	67-74
Salt dip (flint), oval, *not* Fostoria	27-29
Salt/Pepper (2 types), pr.	36-45
Spoonholder	34-42
Sugar bowl, covered, individual, open (handleless)	39-47
Tumbler	37-46
Water bottle	37-46
Wine	28-35

Fifty or more pieces in the set. No goblet. A similar pattern in flint does not form a full circle at the top of the pattern.

Heavy Finecut

(Heavy Panelled Finecut; Finecut Four Panel; Sequoia; original name, Bagware): U. S. Glass (Duncan No. 800 and No. 800 1/2) c. 1891. Clear, amber, blue, canary, nonflint. The panelled and non-panelled versions must be combined for complete sets.

Miscellaneous

Salt dip, oblong; plain side, pattern in base	
Individual	$ 8-12
Master	10-15
Sled, 4½″, flat, oblong	31-42

Panelled, square or rectangular

Bowl	
Berry, flared, 12″ square, panelled, pleated sides	17-24
Oblong 8¾″, 10″, 12″	14-19

Butter on pedestal, square	25-32
Cake basket, round with square stem	30-36
Celery on pedestal	19-23
Compote, low, 7″, 8″ 9″	
Covered	24-38
Open	15-24
Creamer on pedestal, square	19-23
Finger bowl, panelled, deep-fluted	13-17
Goblet	20-25
Pickle, 8⅝″, fan handles	12-17
Pitcher, ½ gal., on pedestal	30-37
Sauce	
Flat, square, panelled pleated sides, flared, 4½″	10-12
Flat, square, flat rim, 4″, 4½″	7-11
Pedestal, 4″ square	9-13
Spoonholder on pedestal, square	14-18
Sugar on pedestal, square	24-30
Tumbler	13-17

Plain, round

Bowl	
Bulbous, 7″, 8″, "Bag"	
Covered	30-36
Open	23-27
Orange, 8″, 9″, high, flared and deep, "Bag"	35-42
Shallow, 7″, "Bag"	17-23
Butter, "Bag"	29-38
Butter pat	10-13
Cake stand, 8″, 9″, 10″	28-38
Catsup (wide mouth cruet), "Bag"	27-33
Celery boat, 11″	16-19
Champagne	22-30
Cheese plate and cover (with plain or scalloped rim, 9″ plate)	36-45
Claret	20-28
Compote, peg for silver-plated base, complete	40-50
Cordial	17-22
Creamer, "Bag"	21-27
Cruet, original faceted stopper	27-33
Finger bowl	
Collared base, scalloped rim, "Bag"	15-18
Cupped, low	13-17
Fluted scalloped rim	14-20
Straight, on plate	19-26
Straight, no plate	11-18
Goblet	20-30
Mustard (salt shaker with mustard top); also made in 800 1/2, larger size	15-25
Nappy, flared, 7½″	13-18
Pickle boat	12-16
Pickle jar	28-34

Pitcher
  Bulbous, ½ gallon, "Bag"   39-47
  Bulbous, 3 pint, "Bag"   33-40
  Tapered, ½ gal. tankard   35-41
Plate
  Cheese, 9", plain or scalloped rim . . .   22-27
  Finger bowl, 5⅜".   8-12
  Plain rim, 7"   14-18
Salt shaker, straight, pattern to top;
  also made with panelled
  neck in 800 1/2.   13-23
Sauce, 4", "Bag"   5-9
Spoonholder
  Bulbous, "Bag"   17-23
  Straight, flat base, "Bag"   15-20
Sugar, "Bag," atypical (squat,
  similar to butter)   25-35
Syrup   40-48
Tray
  Brandy: rectangular, handled. "Brandy
  sett" is oil/vinegar cruet and
  1 oz. cordials   32-39
  Wine: (also appears with two different
  decanters and wines, each with
  different engraving   30-35
Wine   16-22

Plain, square or rectangular

Compote, 7⅝", covered   28-36
Cordial   18-23
Goblet.   20-25
Sauce, ice cream, 5"   12-14
Tray, ice cream
  Handled   31-37
  No handles   25-30
Wine   17-25

This writer has observed that the bulbous pieces appear to be more refined than the rest of the line, slightly lighter in weight and more brilliant in quality. Bagware ("Bag") is indicated above when it appears in original ads.

Heavy Gothic

(Whitton): U.S. Glass Company, 1892. Clear, clear or stained with ruby; nonflint.

Butter dish . . . . $ 32-40
Celery.   15-18
Compote, covered, 6½" dia.   36-41
Creamer (ill.)   24-27
Dish, oblong.   8-11
Goblet.   20-26
Pitcher   39-47
Sauce, footed, 4", 5"   6-12
Spoonholder.   16-19
Sugar bowl, two sizes   30-35

Heavy Gothic

Tumbler.   14-18
Wine   18-23
Ruby stained, 100 percent more.

Heavy Jewel

Heavy Jewel

Fostoria Glass Company, 1900. Clear, nonflint.

Butter dish . . . . $ 30-34
Creamer.   24-27
Pitcher (ill.)   38-46
Spoonholder.   16-19
Sugar bowl
  Covered   28-33
  Open   15-20
Tumbler.   15-18
No goblet.

Heck

(Erroneously Teardrop Row, a case of mistaken identity; Double Prism): Model Flint Glass, Albany, Indiana, c. 1890. Clear, nonflint.

(continued)

Bowl, 6″, 8″ berry	$ 20-27
Butter, covered	34-42
Celery tray, straight or flared rim	19-27
Celery vase	25-35
Cologne	20-26
Compote	
Covered, high, 6″, 7″, 8″	29-40
Open, jelly, 4½″	15-21
Cracker jar	42-55
Goblet	25-32
Pitcher	
Pattern all over, pointed rim, ½ gal.	34-43
Tankard, pattern on lower band, ½ gal.	35-45
Salt shaker	17-22
Sauce, 4½″ berry	10-12
Spoonholder	24-30
Sugar	31-38
Tumbler	17-25
Wine	20-30

Helene

(Recently renamed Zippered Spearpoint): Central, c. 1898. Clear, nonflint

Butter	$ 24-30
Creamer	20-25
Spoonholder	16-19
Sugar, covered	22-27

Information on additional pieces welcomed.

Henrietta

Henrietta

(Erroneously called Hexagon Block or Big Block): Columbia Glass Company, 1889, and U. S. Glass Company. Clear, green, nonflint.

Bowl	
Berry	$ 18-22
Rectangular, 5″ x 8″	14-19
Butter dish	28-36
Cake stand, 10″	39-42
Creamer	15-22
Mustard	30-35
Olive, handled	17-20
Pitcher, water (ill.)	38-44
Rose bowl, covered	40-48
Salt shaker	
Hotel	30-35
Regular	16-21
Sauce	9-12
Saucer	12-15
Shade	30-34
Spoonholder	16-20
Sugar bowl, covered, handled	30-35
Sugar sifter	30-35
Tumbler	27-37
Vase	20-25

Emerald green or ruby stain, 60 percent higher. Sugar sifter, hotel salt, and mustard (different top) are same pieces. No goblet or toothpick.

Heron

Heron

Indiana Tumbler & Goblet (National) Company, late 1890s. Clear and chocolate.

Pitcher, water	
Chocolate	$274-312
Clear (ill.)	155-172

140

Herringbone

Herringbone

Maker unknown, late 1870s. Clear, non-flint.

Butter bowl . . . . $ 30-37
Celery   25-30
Compote, open, 5½" dia.   17-22
Creamer   22-28
Goblet (ill.)   23-28
Pitcher, water   34-42
Sauce, flat   5-8
Spoonholder (pedestal)   18-22
Sugar bowl
    Covered   30-34
    Open 20-25
Wine   25-30
Color, 50 percent more than clear prices listed.

Hexagonal Bull's Eye

Hexagonal Bull's Eye

(Hexagon Block is a different pattern): Dalzell, early 1890s. Clear, nonflint.

Butter dish, covered . . . . $ 39-42
Celery vase   26-31
Creamer   23-30
Goblet   30-35
Pitcher (ill.)   42-47

Sauce   10-13
Spoonholder   17-22
Sugar
    Covered   34-38
    Open 16-21
Tumbler   16-19
Wine   29-34

Hidalgo

Hidalgo

(Frosted Waffle): Adams & Company, Pittsburgh, 1885 and U. S. Glass after 1891. Crystal, plain and engraved; also frosted.

Bowl, 8", 9" . . . . $ 23-27
Bread boat, 13"   34-39
Butter dish   34-38
Celery   21-25
Compote, covered, open, high,
    scalloped edge 30-34
Creamer (scarce)   30-34
Cruet   45-50
Cup and saucer   19-27
Egg cup, flat   20-25
Goblet (typical form)   18-24
Pitcher, milk (ill.)   35-42
Salt dip, master, 2⅞" sq.   24-29
Salt/Pepper, pr.   25-32
Sauce
    Flat, handled   9-12
    Footed 12-17
Spoonholder   15-18
Sugar bowl, covered   32-35
Syrup   48-53
Tumbler   14-18

Frosted, 15 percent higher; ruby stain, 80 percent higher; amber stain, 50 percent higher than clear prices listed. Some frosted pieces have cut stars, add 10 percent. Engraved, 20 percent more. The 13" bread boat mistakenly called celery.

High Hob

Westmoreland No. 550, c. 1912. Clear, nonflint.

Bonbon, 4½" dia., footed	$ 10-13
Bowl	
Bell, 9".	14-17
Flared, 9"	15-20
Punch, 9", two pieces.	50-62
Round, 8", 9".	13-17
Butter, covered	24-30
Celery tray, 10", curled.	12-18
Celery vase, concave or straight	15-19
Creamer.	14-18
Cruet, 6-panelled spire stopper	22-29
Cup, sherbet, straight	5-10
Goblet, straight or bell.	17-22
Pitcher, ½ gal.	25-32
Plate	
7"	10-17
10" bread	16-21
Salt shaker	13-17
Sauce	
4" flat	3-7
4½" bell	5-8
Spoonholder.	11-14
Sugar, covered, handled	18-24
Sweetmeat, tall, flat rim	10-13
Tumbler	
Iced tea	10-15
Water	10-15
Vase, 7" cupped, flared, straight,	
or crimped.	15-22
Wine, belled or straight	14-19

Hobbs Diamond and Sunburst

Hobbs Diamond and Sunburst

(Diamonds with Double Fan): Hobbs, Brockunier & Company, 1880s. Clear, nonflint.

Butter dish, covered	$ 24-27
Creamer (ill.)	16-21
Goblet.	29-37
Spoonholder.	14-17
Sugar bowl, covered	22-25

Hobnail

Hobnail

Many companies made a hobnail pattern, including New Brighton Glass Company, A. J. Beatty Company, McKee & Bros., Gillinder Bros., and others. The piece illustrated is the sugar shaker, also called a "hotel salt," in Dewdrop (original name) by U. S. Glass (Columbia), c. 1891. It came in clear and colors and has been in continuous production. Color and opalescent.

Some of the pieces made were berry bowls, perfume bottles, creamers, celerys, cordials, bone dishes, mugs, pitchers, salts (ill.), glass shades, spoonholders, sugar bowls, toothpick holders, trays, tumblers, vases, wines. There are many "safe" hobnail patterns such as Double Eye Hobnail, Hobnail with Fan Top, and the two following patterns.

Hobnail Band

(Erroneously Garter Band): One of the hobnail group, around 1890. Clear, nonflint.

Creamer (ill.)	$ 29-36
Goblet.	24-34
Pitcher, 8" high, straight sides	35-40

Not reproduced. Please write if you can add to the listing.

Hobnail Band

Holly

Hobnail in Big Diamonds

Hobnail in Big Diamonds

(Erroneously Hobnail with Bars): Challinor, Taylor & Company, 1888. Clear.

Bowl, berry	$ 19-23
Butter dish, covered	39-42
Creamer (ill.)	25-30
Pitcher	45-55
Sauce	10-13
Spoonholder	21-24
Sugar	
Covered	31-37
Open	16-19

Berry set has vertical bars, not diamonds, separating hobnails. Confusion in name from Lee calling two different patterns Hobnails with Bars, one of which is also called Hobnail with Curved Bars. Not reproduced.

Holly

Sandwich Glass Company, c. 1870. Clear, nonflint.

Butter bowl	$132-141
Cake stand, 11″	110-134
Compote, covered, high	
standard, 8″ dia.	167-175
Creamer, applied handle	106-121
Egg cup	64-72
Goblet (ill.)	88-96
Pitcher, water	133-150
Sauce, flat	18-24
Spoonholder	58-69
Sugar bowl	
Covered	100-120
Open	50-60
Tumbler, footed	53-63
Wine	98-121

Similar pattern, Holly Band.

Holly Amber

Holly Amber

(Golden Agate): Indiana Tumbler & Goblet (National) Company, January to June, 1903, only. Amber, chocolate (red agate) and clear.

(continued)

Bowl

7½″, 8½″ dia.	$600+
10″ rect.	750+
Butter dish (ill.)	1,200+

Compote

Covered, 8″ dia.	750+
Covered, 6½″ dia.	1,000+
Cruet	1,600+
Mug, 4″	400+
Pitcher, water	2,000+
Salt/Pepper, pr.	1,100+
Sauce	225+
Spoonholder.	550+
Sugar bowl, flat, 4½″ dia.	700+
Syrup	800+
Toothpick.	300+
Tumbler, smooth rim	375+
Vase, 6″	450+

Other pieces made. Clear, 20 to 50 percent of the amber prices listed. Butter dish, covered compote, jelly compote, creamer, cruet, 7½″ plate, toothpick, and tumbler reproduced.

Home

Home

(Square and Diamond Bands): Pioneer Glass Company, Pittsburgh, late 1880s. Clear, nonflint.

Butter dish, covered	$ 20-25
Celery.	18-22
Creamer, 4¾″ high (ill.)	17-21
Pitcher, water	27-32
Spoonholder.	14-16
Sugar bowl covered	20-25
Tumbler.	11-13

Goblet does not appear in the literature.

Holly Band

Holly Band

Maker unknown, attributed to Sandwich, 1870s. Clear, nonflint.

Butter bowl	$ 75-85
Celery (ill.)	55-67
Compote	35-44
Creamer.	48-59
Pitcher, applied handle	90-105
Salt, footed	44-55
Spoonholder.	41-49
Sugar bowl	62-70

Honeycomb

Honeycomb

(Cincinnati; Vernon): Many firms made this pattern: Bakewell, Pears & Company and Lyons, 1860s on. McKee, 1868 on. Early in clear; later in yellow, blue, amber, green, and opalware. Flint, nonflint.

Bowl, 6″, 7″, 8″, 9″, 10″, oval	$ 29-39
Butter bowl, covered.	47-56
Caster bottle, oil or vinegar, oval	32-38
Celery, ...	58-66
Creamer, 5½″ high (ill.)	35-42
Decanter, pint, quart; honeycomb stopper	51-60
Goblet, barrel	40-50
Jelly glass, tall, thin, pedestal	52-62

144

Jug, ½ pt., pt., qt., 3 pts..	40-47
Pitcher, water, applied handle	72-89
Salt/Pepper, pr..	41-50
Spoonholder.	23-29
Sugar bowl	50-58
Tumbler, ½ pt., ⅓ pt., gill.	42-51
Wine	24-31

Cincinnati is a generic name for allover honeycomb patterns; those with the pattern halfway up are "New York" honeycombs. Although Pittsburgh Honeycomb is an overall pattern, it is not a true honeycomb. Round, large bowls, plentiful in other patterns, elusive in Honeycomb.

Sugar bowl	
Covered	36-40
Open	18-22
Toothpick.	31-37
Tumbler.	28-34
Vase.	15-20
Waste bowl (scarce)	28-35

Blue and decorated custard, 90 percent; green, amber, 40 percent higher than clear prices shown. No goblet. Toothpick reproduced in clear, colors, opalescent, chocolate. Contrary to early literature, pattern is known only with the honeycomb. A candlestick called "Jewelled Vermont" in custard is worth $45-55.

Hops Band

(Original name, Maple; Pressed Leaf Band): King and Son, Pittsburgh, c. 1870s. Clear.

Bowl, oval. . . . . $	14-18
Butter bowl	30-38
Cake stand, 9″, 11″.	33-40
Celery.	26-35
Compote	
Covered, high	30-40
Open, low	18-22
Creamer, on pedestal,	
applied handle.	26-31
Egg cup	20-25
Goblet.	20-25
Pickle, scoop shape	13-16
Pitcher, water, applied handle	42-47
Salt, footed	17-21
Sauce, flat.	5-9
Spoonholder on pedestal.	16-21
Sugar bowl on pedestal	
Covered	32-37
Open	24-30
Wine	22-29

Similar pattern, Panelled Grape Band.

Honeycomb with Flower Rim

Honeycomb with Flower Rim

(Inverted Thumbprint with Daisy Band; Vermont, part of States series): Attributed to U. S. Glass, 1899. Clear, blue, amber, green; decorated custard ("ivory"). Usually with gold.

Basket, low (card tray)	
3 sizes . . . . $	30-40
Bowl	30-35
Butter, covered	40-47
Celery.	24-36
Tray.	17-22
Compote	
Covered	48-54
Open	34-42
Creamer (ill. in green)	28-33
Goblet.	35-40
Pickle tray	14-17
Pitcher	51-60
Salt shaker	20-26
Sauce, 2 sizes (larger is waste bowl) . .	13-18
Spoonholder.	20-25

Horn of Plenty

Sandwich Glass, early 1830s; Bryce, McKee, Pittsburgh, 1868, nonflint. Prices are for Sandwich. Opalescent white, canary, clear, flint.

Butter dish	
Conventional knob,	
6″ dia. . . . . $	133-142
Washington's head (rare)	600+
Cake stand (rare)	900+
Celery.	150-172

(continued)

Horn of Plenty

Champagne	126-145
Compote	
Open, 8″ high	95-115
Open, low standard, 12″	115-124
Creamer, 5½″ or 7″ high (ill.).	187-195
Decanter, pint, quart, ½ gal..	110-135
Egg cup	47-56
Goblet.	79-86
Honey, 3¼″	10-15
Lamp, all glass, tall	172-182
Mug, applied handle, 3″ (rare)	145-162
Pitcher, water	450+
Plate, 6″.	73-89
Sauce, 4½″, 5″	12-19
Spoonholder.	40-47
Sugar bowl, pagoda lid.	100-132
Tumbler, whiskey	77-87
Wine (rare)	135-142

Canary, amber, blue, 85 percent higher than clear prices listed. Amber or clear goblet and water tumbler reproduced. Also, glass lamp. Fluted dish from tumbler mold is pre-WWII production.

Horsehead Medallion

Portland Glass Company attribution, 1870s. Clear; rare in milk-white, nonflint.

Butter.	$ 70-80
Celery.	89-97
Compote	
Covered	88-110
Open	62-71
Creamer.	54-75
Egg cup	60-70
Spoonholder.	32-38
Sugar bowl	
Covered	62-68
Open (ill.)	30-36
Toothpick.	60-70

Horsehead Medallion

Milk-white, 100 percent higher than clear prices listed. Egg cup may be toothpick. Tree of life frequently on finials and stem knobs.

Horseshoe Stem

Horseshoe Stem

Maker unknown, 1880s. Clear, nonflint.

Cake stand, 8″ dia.	$ 56-65
Compote	
Covered	77-86
Open	33-38
Creamer (ill.)	52-62
Goblet.	58-68
Sauce, footed	12-15
Spoonholder.	26-33
Sugar	
Covered	57-67
Open	30-34
Tumbler.	47-55

Hour Glass

Maker unknown, c. 1880s. Clear, yellow, amber, blue; nonflint.

Bowl	$ 14-18
Butter dish, covered	24-30
Creamer	15-20
Goblet	19-24
Pitcher, water	25-32
Salt	22-28
Sauce, large	6-8
Spoonholder	14-17
Sugar bowl, covered	24-30
Wine	20-25

Yellow, 65 percent; amber, blue, 100 percent higher than clear prices listed. A member of the Finecut group.

Huber

Huber

Several firms made this pattern—Sandwich; New England Glass Company; McKee; Lyons; Bakewell, Pears & Company; others, 1860s and earlier. Clear, flint, and nonflint. Number of panels varies with form.

Bitters bottle	$ 35-42
Bowl, covered, 6", 7"	32-39
Butter dish	40-50
Celery (ill.)	31-37
Champagne	25-30
Compote, covered, high and low standard, 7", 10"	50-66
Cordial	29-33
Creamer	50-60
Decanter	
Bar lip, pint, quart	48-58
With stopper, pint, quart	52-62
Egg cup	
Handled	45-55
Regular	29-33

Goblet, hotel, large, small	18-25
Jug, quart, 3 pints	35-45
Mug	30-35
Pitcher, water, 2 styles	80-95
Salt, celery dip, footed	12-20
Spoonholder	24-28
Sugar bowl, covered	46-56
Tumbler, gill, ½ pt., large and small, taper bar	23-32
Wine	24-33

Flint prices given. Nonflint, 30 percent less. Similar crystal pattern. Add 30 percent for good quality engraving.

Huckabee

(Flute and Cane; Prism and Finecut): Imperial No. 666, c. 1920s. Clear, nonflint.

Bowl	
Footed, 7¼"	$ 7-10
Fruit, 8½"	6-9
Butter, covered	30-36
Celery, tall	10-14
Creamer	8-11
Cruet, 6 oz.	18-24
Goblet	10-13
Pitcher	
Jug, milk, 22 oz.	14-19
Tankard, water, 51 oz.	20-27
Plate, sherbet, 6"	4-7
Salt shaker, aluminum top	10-15
Salver, 7¾"	10-13
Sauce, fruit, 4¾"	3-5
Sherbet, 3½"	4-7
Spoonholder	7-10
Sugar, covered	10-13
Tumbler	5-9

Hummingbird

(continued)

Hummingbird

(Flying Robin): Maker unknown, late 1880s. Clear, canary, amber, blue; nonflint. May be engraved, which does not add to the value.

Butter dish, covered	$ 49-56
Celery	40-48
Creamer, footed	31-36
Goblet	34-40
Pickle dish	18-20
Pitcher, 8″ high (ill.)	40-48
Sauce, flat	13-19
Spoonholder	30-34
Sugar bowl, covered	45-53
Tray, water	58-67
Tumbler	32-42

Canary, 25 percent; amber and blue, 50 percent higher than clear prices listed.

Humpty Dumpty Mug

Humpty Dumpty Mug

(Humpty Dumpty shown): maker unknown, a novelty of the 1880s. Clear, pink.

Mug, 3½″ high (ill.)	$ 58-67

"Tom, Tom, the piper's son" is shown on other side. Metz confused him with the Tom Thumb of Barnum Circus fame, but the error in the literature persists. A pink mug, bowl, and plate confirmed.

Hundred Eye

Westmoreland, c. 1934, their Thousand Eye pattern, called Hundred Eye by early authors who believed it to be older.

Ashtray, turtle	$ 5-9
Basket, 8″, handled, flat	12-19
Bowl	
Belled, 11″	9-12
Crimped oblong, 11″	9-12
Flared, 12″	13-16
Round, 11″	9-12
Triangular, 11″	12-15
Two handles, 10″	14-18
Candelabra, two-light, single	12-16
Candlestick, 5″	8-10
Cigarette box and cover, turtle	12-16
Claret, 5 oz.	8-10
Cocktail, 3½ oz.	8-10
Compote, 5″ dia.	7-11
Cordial, 1 oz.	7-11
Creamer, medium	8-12
Cup and saucer	10-14
Goblet, 8 oz.	14-19
Mayonnaise, footed, glass ladle	10-16
Nappy, round, 7½″, one handle	7-12
Pitcher, ½ gal. jug with ice lip	20-25
Plate	
6″, 7″	5-9
8½″, 10″	8-12
14″, 18″	14-22
Relish, 5 sections, 10″ round	15-20
Salt shaker	11-15
Sauce (nappy), flat, 4½″ and 5½″	4-8
Sherbet	
High foot	7-11
Low foot	5-8
Sherry, 3 oz.	10-13
Sugar, open, handled, medium	8-12
Tumbler	
Cocktail, Old Fashioned, 6 oz.	6-10
Footed, 5, 7, 9 oz.	6-14
Ginger ale, 5 oz.	5-10
Iced tea, footed or flat, 12 oz.	7-11
Parfait	6-10
Water, 8 oz.	7-10
Whiskey, 1½ oz. (shot glass)	5-8
Wine, 2 oz.	10-13

Hundred Leaved Rose

Hundred Leaved Rose

Maker unknown, 1880s. Clear, nonflint.

Bowl	$ 25-35

148

Butter dish, covered 31-36
Creamer. 22-26
Pitcher (ill.) 38-43
Sauce, flat. 6-9
Spoonholder. 16-20
Sugar bowl
  Covered 29-33
  Open 15-19
Goblet?

In Remembrance Platter

Imperial

(No. 261): Imperial Glass Company, Bellaire, Ohio, c. 1901. Clear, nonflint.

Butter dish, covered . . . . $ 23-30
Celery tray 9-14
Compote 15-20
Creamer. 20-26
Goblet. 13-18
Pitcher, milk, water 22-32
Spoonholder. 11-16
Sugar bowl, covered 21-29
Tumbler. 10-15
Wine 12-16

Indiana

(Prison Windows): U. S. Glass (Gas City, Indiana) c. 1897. Clear or with gold, nonflint.

Butter. . . . . $ 35-42
Celery tray 20-26
Creamer. 29-34
Cruet 32-38
Jelly dish, round, one handle. 21-26
Salt shaker 19-24
Spoonholder. 23-28
Sugar 35-40

This Indiana is the authentic pattern for the States series, rather than Feather or Cord Drapery. A butter dish in the literature is erroneously labeled "Doric."

In Remembrance Platter

A memorial platter issued after Garfield's assassination in 1881. Garfield shares a place with Lincoln and Washington. Clear with frosted portraits. Nonflint.

Platter (ill.) . . . . $ 84-99

Intaglio

Intaglio

Northwood Glass Company, 1890. Clear, custard, opalescent, blue, deep green, nonflint.

	Colored Opalescent	Custard
Berry set		
Large bowl.	$ 83-119	$169-180
Small bowl, sauce .	26-33	68-78
Butter, covered . . .	120-136	190-220
Compote, jelly. . . .	43-51	64-75
Creamer (ill.)	53-69	92-108
Cruet	100-130	189-225
Pitcher, water	171-189	182-192
Salt/Pepper, pr. . . .		139-184
Spoonholder.	43-54	87-99
Sugar, covered. . . .	83-93	132-159
Tumbler, water . . .	27-37	59-70

149

(continued)

Custard prices are for pieces with good paint. Clear opalescent, 60 percent less than colored opal prices listed.

Creamer.	$ 15-21
Cruet	24-30
Toothpick.	28-33

Other pieces?

Interlocked Hearts

Interlocked Hearts

(Wish Bone): Maker unknown, c. 1890s. Clear, nonflint.

Creamer (ill.)	$ 21-28
Goblet.	18-24
Pitcher, water	30-37
Tumbler.	12-17
Wine	13-19

Interlocking Crescents

(Double Arch; U. S. Columbia): The King Glass Company, Pittsburgh, c. late 1880s. U. S. Glass, 1892. Clear, ruby stain, frosted. Nonflint.

Butter dish, covered	$ 25-35
Compote, open	19-28
Creamer.	22-28
Goblet.	21-26
Salt shaker (scarce) frosted	18-25
Spoonholder.	13-19
Sugar bowl, covered	25-34
Toothpick.	30-40

Ruby stain, add 50 percent to clear prices listed.

Inverted Eye

National Glass Co., c. 1900, their No. 519 pattern.

Iron Kettle

Iron Kettle

(Sanborn): Challinor Taylor & Company, and U. S. Glass, 1885. Clear, nonflint.

Bowl, covered, 7″, 8″	$ 25-35
Butter dish, covered, 6″	28-33
Creamer (ill.)	20-25
Spoonholder.	13-18
Sugar bowl, covered	24-29

Documentation in color would be appreciated.

Ivy-in-Snow

Ivy-in-Snow

(Forest Ware): Cooperative Flint Glass Company, Beaver Falls, Pennsylvania, late 1880s. Clear or clear with foliage stained red, green, or gold.

Butter dish, flat, ivy leaf finial	$ 33-41

150

Cake stand, square, small	31-39
Celery.	60-70
Compote, covered; small, medium, large, high standard; ivy leaf finial	39-58
Creamer (ill.)	24-30
Cup and saucer	28-34
Goblet.	24-34
Jam jar	31-40
Pitcher, water	36-49
Plate, 7".	15-20
Sauce, flat, round, 4", 6"	7-12
Spoonholder.	20-26
Sugar bowl, ivy leaf finial	30-40
Syrup	72-80
Tumbler.	21-27
Wine	24-34

In extended production in clear and milk glass. Ruby stain, add 250 percent to clear prices listed.

Jacob's Coat

Jacob's Coat

Maker unknown, 1880s. Clear, amber, blue, green; milk glass (scarce); nonflint.

Butter bowl, covered.	$ 40-48
Celery.	28-37
Creamer (ill.)	26-34
Saucedish	6-10
Spoonholder.	20-23
Sugar bowl, covered	32-36

Amber, blue, green, 50 percent higher than clear prices listed. No goblet proof although it's listed in the literature. Butter is known in milk glass.

Jacob's Ladder

(Maltese): Bryce Bros., Pittsburgh, 1870s. Clear, amber, yellow; colors scarce; nonflint.

Bowl, 6" dia. (butter base)	$ 22-29

Jacob's Ladder

Butter dish, covered, Maltese Cross finial	61-68
Cake stand, 11"	47-55
Caster set, 4 bottles	98-115
Celery.	25-38
Compote	
Open, large, high standard	36-45
In silver-plated holder	90-104
Creamer, footed	34-40
Cruet, Maltese Cross stopper	74-85
Dish, oval	19-27
Dolphin compote (rare)	270-290
Goblet.	52-66
Marmalade, Maltese Cross finial . . .	59-65
Pitcher, water, applied handle (ill.) .	139-151
Plate, 6".	18-28
Salt, master	28-38
Sauce	
Flat, footed, 3½", 4", 5".	10-17
Footed, 4½"	11-15
Spoonholder.	30-39
Sugar bowl, covered, Maltese Cross finial	52-62
Syrup, 2 types	68-79
Tumbler, ½ pint	40-46
Wine	34-39

Colors, 150 percent higher than clear prices listed. Also see Late Jacob's Ladder.

Jardiniere

Maker unknown, c. 1887. Clear, nonflint.

Butter dish, covered	$ 30-38
Creamer.	25-31
Spoonholder.	21-24
Sugar bowl, covered	35-40

Other pieces?

Jefferson's Number 251

Jefferson's Number 251

(Idyll): Jefferson Glass Company, Steubenville, Ohio, 1904. Clear, apple green, sapphire blue with gold; blue and ruby stain is mentioned in the literature.

Berry bowls, 8″, ...	$ 18-25
Butter dish, covered	31-38
Condiment set (cruet, shakers,	
toothpick, on tray)	143-174
Creamer.	34-44
Cruet, handled (ill.)	40-50
Jug, ½ gal.	46-52
Salt/Pepper, pr.	38-48
Spoonholder.	20-30
Sugar bowl, covered	28-34
Toothpick	35-40

Colors and opalescent, 100-150 percent higher than clear prices listed. Kamm describes in turquoise or green opaque, possibly done in abbreviating "opalescent"?

Jefferson's Number 271

Jefferson's Number 271

(Dolly Madison): Jefferson Glass Company, Follansbee, West Virginia, 1907. Clear, blue, green, also gold trimmed. Nonflint.

Bowl, 8″	$ 22-29
Butter dish, blue	30-35
Creamer.	23-26
Nappy, 4″ and 8″.	25-34
Pitcher, water, ½ gal.	36-44
Sauce	10-13
Spoonholder.	21-24
Sugar bowl, covered	30-35
Tumbler (ill.)	16-20

Blue or green (with good gold), add 150 percent.

Jersey

Jersey

(The Kitchen Stove): McKee Bros., 1894. Clear, nonflint.

Butter dish, covered	$ 39-47
Compote, open	
High standard	36-46
Low standard	29-34
Creamer, 6″ high (ill.)	30-39
Goblet.	30-34
Pitcher, ½ gal.	56-66
Spoonholder.	37-47
Sugar bowl, covered	40-49

The goblet is shown in one reference book as "Diamond and Fan" and also as "Variegated Daisy and Prism Arc." There is an early flint Jersey pattern.

Jersey Swirl

(Swirl): Windsor Glass Company, Pittsburgh, 1887. Clear and color: canary, amber, blue; nonflint.

Jersey Swirl

Butter dish, covered . . . . $ 35-45
Compote
   Covered 38-46
   Open 30-35
Creamer. 22-28
Goblet
   Buttermilk (ill.) large 30-39
   Regular size 27-36
Pitcher, water 47-55
Plate, 10″, 12″ 22-30
Salt dip, flat 11-15
Sauce, collared base 8-12
Spoonholder. 17-23
Sugar bowl
   Covered 32-41
   Open 19-26
Tumbler. 18-25
Wine 25-35

Canary, 40 percent; blue or amber, 60 percent higher than crystal prices listed. Reproduced in goblets, covered compotes, nappies, plates (2 sizes), salt dips and sauces. Pedestal salts are reproductions.

Jewel and Festoon

Jewel and Festoon

(Loop and Jewel; original name, Venus): Beatty-Brady, late 1880s. Clear, nonflint.

Bowls, 6″, 7″, 8″ . . . . $ 17-29
Butter dish, covered, flat 34-39
Creamer, on pedestal (ill.) 25-29
Cup 13-17
Dish, sq., 5″ 15-20
Goblet. 38-47
Pitcher 42-47
Relish dish, rectangular, 8″. 18-24
Salt/Pepper, pr. 40-46
Salt shaker in milk glass 17-29
Sauce, flat, 4″, 4½″. 11-15
Spoonholder on pedestal,
   beaded rim 18-21
Sugar
   Berry, 3 handles 24-29
   Bowl, covered, on pedestal 33-36
   Individual, 3 handles. 26-30
Syrup 44-51
No goblet.

Jewel with Dewdrop

Jewel with Dewdrop

(Kansas): Co-operative Flint Glass Company, 1870s; issued by U.S. Glass Company, in 1907 as Kansas. Clear, color stained, nonflint.

Bowl, berry, 8½″. . . . . $ 20-30
Bread, motto 35-40
Butter, covered
   Flanged 69-80
   Regular 50-58
Cake stand, 8″, 9″, 10″ 43-70
Celery 35-44

(continued)

Compote
Covered, high standard,
  deep bowl   68-77
Open, high standard   60-64
Creamer.   25-32
Goblet.   49-57
Jelly, covered   50-60
Nappy (bowl) 6″, 7″, flared, deep . . .   25-30
Pitcher, water, qt. (ill.).   40-46
Preserve, 8″ oval   39-43
Salt/Pepper, pr.   66-80
Spoonholder.   29-33
Sugar bowl, covered   45-54
Syrup   105-125
Toothpick holder   50-60
Tumbler.   32-38
Wine   45-53

Inferior quality goblet, small mug are later production, States series. Color stained, add 25 percent.

Jeweled Heart

Jeweled Heart

Northwood Glass Company, 1900s. Clear, colored, carnival, opalescent, nonflint.

	Clear Opalescent	Colored Opalescent
Butter.	$72-81	$138-150
Cruet, clear, colored (ill.)		162-178
Pitcher	52-59	134-150
Pitcher, Carnival (rare)		485-522
Syrup	98-112	123-149
Tumbler Carnival		68-77

Toothpick, goblet (not originally made), creamer and sugar reproduced.

Jeweled Moon and Star

(Original name, Imperial): c. 1897, Cooperative reportedly bought the molds from Wilson Glass Company, Tarentum, Pennsylvania, 1890. Clear or with frosted moons; also amber and blue; may have gold trim.

Bowl, 6¾″ round . . . . $ 15-18
Butter dish, covered, on pedestal . . .   40-45
Carafe.   40-50
Celery.   30-38
Compote
Covered, large   52-60
Open, 9″ dia.   37-45
Creamer.   33-39
Cruet   33-39
Goblet.   48-58
Jelly, covered   40-47
Pitcher, water, bulbous,
applied handle   64-72
Salt shaker   25-32
Sauce, 4″ flat   8-11
Spoonholder.   31-35
Sugar bowl, covered   45-55
Syrup   70-80
Tray, water   44-53
Tumbler.   42-50
Wine   39-49

No toothpick. Seventy pieces advertised. Confusion exists with Moon and Star (Palace) pattern. Jeweled Moon and Star has not been reproduced. Frosted, add 20 percent; color, add 150 percent.

Jubilee

Jubilee

(Isis; Radiant Daisy and Button): McKee Glass Company, 1894. Clear, scarce in ruby stain; nonflint.

Butter.	$ 19-26
Celery tray	14-17
Compote	
Open, high, 7″ dia.	22-26
Open, low, 7″ dia..	18-20
Celery tray	14-17
Creamer (ill.)	13-17
Dish, deep, oblong, 8″	15-20
Goblet.	14-18
Pickle dish, 7″ long.	23-33
Pitcher, water	42-52
Plate, 9″	10-18
Spoonholder.	11-15
Sugar bowl, covered	18-23
Tumbler.	12-14
Wine	16-20

Tumbler known in ruby. There is another Jubilee .pattern (Hickman) also by McKee. Confusing pattern is Robinson's Puritan mistakenly labeled Isis, shown in ruby stain.

Jumbo

Photo: Mr. and Mrs. A.M. Zinkeler, Chattanooga, Tenn.

Jumbo

Canton Glass Company, Canton, Ohio, 1883. Also made by Aetna Glass Co., Bellaire, Ohio, same period. Clear, nonflint.

Butter dish	
Oblong, Jumbo	290-326
Round, Barnum's head.	$335-365
Caster set, 3 bottles	448-486
Compote, covered	330-360
Creamer.	125-147
Goblet (rare)	420-458
Pitcher	540-585

Spoon rack, rare (ill.)	530-564
Spoonholder.	130-162
Sugar bowl, covered	360-440

The spoon rack is one of the rarest pieces of pattern glass in America today. Goblet and three-bottle caster set not part of true Jumbo pattern. There are elephant patterns that are plain with elephant finials, Jumbo and Barnum, and odd pieces like the elephant wall matchholder.

King's Breastplate

(Star of David; Pimlico): New Martinsville, c. 1902. Clear; emerald green goblet known.

Bowl	$ 15-19
Butter.	24-32
Compote, jelly.	13-17
Creamer.	19-23
Cruet, faceted stopper	24-31
Goblet.	16-20
Jar, dresser (plated top)	15-21
Pitcher, ice lip.	29-36
Salt shaker	14-19
Sauce, flat, 4½″	6-8
Spoonholder.	13-18
Sugar	
Hotel, divided metal lid	23-29
Regular	22-30
Tumbler.	10-13

Add 20 percent for gold decoration in excellent condition. No toothpick. Goblet produced from 1957 to 1970 in solid red and possibly other colors never made in original, as well as milk glass.

King's Curtain

King's Curtain

Maker unknown, 1880s. Clear, nonflint.

Butter dish, covered	$ 31-37
Cake stand	29-36

155

(continued)

Creamer.	20-26
Goblet.	19-23
Pitcher, water (ill.)	32-40
Plate, 7″.	14-19
Salt shaker	29-38
Saucedish, flat.	5-9
Spoonholder.	14-20
Sugar bowl	
Covered	27-34
Open	15-19
Wine	20-25

King's 500

Photo: Mr. and Mrs. A.M. Zinkeler, Chattanooga, Tenn.

King's 500

(King's Comet; erroneously Parrot; also called Bone Stem in goblet): King, Son & Company, Pittsburgh, 1891. Clear or partially frosted; transparent blue, medium green; usually with gold.

Bowl, berry, blue	$ 39-49
Butter, covered, blue,	
gold eyes.	99-110
Creamer, blue.	40-50
Cruet, blue (ill.)	122-137
Goblet, clear with frosting	46-57
Lamp (rare)	
Banquet, 13″.	140-160
Finger, pedestaled	84-95
Salt shaker	37-47
Spoonholder.	38-44
Sugar bowl	68-75

Probably the usual pieces, the usual prices for a glass of this date. The cruet shown is a beautiful blue.

Klondike

Klondike

(Dalzell's original name, Amberette; English Hobnail Cross): Dalzell; Beatty, who called it Klondike; and also Hobbs, their No. 321. Clear or frosted with color: amber, lilac/gold; nonflint.

Bowl, 8″.	$229-239
Butter dish, covered	400-420
Celery.	172-185
Champagne	650+
Creamer (ill.)	182-200
Cruet	500+
Cup.	89-97
Goblet.	400-430
Pitcher, square, tankard.	650-680
Relish.	67-75
Salt/Pepper, pr.	260-270
Sauce, flat, footed	69-82
Spoonholder.	188-202
Sugar bowl	
Covered	320-330
Open	179-194
Syrup.	600+
Toothpick holder, 2 types	345-367
Tray, 11″ x 8½″	142-155
Tumbler.	142-152
Vase, 8½″ high	228-237

Amberette is also used to describe other patterns. Klondyke is different pattern.

Knights of Labor

156

Knights of Labor

Bakewell, Pears & Company, Pittsburgh, 1879. Clear, canary, amber, blue; nonflint. Only the plates are known in color.

Mug
"Arbitration"	$ 69-81
Regular	51-65
Plate, bread (ill.)	108-116

Colors, 100 percent higher than clear prices listed.

Krom

Krom

Maker unknown, c. 1830s. Clear, flint.
Goblet (ill.)	$ 53-67

Lacy Daisy, New Martinsville's

New Martinsville, c. 1905. Clear, nonflint.

Condensed milk or pickle jar	
flat lid	$ 33-41
Mayonnaise bowl, 3 feet	21-29
Mayonnaise spoon, handle matches	
pattern on mustard handle	10-13
Mustard mug	32-40
Salt dip, individual, square	13-16

This version has crosshatching on the buttons.

Lacy Daisy, Westmoreland's

(Crystal Jewel, Daisy): Westmoreland, c. 1910-1930. Clear, amber; olive dish known in emerald green, and toy berry set that has a pale green tint in the glass was also made. Individual salt dip known in milk glass.

Bonbon (high open compote)	$ 30-35
Bowl, 8″	22-27
Butter	32-37
Celery tray, 10″ plate, folded	20-26
Creamer	23-28
Cruet	31-38
Olive, one handle	16-21
Pickle, 7″ plate, folded	14-17
Plate, 7″, 10″	15-25
Salt dip, round individual	6-9
Sauce, 4″ (toy master berry)	15-20
Spoonholder	16-19
Sugar	30-35
Toy berry set	
Individual (individual salt dip)	6-9
Master (master salt dip)	15-20

This version has a boxed star on the buttons. Milk glass add 50 percent; colors add 200 percent. No goblet or tumbler, but Floral Oval (Pittsburgh Daisy) stemware and tumbler, which has the same basic pattern elements, combines well. Confusing pattern: U. S. Daisy.

Lacy Dewdrop

(Beaded Jewel): Co-Operative Flint Glass Company, Beaver Falls, Pennsylvania, c. 1890; Phoenix (milk glass) after 1929. Clear, milk glass, nonflint.

Bowl, berry	$ 18-23
Butter dish, covered	30-40
Creamer	22-26
Goblet	24-28
Mug	21-27
Pitcher, water	36-41
Spoonholder	17-20
Sugar bowl	
Covered	32-36
Open	15-20
Tumbler	20-25

Milk glass, 30 percent higher than clear prices listed. Reproduced in milk glass water set, goblet, other pieces.

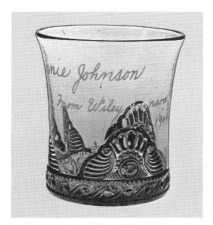

Lacy Medallion

Lacy Medallion

(Original name, Jewel; also see Colorado): U.S. Glass Company, c. 1908. Souvenir type, dark blue, green, ruby stain; opaque white, sometimes with flowers painted on sides, and clambroth, usually gilded. Prices are for green souvenir.

Creamer, toy	18-23
Cup	$ 40-47
Mug, 2 oz., 4 oz., 6 oz.	23-32
Salt shaker, flat base.	32-39
Sugar, open, toy	18-23
Tankard, 6 oz..	28-35
Toothpick (narrower than toy sugar). .	19-24
Tumbler (ill.)	29-34
Wine	17-20

Grouped with Colorado pattern, but glass scholars differentiate souvenir pieces as "Lacy Medallion."souvenirs in clear, 20 percent less; ruby worth 40 percent more than green prices listed.

Lacy Spiral

Lacy Spiral

(Colossus): Maker unknown, late 1880s. Attributed by Canadians to Burlington Glass Works. Clear, nonflint.

Bowl	$ 26-33
Butter dish, covered	37-47
Compote	
Covered, 6½" dia. x 10½" high	49-55
Open, 6½".	29-36
Creamer (ill.)	31-36
Goblet.	31-38
Pitcher, water (ill.)	55-62
Relish dish	11-16
Sauce, flat.	6-9
Spoonholder.	24-30
Sugar bowl, covered	34-40

Ladder with Diamond

Tarentum, c. 1903. Clear or scarce ruby stain, either with gold. Nonflint.

Butter.	$ 30-40
Celery.	19-24
Creamer	
Berry	13-17
Regular	22-26
Cruet, original faceted stopper.	28-33
Cup	6-10
Goblet.	18-22
Pitcher	30-40
Plate, 9¼".	19-23
Spoonholder.	15-20
Sugar	
Berry, open	13-17
Regular	30-36
Toothpick.	28-35
Tumbler.	13-16
Vase.	14-18

A cheese dish appears in the original ads, but appears to be the same as a conventional butter dish. Duncan's "Crown" is also called Ladder with Diamond. Their version of this pattern has the large diamond filled with diamonds, rather than buttons. Ruby add 200 percent.

Lafayet

Boston and Sandwich Company, 1830s. Boat-shaped salt dish. One reason this is a rare piece is because it's signed "Sandwich" inside the base and "B. & S. Glass Co." on the stern. This example is missing the coiled bowsprit. Known in crystal,

Lafayet

blue-green, purple-blue, cobalt; crystal and blue opalescent; opaque white, pale blue.

Crystal	$275+
Colors	425+
Opalescent colors	500+
Opaque	
Blue	600+
White	400+

Ten types are known and value depends on color and type.

Large Stippled Chain

Large Stippled Chain

Maker unknown, 1870s. Clear, nonflint.

Butter	$ 35-40
Creamer (ill.)	31-36
Goblet	26-30
Pitcher	66-74

Spooner	23-28
Sugar bowl	
Covered	35-40
Open	26-30

Late Crystal

Late Crystal

Richards & Hartley Company, 1888; also, McKee Bros., 1894, U.S. Glass Company, 1898 and others. Clear, nonflint.

Butter	$ 29-39
Celery	20-24
Compote	
Covered, low and high foot	39-47
Open, low foot only	22-29
Creamer	20-25
Egg cup	10-18
Goblet	10-18
Pitcher, water (ill.) (McKee)	42-54
Salt/Pepper, pr.	22-32
Sauce, flat or footed	4-7
Spoonholder	13-19
Sugar bowl	29-36
Tumbler	10-14
Wine	10-16

The pitcher shown took a metal lid that was attached through the upper handle. McKee made the pitcher, called a covered jug, in 6 oz., 10 oz., 16 oz., and 32 oz. sizes. The original ads do not indicate a rayed base, but the rest of the details are those of the McKee version.

Late Diamond Point Band

(Scalloped Diamond Point; Panel with Diamond Point): Central Glass Company, Wheeling, West Virginia, 1870s. Nonflint.

(continued)

Bowl, round, oval	$ 16-24
Butter dish, covered	29-36
Cake stand, 8″-12″ (5 sizes).	32-42
Cheese dish, covered, 8″	44-53
Compote, open, 7½″ high standard. . .	30-35
Creamer (ill.)	31-37
Goblet.	23-33
Pickle jar	50-60
Pitcher	51-60
Plate, 5″-9″ (5 sizes)	10-20
Sauce, 4″, flat or footed	5-8
Spoonholder.	20-25
Sugar bowl, covered, open	32-40
Wine	20-27

Compote known in rare cobalt with crystal stem; wine known in turquoise blue.

Late Panelled Grape

Late Panelled Grape

(Erroneously Darling Grape): Indiana Glass Company, after 1907. Clear or painted, nonflint.

Bowl	
Berry	$ 23-30
Salad, 7½″, legged	24-31
Butter dish, covered	35-42
Creamer (ill.)	34-41
Dish, covered	24-29
Goblet.	23-32
Pitcher, milk, water	46-52
Sauce, 4½″, legged.	8-11
Spoonholder.	23-28
Sugar (no grapes on lid)	25-31
Tumbler.	16-25
Wine	24-32

Add 30 percent for good gold with purple grapes.

Late Panelled Grape

Late Panelled Grape

(Also see Grape Jug): Jenkins, after 1900. Clear, nonflint.

Bowl, berry	$ 17-23
Butter dish, covered	26-31
Creamer (ill.)	27-32
Goblet.	22-27
Pitcher	
Milk.	31-41
Syrup	31-40
Water	30-40
Wine	22-29

Late Swan, Opaque

Late Swan, Opaque

Westmoreland Specialty Company, Grapeville, Pennsylvania, 1891-1892. Opaque white and opaque turquoise, nonflint.

Sugar bowl, covered
Opaque turquoise (ill.) 92-103
Opaque white . . . . $ 94-105

Late Thistle

Late Thistle

Cambridge, Ohio, c. 1903. Clear, emerald green; gold trim. Nonflint.

Butter dish, covered . . . . $ 47-53
Cake stand, small 40-47
Compote
Covered 49-54
Open 38-46
Honey dish, covered 35-43
Pitcher (ill.) 61-67
Sugar bowl 47-57
Tumbler 39-48

Lattice

(Diamond Bar): King, Son & Company, Pittsburgh, 1880. Clear, nonflint.

Bowl, 8″, oval . . . . $ 14-17
Butter dish, covered 32-37
Cake stand, 8″ 32-37
Celery 24-32
Compote, covered, high
standard, 8″ 37-47
Creamer (ill.) 21-26
Goblet 28-36
Pitcher, water 54-62
Plate, 10″ 14-25
Platter, clear, "Waste not,
want not" (11½″ x 7½″) 40-48
Sauce, flat, footed 5-10

Lattice

Spoonholder 15-18
Sugar bowl, covered 30-36
Syrup 46-55
Wine 20-30

Leaf and Dart

Leaf and Dart

(Original name, Pride): Sandwich, early; Richards & Hartley, 1870s. Clear, usually nonflint.

Butter dish, covered, flanged
bowl, (flat) . . . . $ 50-60
Celery vase, diamond band 35-44
Compote, 8″, low foot 32-39
Cordial 42-51
Creamer (ill.) 38-42
Egg cup, round ornaments 22-28
Goblet 28-34
Pitcher, water 145-165
Salt, footed 27-33
Spoonholder 24-32

161

(continued)

Sugar bowl, covered   42-48
Tumbler, footed, water   23-29
Wine   34-43

Leaf and Flower

Leaf and Flower

Hobbs, Brockunier & Co., Wheeling, West Virginia. A Wheeling, West Virginia, product made in the 1890s. Clear; clear and frosted with amber or green flowers; ruby stain.

Basket, celery (handled) . . . . $ 41-47
Bowl, 7″, 8″, 9″   39-44
Butter bowl, covered.   85-95
Caster set, 4 plain pieces
  on leaf tray   89-95
Celery vase (ill.)   70-80
Creamer.   42-49
Pitcher, water (ill.)   51-60
Salt shaker   38-43
Sauce, flat, 4½″, 5″.   24-27
Spoonholder.   34-40
Sugar   58-65
Syrup   158-175
Tray, celery   30-40

No goblet. Prices are for frosted/amber. Clear/frosted, deduct 50 percent; ruby, add 20 percent.

Leaf Bracket

Indiana Tumbler & Goblet (National) Company, Greentown, Indiana, 1900. Crystal, milk glass, chocolate, Nile green, cobalt, nonflint.

Berry bowl . . . . $ 55-63
Butter dish   152-169

Leaf Bracket

Celery tray   59-68
Creamer.   61-70
Cruet (ill.)   118-126
Salt/Pepper, pr.   100-126
Spoonholder.   70-80
Sugar, covered.   128-141
Tumbler.   50-60

Chocolate prices listed. Butter known in cobalt, olive, and sauce in milk glass. Nile green listings would be welcomed.

Leafy Scroll

U. S. Glass (Glassport) c. 1896. Clear, nonflint.

Butter. . . . . $ 24-30
Cake stand   29-36
Compote, high, covered   34-40
Cracker jar   32-40
Creamer.   18-23
Goblet.   19-22
Pitcher   31-37
Spoonholder.   15-18
Sugar   22-27
Tumbler.   12-15

Legged Trough

Maker and date unknown. Berry spray on underside. How many pieces other than the creamer (sugar, tumbler, etc.) were made is unknown to the editors. It must have taken some doing to remove it from the mold! If you know—*write!*

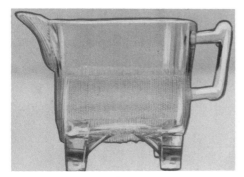

Legged Trough

Lens and Star

(Star and Oval): O'Hara Glass Company, Pittsburgh, c. 1886. Clear or with frosted lenses; nonflint.

Bowl, waste	$ 16-25
Butter dish, covered	42-51
Celery	23-31
Creamer	28-32
Pitcher, water	45-54
Sauce	8-10
Spoonholder	16-20
Sugar bowl, covered	35-44
Syrup	40-50
Tray, handled, (water)	40-49
Tumbler	19-27

No goblet. Clear worth 20 percent less than frosted prices given.

Liberty Bell

(Centennial): Gillinder & Company, Philadelphia. Made for 1876 Centennial. Rare in milk glass. Nonflint.

Butter dish, covered	$140-150
Celery	80-90
Child's table set (4 pc.)	170-178
Compote, open, 6″, 8″	79-89
Creamer	
Plain handle	102-112
Reeded, applied handle	129-137
Goblet	68-75
Pitcher, water	539-575
Plate, 6″, 8″, 10″	75-102
Platter, 9¼″ × 13″, Independence	
signers' names on border (ill.) . . .	154-179
Salt	
Celery dip, individual, oval	29-35
Salt/Pepper, pr.	138-148
Spoonholder, pedestal base	90-111
Sugar bowl	
Covered	121-132
Open	47-57

Milk glass, 150 percent higher than clear prices listed. Reproduced.

Liberty Bell

Liberty Bell Novelty Bank

Liberty Bell Novelty Bank

This bell was made for the St. Louis Exposition in 1903.

Liberty Bell bank (ill.) . . . . $ 49-58

Lightning

Lightning

(Chain Lightning): U. S. Glass Company
(Tiffin), Gas City, Indiana, 1890s. It was
called Chain Lighting in the factory. Clear,
nonflint.

Bowls, several styles	$ 15-22
Butter, covered	24-30
Cake stand	22-29
Celery vase	15-19
Compote	
Covered	45-53
Open	34-42
Creamer	
Berry tankard	12-16
Regular (ill.)	17-22
Goblet	34-42
Pitcher, water (2 types)	47-56
Sauce, flat	5-7
Spoonholder	37-45
Sugar bowl	
Berry	12-16
Regular	24-28
Wine	15-20

Lily-of-the-Valley

Lily-of-the-Valley

Sandwich, 1870s. Clear, etched, nonflint.

Butter dish, footed, on	
three feet	$112-127
Celery	38-44
Compote, covered, high standard	84-93
Creamer, on three feet	
pressed handle (ill.)	59-64
Cruet, tall stopper, pedestal	105-119
Dish, oval	30-34
Goblet	44-52
Sauce, flat	11-15
Spoonholder, on three feet	49-58
Sugar bowl, on three feet	88-105
Wine (scarce)	65-95

Lincoln Drape

Lincoln Drape

Sandwich, late 1860s. Clear, milk-white,
sapphire blue (both rare); flint.

Butter dish	$110-125
Celery	114-126
Compote	
Covered	139-156
Open, low standard	60-69
Creamer	132-140
Decanter	250+
Egg cup	46-54
Goblet (ill.)	78-88
Pitcher, water	362-371
Plate, 6″	78-85
Spoonholder	46-54
Sugar bowl, open	65-74
Tumbler	111-125

Colors, 100 percent higher than clear prices listed.

Lined Band Round Thumbprint

Maker unknown, c. 1860. Clear, flint.

Champagne	$ 50-56
Compote, open	48-55

Lined Band Round Thumbprint

Goblet.	32-41
Tumbler, footed	27-36
Wine (ill.)	37-46

Lion

Lion

(Frosted Lion): Gillinder & Sons, Philadelphia, 1870s. Clear, frosted.

Bread plate, frosted center	
oval, 12¼"	$ 78-96
Butter dish, lion's head finial	110-117
Celery, etched	79-87
Compote, 7"	
Covered, high standard	155-164
Covered, low standard, oval	115-122
Creamer, frosted lion on base	73-79
Goblet.	69-78
Marmalade jar (ill.)	85-95
Pitcher	
Milk	370-410
Syrup, metal top	238-244
Water	210-224
Sauce, footed	19-25

Spoonholder.	57-64
Sugar bowl, rampant lion finial . . .	77-87
Wine, frosted	184-215
Reproduced.	

Lion and Baboon

Lion and Baboon

Maker unknown, a humorous design of the 1880s. Clear or with frosted heads.

Butter dish, covered	$169-175
Creamer (ill.)	113-122
Compote, covered	143-164
Spoonholder.	90-100
Sugar bowl, covered	142-156

Kamm lists a miniature four-piece table set. Do you have it?

Lion Head

Lion Head

Miniature set, possibly Gillinder & Sons, c. 1870s. Clear or frosted, nonflint.

5-piece table set (ill.)	$375-400

Little Owl

(Menagerie): Bryce, Higbee & Company, Pittsburgh, mid-1880s. This is part of a Menagerie Toy Set that includes "Bear"

165

(continued)

Little Owl

covered sugar, "Fish" spoonholder, "Turtle" butter dish. Crystal, amber, and blue. Opaque, glass-eyed Challinor versions are not part of the set. Reproductions (1970s?) in chocolate or purple slag by Imperial.

Creamer, 3¾" high (ill.) . . . . $ 75-100

Little River

Little River

Maker unknown, 1870s. Clear, possibly colors.

Pickle caster in frame . . . . $ 92-110
Pickle jar (ill.) 60-67
Same family as Cape Cod, Canadian, and New England.

Log Cabin

Log Cabin

Central Glass Company, Wheeling, West Virginia, 1875. Clear, nonflint. Rare in colors.

Butter dish	$290-315
Compote, covered, on	
stand (ill.)	250-260
Creamer.	127-142
Mustard, "Tecumseh," not part	
of pattern	79-88
Pitcher, water	287-294
Sauce	30-39
Spoonholder.	104-115
Sugar bowl (rare), covered	193-204

Sugar and creamer reproduced recently.

Loganberry and Grape

(Blackberry and Grape; Raspberry and Grape): Dalzell, Gilmore & Leighton, mid-1880s. Clear, nonflint.

Butter dish, covered	$ 50-60
Celery.	35-42
Creamer, 7" high, pedestal	41-49
Goblet, jelly, rounded bowl	16-21
Pitcher, water (ill.)	50-60
Tumbler.	20-24

Loganberry and Grape

Part of a grouping from same molds, including Cherry and Fig, Strawberry and Currant, and Cornucopia. Editors have not seen better type of goblet, but it should exist. Kamm refers to two types. Some obvious reproductions in clear and colors that were not made in the original.

Long Buttress

Fostoria c. 1904, and New Martinsville (salve jar, known). Clear or with iridized finish (known in toothpick).

Butter.	$ 29-34
Celery.	18-20
Creamer	
Individual	12-15
Regular	19-22
Pickle jar, metal lid	30-36
Pin tray, oblong, metal lid	14-17
Pomade, metal lid ("salve")	13-16
Salt dip, individual	10-12
Salt shaker	11-15
Spoonholder.	14-16
Sugar	
Individual, handled	13-16
Regular	25-31
Syrup	33-39
Toothpick	27-33
Tumbler.	12-15

No goblet. Confusing patterns: Portland (some Long Buttress pieces are mistakenly shown in museum collections of Portland pattern), and New Martinsville's Placid that has flat rather than grooved buttresses. Iridized finish add 25 percent.

Long Maple Leaf

Long Maple Leaf

Maker unknown, c. 1890. Clear, nonflint.

Creamer, 4⅝″ high (ill.) . . . . $ 25-32

Loop

Loop

(O'Hara; Seneca Loop): Made from the 1850s by O'Hara Glass Company, Curling/Ringwalt, and James B. Lyon & Company, 1860s. Then Gillinder & Sons; Portland Glass Company, 1870s, who called it Portland Petal. McKee first shows in 1880. Nonflint and flint.

Butter bowl, covered.	$ 56-64
Cake stand	162-179
Celery.	51-63
Compote	
Covered, high standard, 8″, 9″ dia. .	90-125
Open, 9″ dia., lobed rim	64-78
Creamer, 6″ high, pressed	
handle, nonflint	33--41
Egg cup	31-40
Goblet.	28-38
Pitcher, water, applied handle	150+
Spoonholder.	28-37

167

(continued)

Sugar bowl
Covered   64-72
Open   30-35
Wine   34-39

Prices are for flint, except creamer. Nonflint worth half. O'Hara is a generic name used by many factories.

Loop and Dart with Round Ornaments

Loop and Dart with Round Ornaments

Portland Glass Company, Portland, Maine, c. 1869. Clear, nonflint and flint.

Butter dish, covered . . . . $ 49-55
Butter pat.   23-32
Compote, covered, high   70-77
Creamer.   39-45
Egg cup   25-34
Goblet (ill.)   29-34
Pitcher, water   79-99
Spoonholder.   32-41
Sugar bowl
Covered   43-51
Open   30-36

Nonflint, 25 percent lower than flint prices listed.

Loop and Moose Eye

(Bull's Eye and Loop): Was called "Mirror" in McKee's 1864-1868 catalogs. Clear, flint.

Creamer, pressed handle. . . . . . . $ 35-42
Egg cup   30-36
Goblet.   37-47

Loop and Moose Eye

Sugar bowl, covered   45-55
Tumbler.   42-48

The pattern McKee called "Mirror," shown as early as 1864 up to 1868 in their catalogs, is indeed "Loop and Moose Eye." Shown in Metz 18 No. 149, her Millard 108 reference is incorrect: his "Loop and Moose Eye" does not match hers, and she acknowledges the stems are different, but failed to notice that in hers, the eyes are over the loops, and in Millard's, they are offset. Millard's photo is also Lee VG 57, "Bull's Eye and Loop." Unitt copied the Metz error. Also see Mirror listing.

Loop with Dewdrop

Loop with Dewdrop

Earlier maker unknown; Produced by U.S. Glass Company, 1892. Nonflint.

Bowl, 5″, 6″, 7″, 8″ . . . . $ 14-18
Butter dish, covered   32-37
Compote, open, jelly, ...   14-18
Creamer (ill.)   18-23
Goblet.   19-25
Pitcher, water   33-43
Plate, bread (oval)   23-28
Salt shaker (scarce)   22-28

Sauce, flat.	4-7
Spoonholder.	11-16
Sugar bowl, covered	32-37
Syrup.	41-53
Tumbler.	12-17
Wine (uncommon).	24-30

No toothpick.

Loops and Drops

Loops and Drops

(New Jersey): Maker unknown, c. 1890s. Clear, ruby-flashed, nonflint.

Butter dish, covered (ill.)	$ 48-53
Creamer.	49-53
Goblet.	31-37
Spoonholder.	34-41
Sugar bowl, covered	50-55

Ruby-flashed, 50 percent higher than clear prices listed.

Lorraine

New Martinsville, c. 1903. Clear, with frosted appearance because of tiny rosetted stars making up the pattern; or with key band in ruby stain. Nonflint

Butter.	$ 35-42
Creamer.	29-32
Pitcher	45-55
Spoonholder.	25-30
Sugar	32-37
Tumbler.	17-21

Ruby stain add 100 percent to clear prices listed for this elusive pattern.

Louis XV

Northwood Glass Company, Indiana, Pennsylvania, 1898. Clear, custard, green. Flint and nonflint.

Louis XV

	Custard
Berry set	
Large bowl.	$112-136
Small bowl.	36-45
Butter dish, covered.	184-210
Creamer.	73-89
Cruet	169-177
Pitcher, water.	190-230
Salt/Pepper, pr.	153-162
Spoonholder.	83-91
Sugar bowl, covered (ill.).	110-130
Tumbler, water	59-68

Louise

(Starred Jewel): Fostoria, c. 1901. Clear, nonflint.

Butter.	$ 27-33
Compote, high, covered	32-41
Creamer.	19-24
Salt shaker	14-19
Sauce, flat.	5-8
Spooner.	14-17
Sugar	25-30
Toothpick.	30-34

Goblet does not appear in the literature.

Louisiana Purchase Exposition

The World's Fair held in St. Louis, Missouri, 1904, to commemorate the centennial of the Louisiana Purchase. Plates and iced tea (or beverage) glasses were popular souvenirs. Crystal, crystal with frosted center, milk glass.

169

(continued)

Louisiana Purchase Exposition

Plate, "Festival Hall," Forget
Me Not rim, 7¼" dia. . . . . $ 30-36
Tumbler (ill.) 23-32

Lucere

(Erroneously Lucerne): Fostoria, c. 1905.
Clear or with gold, nonflint.

Bowl, oval . . . . $ 17-22
Butter. 33-40
Champagne 27-33
Cracker jar 46-52
Creamer. 20-25
Cup 10-13
Goblet. 21-26
Jelly
High foot, 4¾" dia. x 4½" high 14-19
Low foot, 4" 10-13
Plate, 8½". 17-24
Salt shaker 13-17
Spoonholder. 14-18
Sugar 30-34
Toothpick. 30-36
Wine 25-29

The pattern is Fostoria's 1515 and variations in
some of the forms such as the salt shakers are
numbered 1515 1/2.

Lutz

(Ball and Swirl): McKee Bros., Jeannette, Pennsylvania, 1894. Clear, nonflint.

Creamer, 6", tankard. . . . . $ 21-27
Also see Ray listing.

Madison

(Original name, Crystal): James B. Lyon
& Company, Pittsburgh, c. 1860.

Madison

Butter, covered bowl, 7" dia. . . . . . . $ 69-75
Compote
Covered, 6", 7" dia., high 90-98
Low foot, 7" 72-82
Creamer, applied handle. 64-70
Spoonholder, 5¼" pedestal,
lobed rim 41-46
Sugar bowl, complete (base ill.) 63-74

In the same ad, Lyon used the name "Crystal"
for this and three other patterns. Goblet?

Magna

Co-operative, c. 1898. Clear or with gold,
nonflint.

Butter. . . . . $ 23-29
Creamer. 16-20
Goblet. 17-21
Salt, flat master 11-15
Salt shaker 12-16
Spoonholder. 14-17
Sugar 20-25

Confusing patterns: Rex, Josephine's Fan.

Magnet and Grape, Frosted Leaf

Magnet and Grape, Frosted Leaf

Magnet and Grape, Frosted Leaf

Traditionally attributed to Portland, and Sandwich, 1860s. Clear flint glass with frosted leaf.

Butter dish	$131-140
Celery	200-207
Champagne	128-140
Compote, open (scarce)	148-162
Creamer (ill.)	172-196
Egg Cup (ill.)	81-95
Goblet	56-65
Salt, master	50-60
Sauce	13-19
Spoonholder	62-74
Sugar	
Covered	112-122
Open	39-43
Tumbler	114-128
Wine	127-149

Reproduction creamer and sugar, goblet embossed "MMA".

Magnet and Grape, Stippled Leaf

Attributed by early authors to Sandwich, 1870s. Clear glass with stippled leaf, nonflint.

Butter dish, acorn knob	$ 39-46
Compote, open	28-33
Creamer	42-48
Goblet	27-34
Pitcher	90-101
Salt, footed	22-29
Saucedish, 4"	5-8
Spoonholder	25-31

Sugar bowl	34-42
Wine	32-39

Lighter weight with less brilliance than the Frosted Leaf version. Also comes with clear leaf.

Maine

Maine

(Stippled Panelled Flower): U.S. Glass Company, Pittsburgh, early 1890s. Clear, emerald green. Also with flowers and leaves, color stained.

Bowl, 6", 7", 8"	$ 21-25
Creamer (ill.)	25-32
Dish, relish	13-19
Mug, handled	31-40
Pitcher	42-52
Sauce, flat	10-14
Spoonholder	23-32
Sugar bowl, covered	34-44
Toothpick holder (rare)	80-92
Tumbler	16-21

Green, 100 percent higher than clear prices listed.

Maize

(continued)

Maize

W. L. Libbey & Son Co., Toledo, Ohio, 1889. Iridized crystal; opaque white; and ivory (custard); the latter two with leaves colored blue, brown, green, or yellow. Blown molded.

Bowl
    Berry, 9", white, green leaves $132-149
    Finger, 5" 40-47
Celery vase, white, green leaves . . . 118-135
Creamer. 70-80
Decanter, qt., clear,
    gold husks 153-169
Pitcher, syrup, clear,
    green leaves (ill.). 174-189
Spoonholder, white, green leaves. . . 72-89
Sugar bowl, covered, clear 114-129
Toothpick holder
    Ivory, blue leaves 234-252
    Ivory, brown leaves 193-210
Tumbler, ivory; no paint. 48-52

Recent (and obvious) reproductions. Two sizes of tall lamps, and a parlor lamp were also made and are very rare.

Manhattan

Manhattan

U.S. Glass Company, 1902. Clear, gilt in the sunken circles; rose stain with gilt; nonflint.

Bowl, berry, 7", 8", 8½", 9½",
    10", 11", 12½" . . . . $ 15-32
Bowl, punch, large, cups 120-140
Butter dish 37-44
Cake stand 45-55
Celery vase, tall 22-29
Compote, 9½", 10½". 40-47
Creamer, individual, large 17-33
Pitcher, syrup (ill.) 50-58
Plate, 5", 9½", 11", 12" 15-22

Sauce, 5" footed, 4½" flat 10-15
Spoonholder. 19-24
Sugar bowl
    Covered 37-44
    Open, individual 15-21
Tumbler, iced tea, water. 18-24
Water bottle. 37-42

Rose stain 100 percent higher than clear. Reissued in inferior quality, Depression era, slight variation.

Manhattan

Manhattan

Tarentum Glass Company, Tarentum, Pennsylvania, 1895. Clear and with ruby stain. Nonflint.

Butter dish, covered (ill.) . . . . $ 35-42
Cake stand 35-42
Celery. 24-30
Creamer. 18-22
Cruet 31-39
Pitcher, water 37-43
Spoonholder. 21-26
Sugar bowl, covered 37-42
Tumbler. 13-18
Wine 23-32

Original ads show two spellings: Manhattan (probably correct) and Manhatton. Ruby stain worth 60 percent more.

Maple Leaf

Formerly attributed to Northwood Glass Company, 1890s and now known to be Dugan. Custard, Carnival, and limited opalescent in clear, blue, green. Nonflint.

Berry set
    Large bowl, pedestal, custard . . . $295-325
    Small bowl, custard 79-89

Maple Leaf

Butter dish, covered, custard	195-218
Carnival marigold	70-80
Carnival vivid	111-128
Creamer, custard (ill.)	90-116
Carnival marigold	44-53
Carnival vivid	65-73
Ice cream set, Carnival	
Large bowl	
Carnival vivid	117-123
Marigold.	63-69
Small bowl	
Carnival vivid	35-40
Marigold.	29-36
Pitcher, custard	268-285
Carnival marigold	87-94
Carnival vivid	160-175
Spoonholder, custard	89-110
Carnival marigold	49-60
Carnival vivid	63-71
Sugar bowl, covered, custard.	145-165
Carnival marigold	41-50
Carnival vivid	77-92
Tumbler, custard	89-97
Carnival marigold	29-34
Carnival vivid	35-42

Maple Leaf

Maple Leaf

(Leaf): Gillinder & Sons, Greensburg, Pennsylvania, late 1880s. Clear or frosted, canary, amber, blue, nonflint. Mostly oval with log feet.

Butter dish, 6¼" oval	$ 63-74
Celery vase	40-49
Creamer.	42-49
Finger bowl (ill.).	24-30
Goblet, branch stem	48-54
Pitcher, large	72-82
Plate, 10½", Grant Peace	45-52
Sauce, 5", 6", footed	17-24
Spoonholder.	35-40
Sugar bowl	51-60
Tumbler.	30-38

Colors, 60 to 100 percent higher than the clear prices listed. Reproduced in clear and colors, especially goblet.

Marlboro

(Heart Plume, Rayed Pineapple, Rayed Divided Diamond Heart): U. S. Glass (Bryce), c. 1907. Clear or rose stained. Some with gold.

Bonbon, heart shaped	$ 13-17
Butter.	28-35
Creamer.	14-18
Cruet	30-37
Goblet.	29-35
Pitcher	
½ gal.	38-45
3 pint	32-37
Salt shaker	16-20
Spoonholder.	15-18
Sugar	25-30
Wine	25-30

Add 40 percent for rose stain. Confusing patterns: Rayed Heart, Cambridge's Sweetheart, and Ripley's Iverna.

Marquisette

Co-Operative Flint Glass Company, Beaver Falls, Pennsylvania, c. early 1880s. Clear, nonflint.

Butter dish, covered	$ 42-48
Celery.	33-38
Compote	
Covered, large, high standard	60-68
Open	22-32
Creamer, applied handle, 5⅝" high . .	39-47
Goblet.	22-29
Spoonholder.	24-29
Sugar bowl	
Covered	40-50
Open	17-22
Wine	29-36

Marsh Ferns

Riverside Glass Works, Wellsburg, West Virginia, c. 1889. Clear, engraved; nonflint. This was their No. 327.

Bowl	$ 19-24
Butter, flat, straight sides	34-40
Compote, high standard	
7″ dia., open	26-32
Creamer, tankard, 6″ high,	
applied handle	33-39
Goblet	37-46
Pitcher, ½ gal., applied handle	49-55
Spoonholder, flat base	14-19
Sugar bowl, covered	30-37

Prices are for engraving. Clear worth 25 percent less.

Marsh Pink

Marsh Pink

Maker unknown, Ohio, 1880s. Clear, rare pieces in amber; nonflint.

Bowl, open and covered	$ 20-27
Butter dish, covered	48-58
Cake stand, small	27-32
Compote, covered	52-62
Jam jar	42-51
Pitcher (ill.)	52-60
Spoonholder	22-29
Sugar bowl, covered	37-44

Amber, 150 percent higher than clear prices listed.

Maryland

U.S. Glass Company, one of their States series. Clear, with gold, nonflint.

Bowl	$ 33-42

Maryland

Butter dish, covered	42-50
Compote, open	41-50
Custard	23-36
Creamer	35-44
Cruet	27-35
Honey dish	12-16
Goblet	37-44
Pitcher, water, with gold (ill.)	45-53
Plate, bread	28-34
Sauce	11-15
Spoonholder	40-44
Sugar bowl, covered	37-46
Tumbler	39-47
Wine	35-43

Mascotte

Ripley & Company, Pittsburgh, c. 1884, clear, plain or engraved. Reissued by U.S. Glass Company after 1891. Nonflint.

Butter dish	
Plain	$ 45-57
Horseshoe-shaped, marked	
"Maud S." (rare)	88-107
Celery, etched	33-41
Compote, 7″, 8″	
Covered	49-60
Open	32-44
Creamer	33-39
Dish	22-31
Goblet	31-36
Spoonholder	24-29
Sugar bowl, covered	42-47
Tumbler	22-27
Wine	27-35

The cylinder and globe apothecary jars and the four- and five-piece stack sets were reissued by Tiffin and appear in a 1956 catalog.

Masonic

(Inverted Prism; Prism with Double Block): McKee Glass Company, Jeannette, Pennsylvania, and National Glass Company, c. 1894. Clear, chocolate, ruby stain, amber stain; nonflint.

Bowl, berry, 9″, toothed rim	$ 24-34
Butter bowl	
Covered, flat or pedestal	47-54
Open, flared or straight	18-22
Cake stand, 9″, 10″	40-50
Creamer	30-38
Dish, oblong	12-16
Honey, square, covered	52-65
Pitcher, water	58-66
Sardine box, open, rectangular	21-25
Spoonholder	24-29
Sugar bowl, covered	44-54
Toothpick	
Plain	36-42
Ruby stain	180-200
Tumbler	28-33

Vase and handled triangular nappy are the only known pieces in chocolate. An 1897 Sears catalog shows 39 pieces for $2.75!

Massachusetts

Massachusetts

(Geneva): U.S. Glass Company, 1898. Clear, cobalt, emerald green, ruby stain, nonflint.

Basket, toy	$ 100+
Butter dish, covered	50-58
Cologne, 7½″ high	33-42
Creamer	28-33
Cruet, miniature with stopper,	
(3½″ to spout)	62-72

Dish, candy	14-19
Goblet	38-40
Jug, rum (ill.)	67-89
Pitcher, water	65-73
Plate, 8″	39-43
Salt shaker	20-26
Shot glass	12-18
Spoonholder, handled	19-24
Sugar, covered, handled	39-43
Table lamp	64-73
"Teapot" (intended as rum	
jug) (ill.)	109-121
Toothpick	52-64
Vase, 6⅝″, 10″	16-28
Water bottle	49-54

Butter dish recently reproduced in clear, pink, light green. Emerald green worth 50 percent more (toothpick, 150 percent); cobalt or ruby worth 100 percent more.

William McKinley Campaign Items

William McKinley Campaign Items

Most were made by McKee & Bros. in 1896. Nonflint.

Bread plate, "His Will Be Done"	
8″ x 10½″ oval (ill.)	$ 39-48
Mug	
Covered	62-72
Open	34-41
Plate	
"Protection and Plenty," 7″, 9″ . . .	39-49
Openwork, "Gothic" edge, 9″ dia.	
Black amethyst	69-79
Opaque white	49-55
Colored decal portrait	36-42
Platter, rectangular, 7¾″ x 10½″,	
"Gold Standard" ("Feather Duster" or	
"Huckel" pattern)	200+
Tumbler	

(continued)

Clear, "Protection and Plenty"
in base   52-62
Frosted   59-68

Medallion

Medallion

(Spades; Hearts and Spades): Maker unknown, 1880s. Clear, yellow, amber, blue, apple green; nonflint.

Butter dish . . . . $	38-47
Cake stand	40-47
Celery vase	27-34
Compote, covered, high	
standard	46-54
Creamer	28-34
Goblet	24-29
Pitcher, water (ill.)	49-60
Sauce, flat, footed	6-11
Spoonholder	17-24
Sugar bowl, covered	29-38
Tumbler	13-19
Wine	20-27

Yellow, amber, blue, 40 percent; apple green, 75 percent higher than clear prices listed.

Medallion Sunburst

(Tiffany): Unmarked Higbee, c. 1905. Clear, nonflint.

Banana dish, flat . . . . $	16-19
Banana stand	28-35
Bowl	
Round	14-17
Square, 8″	15-20
Butter	25-35
Butter pat (erroneously described as	
cup plate or lens cover)	5-10
Cake stand	24-29

Celery	
Tray	15-19
Vase	17-21
Compote, high covered	31-38
Creamer	
Individual	10-13
Regular	19-26
Cruet	24-30
Cup	6-9
Goblet	15-20
Jam or pickle jar has a diamond in	
the design not found in	
other pieces: complete	30-36
Mug	10-14
Mustard (flat rim, patterned lid has	
spoonhole)	30-38
Olive, one handle	14-18
Pitcher	
Milk	22-29
Water	26-31
Plate	
Round, 6½″, 7½″, 9½″	12-18
Square, 7¼″	14-19
Relish	10-12
Salt dip, individual	8-11
Salt shaker	14-19
Sauce, 4″, 4½″	6-8
Spoonholder	15-18
Sugar	
Individual handled, covered	16-20
Regular, no handles	24-27
Toothpick (scalloped rim)	22-26
Tumbler	12-15
Vase, set of three graduated	30-39
Wine	18-23

Confusing name: Sunburst Medallion, a different pattern.

Melrose

Brilliant Glass Works, Brilliant, Ohio, 1887-1888, continuing in 1889 by Greensburg Glass Company, Greensburg, Pennsylvania. Clear, ruby stain, plain or etched; nonflint.

Butter dish, covered, flanged . . . . $	43-52
Cake stand	30-37
Celery, 6″ high, flat rim	25-32
Compote, covered, high	
standard, 6″, 8″	39-48
Creamer, tankard, 5¼″ high	27-36
Goblet	19-25
Pitcher	
Quart	40-46
½ gal.	42-47

Plate, 7″, 8″	12-16
Spoonholder.	23-27
Sugar bowl, covered	39-46
Tumbler.	18-25
Wine	18-22

Etched, 20 percent higher than clear prices listed. If you are desperate for a butter base, the lid will fit a 7″ plate!

Mephistopheles

Pitcher, applied handle, clear	78-85

Memphis

Memphis

(Doll's Eye): Northwood Glass Company, 1908-1910. Clear, emerald with gold; Carnival. Prices are for green with good gold.

Berry set	
Bowl.	$ 40-46
Sauce	14-19
Butter dish, covered	100-115
Creamer.	43-55
Fruit bowl and base	62-71
Pitcher, water (ill.)	159-167
Punch set (Carnival marigold or green)	
Bowl and base	169-185
Cup	22-32
Spoonholder.	47-56
Sugar bowl, covered	68-75

Clear worth 30 percent less.

Mephistopheles

Germany; also made in this country, late 1800s. Clear, frosted, opaque.

Ale glass, "Germany," frosted	$ 51-59
Mug, opaque white (ill.)	54-63

Michigan

Michigan

(Loop and Pillar): U.S. Glass Company, c. 1893. Clear; some pieces with combinations of two stains, with or without painted decorations; nonflint. Ruby stained scarce.

Bowl, berry, 7½″, 8½″, 10″	$ 27-34
Butter dish, covered	
Large	42-50
Toy	84-97
Creamer	
Individual, tankard, 6 oz..	21-28
Large	27-35
Toy	36-42
Cruet	34-42
Goblet (ill.)	37-42
Pitcher, tankard.	45-54
Salt/Pepper, pr., 3 types	38-47

(continued)

Spoonholder

Large	24-30
Toy	36-42

Sugar bowl, covered

Large	47-54
Toy	30-38

Toothpick (larger than toy

spooner)	60-70
Tumbler	39-42
Wine	34-42

Toothpick reproduced in several colors.

Millard

(Fan and Flute): U. S. Glass (Hobbs), c. 1893. Clear or with panels in amber or ruby stain, with or without engraving.

Bowl, 7″, 8″, 9″	$ 14-17
Butter	30-36
Cake stand	33-38
Celery tray	16-19
Celery vase	19-25
Compote, open, 6″,7″, 8″, 9″	18-30
Creamer	22-26
Cruet	26-33
Cup	10-12
Dish, oblong, 7″, 8″, 9″, 10″	14-20
Goblet	20-24
Pitcher	31-37
Plate, 7″, 9″, 10″	15-20
Salt shaker, clear	16-20

Sauce

Flat, 4″, 4½″	5-8
Footed, 4″	10-13
Ice cream, 5″	10-13
Spoonholder	15-18
Sugar	23-28
Syrup	34-40
Toothpick	27-33
Tumbler	13-16
Wine	20-24

For engraved amber stain, add 100 percent; engraved ruby stain, add 200-250 percent to clear prices listed. Clear with engraved panels add 30 percent. Similar pattern: Kentucky.

Minerva

Sandwich glass, 1870s. Clear, nonflint.

Butter dish, covered	$ 69-77
Cake stand, 8″, 10″	96-114

Compote, high and low

standard, 7″ dia.	92-101
Creamer	43-52
Goblet	88-97

Minerva

Marmalade jar, w/lid	79-88
Pitcher, water, 9½″ high	130-160

Plate

Closed handles, 8″ plus handles	54-63
Large, 10″ plus handles, "Mars"	52-56

Platter, "Give Us This Day,"

oval, "Minerva"	66-74

Sauce, flat round, footed

round, 3¾″, 4¼″ dia.	10-15
Spoonholder	34-39
Sugar bowl, lid perfect, (ill.)	82-91

The four- piece table set was made in two types, so the lids and bases are not interchangeable.

Minnesota

(Erroneously Muchness; U. S. A.): U.S. Glass Company, c. 1898. Clear, ruby (scarce), or green with gold decoration, nonflint.

Bowl, 9½″, 10″, oval

Berry, round,	$ 25-30
Flared edge, 5″	10-13
Butter dish, covered	42-49
Celery tray, 10″, 13″	19-27

Compote, open

Round, 6″, 7″, 8″	32-42
Square, 6″, 7″, 8″	32-42
Creamer	26-31
Goblet	24-29
Humidor, metal jewelled top	125+
Pitcher, water	48-56
Spoonholder	20-25
Sugar bowl, covered	42-49
Tumbler	14-19

Green with gold decoration, 25 percent higher than prices listed. Embossed advertising found on double toothpicks.

Mirror

Mirror

McKee's "Concave" (1864-1871 catalogs list only pieces indicated below), and others. Clear, flint. The tumbler illustrated and some of the listings refer to a general or "generic" mirror design.

Ale	$ 32-39
Compote, 9", scalloped	
Rim ("Concave")	55-64
Goblet, bulb or plain stem	34-39
Lamp, tall ("Concave," atypical). . .	112-127
Salt dip, individual ("Concave") . . .	11-16
Spoonholder or spill	30-37

It appears that an error has been perpetuated over the years. The pattern McKee called "Mirror," shown as early as 1864 up to 1868 in their catalogs, is not the one pictured here, but is indeed "Loop and Moose Eye" (see). Shown in Metz 18 No. 149, her Millard 108 reference is incorrect: his "Loop and Moose Eye" does not match hers, and she acknowledges the stems are different, but failed to notice that in hers, the eyes are over the loops, and in Millard's, they are offset. Millard's photo is also Lee VG 57, "Bull's Eye and Loop." Unitt copied the Metz error.

Missouri

(Palm and Scroll): U.S. Glass Company, after 1891. Clear, emerald green, nonflint.

Butter dish, covered	$ 39-46
Celery	27-32
Compote, high or low standard.	39-42
Creamer.	27-32
Cruet (scarce)	53-68
Goblet.	39-47
Pitcher, pint, ½ gal..	44-52
Spoonholder.	22-27
Sugar bowl, covered	39-47
Tumbler.	15-20

Blue, green, 50 percent higher than clear prices listed. Metz lists canary and amethyst; confirmation of either would be appreciated.

Mitered Prisms

(Original name, Trump): Model Flint Glass Co., late 1890s. Clear; goblet is listed in blue. Nonflint.

Bowl, 6"	$ 10-13
Butter.	30-35
Cake stand, 9" dia..	28-33
Compote	
Covered, 5" jelly	26-32
Open, 6½" dia. x 6¼" high	14-17
Creamer.	18-22
Cruet, original square peaked stopper	
3½ oz. "sham"; 4 oz..	24-30
Cup (also came with tin lid as jelly	
container)	10-12
Goblet.	15-20
Salt shaker	13-16
Sauce, 4" flat	4-7
Spoonholder, handled	15-18
Sugar, handled	29-34
Syrup	31-37
Tumbler.	13-17
Wine	15-20

A Gem goblet (also made by Model) from an original ad is mislabeled Trump.

Mitred Bars

(Mitred Diamond Points): Bryce Bros., Pittsburgh, c. 1885. Clear, nonflint.

Bowl, oval	$ 25-34
Butter dish, covered	38-44
Cake stand	31-40
Celery.	37-46
Creamer, covered	42-52
Goblet.	38-47
Spoonholder.	28-31
Sugar bowl, covered	38-47
Wine	26-30

Model Peerless

Model Flint Glass Co., c. 1895. Clear or green, may have gold. Nonflint.

Bowl, square crimped	$ 14-19
Butter.	26-30
Cake stand, 11"	33-40
Celery	20-25
Cordial	15-20

(continued)

Cracker jar	32-38
Creamer	17-20
Cruet	24-28
Decanter, patterned stopper	
Pint	29-35
22 oz.	36-42
Olive, one handle	13-18
Salt shaker	16-19
Spoonholder	13-16
Sugar	20-25
Toothpick (scarce)	34-40
Tray, cordial	26-32
Whiskey (shot glass)	10-12
Wine	13-16

Green worth 100 percent more. A cordial tray pictured in the literature is called Thumbelina, a case of mistaken identity. Company prefix needed as there are other Peerless patterns. Goblet does not appear in the literature.

Monkey

Monkey

George A. Duncan and Sons, Pittsburgh, 1880s. Clear and opalescent, nonflint.

Bowl, waste	$115-127
Butter dish, covered	171-180
Celery	61-70
Creamer	118-126
Jar, pickle	59-68
Mug, 2 styles	80-90
Pitcher (ill.)	258-266
Spoonholder	120-130
Sugar	
Covered	177-187
Open	96-105
Toothpick holder	77-86
Tumbler	82-90

Opalescent, 90 percent higher than clear prices listed. Spoonholder and toothpick holder reproduced.

Monroe

Monroe

Maker unknown, made well before the Civil War. Clear and brilliant. Extremely rare in lamp. Shown here because too many patterns remain unidentified as to maker, etc. If you know, write to the Houston Museum, Chattanooga, Tennessee.

Lamp (rare) (ill.) . . . . $ 875+

Moon and Star

180

Moon and Star

Pioneer Glass Company, 1892; Wilson Glass Company, 1890, same name. Imperial, Cooperative Flint Glass Company, 1890s. Mold sold to Phoenix Glass Company, 1937. Many reproductions on market today. Clear, some pieces with color added, also milk glass.

Bowl, berry, 6″, 12½″	$ 23-29
Butter dish, covered	62-70
Cake stand, 6″ dia..	62-72
Celery.	50-60
Compote, covered, 7″, 8″, 10″, high standard	49-80
Creamer..	64-72
Goblet, clear, frosted	44-52
Pitcher, water (ill.)	122-130
Sugar bowl, covered, jeweled.	62-71
Tumbler, footed, flint	58-68
Wine	34-42

Morning Glory

Morning Glory

Sandwich, c. 1860s. Clear, flint.

Compote, open	$195-218
Creamer (rare)	365+
Egg cup	170+
Goblet (ill.)	274-285
Wine	158-167

Goblet and wine reproduced in clear and in color.

Mosque

Maker unknown, c. 1890. Water set described has heavy engraved ferns, identical on all pieces; a different fern engraving is known on the goblet.

Water set	
Goblet.	$ 18-24
Pitcher	34-39
Tray.	30-36
Waste bowl	21-25

Other pieces?

Murano

(Leaf and Fan): Greensburg, c. 1894. Clear, nonflint.

Cruet	$ 26-30
Salt shaker	14-18

A Murano pattern also by Greensburg is described in the literature as "an over-all floral simulating engraving," obviously not this one. Information, please!

Nail

Nail

Bryce Bros., Pittsburgh, 1885, and U. S. Glass after 1891. Crystal, or with ruby stain, etched.

Bowl	
Berry, 8″.	$ 22-27
Waste	30-35
Butter, covered	38-46
Creamer, 4½″ high (ill.)	28-33
Goblet	30-35
Pitcher, water	68-72
Salt/Pepper, pr..	45-65
Sauce, 4″ flat	8-11
Spoonholder..	22-27

(continued)

Sugar bowl

Covered	34-38
Open	18-26
Tumbler.	15-20
Vase, 7″	15-20

With ruby stain, 100 percent higher than clear prices listed. Etched, 30 percent more.

New England Pineapple

Creamer.	155-170
Decanter, with patterned stopper	150+
Goblet (ill.)	54-63
Sauce	12-15
Spoonholder.	40-46
Sugar bowl, covered	112-122
Tumbler, water	84-92

Goblet and wine reproduced.

Nailhead

Nailhead

(Gem): Fragments found at Sandwich are not proof of origin. Bryce, Higbee & Co., Pittsburgh. Nonflint.

Bread plate, 9″ round	$ 30-36
Butter dish	42-48
Cake stand, 4″ high, (common).	20-25
Celery.	28-34
Compote, covered, 6″	46-59
Creamer.	29-34
Goblet.	24-29
Pitcher, water (ill.)	47-55
Plate, round, 9″, square, 7″	17-34
Sauce	8-12
Spoonholder.	18-23
Sugar bowl, covered	35-43
Tumbler (scarce)	40-50
Wine	16-22

Kamm mentions orange decoration "in the grooves" and "clear aquamarine."

New England Pineapple

Boston & Sandwich Glass Company, c. 1860s. Clear, flint. Colored pieces rare.

Butter dish, covered	$143-155
Champagne	130-145
Compote, open	60-68

Niagara

Fostoria Glass Company, Moundsville, West Virginia, c. 1900. Clear, nonflint.

Bowl, berry	$ 10-16
Butter dish, covered	28-36
Celery vase	15-22
Creamer.	16-24
Pitcher, 2 qt.	25-32
Salt shaker	10-15
Sauce, 4″, flat	3-5
Spoonholder.	14-19
Sugar bowl, covered	30-35
Syrup	31-39
Tumbler.	10-13

U. S. Glass made a different Niagara pattern.

Northwood's Near-Cut

(Northwood No. 12; Locket; erroneously Dixie): trademarked Northwood, c. 1905. Clear or emerald green, either may have gold; ruby stain. Also made in carnival. Nonflint.

Basket, handled	$ 89-95
Bowl, 8¾″, 10″	27-33
Butter.	50-60

Compote	34-44
Creamer	36-41
Goblet	35-40
Pitcher	48-59
Plate	27-35
Salt shaker	24-30
Sauce, flat	14-17
Spoonholder	28-33
Sugar	42-49
Tumbler	18-23

Emerald green with good gold worth 150 percent more; ruby stain add 200 percent to clear prices listed.

Notched Bar

(Ball; Canadian "Crown," no proof of Canadian origin): McKee & Bros., Jeannette, Pennsylvania, c. 1894, at least up to 1917. Clear, nonflint. Rarely etched.

Butter dish, covered	
(cheese dish)	$125+
Creamer, individual, 4″ high	31-38
Cruet, original Maltese	
Cross stopper	30-40
Jar, jam or mustard, small, covered .	40-47
Spoonholder, small	31-42
Sugar bowl, covered, individual . . .	43-50

Jam jar known with embossed advertising in base. Although the butter is listed here, the cheese plate with the dome is the only "butter" we know of. The cruets are small.

Nova Scotia Buttons and Bows

(Swirl with Beaded Band): c. 1890. Clear, nonflint.

Bowl, 8″, 10″	$ 16-24
Butter	52-65
Creamer	40-45
Goblet	30-36
Honey, 3″	10-12
Pitcher	
Milk	39-43
Water, ½ gal.	42-49
Sauce, 4″	12-15
Spoonholder	29-33
Sugar	41-51
Wine (cordial)	33-39

Nova Scotia Grape and Vine

Nova Scotia Grape and Vine

(Ramsey Grape): Nova Scotia, Canada, late 1880s. Nonflint.

Bowl, 3″ x 7″ dia.	$ 30-36
Butter, covered	77-89
Cheese dish, covered	100-118
Compote	
6½″ dia., covered	65-73
Open	40-46
Creamer	42-47
Goblet	68-78
Pitcher, water, 9″, ½ gal. (ill.)	54-69
Plate, bread, 10¾″	50-60
Spoonholder	39-43
Sugar, covered	62-71

Confusing pattern, Jenkins Grape.

Nova Scotia Starflower

(Dewdrops with Flowers; Quantico): c. 1900. Clear, nonflint.

Butter	$ 42-48
Cake stand	30-37
Compote, open, high	30-38
Creamer	35-41
Goblet	36-42
Pitcher	50-60
Sauce, flat	10-14
Spoonholder	23-29
Sugar	39-45

At least two different blanks with pattern variations are included under this name and are probably two distinctly different patterns.

Nova Scotia Tassel and Crest

(Pins and Bells): Humphrey Glass Co., Nova Scotia, Canada, c. 1890. Clear, nonflint.

183

(continued)

Butter.	$ 55-65
Compote, covered,	
7" dia. x 10" high with lid	59-66
Creamer.	37-42
Pickle dish	20-26
Pitcher	52-62
Sauce, flat, 4"	12-16
Spoonholder.	28-33
Sugar	50-60

Nursery Tales

(Nursery Rhyme): U. S. Glass Company, 1880s. A miniature set; each piece shows different characters from old nursery tales. Clear, blue; opaque white, blue; nonflint.

Child's 4-piece set (butter	
dish, creamer, spoonholder,	
sugar bowl), clear	$210-235
Punch set with 6 cups, clear	195-220
Sauce (master berry), 4"	50-58

Opaque white, 50 percent; opaque blue, 100 percent; clear cobalt, 400 percent more than clear prices listed.

Occidental

Federal, c. 1910. A silvery glass with the design pressed to simulate engraving.

Pitcher	$ 32-36
Tumbler.	14-18

The water set probably came with a metal tray. Other pieces?

Octagonal Beehive Deep Dish

Octagonal Beehive Deep Dish

Boston and Sandwich, 1830-1850. It is 9¼" in diameter and was used to hold a compote. Clear, blue, yellow; flint.

Beehive dish (ill.)	$ 150+
Compote to match	
(extremely rare)	650+

A 7" bowl, 7¾" pink plate, 9½" green, and 9½" clear with purple stain are among the modern Duncan versions, nonflint, but almost identical. Heisey produced a similar line.

Odd Fellow

Odd Fellow

Probably Adams & Company, Pittsburgh, early 1880s, assuming Kamm's attribution is correct on the Horseshoe/Good Luck pattern. This goblet is made from the same mold. Clear, nonflint.

Goblet (ill.)	$ 35-42

No other pieces are known.

O'Hara Diamond

(Ruby Star; Sawtooth and Star): U.S. Glass Company (O'Hara), c. 1891. Clear, ruby stain, nonflint.

Bowl, 8", sawtooth edge	$ 24-32
Creamer.	35-42
Cup/saucer, custard	32-36
Goblet.	30-34
Pitcher, tankard.	45-54
Spoonholder.	34-42
Sugar bowl, covered	42-50
Tray	
Water, piecrust edge	50-60
Waste bowl	50-60

184

Ruby stain, 80 percent higher than clear prices listed.

Oneata

(Chimo): Riverside, c. 1907. Clear or amethyst stained. Nonflint.

Butter (lid atypical)	
Regular	$ 30-34
Toy	72-85
Creamer	
Regular	22-26
Toy	40-46
Cup, toy.	17-22
Goblet.	20-26
Punch bowl, toy	110-128
Spoonholder	
Regular	16-20
Toy (toothpick)	35-40
Sugar (lid atypical)	
Regular	30-34
Toy	60-70
Toothpick	35-40

Reproductions in clear and color in toy spooner (toothpick) and toy creamer.

One-Hundred-and-One

One-Hundred-and-One

(101): Maker unknown, late 1870s. Clear, nonflint. Canadian attribution based on the so-called "Burlington Mark" on applied handles is considered invalid by glass scholars. A Duncan catalog is known showing a scalloped-rim 4″ flat sauce, no beading in the ovals, and is the only possible evidence of origin so far.

Butter bowl, covered.	$ 48-55
Celery, pedestal, scalloped rim	59-67
Compote, covered, high foot, 7″ dia. . .	70-72

Creamer, pressed handle.	27-32
Goblet.	33-43
Lamp	
Flat, applied handle	53-63
Tall	85-99
Pickle, oval, tapered end.	12-17
Plate	
7″, 8″, 9″	18-28
Bread, round, "Give us this day", 9½″ (ill.)	50-59
Relish dish, oval, deep	21-27
Salt/Pepper, pr.	42-52
Sauce, flat, 4″, flat rim	7-10
Spoonholder, flat rim	50-54
Sugar bowl	40-48

Beading between ovals varies from 1 to 3 rows, depending on form.

Open Plaid

(Open Basketweave, Plaid): Attributed to Central Glass Co., c. 1885 and U. S. Glass, c. 1891. Clear, nonflint.

Butter.	$ 25-32
Compote, covered	30-36
Creamer, 5½″	17-21
Goblet.	16-21
Salt, flat master	18-23
Spoonholder.	15-18
Sugar	22-28
Tumblers: champagne (juice), water	14-17

Opposing Pyramids

Opposing Pyramids

(Flora): Bryce, Higbee and Company, late 1880s. Formerly attributed to Greensburg, a Kamm mixup.

Butter dish, covered, flanged	$ 32-39
Creamer.	22-27

(continued)

Goblet (ill.)	16-20
Pitcher, water, qt., ½ gal.	39-47
Spoonholder.	13-16
Sugar bowl, covered	30-40
Tumbler.	12-16
Wine	14-17

Optic

(U. S. Optic): U.S. Glass Company, c. 1892. Clear, "Colonial" type, panelled, nonflint.

Bowl, berry, 8".	$ 10-15
Butter dish, covered	20-26
Creamer.	12-15
Pitcher, water, 3 pint	18-24
Spoonholder, handles	10-13
Sugar bowl, covered, handles	16-19
Toothpick holder	24-35

Oregon

(Skilton): Richards & Hartley Glass Company, Tarentum, Pennsylvania, c. 1888. Clear, or stained with ruby; nonflint.

Butter dish, covered	$ 42-51
Celery.	24-30
Compote, covered, 8" dia.	48-57
Creamer.	30-35
Goblet.	37-42
Pitcher, water, ½ gal.,	
pressed handles	50-57
Sauce, footed, 4".	10-13
Spoonholder.	21-25
Sugar bowl, covered	35-46

Ruby blocks, 100-150 percent higher than clear prices listed. The 1/2 gallon tankard is atypical with the pattern at the base consisting only of a band of the smaller blocks above the convex prisms. The fans and larger blocks are missing. The handle is applied; four sizes of the tall lamps are known, also atypical, with alternating large blocks and prisms.

Oriental

Maker unknown, c. 1885. Clear, nonflint.

Butter, covered	$ 38-42
Creamer.	26-32
Spoonholder.	22-28
Sugar, covered.	35-40

There are many patterns with oriental motifs, but this is the only one with straight buttressed legs. Other pieces?

Orinda

National Glass Works (Lancaster No. 1492): Clear, ruby stain, milk glass.

Butter.	$ 24-29
Creamer.	15-20
Salt shaker	10-14
Spoonholder.	13-17
Sugar	20-25
Toothpick.	30-36

Milk glass add 20 percent; ruby stain add 200 percent to clear prices listed. Goblet?

Orion Thumbprint

Orion Thumbprint

(Orion Inverted Thumbprint): Canton Glass Company, Canton, Ohio, and Marion, Indiana, 1880s. Clear, probably amber, blue, green, and yellow; nonflint. Lee lists opaque white, black and blue.

Butter dish, covered	$ 40-45
Celery.	29-35
Compote, high	
Covered	46-55
Open	24-28
Creamer (ill.)	31-40
Goblet.	22-28
Platter, oval, Daisy and	
Button center	25-30
Sauce, footed	4-7
Spoonholder.	30-32
Sugar bowl	
Covered	39-42
Open	20-24

Yellow, 45 percent; amber, green, 65 percent; blue, 100 percent higher than prices listed for clear.

Ornate Star

(Divided Star; recently called Ladders and Diamond with Star): Tarentum, 1907-1912. Clear, ruby stain; either may be gilded. Scarce in custard.

Butter.	$ 28-34
Creamer, 4½″ high	16-20
Goblet.	20-25
Spoonholder.	14-17
Sugar, covered.	25-31
Vase, swung .	17-22
Wine	15-18

Ruby stain add 80 percent.

Oval Loop

(Question Mark): U. S. Glass Company (Richards & Hartley), Pittsburgh, c. 1890. Clear, nonflint.

Bowls, round, oval.	$ 14-24
Butter dish, covered	36-42
Celery.	24-30
Compote, covered	44-50
Creamer.	27-31
Goblet.	26-32
Pitcher	47-51
Shaker, sugar	33-42
Spoonholder.	15-18
Sugar bowl, covered	40-42
Tumbler.	13-16
Wine	20-25

Oval Mitre

McKee & Bros., Pittsburgh. Only the oval dish first shown 1859-1860 catalog, with its last appearance in 1868. Clear, flint.

Butter dish, covered	$ 54-65
Compote	
Open, 6″, 8″	52-59
Covered, high standard	89-110
Creamer.	54-64
Dish, 8″ oval	22-29
Goblet.	33-38
Sauce, flat.	9-12
Spoonholder.	30-36
Sugar bowl	
Open	73-78
Covered	51-60

Oval Panels

Maker unknown, c. late 1880s. Nonflint.

Goblet		
Amber.	$	32-37
Blue.		42-48
Clear		16-21
Yellow.		42-48

Millard gives King Brothers as the maker; the photo in Lucas is grouped with Richards and Hartley goblets but is not indexed and the text seems to be missing.

Owl and Possum

Owl and Possum

Traditionally Portland, 1880s. Clear, nonflint.

Goblet (ill.)	$ 77-84

Paling

(continued)

Paling

(Banded Paling): O'Hara Glass Co., Ltd., their No. 80 pattern, c. 1890. Clear, nonflint.

Butter dish, covered . . . . $ 31-39
Creamer (ill.) 21-29
Goblet, 3 types 16-24
Spoonholder, pedestal 17-22
Sugar bowl, covered 30-39

Three types of goblets by O'Hara: plain or prism stem (tapered bowl), and U-shaped bowl, no bands. Creamer also known in prism stem.

Palm Beach

U.S. Glass Company, c. 1909. Clear; decorated milk glass; Carnival; yellow, blue opalescent; nonflint. Prices are for yellow opalescent.

Butter dish, covered $230-265
Creamer 89-97
Pitcher, water 252-289
Sauce 33-39
Spoonholder 74-84
Sugar bowl, covered 122-135
Tumbler 61-74

Blue, add 25 percent. Reproduced in milk glass.

Palm Leaf

(Oriental): Maker unknown, 1880s.

Celery vase . . . . $ 20-30

This is a "loner" and not part of the Oriental or other similar pattern. No other pieces are known.

Palm Leaf Fan

Palm Leaf Fan

Bryce, Higbee, c. 1904. Clear, nonflint.

Bowl, large . . . . $ 15-21
Butter dish, covered 32-42
Cake stand, large 30-38
Celery vase 28-35
Compote
  Covered 41-48
  Open 21-26
Creamer, 5½" high (ill.) 26-30
Pitcher, water 43-49
Sugar, covered 32-42
Wine 24-29

Palmette

Palmette

Maker unknown, c. 1870s. Clear, nonflint.

Butter dish, covered . . . . $ 49-59
Cake stand 48-59
Celery 35-42
Compote
  Covered, low standard 65-74
  Open, 8" high 34-39
Creamer applied handle 49-54
Goblet 35-40
Pitcher (with applied handle,
  rare) 110-130
Salt, master (ill.) 22-28
Spoonholder 28-34
Sugar bowl, covered 39-45
Tumbler, footed 32-39
Wine 48-55

Panama

(Fine Cut Bar; Millard's "Viking"): U.S. Glass Company, c. 1904. Clear, nonflint.

Butter dish, covered . . . . $ 34-39

Panama

Compote, covered	34-38
Creamer, 5½″ high	29-38
Cruet	30-36
Decanter	33-41
Goblet.	25-30
Salt/Pepper, pr.	30-38
Spoonholder.	19-29
Sugar bowl, covered	40-42
Tumbler.	12-16
Wine (ill.)	16-20

At least 56 pieces. A patterned tray to hold the salt and pepper shaker is known.

Panel and Cane

Panel and Cane

Maker unknown, 1890s. Clear, nonflint.

Butter dish, covered	$ 20-26
Creamer, 5½″ high (ill.)	15-18
Goblet.	33-42

Spoonholder, pedestal	10-14
Sugar bowl, covered, pedestal	18-24

Panel and Star

(Column Block): O'Hara Glass Company, Ltd., Pittsburgh, c. 1880, and U. S. Glass. Clear, amber, vaseline, blue; nonflint.

Butter dish, covered	$ 33-40
Celery	31-37
Creamer	32-36
Cruet, miniature, applied handle. . . .	40-50
Goblet.	35-41
Jar, pickle, open	28-32
Pitcher, ...	44-52
Sauce, footed	10-13
Shaker, salt	20-29
Spoonholder.	20-25
Sugar bowl, covered	34-43
Toothpick (rare).	38-45

Colors worth 60-100 percent more.

Panelled Acorn Band

Panelled Acorn Band

Attributed to Sandwich, 1870s. Clear, nonflint.

Butter dish, covered	$ 40-45
Compote	
Covered	56-62
Open	32-40
Celery vase	34-39
Creamer, applied handle.	41-48
Egg cup	30-35
Goblet.	30-40

189 (continued)

Pitcher (ill.)	88-97
Sauce, flat, footed	7-10
Spoonholder	30-35
Sugar bowl, covered	40-45

The same as Acorn Band, but has leaves dividing the panels.

Panelled Cable

Panelled Cable

(Original name, Acme): Bryce/U. S. Glass, 1880s through 1890s. Clear, nonflint.

Butter bowl, flanged	$ 20-28
Creamer, 4¾" high (ill.)	15-18
Cup	6-10
Spoonholder	13-16
Sugar, covered	20-26

A cup is known made from this mold, but with pointed hobnails added, and seems to be unidentified in the literature.

Panelled Cane

(Cane Column): Claimed by Portland, Maine, and known as "Jewel," 1870s. Clear, canary, amber, blue; nonflint.

Butter dish, covered	$ 34-39
Creamer, 5¾" high, pedestal	29-33
Goblet (ill.)	19-24
Sauce, flat	4-9
Spoonholder	19-23
Sugar bowl, open	20-28
Wine	20-27

Panelled Cane

Canary, 75 percent; amber, 85 percent; blue, 100 percent higher than clear prices listed. Cane and Rosette is the companion pattern made from the same molds.

Panelled Cherry

Panelled Cherry

(Cherry Thumbprints; Cherry with Cable): Northwood Glass Company, 1880s. "N" sometimes found in bottom. Clear, cherries red, leaves gold; nonflint.

Butter dish, covered	$ 83-92
Creamer	49-54
Pitcher, water (ill.)	100-125
Sauce, flat,	17-22
Spoonholder	39-47
Sugar bowl, covered	72-82
Tumbler	28-33

Prices are for decoration in excellent conditon. Clear worth 50 percent less.

Panelled Cosmos

(Flower Medallion; original name, Eclipse): Indiana Glass Co., Dunkirk (1907-1930s). Clear, or painted with crimson flowers and gold trim. Four-piece table set in ad as "Tea Set."

Bowl
Berry, round, 10″ flat	$ 12-16
Salad, 7½″, three feet	15-20
Butter, covered	23-29
Celery tray, 10½″	13-16
Celery vase, handled	15-19
Compote, jelly	11-14
Creamer	14-20
Goblet	15-21
Pickle dish, oval	9-12
Pitcher, water, ½ gal.	24-30

Sauce
Berry, 5″ flat	4-7
Salad, 4½″, three feet	6-9
Spoonholder, handled	13-16
Sugar, covered, handled	20-25
Tumbler	10-13

Color stained, add 30 percent.

Panelled Daisy

Panelled Daisy

(Original name, Brazil): Bryce Bros., Pittsburgh, c. 1888, and U. S. Glass, 1890s. Clear, nonflint; amber, rare.

Bowl, waste	$ 25-32
Butter dish, covered	40-48
Cake stand, 8″, 9″, 10″, 11″, high standard	37-55
Creamer	31-35
Goblet	30-36

Pitcher
Water	48-56
Syrup	60-62
Plate, 7″ round, 10″ sq. (ill.)	34-39
Salt/Pepper, pr.	47-54
Spoonholder	24-28
Sugar bowl, covered	44-48

Amber, 300 percent higher than clear prices listed. Goblet reproduced. The butter also comes with a fancy flange and spiral-ribbed finial, worth about 30 percent more.

Panelled Dewdrop

Panelled Dewdrop

(Striped Dewdrop): Campbell, Jones & Company, Pittsburgh, c. 1878. Clear, nonflint. Two types: plain base; rows of dewdrops on base.

Butter dish, covered	$ 36-42
Celery (ill.)	33-38
Champagne	33-37
Cheese, covered	52-62
Cordial	27-32
Creamer, applied handle	34-39
Goblet, dewdrops on base	31-36
Mug, applied handle	34-41
Pitcher, water	42-48
Platter, bread (motto)	32-38
Relish	10-14

Sauce
Flat	6-9
Footed	9-12
Spoonholder	16-20
Sugar bowl, covered	36-39
Tumbler	24-30
Wine	25-30

(continued)

Rows of dewdrops on base, 20 percent higher than plain base prices listed. Confusing pattern: Beaded Panels.

Panelled Forget-Me-Not

Panelled Forget-Me-Not

(Original name, Regal) Bryce Bros., Pittsburgh, 1870s, also attributed to Doyle. Clear, amber, yellow, blue. Kamm reported the pitcher in "reddish-amethyst," which would be rare.

Bowl, covered	$ 28-35
Bread plate, oblong	32-36
Butter dish, covered	44-52
Cake plate on standard	32-45
Celery, pedestal	31-36
Compote, covered, high	
standard, 8″ dia.	57-63
Creamer.	28-34
Goblet.	39-48
Jam jar, open (ill.)	32-38
Pickle dish, tapered	22-27
Pitcher, two sizes	36-49
Sauce, flat, footed	10-15
Spoonholder.	23-30
Sugar bowl, covered	39-46
Wine (scarce)	40-47

Colors, 40-50 percent higher than clear prices listed. Amethyst, 200 percent higher. See Panelled Ivy for similar pattern.

Panelled Grape

(Heavy Panelled Grape): D. C. Jenkins Glass Company, Kokomo, Indiana, c. 1904. Clear or decorated. Nonflint.

Bowl, round, covered	$ 33-40
Butter dish	47-59
Compote, covered	60-72

Panelled Grape (Number 507)

Creamer, 4½″ high (ill.)	40-48
Pitcher	68-76
Sauce, footed and flat	20-27
Spoonholder.	27-32
Sugar bowl	
Covered	42-51
Open	28-32
Toothpick.	40-50

Heavily reproduced in milk glass and colors.

Panelled Heather

Panelled Heather

Maker unknown, early 1890s. Clear, nonflint. Frequently with gilt.

Bowl	
Berry, 7½″.	$ 15-20
Footed salad, 4½″	8-12
Oval, footed, 6½″	10-16
Butter dish	33-38
Cake stand	30-40
Celery, handled	21-29
Compote, covered, jelly	40-49

Creamer
Berry, on pedestal	. . . .	14-19
Regular, flat (ill.)	. . . .	20-25

Cruet, pointed panelled stopper	. . . .	33-41
Goblet	. . . .	24-34
Pitcher, medium	. . . .	32-37
Spoonholder	. . . .	32-37

Sugar bowl
Berry, pedestalled, handled, open	. .	18-22
Covered	. . . .	26-34
Regular	. . . .	14-19

Tumbler	. . . .	15-22
Wine	. . . .	21-26

Panelled Hobnail

Panelled Hobnail

Bryce Bros., c. 1885. Clear, amber, green, blue, opaque white, vaseline, canary; nonflint.

Butter dish, covered	. . . .	$ 34-38

Compote
Covered	. . . .	32-37
Open	. . . .	23-28

Creamer (ill.)	. . . .	25-31
Goblet	. . . .	20-27
Pitcher	. . . .	30-40

Sugar bowl
Covered	. . . .	37-45
Open	. . . .	20-24

Wine	. . . .	22-29

Amber, canary, opaque white, 60 percent higher; blue, green, 80 percent higher than clear prices listed. Not reproduced.

Panelled Honeycomb

Maker unknown. Clear, nonflint.

Butter dish	. . . .	$ 39-46
Celery	. . . .	25-31

Panelled Honeycomb

Compote	. . . .	39-44
Creamer, pewter lid missing (ill.).	. . .	25-32
Pitcher	. . . .	49-54
Spoonholder	. . . .	24-32
Sugar bowl, covered	. . . .	38-46

Only the creamer and sugar are a certainty.

Panelled Ivy

Panelled Ivy

Maker unknown, but is so like Panelled Forget-Me-Not, attributed to Bryce Bros., late 1880s. Clear; amber goblet known. Nonflint.

Butter dish, covered	. . . .	$ 38-44
Cake stand	. . . .	33-42
Celery	. . . .	25-38

Compote
Covered	. . . .	48-57
Open	. . . .	32-37

Goblet	. . . .	35-42

(continued)

Pitcher (ill.) 39-44

Color, at least 60 percent higher than clear prices listed. Same as Panelled Forget-Me-Not, but with ivy. Lee shows the sauce as "Cape Cod."

Panelled Oak

Panelled Oak

Lancaster Glass Company, early 1900s. Clear, nonflint.

Butter dish, covered . . . . $ 28-34
Celery vase 19-24
Creamer. 20-26
Pitcher (ill.) 33-39
Spoonholder. 14-18
Sugar bowl, covered 28-34
Tumbler. 12-17
Goblet?

Panelled Ovals

Maker unknown, c. 1860s. Clear, flint.

Butter dish, covered . . . . $ 50-62
Compote
  Open 32-39
  Covered 57-66
Creamer, applied handle. 60-68
Egg cup 37-42
Goblet. 48-57
Spoonholder, flat rim, pedestal 35-40
Sugar bowl
  Open 25-34
  Covered 42-48

Panelled Pleat

(Original name, Ladders): Robinson Glass Company, Zanesville, Ohio, c. 1894. Clear, nonflint.

Bowl . . . . $ 17-21
Butter dish, covered 36-42
Creamer. 29-38
Goblet. 26-32
Spoonholder, flat rim 24-31
Sugar bowl, covered 30-34

Production may have been limited, as few pieces are seen in this pattern. Erroneously referred to as "Zipper."

Panelled Primula

Panelled Primula

Maker unknown, 1900s. Clear, nonflint.

Butter dish, covered . . . . $ 37-44
Cake stand 38-46
Celery vase 29-34
Compote
  Covered, high standard 49-54
  Open, high or low standard. 36-42
Creamer. 25-34
Pitcher, water (ill.) 43-52
Spoonholder. 21-28
Sugar bowl, covered 32-37
Tumbler. 17-21

Only the pitcher is confirmed.

Panelled "S"

Maker unknown, 1880s. Clear, nonflint.

Butter dish, covered . . . . $ 31-39
Celery. 27-31
Compote, open 34-39
Creamer. 24-28

Panelled "S"

Goblet(ill.)	19-25
Plate	15-24
Pitcher, water	33-43
Spoonholder.	14-18
Sugar bowl, covered	31-39

Only goblet confirmed.

Panelled Sawtooth

Panelled Sawtooth

(Fluted Diamond Point): Attributed by Kamm to Duncan & Miller Glass Company, Washington, Pennsylvania, 1880s, and U. S. Glass Company. Clear, nonflint.

Butter dish, covered	$ 29-35
Cake stand	32-38
Celery	22-27
Creamer, 5½" high	23-29
Goblet.	32-41
Pitcher (ill.)	32-38
Spoonholder.	21-29

Sugar		
Covered	32-36
Open	15-20
Wine	18-21

Panelled Star and Button

Panelled Star and Button

(Sedan): Maker unknown, 1890s. Clear, nonflint.

Butter dish, covered	$ 30-36
Creamer (ill.)	22-27
Goblet.	16-22
Salt, master (flat)	19-23
Sauce, flat.	4-6
Spoonholder, pedestal	15-19

Sugar bowl	
Covered	30-36
Open	14-19
Wine	14-17

A rare pickle dish in purple slag with traces of white is confirmed.

Panelled Stippled Scroll

Westmoreland's Princess Feather, 1924-1960s. Clear, nonflint.

Compote, jelly, footed	$ 34-39
Creamer.	14-19
Goblet (ill.)	15-18
Pitcher, water, 54 oz.	50-60
Sugar bowl	15-20
Tumbler, footed, 8 oz., 9 oz., 10 oz. . . .	12-17
Wine	15-18

Color, 30 percent more than clear prices listed. Unitt uses this name, but shows another Depression pattern, Duncan's "Early American Sandwich." Amber made 1960s.

Panelled Strawberry

Panelled Strawberry

(Strawberry with Roman Key Band): Indiana Glass Company from 1913, their No. 127 pattern. Clear, foliage and berries burnished gold; also, maroon to pink; nonflint.

Butter dish	$ 48-54
Creamer, 4½" high	32-37
Goblet.	31-38
Pitcher, ½ gal. (ill.)	55-62
Sauce	10-14
Spoonholder, handled	30-38
Sugar bowl, covered, handled	39-47
Tumbler.	22-29

Prices are for paint in good condition.

Panelled Sunflower

Panelled Sunflower

Attributed to Jenkins Glass Company, Dunkirk, Indiana (1906-1932) based on similarity of design, ribbed collars, lid treatment, especially on jugs and bowls, and panelled forms.

Creamer, 4¾" high, patterned glass lid is 1⅞" dia.	
Covered	$ 42-50
Open.	31-36
Goblet (ill.)	16-21
Mug.	32-36
Toothpick.	40-46

Creamer, goblet, mug, toothpick confirmed. Kamm calls the creamer "Sunflower, Container."

Panelled Thistle

Panelled Thistle

(Original Higbee name, Delta): J. B. Higbee Glass Company, Bridgeville, Pennsylvania, 1910. Jefferson Glass Company, Toronto, Ontario, and Dominion Glass Company in the 1920s. Clear, nonflint.

Basket, 3 sizes	$ 62-85
Bowl, berry, 6½", 7", 8½", 9", footed	32-44
Butter dish, flanged	45-52
Cake stand, 9¾" dia..	25-34
Celery, tall, handled	28-34
Celery tray, 10"	21-26
Compote, open, 5" (sweetmeat), 8" . . .	26-33
Creamer, knob feet, Bee	34-39
Cruet, no stopper	31-39
Dish, honey, covered, square.	54-66
Goblet, flared or straight.	24-39
Pickle dish, 8¼"	13-17
Pitcher, qt. (ill.), ½ gal.	59-69
Plate, 7¼", 8¼", 9½", 10¼"	19-39
Salt dip, feet (individual)	12-16

Salt/Pepper, pr.	55-64	
Spoonholder, 2 handles	23-28	
Sugar bowl, 2 handles, covered.	41-52	
Toothpick.	44-54	
Tumbler, water	21-28	
Wine, flared or straight	19-27	

On reproduction pieces (we call the bee the "Higbee Hornet"), the body is elongated, rather than rounded. Colored salt dips are fakes. Clear fakes larger than originals, which are 1″ high. Many reproductions, but variation in form does not necessarily mean it is a reproduction. The butter comes with a flat, flanged base and also with two handles and straight sides. The bulbous toothpick is genuine; the skinny flared a reproduction. With Bee mark, 25 percent higher, except for the Canadian market.

Spoonholder, scalloped rim	22-30	31-38
Sugar bowl		
Covered with spoon rack	49-54	59-69
Open	24-30	30-35

Minor detail variations are known and are not an indication of reproduction. The creamer comes with a ringed waist. The spoonholder with plain or scalloped rim, 20 percent more. Metz lists a goblet, but the one she lists may be Millard's Panelled Wheat, which we know as "Wheat in Shield," which is not the pattern listed here.

Panelled Wheat

Panelled Wheat

(Wheat): Hobbs, Brockunier & Company, Wheeling, West Virginia, patented February 28, 1871. Clear and milk glass.

	Clear	Milk Glass
Butter dish, collared base with drain insert	$37-42	$ 47-52
Compote		
Covered, 11″ high . . .	69-72	120-134
Open, low	30-36	40-50
Creamer, 5¾″ (ill.). . . .	28-37	34-39
Pitcher, water		118-124
Relish, 8″ no panels . . .	13-18	34-39
Sauce, flat.	12-18	23-32

Pansy and Moss Rose

Pansy and Moss Rose

(Pansy, Moss Rose; Lily-of-the-Valley): Maker, date unknown. Clear, amber, blue; nonflint.

Butter.	$ 35-42
Creamer, 4½″ high (ill.)	24-29
Spoonholder (not confirmed)	18-23
Sugar, covered.	35-42

Amber, blue, 50 percent more than clear prices listed.

Paris

(Roughneck, Victory, Zipper Cross; erroneously Little Ladders): Higbee, c. 1910; New Martinsville purchased the molds shortly afterwards. Also attributed to Portland. Clear, nonflint.

197

(continued)

Bowl

Deep, 7½" . . . . $ 10-13

Fruit, 9" shallow or extra deep 12-15

Butter, covered 25-30

Cake stand

Regular, 9¼" dia. 26-31

Toy 28-35

Celery vase, 7¼". 17-20

Compote

Jelly 11-15

Open, 8½" 14-18

Creamer 15-18

Cruet 21-25

Goblet. 24-29

Mug 12-15

Pitcher

Squat jug, 8" 23-28

Straight (lacks horizontal design
element, so is zippers to
top), 3 pt. jug. 25-32

Plate

Round, 8" 13-16

Square, 7" 15-21

Rose bowl, 3" dia. 17-22

Salt shaker 15-20

Spoonholder. 13-16

Sugar, covered. 25-30

Vase, 9½" 16-22

Wine 18-22

Parrot

Parrot

(Owl in Fan): Possibly Richards & Hartley, Tarentum, Pennsylvania, 1880s. Clear, nonflint.

Goblet (ill.) . . . . $ 47-53

Bird Chasing Insect 84-99

Wine (rare) 73-87

Any other pieces?

Pathfinder, Late

(Millard's Pathfinder; Omnibus): U. S. Glass, c. 1911. Clear, may have gold. Nonflint.

Bowls, each . . . . $ 10-18

Belled, 5", 6", 7½", 8½"

Berry, 6", 7", 8"

Deep, 8", 9"

Shallow, 9"

Butter. 19-23

Celery

Tray, 10¼" x 5½" 12-16

Vase, handled 13-17

Compote, open, flared 15-20

Creamer

Berry 10-13

Regular 13-16

Cup 4-8

Dish, curled, handled 12-15

Goblet. 16-21

Pickle, 8" x 4¾" 8-11

Plate, 7½" 10-14

Salt shaker 10-15

Salt/Pepper on handled glass tray . . . 32-38

Sauces, each 4-8

Belled, 4½"

Berry, 4", 4½"

Deep, 4"

Spoonholder, handled 12-14

Sugar

Berry, open, handled 10-14

Regular, covered, handled 16-20

Syrup 26-32

Tumbler. 8-11

Wine 12-16

Some examples have a yellowish tint to the glass. Don't confuse this nonflint glass with earlier flint Pathfinder.

Pattee Cross

(Broughton; Gloria): U.S. Glass Company, c. 1900. In 1912, Sears, Roebuck listed it in their catalog under the name Gloria. Clear, green, nonflint. Occasionally found with rose stain.

Bowl, 8" . . . . $ 14-20

Butter dish, covered 33-38

Celery tray 16-21

Compote

Jelly 16-19

Open, 8" 32-37

Creamer

Flat, regular 14-19

Tankard (is toy water) 30-39

Cruet 30-35

Goblet. 19-26

Nappy, diamond. 8-12

Olive, handle 10-14

Pickle 9-13

Pitcher, pedestal 30-34

Salt dip (is toy sauce) 11-15

Salt shaker 20-24

Sauce

Flat (is toy berry) 23-29

Footed. 8-10

Spoonholder, handled 12-16

Sugar bowl, covered, handled 34-39

Syrup 39-46

Tumbler. 12-16

Vase, 6", crimped or straight 12-17

Wine 19-22

Green, 40 percent higher than clear prices listed. Prices of 1900 pieces listed. No toothpick.

Goblet, pineapple stemmed,

etched 35-44

Pitcher, water, tankard, band of

pattern at base. 51-59

Spoonholder

Etched (ill.) see footnote 24-33

Pedestal 30-39

Sugar bowl, covered 58-66

Tumbler, etched. 27-33

Wine, etched 35-39

Ruby stain, 100 percent more than clear. Similar pattern, Roanoke, also made by Ripley. Kamm describes a high-foot table set in which the spoonholder has a smooth rim and could be mistaken (or used) for a goblet. She also mentions a hotel set for which the illustration may be a spoonholder. This speculation is based on seven tumblers—six measuring under 4", one measuring 4½ high—owned by Dori Miles.

Pavonia

Pavonia

(Pineapple Stem): Ripley & Company, Pittsburgh, 1885. Clear, ruby stained, etched; nonflint.

Butter dish, covered, etched . . . . . . $ 64-74

Cake stand, etched

Large 52-64

Small 40-42

Celery, etched 37-42

Compote

Covered, high standard, 8" 48-54

Open, high standard 34-39

Creamer, pedestal base, etched 54-62

George Peabody

George Peabody

Henry Greener Wear Flint Glass Works, Sunderland, England, Registry mark Dec. 7, 1869. A hero in the War of 1812, a great philanthropist, honored both in England and America (1795-1869).

Bowl, English registry mark . . . . . . $ 39-44

Creamer, English registry

mark (ill.) 55-68

Mug, English registry mark 45-59

Plate, 6". 41-47

Peacock Eye

Peacock Eye

An early lacy pattern, c. 1840. Many fragments found at Sandwich. Don't confuse the name with Peacock Feather (Georgia). Clear, amethyst, pale yellow; flint.

Bowl, 8″ dia. (ill.)	$ 73-85
Compote, low open,	
9″ dia. x 4½″ high	300+
Mustard pot	
Covered	108-125
Open	62-69
Plate (goes under mustard pot) . . .	49-58
Sauce	24-31

Peacock Feather

Peacock Feather

(Original name, Georgia): U.S. Glass Company, c. 1908, as part of their States series. Clear, nonflint. Decorated with gold paint; lamps are listed in blue.

Bowl, berry	$ 23-27
Butter dish, covered	41-48
Cake stand, 9″, 10″, 11″.	36-52
Celery tray	22-29
Compote	
Shallow, high standard.	26-35
Covered, high standard	44-53
Creamer	
Regular	29-33
Toy, 2″ high	62-75
Dish, oval, deep	20-25
Lamp	
Hand	38-46
Tall	54-69
Pitcher, water (ill.)	52-68
Salt/Pepper, pr.	45-53
Spoonholder.	24-29
Sugar bowl, covered	37-42
Tumbler.	33-40

Colors, 50 percent higher. No goblet or toothpick.

Pendleton

Pendleton

Maker unknown, late 1860s, early 1870s. Clear; flint and nonflint.

Butter dish	$ 47-59
Celery vase	37-48
Creamer, applied handle.	45-56
Goblet.	29-38
Pitcher, syrup, metal cap (ill.)	150+
Spoonholder.	36-41
Sugar bowl, covered	52-60
Tumbler.	40-46

Only goblet and syrup confirmed. Prices are for flint. Nonflint worth about half.

Pentagon

Maker unknown, c. 1890. Clear, ruby stained; nonflint.

Pentagon

Butter dish, covered	39-46
Celery	30-37
Creamer (ill.)	25-32
Goblet	17-23
Mug	16-20
Nappies, fruit, 5″, 6″, 7″, 8″	19-27
Pickle, handles	12-16
Pitcher, ½ gal.	40-50
Spoonholder	16-21
Sugar bowl, covered	40-47
Tumbler	18-22
Wine	20-26

Creamer, tankard, 6″ high . . . . $	29-33
Decanter (flat base)	43-49
Pitcher, water, tankard (ill.)	57-67
Salt shaker (rare)	40-50
Wine	20-26

Pert

Pert

Maker unknown, c. 1880. Confused attributions to Bryce Bros. who made a "Pert Set" (Ribbed Forget-Me-Not). Clear, nonflint, toy set.

Butter dish, covered, 2¾″ high . . . . . $	85-95
Creamer, 3½″ high (ill.)	73-84
Spoonholder, 3″ high	66-70
Sugar bowl, covered, open, 5″ high . . .	52-64

No other pieces.

Persian

Persian

(Three Stories; Block and Pleat): Bryce, Higbee & Company, Pittsburgh, c. 1885. Clear, nonflint. Mug known in amber. Blue is probable.

Bowls, oval, 8″, 9″, 10″ . . . . $	23-31
Bread plate, oval	25-32

Petal and Loop

(Atypical): Sandwich and other New England factories, 1850s. The piece shown here is Sandwich; the bowl part is not the petal motif, but the loop design on the base of the standard is the one found on "Petal and Loop" pieces. Flint in crystal, blues, vaseline, amethyst; opaque and fiery opal. (continued)

Petal and Loop

Candlestick	$ 59-68
Compote (ill.)	127-140
Dish, low, with flared petals bowl . .	51-69
Sauce	12-16
Sugar, covered.	94-125

Colors worth 100-500 percent depending on form.

Philadelphia

New England Glass Company, c. 1860s. Clear, flint.

Bowl, covered	$ 43-52
Celery.	38-48
Egg cup	38-46
Goblet.	50-60
Spoonholder.	30-38
Sugar bowl	
Covered	49-55
Open	29-38
Wine	39-46

Picket

Picket

(London; Picket Fence): King Glass Company, Pittsburgh, 1880s. Canadian attribution, Burlington Glass Works. Clear, nonflint.

Bread plate, 8″ x 13″	
Stuart's "McCormick Reaper" . . .	$138-152
Stuart's "Mulberry"	54-68
Butter dish, covered	54-63
Celery vase	45-52
Compote (made in 4″—8″ sizes)	
Covered, 6″, 8″, high foot	58-64
Open, peg type, in plated base . . .	79-87
Creamer, 5″ high.	35-42
Goblet.	39-44
Marmalade jar (pickle jar)	50-60
Match holder	32-37
Pickle jar, with cover	42-48
Pitcher, water (ill.)	54-64
Salt	
Flat, oblong, master	26-30
Individual with feet	12-16
Sauce, feet, or flat with tab	12-16
Spoonholder.	31-37
Sugar bowl, covered	48-56
Tray for water set	62-78

Pigs in Corn

Pigs in Corn

Maker unknown, 1875-1885. Clear, goblet only. Comes with corn bent to right or left.

Goblet (ill.)	$250-275

Pilgrim Bottle

Pilgrim Bottle

Attributed to Belmont Glass Company, Bellaire, Ohio, c. 1882. Clear, amber, blue, canary. May be engraved.

Butter.	$ 48-55
Creamer.	34-41
Cruet	48-53
Salt shaker (Peterson 168m), rare	32-42
Spoonholder.	30-36
Sugar, covered.	44-52
Syrup (ill.)	64-78

Toothpick not yet confirmed. Colors, add 40 percent to 100 percent to clear prices listed.

Pillar

Pillar

Bakewell, Pears & Company, Pittsburgh, c. 1850s. Clear, flint.

Ale (ill.)	$ 40-52
Bottle, bar, 7″	44-52
Claret	50-60
Cordial	70-78
Creamer.	100-128
Decanter, no stopper	59-64
Goblet, heavy or light type (knob stem varies)	49-55
Sauce, flat.	12-15
Sugar bowl, covered	84-96

Pillow and Sunburst

Pillow and Sunburst

(Elite): Westmoreland Specialty Company, 1891; again in 1896, and again in 1917. Clear, amber, ruby stained; some pieces are gilded.

Butter dish, covered, large dated finial	$ 40-47
Celery.	28-34
Compote	
Covered	45-54
Open	20-29
Creamer, 3½″ high, individual (ill.).	14-18
Pitcher, water.	42-47
Spoonholder, large.	23-28
Sugar bowl, large	38-47

Confusing pattern "Sydney." There are three types of finials and some are dated "2-25-96." Oval forms seem to have been made only in the smaller size. The goblet, if it exists, must be scarce, since it is not in the standard reference books.

203

Pillow Bands

Pillow Bands

Kokomo Glass Company, c. 1904, their No. 450 pattern, Kamm attribution. Clear and colors, nonflint.

Berry bowl	$ 20-28
Butter dish	38-44
Celery	23-30
Compote	
Covered	40-47
Open	22-28
Creamer, 4⅜″ high (ill.)	24-29
Pitcher	39-47
Spoonholder.	16-19
Sugar bowl, covered	39-44

Colors, 50 percent more than clear prices listed. More information needed. Proof of creamer only. Similar design "Guttate."

Pillow Encircled

Pillow Encircled

(Midway): Model Flint Glass Company, Albany, Indiana, c. 1900; National Glass Company (Cambridge) to 1904. Clear and ruby stained, nonflint. Also comes engraved.

Bowl, nut, 7″, 8″	$ 16-21
Butter dish, covered	35-42
Cake stand, 10″	40-46
Compote	
Covered, 5″, 6″, 7″, 8″	32-47
Open	20-30
Creamer.	29-39
Pitcher, qt., ½ gal. (ill.)	40-48
Sauce, 4″.	4-8
Spoonholder.	14-18
Sugar bowl	
Covered	32-36
Open	16-22
Sugar shaker	33-39
Tumbler.	12-17

Ruby stain 60 percent higher than clear prices listed. Confusing pattern is Hero, which when ruby stained is called Ruby Rosette. Pillow Encircled has a straight band above the "pillows." Probably Barrett copied from Metz who started the problem when she showed the "Hero" tumbler, giving the Kamm reference but overlooking the difference in the patterns. Pillow Encircled/Midway in ruby stain is simply that. It is not Ruby Rosette although it appears in current publications that way. No goblet or toothpick.

Pineapple

Pineapple

Maker unknown, 1880s. Clear, opaque white (scarce). Nonflint.

Butter dish, covered	$ 54-69
Celery, handled	35-45
Creamer	
5¼″ high (ill.)	45-50
Plain handle	39-44

Spoonholder, ring handles	34-38
Sugar bowl	
Covered	50-60
Open	28-36
Tumbler	33-39

White, 100 percent more than clear prices listed. The creamer, shown with its supported ring handle, is known in opaque white; but Kamm shows a different handle, also pressed.

Pineapple and Fan

Pineapple and Fan

(Cube with Fan; Holbrook): Adams & Company, Pittsburgh; later by U.S. Glass Company, 1891. Clear, emerald green, ruby stain, nonflint.

Bowl, berry, 8″, 9″	$ 17-27
Butter dish, covered, flat base	38-44
Cake stand	30-40
Celery	37-44
Creamer, large (ill.)	26-32
Cup (custard)	6-10
Goblet	19-24
Mug, small	8-12
Piccalilli jar, covered	37-42
Pitcher	
½ gal., ¾ gal., tankard	46-55
1 qt., 1 pt., water	36-41
Salt dip, individual	8-10
Sauce, 4″, 4½″	4-9
Spoonholder, laydown type	24-32
Sugar bowl, large, covered	35-45
Tumbler, water	10-14
Wine	15-20

Emerald green, 50 percent; ruby stain, 100 percent higher than clear prices listed. The cubes are beveled flat squares, which differentiate it from confusing patterns having flat or pointed (convex) diamonds.

Pioneer's No. 15

Pioneer's No. 15

(Bamboo): Pioneer Glass Company, Pittsburgh, c. 1890s. Clear, nonflint.

Bowl, 8″ berry, crimped	$ 19-25
Butter dish, covered, concave,	
flanged base	29-38
Celery	24-29
Creamer, flat	22-29
Pitcher, ½ gal.	40-47
Sauce, 4″, flat	5-8
Spoonholder, flat, scalloped rim	15-20
Sugar bowl, covered	29-38
Tumbler (ill.)	10-14

Metz lists a ruby-stained tumbler, but ruby stain in this pattern is certainly elusive, if indeed it exists! Confusing patterns: Broken Column, especially from the Pioneer factory catalog; and Westmoreland's No. 15, the forerunner of the Pioneer version.

Pioneer's Victoria

Pioneer's Victoria

Pioneer Glass Company, 1885. Crystal, usually with ruby stain. Some pieces are engraved. Prices are for ruby.

205

(continued)

Butter dish, covered	$100-128
Celery.	66-77
Creamer.	32-40
Cruet, long pressed spout curves up opposite lower handle; original ruby stopper (rare).	350+
Cup.	29-39
Goblet.	62-75
Molasses (squat syrup)	134-152
Pitcher, water (ill.)	148-165
Sauce	22-29
Spoonholder.	42-49
Sugar bowl	85-97
Tumbler.	30-39
Wine	62-75

Clear worth about 50 percent less. The companion pattern by the same company is called "Beauty" in which the design is extended to the top of the piece with diamond motif repeated near the rim.

Plaid

Plaid

(Zenith Block): Maker unknown, seldom seen pattern of the 1880s. Clear, nonflint.

Butter.	$ 32-37
Celery, pedestal, flat rim.	24-29
Creamer.	29-33
Goblet.	20-25
Pickle dish	13-17
Pitcher, water (ill.)	36-40
Spoonholder, pedestal, flat rim	16-20
Sugar bowl, open	19-21

If you have other pieces, please write. Metz lists as Plaid (no illustration) and Zenith Block, which she took from Millard.

Pleat and Panel

Pleat and Panel

(Original name, Derby): Bryce Bros., Pittsburgh, 1870s. Clear, amethyst, yellow, blue, nonflint. Most forms are square or rectangular.

Butter dish, covered	$ 54-69
Cake stand, 9″.	32-40
Compote, covered, 8″	38-45
Creamer (ill.)	34-39
Goblet.	25-37
Lamp, 9¼″ high, clear font.	110-135
Pickle dish, 7″	14-19
Pitcher, water	55-66
Plate, square, 3½″, 6″, 7½″, 8½″ . . .	24-35
Platter, handled	39-47
Salt/Pepper, pr.	53-60
Spoonholder.	29-37
Sugar bowl, covered	48-55

Colors, 75 percent higher than clear prices listed. The 7½″ plate and goblet reproduced.

Pleating

(Flat Panel): Bryce Bros., Pittsburgh; Gillinder & Sons, Philadelphia, c. 1880s. Reissued by U.S. Glass Company, c. 1891. Clear, ruby stain; either may have frosted panels or engraving.

Bowl, 8″ round, 9″ oval	$ 15-22
Butter dish, covered	34-39
Cake stand	31-38
Celery	22-28
Claret	30-36
Compote	
Covered, 8″	40-48
Open, 5″	15-20
Creamer.	24-32

Goblet.	19-25
Pickle dish	10-14
Pitcher, water	39-46
Plate, 6″—10″	13-25
Salt shaker	15-19
Sauce, 3½″, 4″	4-8
Spoonholder.	14-18
Sugar bowl, covered	36-41
Toothpick.	18-23
Tumbler.	11-16

Ruby stain worth about 100 percent more. Confusing pattern Regina.

Plume and Block

Plume and Block

(Feather and Block): Richards & Hartley Glass Company, Tarentum, Pennsylvania, 1885, U. S. Glass after 1891. Clear, clear with ruby stain; nonflint.

Butter dish, covered	$ 38-45
Celery (ill.)	28-36
Creamer.	28-37
Pitcher, qt.	40-49
Spoonholder.	22-27
Sugar bowl, covered	38-44

Ruby stain worth 80 percent more.

Plume

Plume

Adams Glass Company, 1874. Clear, ruby; or etched; nonflint.

Bowl, open, covered,	
6″, 7″, 8″	$ 36-49
Butter dish, covered	46-54
Cake stand, 9″, 10″	43-50
Celery (horizontal or vertical plume)	31-36
Compote	
Covered	44-52
Open, scalloped top	35-43
Creamer (ill.)	33-39
Goblet.	31-36
Pickle dish	13-18
Pitcher, water	58-66
Sauce, 4″, flat or footed	8-12
Spoonholder.	25-29
Sugar bowl, covered	43-48
Tumbler.	24-30

Ruby stained 25 percent higher than clear prices listed. Goblet reproduced.

Plutec

207

(continued)

Plutec

McKee Glass Company, Jeannette, Pennsylvania, c. early 1900s. Clear, nonflint. Most pieces marked "Prescut."

Bowl, nut	$ 17-22
Butter dish, covered	34-43
Cake stand, 8½".	29-34
Creamer.	18-22
Decanter, wine	45-54
Dish, pickle (spoon tray).	13-17
Pitcher, water, ½ gal., qt.	39-46
Spoonholder.	16-20
Sugar bowl, covered	34-37
Tray, wine.	31-37
Wine (ill.)	15-20

Pointed Jewel

Pitcher	35-39
Spoonholder.	15-18
Sugar bowl, covered, no handles	30-34
Tumbler.	14-18
Wine	22-29

Pointed Cube

Pointed Cube

Maker unknown, c. 1880s. Clear or frosted, nonflint.

Decanter	$ 30-38
Tray, wine.	23-31
Wine (ill.)	14-18

Frosted, 20 percent higher than clear prices listed.

Pointed Jewel

Columbia Glass Company, Findlay, Ohio, 1880s; later U.S. Glass Company, 1892. Clear, nonflint.

Butter dish, covered, handled	$ 31-36
Creamer, tankard (ill.).	20-24
Custard cup	10-12
Goblet.	20-25

Polar Bear

Polar Bear

(Original name, Arctic; Iceberg; Alaska): Crystal Glass Company, Bridgeport, Ohio, 1880s. Clear; partly frosted, nonflint.

Bowl, waste	$ 89-94
Butter dish	195-212
Creamer.	142-157
Goblet	
Clear	74-87
Frosted	108-114
Pitcher, water, frosted (ill.)	284-293
Spoonholder.	92-110
Sugar bowl, covered	136-146
Tray, handled, 11" x 15½"	152-170

Clear worth 20 percent less. The stern of the boat on the water tray is impressed "C. G. C.", the manufactuer's initials.

Popcorn

Popcorn

Attributed by Lee to Sandwich, 1860s. Crystal only. Some pieces have "popcorn ears."

Butter dish, covered	$	42-50
Creamer, 4⅞" high		31-36
Goblet		
With ear.		40-46
Without ear		35-40
Pitcher, water (ill.)		78-92
Sauce		10-12
Spoonholder.		24-28
Sugar bowl, covered		40-50
Wine, with ear.		34-39

"Popcorn ear" pieces, 25 percent higher than clear prices listed.

Portland

Portland

Attributed to Portland, Maine, 1880s. U. S. Glass, later. Clear, gold, ruby stain; nonflint.

Basket, handled, large	$	92-105

Butter dish, covered	40-50
Candlestick	60-68
Celery.	25-31
Compote, covered, high	40-47
Creamer.	23-27
Cruet (ill.).	35-39
Cup	18-24
Goblet.	25-32
Pitcher, water	39-49
Punch bowl	82-110
Spoonholder.	19-26
Sugar bowl, covered	40-45
Sugar shaker	33-39
Wine	28-34

Add 80 percent for ruby stain.

Post Script

Tarentum, c. 1905. Clear, also with gold, nonflint.

Bowl, berry	$	10-15
Butter.		21-28
Creamer		
Individual		10-12
Table		14-18
Cruet, original faceted stopper		20-26
Goblet.		14-18
Olive, one handle		11-14
Plate		12-16
Salt shaker		10-15
Sauce		3-6
Spoonholder.		12-15
Sugar, covered.		20-26
Wine		12-15

Powder and Shot

Powder and Shot

Some made at Sandwich, early 1870s; other makers unknown. Clear, nonflint and flint; latter more usual.

(continued)

Butter bowl, covered.	$ 80-88
Caster bottle	41-50
Celery.	62-74
Compote, covered, high standard.	88-95
Creamer, applied handle (ill.)	82-92
Egg cup, flint	46-55
Goblet.	55-65
Pitcher, water	136-155
Sauce	12-17
Spoonholder.	39-46
Sugar bowl, covered	74-82

Pressed Diamond

Pressed Diamond

(Zephyr): Central Glass Company, Wheeling, West Virginia. Clear, yellow, amber, blue (scarce); nonflint.

Butter dish, covered	$ 50-58
Celery.	30-39
Creamer, 4¾″ high (ill.)	32-36
Compote	
Covered	50-62
Open	24-29
Goblet.	30-35
Pitcher	49-54
Spoonholder.	24-28
Sugar bowl, covered	58-66
Tumbler.	24-30

Amber, 30 percent; yellow, 70 percent; blue, 125 percent higher than clear prices listed. A few scarce examples made for silver-plated holders.

Pressed Leaf

(N.P.L.): McKee Bros., Pittsburgh, 1868. Attributed to Sandwich; in McKee's catalog as early as 1868 in flint; "N.P.L.", McKee's abbreviation for "New Pressed

Pressed Leaf

Leaf." Central Glass Company, Wheeling, West Virginia, 1881, nonflint.

Butter bowl, covered.	$ 40-47
Compote, covered, high standard, 6″, (sweetmeat), 7″, 8″	54-72
Cordial	44-51
Creamer, applied handle (ill.)	40-45
Dish, oval, 7″, 8″, 9″.	25-38
Egg cup	22-27
Goblet.	27-35
Pitcher, water	88-96
Sauce, flat, 4″	8-11
Spoonholder.	23-28
Sugar bowl, covered	38-44
Wine	38-42

Prices are for nonflint. Flint worth 20 percent more.

Primrose

Primrose

Canton Glass Company, Canton, Ohio, 1880s. Crystal, amber, canary, blue, apple green, opaque-white, turquoise, purple slag, opaque-black, and yellow. Nonflint.

Bowl, berry, round, deep.	$ 19-24
Bread plate, oval, 8″ x 12½″,	
flower handles	33-36
Butter dish	35-40
Cake stand	31-38
Compote, covered, 6″, 7½″, 8″, 9″	30-56
Creamer.	24-28
Egg cup	28-33
Goblet, plain or knob stem.	24-33
Pickle dish	11-14
Pitcher, 7½″ high (ill.)	34-38
Plate, 4½″, 6″, 7″, 8¾″, cake (handled) .	17-32
Sauce, footed, 4″, 5½″; flat	8-14
Spoonholder.	19-22
Sugar bowl, covered	34-42
Waste bowl	21-26
Water tray	32-39
Wine	20-30

Yellow and amber, 20 percent higher; blue, green, 30 percent higher than clear prices listed.

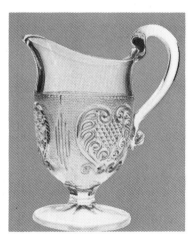

Princess Feather

Princess Feather

(Rochelle): Sandwich called it Princess Feather; Bakewell, Pears, Blackwell & Company called it Rochelle. Clear, opaque white, nonflint.

Butter dish, covered	$ 50-60
Celery	45-53
Compote	
Covered, 6″, 7″, high standard . . .	69-87
Open, 8″, low standard	28-34
Creamer (ill.)	54-62
Egg cup	36-40
Goblet.	35-40
Honey dish or sauce	10-14
Pitcher, ½ gal.	110-132
Plate, 6″, 7″, 8″, 9″, cake.	34-53
Spoonholder.	29-35
Sugar bowl, open	42-52

Opaque white, 50 percent higher than clear.

Printed Hobnail

Printed Hobnail

Maker unknown, 1880s. Clear, amber, canary, blue, green, amethyst; nonflint.

Butter dish	$ 36-44
Celery vase	32-37
Creamer.	24-30
Goblet.	28-32
Mug, handled	12-16
Pitcher, water (ill.)	30-40
Saucedish, 4″	5-8
Spoonholder.	15-19
Sugar bowl	31-41
Tray for water set	32-38
Tumbler.	12-16
Wine	24-29

Amber, canary, 60 percent higher; blue, green, amethyst, at least 125 percent higher than clear prices listed. One of the "safe" hobnails.

Priscilla

Priscilla

(Alexis; Sun and Star): Dalzell, Gilmore & Leighton Company, Findlay, Ohio, 1890s. Clear, with red dots, nonflint.

Bowl, square, 8″, flat, 10½″, rose	$ 35-52
Butter dish, covered	74-85
Cake stand, 10″ dia.	63-79
Celery	45-58
Compote	
Covered, 7″	57-62
5″ high	45-50
Open, 7½″	30-36
Creamer	36-41
Goblet	40-50
Mug	29-35
Pitcher, water	91-100
Spoonholder	29-33
Sugar bowl, covered	47-59
Tumbler (ill.)	25-34
Wine	29-37

With red dots, values 40 percent higher than clear prices listed. Being reproduced in limited forms, most shapes of which were not made originally, and in blue and green, not original colors. Metz and some current publications list a toothpick, but we do not have proof that one exists.

Prism

McKee and others, c. 1860s. Flint and nonflint. Don't confuse it with Bakewell, Pears' Prism and Flute—originally called Prism—a nonflint product, renamed for clarification.

Champagne	$ 37-42
Compote, open	32-42

Prism

Creamer	60-68
Decanter, qt., no stopper	59-67
Goblet (ill.)	30-35
Pitcher	84-92
Wine	39-49

Nonflint, 50 percent lower than flint prices listed. The McKee version has a stem with prisms ending at the stem base in points, with the base disc plain.

Prism and Diamond Point

Shards found at Sandwich. Bryce/U. S. Glass, 1880s, 1890s. Clear, flint, from 1860s; later in nonflint.

Butter dish, covered	$ 54-65
Compote, covered, knob stem	103-112
Creamer, 6½″ high	68-76
Egg cup, double	48-55
Goblet	
Knob stem (flint)	40-50
Plain stem (nonflint)	20-25
Spoonholder	36-41
Sugar bowl, covered	54-62
Tumbler	38-45
Wine	55-64

Prices are for flint; nonflint worth about half.

Prism and Flattened Sawtooth

(Ribbed Pineapple): Maker unknown, 1850s. Clear.

Goblet	$ 60-68
Lamp	74-81

Prism and Flattened Sawtooth

Spoonholder, or spill (ill.) 38-45
Sugar bowl, open 40-50

Prismatic

Maker unknown, c. 1885. Clear, nonflint.

Butter. . . . . $ 17-23
Creamer, 6¼" high 14-16
Sauce, flat 3-5
Spoonholder. 12-15
Sugar 16-20

Goblet not found in the literature. Table pieces have pedestal base.

The Prize

Won first prize for new pattern design, National Glass Co., 1901; McKee, 1910; New Martinsville (salve jar known). Clear or emerald green, may be gilded. Cruet, cup, squat syrup, and toothpick known in ruby stain.

Bowl, collared base, 7", 8" . . . . . . $ 14-18
Bowl, flat base
  Berry (straight) 6", 7", 8";
    flared 7", 10" 14-24
  Finger 15-20
Butter. 34-40
Cake stand, 9" dia. 30-38
Compote
  Jelly, 4½" dia. 16-21
    with lid 28-34
    Regular, 7", 8" 24-32
Cracker jar, covered, 7" high 42-55
Creamer
  Berry 18-22
  Table 23-29
Cruet, 8 oz. (no thumbprint
  and ellipse) 33-39
Cup, no thumbprint and ellipse . . . 10-13

Dish, oblong 7", 9", 10" 14-20
Goblet. 27-34
Mustard, covered 32-42
Olive, 4½" triangular, handleless. . . 15-21
Pitcher, ½ gal.
  Squat (bulbous), stuck handle . . . 41-49
  Tankard, lacks thumbprint
    and ellipse 34-40
Plate, underliner for finger bowl
  (lacks thumbprint
  and ellipse), 5" 12-16
Pomade jar, took metal lid, bulbous,
  1½" top dia. with lid 18-22
Punch bowl, 14", footed 95-118
Salt shaker
  Large, swelled center, no
    thumbprint and ellipse. 14-18
  Squat (narrow neck, bulbous) . . . 19-22
  Tall, straight tapered (no
    thumbprint and ellipse) 14-18
Sauce, flat, 4" (also with collared
  base); 4½" 7-12
Spoonholder. 17-21
Straw jar, covered 49-56
Sugar
  Berry, open, handleless 16-20
  Table, covered 30-36
Syrup
  "Lip can," lid is attached
    to handle and covers the lip;
    stuck handle 39-44
  Molasses: tall, straight, does not
    have thumbprint and ellipse,
    stuck handle 34-40
  Squat syrup, patterned handle . . . 35-45
Toothpick 30-38
Tray, condiment, oblong. 15-20
Tumbler (no thumbprint and ellipse)
  Iced tea 15-21
  Water 13-17
Vase
  Limousine, for metal holder, 6" high
    top dia. 3", bottom ½" 35-42
  Trumpet, 6", 7", 10". 13-23
Water bottle. 33-41
Wine 24-29

Many pieces come without the characteristic ellipse and thumbprint band. Emerald green add 50 percent; ruby stain add 200-400 percent to clear prices listed.

Psyche and Cupid

Maker unknown, 1890s. Clear, nonflint.

Butter dish, covered . . . . $ 64-72
Celery. 40-47

213

(continued)

Psyche and Cupid

Compote, high, low standard, covered .	56-77
Creamer, 7″ high (ill.)	49-58
Goblet.	42-51
Pitcher, water	71-81
Sauce, footed, 3 sizes	15-19
Spoonholder, pedestal, smooth rim . .	36-40
Sugar bowl	47-56
Wine	40-52

Pieces are oversized (note height of creamer). A bread tray is not known.

Quaker Lady

Dalzell, c. 1890. Clear, nonflint. May be engraved.

Bowl	$ 20-25
Butter.	40-44
Creamer.	27-32
Goblet.	30-36
Sauce	12-15
Spoonholder.	20-24
Sugar	34-38

Add 30 percent for engraving.

Quatrefoil

Quatrefoil

Maker unknown, 1880s. Clear, apple green, nonflint.

Bowl	$ 16-20
Butter dish, covered	32-36
Compote, covered, 7″	35-40
Creamer.	20-23
Pitcher (ill.)	32-37
Salt/Pepper, pr.	24-33
Sauce, footed, 4″ dia..	11-15
Spoonholder.	14-18
Sugar bowl	
Covered	24-30
Open	14-21

Colors, 75 percent higher than clear prices listed. No goblet or tumbler yet, despite listings in the literature.

Queen

Queen

(Panelled Daisy and Button; Pointed Panel Daisy and Button): McKee Glass Company, Jeannette, Pennsylvania, c. 1894. Canadian name, "Daisy and Depressed Button." Clear, yellow, amber, apple green, blue.

Butter dish, covered	
Flat base, tapered lid.	$ 58-68
Wavy base, round dome	40-50
Cake stand	39-45
Claret	32-37
Compote	
Covered	41-50
Open, amber, in silver-plated base . .	78-86
Creamer.	30-34
Dish, oval, 7″, 9″	16-22
Goblet.	26-30
Pitcher, water, ½ gal., qt. (ill.)	40-45

Sauce, flat, footed, 4″   5-12
Spoonholder.   21-26
Sugar bowl
   Covered   40-48
   Open   28-36
Wine   20-25

Yellow, 50 percent; amber, apple green, 60 percent; blue, 80 percent higher than clear prices listed. One of the "safe" Daisy and Button patterns, not reproduced.

Queen Anne

Queen Anne

(Bearded Man; Santa Claus; Neptune; Old Man; Old Man of the Woods): LaBelle Glass Company, Bridgeport, Ohio, 1879. Clear, colors, nonflint. May be engraved.

Bowl, covered (in original ad as
   "casserole"), 7″, 8″ . . . . $ 52-68
Butter dish, covered   54-62
Compote, covered, 7″, 8″   52-63
Creamer, head, 5½″ high.   34-42
Milk, head.   50-60
Pitcher, water, ½ gal., head   55-63
Salt shaker, scarce.   30-40
Sauce, footed, 4½″.   10-14
Spoonholder.   29-36
Sugar bowl, open   25-32
Syrup (ill.), head . . . .   125+

Colors, 25 percent higher than clear prices listed. No goblet. The four pitchers have the bearded head.

Quilt and Flute

Quilt and Flute

Maker and date unknown. Blown in the mold. Probably sold as a container for mustard, to be used later for cream and sugar. Clear, nonflint.

Creamer, 3½″ high (ill.) . . . . $ 28-37
Sugar bowl   35-44

Other pieces not known.

Racing Deer

Racing Deer

Indiana Tumbler & Goblet Company, late 1890s. Clear, chocolate.

Pitcher
   Water, chocolate. $350-400
   Water, clear (ill.).   175-195

Radiant

(Dynast): U. S. Glass Company (Columbia), c. late 1880s. Clear, etched, nonflint.

215

(continued)

Bowl	$ 12-15
Butter dish, covered	30-34
Cake plate.	28-33
Celery.	24-27
Compote	
Covered	38-44
Open	23-27
Creamer.	19-23
Goblet.	20-24
Pitcher, syrup	34-40
Salt/Pepper, pr.	30-37
Spoonholder.	14-18
Sugar bowl, covered	30-34
Tumbler.	15-20
Wine	16-19

Clear, etched, same price.

Rainbow

McKee & Bros., Pittsburgh, c. 1894, with a sugar shown in an 1898 catalog. McKee was the first of the manufacturers to use a permanent trademark, "PRES-CUT" 1894, in the glass. Clear, rose pink, emerald green, nonflint.

Bowl	$ 16-20
Butter dish, covered	36-49
Carafe, faceted stopper	35-39
Creamer.	29-34
Decanter, faceted stopper	40-46
Goblet.	42-47
Jar, cigar, gold or silver lid	38-47
Pitcher, water	35-41
Salt dip, individual	10-13
Salt shaker, 2 types	15-19
Sugar, covered.	30-40
Tray, wine.	22-27
Tumbler	
Champagne (juice).	10-14
Whiskey (shot glass)	7-11
Wine	12-17

Listed in the McKee ads as late as 1927. The wine set is shown in a Butler Bros. catalog of 1910. Peterson 24B shows the shaker with bulging sides, calling it "Button and Star Panel," and 169P shows another form, calling it "Rainbow." No proof of butter, goblet, or spoonholder.

Raindrop

Maker unknown, c. 1880s. Clear, canary, amber, blue, emerald green, light green (rare); nonflint.

Raindrop

Bowl (ill.)	$ 12-16
Butter dish, covered, round	32-40
Compote, open, high, swirl stem	28-34
Creamer.	24-32
Egg cup, double	27-35
Pitcher, water	33-39
Plate	14-18
Sauce, flat, footed, 4″	4-8
Tray, water, plain edge, 10½″	30-38

Blue, 70 percent higher; amber, canary, 100 percent higher; light green, 150 percent higher than clear prices listed. Raindrops are graduated sizes on the exterior, whereas Flattened Hobnail has drops that are the same size. No goblet.

Raspberry

Raspberry

Maker unknown, late 1870s. Clear, nonflint.

216

Butter dish, covered	$ 35-42
Creamer , 4⅞" high	29-34
Pitcher, water (ill.)	47-54
Spoonholder.	29-34
Sugar bowl, covered	37-46
Tray.	42-49
Tumbler.	26-34

Goblet not known in the literature.

Ray

Ray

(Ball and Swirl): McKee Bros., 1894. Plain or engraved or ruby-stained or frosted on the plain parts. Nonflint.

Butter.	$ 42-49
Candlestick, single.	31-39
Celery vase, tall	28-32
Compote, open, 9", ...	30-36
Creamer (ill.)	24-30
Goblet.	17-23
Pitcher, tankard (flat;	
pattern on base)	47-54
Saucedish, round, 4", 5", footed.	24-32
Spoonholder.	15-19
Sugar bowl	
Covered	39-42
Open	35-45
Tumbler.	23-29

Ruby-stained, 60 percent more than clear prices listed. The salt shaker is an overall pattern, swirling to right. Lee's sketch of the goblet shows the base with a ring of balls, but the goblet actually has a plain base, and the swirled stem bulbous, not concave and elongated as she shows.

Red Block

Red Block

Doyle & Company (U.S. Glass Company), 1892 and later. Clear with blocks painted red; nonflint.

Bowl, 8", 9"	$ 56-64
Butter dish, covered, dbl. handled . .	68-74
Celery vase, no handles, 6½" high . .	96-115
Creamer, individual	62-73
Dish	
Large	59-69
8", 9", 10".	41-49
Finger or waste bowl (scarce)	72-79
Goblet.	32-38
Mug.	29-35
Pitcher, water (ill.)	120-140
Salt dip	
Individual	51-59
Master, round	86-95
Salt/Pepper, pr.	118-130
Spoonholder, dbl. handled	36-42
Sugar bowl, covered,	
dbl. handled	64-72
Tray, water (rare)	125-140
Tumbler, two rows of blocks	29-34
Wine	35-40

Goblet, mug, wine reproduced. The tumbler with three rows of blocks is scarce. Sugar lids in mint condition are very hard to find.

Regal Block

(Co-op's No. 190): Co-operative Flint Glass Co., c. 1892. Clear, or with gold or engraving. Nonflint.

Bowl, 7", 8"	$ 12-16
Butter.	25-32
Cake stand	25-30
Celery.	16-21
Compote, covered, 7", 8"	28-34

(continued)

Creamer	
Individual	11-14
Regular	17-20
Decanter	28-35
Dish, oblong 7″, 8″, 9″	
(also comes footed)	13-16
Goblet.	15-19
Hat made from tumbler mold	36-40
Jelly, 4½″ handled.	13-16
Pitcher	
Jug or tankard, ½ gal.	29-35
Jug, quart	25-30
Salt shaker	10-14
Sauce, 4½″	4-6
Spooner	12-15
Sugar	
Individual, covered	15-19
Regular	21-26
Syrup	32-36
Tumbler.	10-12
Wine	13-15

Add 20 percent for gold or engraving.

Sauce	8-11
Spoonholder.	25-32
Sugar bowl	40-47
Tumbler.	14-19

Green, 40 percent; blue, 100 percent; amethyst, 200 percent higher than clear prices given. No toothpick (yet!).

Reticulated Cord

Reticulated Cord

O'Hara Glass Company, Pittsburgh, and U. S. Glass Company, 1880s. Clear; amber and blue.

Bread plate, 9½″ + handles	$ 30-36
Butter dish, covered	33-40
Cake stand, large	34-38
Celery vase	24-28
Creamer (ill.)	31-37
Goblet.	19-25
Pitcher, water	39-49
Relish	12-15
Sauce, flat.	5-8
Spoonholder.	15-19
Sugar bowl	
Covered	30-38
Open	18-22
Tumbler.	25-34
Wine	18-26

Color, 125 percent higher than clear prices listed. Stuart lists the bread plate as "Atlantic Cable," associating it with earlier Cable, misdating it as the 1860s.

The Regent

The Regent

(Leaf Medallion): H. Northwood and Co., Wheeling, West Virginia, 1880s. Clear, cobalt, green, amethyst (rare), decorated with gold. Clear prices given.

Bowl	$ 24-30
Butter dish	42-50
Compote, jelly.	21-26
Creamer (ill.)	38-42
Cruet set	80-88
Pitcher, water 8″ high	52-65
Salt/Pepper, pr.	50-58

Rexford

Rexford

(Euclid; Boylan; original name, Alfa): Higbee, c. 1910, occasionally marked, and limited production by New Martinsville. Clear glass only, nonflint.

Butter dish, covered	$ 31-40
Cake stand, 9¾".	29-35
Celery (ill.)	22-31
Creamer.	25-34
Goblet.	24-32
Honey or preserve, covered, round . . .	42-52
Pitcher	37-44
Plate, square, 7"	17-23
Spoonholder.	16-21
Sugar bowl, covered	30-36
Toothpick (not toy spooner)	17-24
Wine	16-24

Confusing pattern, Paden City's "Webb." There is a toy banana stand and cake stand. The toy four-piece set is worth $100-125. Lucas shows the base to the honey.

Ribbed Forget-Me-Not

(Pert): Bryce Brothers, 1880, and U. S. Glass, 1890s. Clear, nonflint, with scarce pieces in amber or blue.

Butter dish, covered, 5¾" dia.	$ 31-38
Creamer (ill.)	30-39
Cup, handled	22-29
Mug, 3¼" high.	22-29
Mustard jar (mug with cover)	32-42
Spoonholder.	24-30
Sugar bowl, covered	33-40

Ribbed Forget-Me-Not

Although larger than average for a toy set, is included in that category. No other pieces known.

Ribbed Grape

Ribbed Grape

Maker unknown, attributed to Sandwich, 1850s. Clear, flint. Opaque white, blue-green, rare.

Butter dish, covered	$105-111
Compote	
Covered, 6", high standard	147-156
Open, low foot, 8"	65-77
Creamer (ill.)	142-148
Goblet, 2 types	50-58
Pitcher	170-180
Plate, 6"	38-45
Sauce, flat.	14-20
Spoonholder.	39-45
Sugar bowl, covered	99-106
Wine	16-22

Colors, 250 percent higher than clear prices listed.

Ribbed Opal

Ribbed Opal

(Beatty Rib): A. J. Beatty Glass Company, Steubenville, Ohio, 1888, and U. S. Glass at Tiffin after 1890. Crystal, and blue, opalescent.

Butter.	$120-130
Creamer	
Individual (ill.)	58-65
Large	61-66
Matchholder, 1¾".	33-39
Mug.	37-46
Pitcher, water	58-64
Salt shaker	36-42
Spoonholder.	41-47
Sugar bowl	
Covered	97-115
Individual, did not take lid.	33-40
Shaker.	72-82
Toothpick, 2½"	52-62
Tumbler, 2 types	40-47
Wine	34-38

White opalescent worth 90 percent less than blue prices given. No stemware, cruet, or syrup. Not reproduced.

Ribbed Palm

Ribbed Palm

(Sprig): McKee & Bros., Pittsburgh, 1868. Clear, flint.

Bowl, 6", flat rim (butter base)	$ 29-32
Butter dish	78-88
Celery.	58-66
Champagne	83-97
Compote	
Covered, 6" (sweetmeat)	108-127
Low	33-39
Open, high, scalloped rim,	
7", 8", 10",.	77-140
Creamer, applied handle.	182-192
Dish, 6", 7", 8", 9", deep,	
scalloped rim	49-58
Egg cup	30-35
Goblet.	34-38
Lamp, three types	98-107
Pitcher, 9" high, applied	
handle, rare (ill.).	170-194
Plate, 6".	32-39
Salt on pedestal	27-35
Sauce, 4".	8-12
Spoonholder.	30-35
Sugar bowl, covered	66-69
Tumbler, ½ pt.	72-87
Wine	57-64

Color, 100 percent higher than clear prices listed.

Ribbon

Bakewell, Pears & Company, Pittsburgh, c. 1870; also George Duncan and Sons. Clear, frosted, nonflint.

Bowl, waste	$ 46-54
Butter dish, covered	68-75
Celery.	44-53
Compote	
Covered, high standard	62-79
Dolphin stem, scalloped	325-355
Open, Dolphin standard,	
rectangular.	185-215
Rebecca	240-268
Round, 8"	79-85
Creamer.	44-50
Dish, cheese, covered	109-114
Goblet.	38-47
Pitcher	55-65
Spoonholder.	29-36
Sugar bowl, covered	59-69
Tray, water	108-116
Tumbler.	32-37
Wine (scarce)	108-119

Goblet and Rebecca compote reproduced. The Fostoria reproduction of the Rebecca compote has more pronounced ring under the bowl and harsher rim scallops. Prices are for frosted. Clear worth 30 percent less.

Ribbon Candy

Ribbon Candy

(Erroneously, Candy Ribbon. Figure Eight; Double Loop; Bryce): Bryce Bros., 1880s; U.S. Glass Company, 1898. Clear, scarce in green. Nonflint.

Bowls, various, open	$ 17-26
Butter dish, covered, flat or footed . . .	36-46
Cake stand, 10″	39-46
Celery	29-38
Claret	40-45
Compote, covered, 7″, 8″	42-52
Cordial	42-48
Cruet	50-54
Cup/saucer	32-42
Creamer	29-35
Goblet	31-39
Honey dish, square, covered	47-55
Pitcher, water (ill.)	40-50
Plate, 6″, 7″, 8″	15-25
Salt shaker	24-30
Spoonholder	15-20
Sugar bowl	
Covered	34-41
Open	15-20
Syrup (scarce)	82-95
Tumbler	23-29
Wine	27-33

Green worth 60 percent more.

Richmond

Nickel Plate Glass Company, Fostoria, Ohio, 1889, and U. S. Glass Company, early 1890s. Clear, ruby stain; nonflint.

Richmond

Bowl, finger	$ 20-26
Butter dish	35-42
Celery	28-35
Creamer, 4½″ high (ill.)	29-37
Goblet	21-28
Mustard, metal top	29-33
Pitcher, water tankard (one row	
pattern at base)	58-68
Salt/Pepper, pr. (scarce)	37-49
Spoonholder	15-20
Sugar bowl	32-36
Tumbler	14-19
Wine	21-28

Pattern direction varies on different pieces (vertical or diagonal). Metz pictures the goblet as Akron Block and next to it the creamer as Bars and Buttons. McCain lists Block and Double Bar as another name for this pattern; similar but lacking the hexagonal buttons, and made at Findlay.

Richmond

221 (continued)

Richmond

Richards & Hartley Glass Company, Tarentum, Pennsylvania, 1885-1891 and U. S. Glass Company. Clear glass only, nonflint.

Butter dish, covered	$ 36-42
Celery (ill.)	29-35
Compotes, open, 7″, 8″,	24-33
Creamer	22-31
Cruet	30-37
Goblet	24-29
Pitcher, qt., ½ gal.	47-56
Sauce, 4″	4-7
Spoonholder	13-18
Sugar shaker	28-37
Sugar bowl, covered	32-40
Tumbler	16-22
Wine	33-43

Forms are generally square. Design elements probably inspired by the earlier Tulip with Sawtooth.

Ring and Block

(Block and Ring, Prism and Block Band; erroneously Persian, a case of mistaken identity): King Glass Co., c. 1891. Clear or with ruby stain, nonflint. May be engraved.

Compote on high standard, covered	$ 35-40
Goblet	17-22
Pitcher, tankard	32-36
Salt dip, individual	12-15

Ruby stain add 100 percent.

Ringed Framed Ovals

Ringed Framed Ovals

An "Oval" pattern attributed to New England and Midwest from the 1840s to the 1860s. Clear, vaseline, apple green, flint.

Goblet	$137-150
Tumbler (ill.)	78-90

Vaseline, 25 percent; apple green, 50 percent higher than clear prices listed.

Ripple

(Ripple Band): Sandwich, 1870s. Made in the closing days of the factory, and by others. Clear, nonflint.

Bowl, oval	$ 18-26
Butter dish, covered	33-39
Champagne	24-31
Compote	
Covered	37-47
Open	26-31
Creamer, applied handle	40-50
Egg cup	15-20
Goblet	17-22
Lamp	29-38
Plate, 6″	12-18
Salt, footed, round or flat oval	19-26
Sauce, flat, round	4-6
Spoonholder	23-32
Sugar bowl, covered	35-42
Wine	30-37

Similar pattern is Herringbone Band in which the band is made of "V's" rather than wavy ripples. Same values.

Roanoke

Ripley and Company, Pittsburgh, 1880s; U. S. Glass Company, 1890s. Clear or with ruby rims; emerald green; nonflint.

Butter dish, covered	$ 38-45
Celery	22-27
Creamer	28-34
Goblet	24-32
Spoonholder	16-19
Sugar bowl, covered	38-45
Tumbler	13-17
Water pitcher, reeded applied handle	42-52
Wine	20-25

Colors, 20-25 percent; ruby stain, 30-40 percent higher than for clear prices listed.

Robin Hood

Roman Rosette

Robin Hood

Fostoria Glass Company, c. 1901. Clear, nonflint.

Butter dish . . . . $ 25-36
Creamer (ill.) 15-20
Goblet. 30-37
Pickle dish, oval 8-11
Pitcher, 3 pint 25-30
Salt shaker 13-17
Spoonholder. 13-17
Sugar bowl 25-30
Syrup 30-35
Tumbler. 12-16

Rock Crystal

McKee Glass Company, Jeannette, Pennsylvania, c. 1894. Clear, colors, opaque decorated, nonflint.

Butter dish, covered . . . . $ 125+
Cake stand 28-36
Celery tray (comb and brush) 10-15
Creamer. 16-21
Cup, custard. 5-10
Glass, sundae 5-10
Goblet. 14-19
Pitcher, qt. jug 41-49
Spoonholder. 26-33
Sugar bowl, covered 32-40

Colors, 50 percent higher than clear prices listed.

Roman Rosette

Bryce, Walker & Company, 1875. Reissued by U.S. Glass Company in 1892, again in 1898. Clear; few pieces in color; clear pieces sometimes decorated with ruby; nonflint.

Bowl, 5″, 6″, 7″, 8″ . . . . $ 15-25
Bread plate, 9″ x 11″ oval,
  no motto. 31-36
Butter dish, covered 44-51
Cake stand, 9″, 10″ 42-51
Caster set, 3 bottles
  on flat glass stand 70-79
Celery. 26-30
Compote, covered, high, low
  standard, 5″, 6″, 7″, 8″ 49-66
Creamer, one pint 29-36
Goblet. 30-36
Mug, large, medium 16-36
Pickle dish 12-17
Pitcher, syrup (ill.) 57-63
Salt/Pepper, pr. 28-40
Sauce, flat, footed 6-10
Spoonholder. 19-24
Sugar bowl, covered 41-46
Wine 62-70

Ruby stain 60 percent higher than clear prices listed. Goblet reproduced.

Romola

Robinson Glass Co., c. 1894. Clear, nonflint.

Bowl, 7″ . . . . $ 10-13
Compote, covered, 6″ dia. 24-29
Condiment set on tray (cruet,
  salt/pepper shakers, mustard) 66-85

223

(continued)

Cordial	16-19
Cruet, faceted stopper	19-24
Goblet.	15-20
Mustard (salt shaker with	
metal mustard lid)	12-15
Pitcher, bulbous base (Globe Jug) . . .	25-30
Salt shaker	10-13
Tray, round condiment (may double	
as cordial tray).	15-18
Wine	15-20

Rose in Snow

Rope Bands

Rope Bands

(Clear Panels with Cord Band; original name, Argent): Bryce/U. S. Glass, c. 1890. Clear; color would be scarce.

Bread plate, 8¾″ x 13″ (see note). . . .	$ 30-36
Butter, covered	31-36
Cake stand, large	30-36
Celery.	21-25
Compote, covered	33-40
Creamer (ill.)	23-29
Goblet.	19-25
Plate, 7″	16-21
Platter	34-42
Spoonholder, pedestal, flat rim	14-17
Sugar	
Covered	35-40
Open	18-22
Tumbler.	11-15

Color, 100 percent higher than clear prices listed. Stuart calls the platter "Four-Petal (Variant)."

Rose in Snow

Kamm states the round form made in Lancaster, Ohio, probably Ohio Flint Glass Company, and both forms by Indiana Glass at Dunkirk. Bryce Bros., Pittsburgh, in the square shape. 1870s. Clear, amber, blue, yellow; nonflint.

Butter dish, round.	$ 44-53
Compote, covered, high	
standard, medium	49-56
Creamer (ill.)	30-39
Dish, oval, large, small (deep)	20-30
Goblet.	28-35
Mug, applied handle, better type. . .	46-54
Pitcher, water	102-112
Plate, 5″, 6″, 7¼″, 9″, (5″ scarce). . . .	19-37
Sauce, flat,	9-13
Spoonholder, round, square	27-32
Sugar bowl, round, square	42-47
Tumbler, water	42-50

Colors, 100 percent higher than clear prices listed. Goblet, mug with pressed handle "In fond Remembrance" and 9″ plate reproduced; the better type mug with the applied handle ends in crimping near the base, usually with a looped end, rather than a plain flat rounded end (reproduction?). Footed 8″ bowls are common and probably later production.

Rose Leaves

Maker unknown, c. 1880s. Clear, nonflint.

Goblet (ill.)	$ 20-27

Rose Leaves

Rose Point Band

Rose Point Band

(Water Lily): Indiana Glass Company, c. 1913. Clear, nonflint.

Butter dish	$ 30-33
Compote, covered, 7½″ dia.	30-40
Creamer (ill.)	24-28
Goblet.	21-28
Spoonholder.	15-19
Sugar bowl, covered	30-35
Tumbler.	16-20
Wine	19-25

Rose Sprig

Campbell, Jones & Company, Pittsburgh, 1886. Clear, amber, yellow, blue; nonflint.

Butter dish	$ 40-47
Cake stand	39-49
Celery vase	32-37

Rose Sprig

Creamer.	31-38
Goblet.	30-38
Mug, applied handle.	40-47
Pitcher, water, two sizes (ill.)	49-53
Plate, 6½″, 8½″, square	18-26
Salt, sleigh, 6″ long, undated	32-40
Spoonholder.	24-31
Sugar bowl, covered	46-52
Tray, water	51-60
Tumbler.	27-35

Colors, 40-50 percent higher than clear prices listed. Salt, sleigh salt reproduced. Stuart's "Rose Sprig" is not this pattern.

Rosette

Rosette

(Original name, Magic): Bryce Bros., Pittsburgh. Later produced by U.S. Glass Company, Tiffin, Ohio, 1890s. Clear, nonflint.

Bread plate, 9″ plus handles	$ 23-29
Butter dish, covered	35-43
Cake stand, 9″, 10″, 11″.	27-42
Celery.	33-37

(continued)

Compote
Covered, high standard,
6″, 7″, 8″.   49-53
Open, footed, 6″, 7″, 8″,
9″, 10″   21-32
Creamer.   22-27
Goblet.   29-36
Pitcher, water,
half gal. (ill.).   39-47
Plate, 7″, 9″   20-30
Relish   15-19
Spoonholder.   17-23
Sugar bowl, covered   28-34

Royal

Sugar bowl, covered (ill.).   40-48
Tumbler.   22-32
Confirmation of a goblet would be appreciated.

Rosette with Pinwheels

Rosette with Pinwheels

Indiana Glass Company, c. 1904. Clear,
nonflint.

Butter dish, covered . . . . $ 30-39
Celery.   26-34
Compote, jelly, open, 4⅝″ dia.   14-18
Creamer (ill.)   22-30
Cup, footed   9-13
Pitcher, water   50-58
Spoonholder.   14-19
Sugar bowl, covered   32-40

Royal

(Royal Lady): Belmont Glass Company,
Bellaire, Ohio, 1881. Clear, nonflint.

Bread plate, 8¾″ x 13½″,
"Crying Baby". . . . . $ 58-65
Butter dish   47-55
Celery, handled   30-37
Compote, covered 8″ high   44-59
Creamer.   34-39
Pitcher, water, ½ gal.   41-48
Salt shaker (very rare)   40-47
Spoonholder, handled   31-38

Royal Crystal

Royal Crystal

(Original name, Atlanta): Tarentum
Glass Company. Tarentum, Pennsylvania,
1894. Clear, ruby stained; nonflint.

Butter dish, covered . . . . $ 50-58
Celery.   27-36
Compote, open, 7¾″.   30-36
Creamer, 5¼″ high (ill.)   31-40
Pitcher, tankard, 9½″ high   57-67
Sauce, flat.   8-11
Spoonholder.   23-32
Sugar bowl
Covered   40-48
Open   22-29

Ruby stained, 50 percent higher than the clear
prices listed.

Royal Ivy

Ruffled Edge Hobnail

Royal Ivy

Northwood Glass Company, Martins Ferry, Ohio, 1889-1890. Clear, or frosted in deep pink fading to colorless; amber craquelle.

Bowl, berry	$ 50-55
Butter dish, covered, ...	112-128
Creamer.	57-64
Pitcher	
Syrup	68-77
Water (ill.).	118-127
Shakers,Salt/Pepper, pr..	62-74
Spoonholder.	40-45
Sugar bowl, covered	69-72
Toothpick holder	43-51
Tumbler.	30-35

All color patterns at least 50 percent higher than clear/frosted prices listed.

Ruffled Edge Hobnail

Northwood, Wheeling, West Virginia, 1903. White opalescent. Nonflint.

Butter dish, covered	$ 47-59
Celery, opalescent (ill.)	35-42
Creamer.	37-47
Spoonholder.	32-37
Sugar bowl	44-52
Tumbler.	30-35

Candleholders, cigarette boxes, powder jars listed in colors are not this pattern. Confusing pattern is Squat Ruffled Hobnail (Hobbs' Hobnail).

Royal Oak

Ruffled Eye

Royal Oak

Northwood Glass Company, Martins Ferry, Ohio, 1889-1890. Deep pink/clear; deep pink/clear, acid finished; pink/clear, amber mottled.

Prices about the same as Royal Ivy.

Ruffled Eye

Indiana Tumbler & Goblet (National) Company, 1890s. Water pitcher only. Nonflint.

(continued)

Amber.				$142-155
Canary				171-177
Chocolate				285-315
Clear				87-95
Emerald green.				148-154

Bowl, berry, dog in base	$ 25-32
Butter dish, dog finial	62-69
Cake stand, no dog	32-37
Celery vase	22-29
Compote, covered, high (dog finial)	40-48
Creamer.	30-36
Cruet	30-34
Goblet.	25-32
Jar, jam, covered	48-55
Jelly compote	20-24
Pickle dish, dog in base	25-31
Pitcher, ½ gal. jug,	
½ gal. tankard (no dog)	32-43
Salt shaker (no dog)	15-21
Sauce, flat (no dog)	8-10
Spoonholder.	25-30
Sugar bowl, covered, dog finial.	54-68
Tumbler, no dog.	15-22

S Repeat

S Repeat

National Glass Company, Pittsburgh, 1903, at Northwood Glass Company. Clear; clear amethyst, blue, apple green, all may be gilded; white, blue opalescent. Nonflint.

Bowl	$ 19-23
Butter dish	31-42
Celery.	24-30
Creamer.	25-30
Cruet	29-33
Decanter	35-41
Jam jar	30-37
Pitcher, water	34-40
Punch bowl	80-96
Salt/Pepper, pr.	36-44
Sauce	9-12
Spoonholder.	21-26
Sugar bowl, covered	30-37
Toothpick.	21-29
Tray.	33-40
Tumbler (ill.)	55-64
Wine	18-25

Opalescent, 100-200 percent more; colors, 50 percent higher than clear prices listed. Cruet reproductions common in translucent colors without gold and with pointed panelled stoppers. Original stoppers are onion-shaped.

St. Bernard

Fostoria Glass Company, Moundsville, West Virginia, c. 1894. Clear, nonflint. Usually engraved.

Sandwich Block

Sandwich Block

Sandwich, early. Flint.

Piece shown in photo is blue perfume with stopper. Rare.

Sandwich Covered Sugar

Attributed to Sandwich. Early flint.

Sandwich Spill

Sandwich glass, early 1850s. Another example of magnificent glass in an Inverted Sawtooth pattern. Flint.

Sandwich Covered Sugar

Sandwich Star

Compote	
Covered, high standard	$ 350+
Open, supported by 3	
dolphins, flint	850+
Amethyst, tall (rare),	
flint	1,350+
Cordial, flint	300+
Creamer, flint	335-365
Decanter, qt. with stopper	118-132
Goblet (rare), flint	420-500
Pitcher, flint (ill.)	1,000+
Relish dish	78-84
Spill holder	45-55
Spoonholder.	45-55

Sandwich Spill

Sandwich Star

Sandwich, early. Clear, clambroth, or amethyst (rare).

Sawtooth

Sawtooth

New England Glass Company, and Sandwich, 1860s. Clear, rare in color; flint and nonflint.

Bowl, berry	$ 33-42
Butter bowl	42-55
Cake stand, 9″, 10″	90-97
Celery vase	49-55
Compote	
Covered, 10″, knob stem	118-126
Open, 6″, 7″, 8″, 10″	35-67

(continued)

Creamer (ill.)	45-55
Decanter, qt.	47-53
Egg cup	30-40
Goblet, knob stem	36-43
Pitcher, water, ½ gal.	70-94
Sauce, 4", 5"	10-16
Spill holder, octagonal	42-51
Spoonholder.	29-34
Sugar bowl	40-50
Tumbler, footed, ...	34-40

Prices are for early flint. Later nonflint pieces such as plain-stem goblets, covered pieces with flat rather than sawtooth rims that interlock, and pieces with pressed handles are worth 30-50 percent less.

Sawtoothed Honeycomb

Sawtoothed Honeycomb

(Original name, Serrated Block and Loop; called Radiant by Union Stopper): Steiner Glass Company, Buckhannon, West Virginia, 1906; again in 1908 by Union Stopper Company, Morgantown, West Virginia. Clear, clear with central honeycombs in ruby with rims in gold; nonflint.

Bonbon, triangular, one handle . . .	$ 14-18
Butter dish	30-37
Creamer (ill.)	21-25
Goblet.	20-29
Punch bowl	
14" dia.	79-88
With stand	98-122
Sauce	
Flat, 4".	5-8
Footed, 4½"	6-10
Spoonholder.	30-37
Sugar bowl, covered	30-37

Syrup	41-49
Toothpick	
Plain	20-25
Ruby souvenir	32-77

Ruby stain, 100 percent more.

Saxon

Adams & Company, Pittsburgh, Pennsylvania, c. 1880. Clear, ruby stain plain and engraved, milk glass.. Reissued after 1891 by the U.S. Glass Company. Nonflint.

Bowl, waste	$ 32-41
Butter dish, covered, flanged	29-35
Celery.	17-22
Claret	18-23
Compote	
Covered	35-40
Open	21-28
Creamer.	22-26
Cruet, plain	34-42
Goblet.	15-20
Mug.	14-17
Pitcher, ½ gal.	30-40
Plate, 6"	33-42
Salt shaker	15-21
Spoonholder, pedestal	14-19
Sugar bowl, covered	28-33
Tray, water	28-34
Tumbler.	12-16
Wine	15-20

Ruby, 80 percent more; Bakewell, Pears made a different engraved or milk glass, 30 percent more.

Scalloped Prism

(Triple Bar): Doyle & Company, Pittsburgh, c. 1880s. Clear, nonflint. Originally called No. 84 by Doyle. Reissued by U.S. Glass Company in 1891.

Butter dish, covered	$ 20-25
Goblet.	13-17
Spoonholder.	11-15
Sugar bowl, covered	20-25
Tumbler.	9-12

Scalloped Tape

(Jewel Band): Maker unknown, 1880s. Clear, amber, canary, blue, apple green.

Butter dish, covered	$ 33-39
Cake stand	30-38
Celery.	22-30

Scalloped Tape

Compote, 8″ dia., covered	43-55
Creamer.	22-29
Dish, covered, triangular, 8″	35-42
Egg cup	19-27
Goblet.	20-28
Pitcher	
Milk	29-35
Water (ill.).	35-45
Plate, bread	25-32
Relish	10-15
Sauce	
Flat	5-9
Footed.	7-11
Spoonholder.	14-18
Sugar	
Covered	27-36
Open	13-19
Wine	19-27

All colored pieces, at least 60 percent higher than clear prices listed.

Scarab

Scarab

Maker unknown, c. 1850. Clear, flint.

Goblet (ill.) $118-130

Other pieces? The goblet is beautiful!

Scroll

(Stippled Scroll): Maker unknown, 1880s. Clear, nonflint.

Butter bowl, covered.	$ 30-38
Compote, covered, high or low	
standard.	34-42
Creamer.	28-35
Egg cup	14-23
Goblet.	18-26
Salt, footed	17-24
Sauce	5-8
Spoonholder.	22-26
Sugar bowl, covered	30-38
Tumbler, footed	15-21

Acorn finials.

Scroll and Daisy

Scroll and Daisy

Maker unknown, c. 1900. Clear, nonflint.

Creamer, 4⅝″ high (ill.) . . . . $ 17-23

Probably sold with mustard in it, to be used as measuring cup. Marked on panel under lip are gradations from 2 oz. to 8 oz.

Scroll with Acanthus

Northwood, c. 1903. Clear, blue, apple green, sometimes enameled; opalescent in clear, green, blue, canary; purple slag.

231

(continued)

Scroll with Acanthus

Butter dish	$ 34-43
Compote, jelly, opalescent colored . .	34-39
Creamer (ill.)	30-35
Cruet, green or blue opalescent . . .	139-165
Pitcher, green opalescent	185-215
Salt shaker, blue with gold	37-43
Sauce, 5″, clear opalescent	15-21
Sugar bowl, no cover	20-26
Toothpick, apple green	59-69
Tumbler, blue opal	39-47

U. S. Glass made a quite different pattern by the same name.

Butter dish	$ 30-36
Cake plate, handled	17-24
Cordial	21-28
Creamer.	19-23
Egg cup, 2 handles.	18-24
Goblet.	23-28
Mustard, covered	26-34
Pitcher (ill.)	77-86
Salt dip, handled	14-19
Spoonholder.	13-19
Sugar bowl, covered	30-35
Wine	20-26

Colors, 50 percent higher than clear prices listed.

Scroll with Star

(Wycliff): U. S. Glass Company; Challinor, Taylor & Company, Tarentum, Pennsylvania; c. 1890. Clear, nonflint.

Bowl, 8″	$ 12-17
Butter dish	23-30
Cup	7-11
Creamer.	18-25
Goblet.	17-22
Plate, 5″, 8″, 10″	10-18
Sauce	4-8
Saucer.	9-12
Spoonholder.	13-16
Sugar bowl, covered	22-29

Scroll with Flowers

Scroll with Flowers

Central Glass Company, late 1870s. Clear. Scarce in amber, apple green, blue. Nonflint.

Scrolled Sunflower

Scrolled Sunflower

Another of those patterns lost on the back roads of time. If you know, write.

232

Butter dish . . . . $ 18-23
Creamer. 14-19
Spoonholder (ill.) 12-16
Sugar bowl 16-21

?

?

Because that's just what it is! An absolutely beautiful piece. Maker unknown, c. 1865. Anyone know its name?

Seashell

(Boswell): Maker unknown, c. late 1870s. Clear, nonflint. May have frosting or engraving.

Butter dish, covered . . . . $ 40-47
Compote, covered 59-67
Creamer. 36-41
Egg cup 30-35
Goblet. 35-42
Sauce, footed 12-17
Spoonholder. 35-41
Sugar bowl, covered 40-48

Covered pieces have seashell stems, and seashell finials.

Seesaw

Probably Gillinder & Sons, c. 1870s.

Plate, 10″ dia. (ill.). . . . . $ 60-72

Seesaw

Serenade Plate

Unproved attribution to Indiana Tumbler & Goblet (National) Company, 1890s, but probably McKee. Chocolate, milk glass.

Serenade plate, 6″ $134-138
Serenade plate, 8″ 150-165

Prices given are for chocolate; milk glass, 70 percent lower.

Sharp Sunburst and File

(Westmoreland No. 920): Westmoreland, c. 1912. Clear or with ruby stained files. Nonflint.

Bowl, 8″ . . . . $ 13-16
Butter. 30-34
Compote, 6″ dia., open 16-20
Creamer. 21-24
Goblet. 20-25
Sauce, 4″. 5-7
Spoonholder, flat, no handles 14-17
Sugar, handled 30-34
Tumbler. 12-16
Wine 14-18

Shell and Jewel

Shell and Jewel

(Victor): Westmoreland Glass Company, 1893, originally called it Victor. A water pitcher by Fostoria is documented. Clear, amber, blue, green, nonflint. Covered creamer, sugar in iridescent (Carnival) colors.

Butter dish, covered	$ 55-65
Cake stand	50-60
Compote, open, high foot	36-42
Creamer (ill.)	30-38
Pitcher, water	36-42
Spoonholder.	22-26
Sugar bowl	42-51
Tumbler.	18-25

No goblet made. Colors, 100 percent higher than clear prices listed. Poor quality cake stand, flat rim sauces common.

Shell and Ribbing

Shell and Ribbing

This is blown, three-mold glass, c. 1850s, probably Sandwich. Not pressed glass but we thought you'd like to see one of the rarest types of glass in the world. Made in clear, light blue and sapphire blue. Shown with original stopper.

Shell and Tassel

Shell and Tassel

(Shell and Spike): Duncan, c. 1880, and Portland, Maine. Made in round and square forms. Clear, blue; rare in amber. Nonflint.

Berry set, 7 pcs.	$108-130
Butter dish, round, covered,	
dog finial	55-64
Cake stand, 7″ square	39-48
Celery vase, square	40-50
Compote	
Covered	30-37
Open, high standard, 8″ square . . .	39-44
Creamer (ill.)	39-44
Goblet, 2 types	32-46
Pitcher, square	43-52
Platter, 11″ rectangular	58-68
Salt shaker (scarce)	49-55
Spoonholder, round	27-39
Sugar bowl, round, dog finial.	70-78
Vases, oval, pr.	155-165

Colors. 100 percent higher than prices listed for clear. Goblet reproduced.

Sheraton

(Original name, Ida): Bryce, Higbee & Company, Pittsburgh, 1880s,. Clear, amber, blue, nonflint.

Sheraton

Bowl, berry	$ 14-21
Butter dish	28-36
Compote, covered	36-44
Creamer.	18-24
Goblet.	20-25
Pitcher, water (ill.)	29-39
Sauce, flat or footed	12-16
Sugar bowl, covered	27-32
Tumbler.	29-37
Wine	20-25

Amber, blue, 40-50 percent higher than clear prices listed.

Shimmering Star

Shimmering Star

(Beaded Star): Maker unknown, 1880s. Clear, nonflint.

Butter dish, covered	$ 26-33
Cake stand	27-37
Creamer (ill.)	19-24
Sauce, flat.	5-8
Spoonholder.	15-20
Sugar bowl	
Covered	25-35
Open	13-18
Tumbler.	15-20

Confusing pattern, Bevelled Star.

Shoshone

Shoshone

(Victor; Blazing Pinwheels): U.S. Glass Company c. 1895. Crystal; ruby-stained, amber-stained; emerald green; cobalt Gainsborough olive known. Nonflint.

Banana stand (ill.).	$ 32-40
Butter dish, covered	35-43
Compote, low jelly.	16-21
Creamer.	25-32
Goblet.	25-34
Pitcher	40-49
Spoonholder.	18-24
Sugar bowl	31-38

Colors, 100 percent higher than clear prices listed. Cobalt 150 percent higher.

Shrine

Shrine

Beatty-Brady, c. 1880s. Clear, nonflint.

Bowl	$ 25-32
Butter dish, covered	52-65
Compote, jelly.	31-37
Creamer (ill.)	33-42
Goblet.	43-55
Sauce	12-16
Spoonholder.	25-33

(continued)

Sugar bowl
Covered   45-52
Open   20-25
Toothpick (scarce).   60-75
Tumbler, regular   30-35

Shuttle

Shuttle

(Hearts of Loch Haven): Indiana Tumbler & Goblet (National) Company, 1900. Chocolate, clear, colors, nonflint.

Bowl . . . . $ 28-35
Butter dish   40-50
Cordial   25-30
Creamer.   25-30
Goblet (scarce)   38-45
Mug (ill.)   18-25
Pitcher, syrup, tankard   30-40
Punch cup.   12-16
Salt/Pepper, pr.   80-100
Saucedish   10-15
Spoonholder.   21-29
Tumbler.   28-37
Wine, good impression.   14-19

Chocolate, 200-300 percent higher.

Side Wheeler

Maker unknown, c. 1885. Clear or with engraved panels. Nonflint.

Butter. . . . . $ 28-32
Creamer.   20-23
Goblet.   19-23
Salt shaker, handled.   14-18
Spoonholder.   15-19
Sugar   25-30

Add 20 percent for engraving.

Singing Birds

Singing Birds

Northwood Glass Company, Wheeling, West Virginia, 1900s. Clear, custard, Carnival, opalescent, nonflint.

Berry set, large bowl
Marigold. . . . . $ 50-60
Vivid   77-84
Butter dish, covered
Clear   38-44
Marigold.   77-97
Vivid   169-185
Creamer
Clear (ill.)   52-62
Marigold.   56-64
Vivid   70-75
Mug
Custard, marigold, vivid   37-42
Color, non-iridescent.   40-46
Pitcher
Marigold.   80-88
Vivid   132-142
Sauce
Marigold.   24-32
Vivid   26-37
Sugar bowl, covered
Clear   48-57
Marigold.   62-72
Vivid   77-86
Spoonholder
Clear   38-42
Marigold.   50-60
Vivid   67-74
Tumbler
Marigold.   35-44
Vivid   35-46

Vivid colors are green, purple. Mugs in pastel or pastel opalescent are very rare and some are valued at $500-$1,000, and more.

Single Rose

(Wild Rose): Northwood. Clear, rose and green; gilded; nonflint.

Butter dish, covered	$ 32-40
Creamer.	24-28
Pitcher, water	35-42
Salt shaker	19-24
Spoonholder.	21-26
Sugar bowl, covered	30-37
Tumbler.	18-25

Rose, 30 percent; green, 40 percent higher than clear prices listed.

Siskyou

Siskyou

Maker unknown, c. 1880s. Clear, non-flint.

Goblet (ill.) . . . . $ 14-19

Slashed Swirl

Slashed Swirl

Riverside Glass Company, Wellsburg, West Virginia, 1891. Clear, nonflint.

Butter dish, covered	$ 25-30
Cake stand	29-36
Carafe.	33-37
Celery.	21-28
Compote, open	22-27
Creamer.	22-30
Goblet.	15-20
Pickle dish	11-14
Pitcher, water (ill.)	40-49
Salt/Pepper, pr., 2 types	28-38
Spoonholder.	13-17
Sugar bowl	25-30
Tumbler.	10-14
Wine	12-16

Slewed Horseshoe

Slewed Horseshoe

(Radiant Daisy; U. S. Peacock): U. S. Glass Company, c. 1908, and into the 1920s. Clear, Carnival; nonflint.

Bowl	$ 14-19
Butter dish	24-30
Creamer.	16-20
Cup	6-9
Goblet.	22-28
Pitcher, syrup, with top (ill.)	31-41
Sauce	5-8
Spoonholder, handled	14-17
Sugar bowl, covered, handled	22-28

Punch bowl on tray made after World War II.

Smocking

Sandwich Glass and others, 1840s. Clear, flint.

Butter dish, covered	$ 99-119
Compote, open, 6″ high, 7¾″ dia.. . .	72-81
Creamer, applied handle	
(rare)	101-119

237

(continued)

Smocking

Goblet, knob stem	70-78
Lamp, 9″ high	136-144
Spill or spoonholder	39-45
Sugar bowl, covered (ill.).	78-90

Many different types of goblets.

Smooth Diamond

Smooth Diamond

(Double Icicles; Early Diamond): Green-town, c. 1900. Clear, cobalt, green, chocolate; nonflint.

Butter dish	$ 40-47
Creamer (ill.)	30-40
Dish, rectangular, 5″ x 8″.	20-26

Goblet.	28-34
Pitcher, water	50-60
Sugar bowl, covered	40-48
Tumbler.	27-36
Wine	30-37

Prices are for clear. Not all pieces in all colors.

Snail

(Original name, Compact; Idaho): George Duncan & Sons, Pittsburgh, c. 1880s, clear. After 1891, by U.S. Glass Company, who added ruby stain, sometimes engraving through the color. Nonflint.

Bowls, berry.	$ 33-42
Butter dish, covered	70-88
Cake stand	85-110
Celery.	47-54
Compote, covered, large	100-125
Creamer, regular.	46-52
Goblet.	60-67
Pitcher, water (tankard)	88-97
Spoonholder.	32-38
Sugar bowl	50-60
Tumbler.	37-45

Engraved, 30 percent higher than clear prices listed. Confusing pattern, Halley's Comet.

Snakeskin and Dot

Snakeskin and Dot

Maker unknown, late 1870s. Clear, occasionally found in deep blue and amber.

Celery vase	$ 21-29
Creamer (ill.)	20-24

238

Goblet. 16-22
Plates, 4½" to 7". 10-16
Sugar bowl, covered 25-32

Deep blue and amber, 50 percent higher than clear prices listed. The small plates are found in wire baskets and were used for calling cards.

Snow Band

(Puffed Bands): Maker unknown, c. early 1880s. Clear, dark blue, nonflint.

Butter dish . . . . $ 23-29
Compote
  Covered 22-30
  Open 15-20
Creamer. 15-20
Goblet. 26-35
Relish 8-11
Sauce, flat 4-6
Spoonholder. 14-18
Sugar bowl, covered 20-26
Wine 13-16

Blue, 40 percent higher than clear prices listed.

Snowdrop

(Ashland): Portland Glass Company, Portland, Maine, c. 1880s. Clear, nonflint.

Bowl . . . . $ 15-22
Goblet. 30-40
Sauce, shell shape
  (ice cream), 6" long. 12-16
Tray, ice cream, 13½" long. 38-46

Snowflake

Snowflake

(Fernland): Cambridge Glass Company, c. 1909. Clear, emerald green, blue, nonflint.

Butter dish . . . . $ 28-34
Celery, 6¼" high. 20-26
Compote, open, 8" 17-22
Creamer (ill.) 22-27
Pitcher, qt., 8¾" high 30-36
Plate, bread 16-23
Salt shaker 18-25
Spoonholder. 15-20
Sugar bowl, covered 27-32
Toothpick 20-25
Toy set (4- piece table set) 76-89
Tumbler. 11-15

Colors, add 100 percent.

Southern Ivy

Southern Ivy

Maker unknown, mid-1880s. Clear, nonflint.

Bowl, berry . . . . $ 14-19
Butter dish, covered 27-36
Creamer. 21-27
Egg cup 18-26
Pitcher, water (ill.) 34-39
Saucedish, 4" 6-9
Spoonholder. 15-19
Sugar bowl, covered 27-36
Tumbler, water 17-23

No goblet made?

Spanish-American

(Dewey or Gridley): Beatty-Brady Glass Co., Dunkirk, Indiana, late 1890s.

Pitcher, water, Admiral Dewey,
  cannon balls around base (ill.) . . . . $ 66-75

(continued)

Spanish-American

Tumbler, matches pitcher 38-46
Pitcher, water, "You may fire
when ready, Gridley" 77-90
If you can confirm Gridley pitcher, please write.

Spearpoint Band

Spearpoint Band

(Original name, Gothic): McKee, c. 1900.
Clear, ruby stained with or without frosted
band.

Bowl, 7", 8" . . . . $ 14-17
Butter
  English 32-36
  Regular 30-35
Cake stand, 8" 30-35
Celery
  Tray, 11¾" 16-21
  Vase 22-27

Compote
  High, covered, 6", 7", 8" 34-45
  High, open, scalloped rim, 6", 7", 8" . . 24-33
  Low, jelly, open 14-17
Creamer
  English, 6 oz. 17-20
  Regular 20-24
Cruet 33-37
Dish, oval: graduated sizes 5"-11" 12-23
Olive, one handle 14-18
Pickle tray, 9¼" 12-15
Pitcher, ½ gal. (ill.) 33-39
Salt shaker 14-18
Sauce, flat, 4", 4½" 5-9
Spoonholder 14-18
Sugar
  English (open, on pedestal) 27-30
  Regular 31-34
  Sifter (muffineer) 25-30
Syrup 35-41
Toothpick 24-29
Tumbler, iced tea, water 13-17

Ruby stain worth 100 percent more, plus 20 percent for frosted band; cruet, syrup, covered compotes worth 300 percent more.

Spiral and Maltese Cross

Maker unknown, c. early 1880s. Clear,
nonflint.

Butter dish, covered . . . . $ 32-40
Creamer 29-38
Spoonholder 21-29
Sugar bowl, covered 32-40

Spiralled Ivy

Spiralled Ivy

One of the less frequently seen Ivy patterns, mid-1880s. Maker unknown. Clear,
nonflint.

Butter dish, covered	$ 32-45
Creamer.	27-36
Pitcher, water (ill.)	33-43
Sauce	9-12
Spoonholder.	20-24
Sugar bowl, covered	34-42
Tumbler.	17-21

No goblet.

Spirea Band

Spirea Band

(Square and Dot; Squared Dot): Bryce, Higbee & Company, c. 1885. Clear, amber, blue, canary, nonflint.

Butter dish, covered , 2 types	$ 30-35
Cake stand	29-33
Celery.	24-28
Compote	
Covered, low.	41-48
Open	20-24
Creamer.	18-24
Goblet.	19-24
Pitcher, water (ill.)	39-46
Platter, oval	20-23
Salt/Pepper, pr.	28-34
Spoonholder.	14-18
Sugar bowl, open	15-19
Tumbler.	17-22
Wine	18-26

Amber, canary, blue, 65 percent higher than clear prices listed. Green listed in the literature but not confirmed.

Sprig

Bryce, Higbee & Company, Pittsburgh, early 1880s. Clear, nonflint.

Bowl, berry	$ 29-34
Butter dish on pedestal	35-43

Sprig

Cake stand	31-40
Celery.	32-37
Compote	
Covered, high, 10″	52-61
Open, low standard	30-35
Creamer.	24-32
Goblet.	28-35
Pitcher, water (ill.)	54-63
Platter, oval	30-36
Sauce, flat, footed	8-11
Spoonholder.	24-27
Sugar bowl, covered	37-44
Tumbler.	17-24
Wine	35-47

The same molds were used to make "Royal," which lacks the sprig.

Square Lion Head

Square Lion Head

(Atlanta Clear Lion Head): Fostoria Glass Company, Moundsville, West Virginia, 1895. Clear, frosted (camphor), ruby. Clear and ruby may be engraved. Nonflint.

Bowl, berry (ill.)	$ 33-41
Butter dish, covered	67-77
Cake stand, large, square	89-108

241

(continued)

Compote
Covered, 5″, square stem	144-152
Open, 5″, square stem	139-150
Creamer.	50-57
Goblet, round	42-56
Jam jar	69-74
Pickle dish	49-54
Salt, master	53-62
Sauce, flat.	15-20
Spoonholder.	38-45

Sugar bowl
Covered	55-62
Open	31-39
Toothpick holder	39-46

Tumbler known in ruby stain.

Squirrel-in-Bower

Pitcher
Water, chocolate.	300-400
Water, tree bark handle	210-242
Sauce, flat.	38-48
Spoonholder.	76-89

Sugar bowl
Covered (ill.).	190-218
Open	50-66

This is not the Greentown version of which only
the smooth handle pitcher is known.

Squared Star

Squared Star

(Spear Head): Maker unknown, c. 1880s.
Clear, nonflint.

Butter dish	$ 31-39
Celery (ill.)	30-39
Creamer, applied handle.	35-40
Goblet.	20-25
Pitcher, bulbous, applied handle. . . .	67-75
Spoonholder.	30-35
Sugar bowl, covered	35-45

Pieces are larger than average.

Squirrel-in-Bower

Maker unknown, 1880s. Clear. Nonflint.

Butter dish, covered,	
squirrel knob	$200-229
Creamer.	143-165
Goblet (extremely rare)	585+

Star and Dart

Star and Dart

Maker unknown, c. 1850s. Clear, flint.

Butter dish, covered (ill.)	$ 50-58

If you have information concerning **any** pattern, please let us hear from you. If you don't
agree with the prices quoted, please, let us hear
from you. If you think the piece illustrated is a
spoonholder rather than a celery (etc.), please
let us hear from you. Constructive criticism is
always welcome.

Star and Pillar

Star and Pillar

(Original name, Paris; Stars and Bars): McKee, c. 1880. Clear, nonflint.

Butter dish, covered, 6″ dia.	$ 40-49
Celery	32-41
Champagne	30-38
Compote, covered, low, 7″, 8″	49-55
Creamer	30-35
Goblet	31-46
Pitcher, water, ½ gal.	50-60
Plate, 11″ dia., "Do unto others," etc.	
Fruit center	40-49
Shell center	36-42
Salt dip, master	29-36
Sauce, footed, 3½″, 4″, 4½″	10-14
Spoonholder, pedestaled	24-29
Sugar bowl, covered	41-50
Tumbler	30-39
Wine	30-38

Butter was made plain or flanged.

Star and Punty

Star and Punty

Sandwich and also made by McKee, 1850s. Clear, canary, jade green, cobalt, flint.

Cologne bottle	$227-240
Creamer (ill.)	230-275
Pitcher	585+
Spill	79-95
Sugar bowl	282-292
Syrup	385-415
Whale-oil lamp	750+

Star Band

Star Band

(Bosworth): Indiana Glass Company, Dunkirk, 1907-1913. Advertised as "Our New Wonder Assortment." Clear, nonflint.

Butter dish	$ 20-25
Celery, flat base, handled	13-18
Compote, jelly	10-14
Creamer	15-19
Goblet	13-17
Pitcher (ill.)	20-25
Spoonholder	10-14
Sugar bowl, cover lacks "stars"	17-21
Vase, 6½″, pedestal	12-16
Wine	12-15

Star-in-Bull's-Eye

U.S. Glass Company, 1905. Clear, gold trim, nonflint. Also comes with rose stain.

Bowl, berry	$ 20-24
Butter dish	30-39
Cake stand	31-40
Celery vase	26-32

(continued)

Star-in-Bull's-Eye

Compote
Covered, high	36-44
Open, 6″ dia., fancy rim	21-27
Creamer.	20-26
Cruet, 4″.	24-29
Dish, diamond shape	9-13
Goblet.	19-24
Pitcher, water	37-45
Spoonholder.	17-22
Sugar bowl, covered	25-35
Toothpick	
Double	32-38
Single	29-35
Tumbler, gold band (ill.).	14-19
Wine	15-22

Rose stain, add 30 percent; gold, add 10 percent.

Star in Honeycomb

Star in Honeycomb

(Laverne): Bryce Bros., Pittsburgh, late 1880s. Clear, nonflint.

Butter dish, covered	$ 45-54

Compote
Covered	40-47
Open	35-44
Cake stand	42-51
Creamer.	42-48
Goblet.	25-37
Pitcher (ill.)	43-49
Sauce, flat	23-32
Spoonholder.	24-33
Sugar bowl, covered	52-61
Tumbler.	31-40
Wine	20-28

Star Pattern

Star Pattern

Generic name given only for filing purposes. No one can find it in any book. 8-pointed stars. Not made by U. S. Glass Company, possibly not American. Anyone know?

Star Rosetted

McKee & Bros., Pittsburgh, 1875. Clear, nonflint.

Butter dish	$ 31-37
Compote, open, high standard	20-27
Creamer.	22-26
Goblet.	20-29
Pickle, oval	12-16

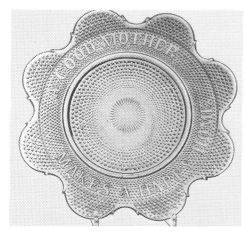

Star Rosetted

Pitcher, water	39-49
Plate	
10″, "A Good Mother" (ill.).	45-56
7″, feather center.	12-19
Sauce	
Flat	5-10
Footed.	8-13
Spoonholder.	13-19
Sugar bowl, covered	30-35

The 7″ plate comes in amber, canary, blue, pale green.

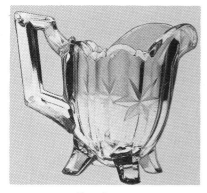

Starlyte

Starlyte

(Colonial; Dunkirk's; erroneously Chippendale): Indiana Glass Company, 1907, probably into the 1920s. Clear, may have cut star as shown.

Butter dish	$ 15-21
Celery vase, two handles	15-19
Compote, jelly	10-14
Creamer (ill.)	12-15
Goblet.	13-17
Salt shaker	7-10
Spoonholder.	10-13
Sugar bowl, covered	15-21
Tumbler.	8-11

The goblet is shown in the literature as Flute with Beaded Stem.

Starred Scroll

Starred Scroll

(Crescent and Fan): Maker unknown, c. early 1900s. Clear, nonflint.

Butter dish, covered	$ 30-37
Celery	21-29
Creamer.	20-24
Jug, syrup (ill.)	28-34
Spoonholder.	17-23
Sugar bowl, covered	30-37
Wine, large (champagne)	15-24

Stars and Bars

(continued)

Stars and Bars

(Daisy and Cube): Bellaire and U. S. Glass, c. 1891. Clear, amber, blue, and scarce in canary.

Bitters bottle	$ 42-55
Butter dish	32-41
Cake stand	39-43
Cigar lighter (rare)	450+
Creamer, 5½″, applied handle (ill.). .	35-42
Cruet	24-30
Cup	18-25
Dish, oval	20-25
Jam jar	34-42
Night lamp with patterned shade . .	110-130
Pickle and olive set in holder.	64-88
Pitcher, milk	47-52
Plate, ice cream	30-40
Spoonholder.	22-26
Sugar bowl, covered	35-42
Toothpick	
Potty	36-41
Regular	40-50
Tray, condiment.	23-30

No goblet. There are other patterns with this name. Miniature creamer illustrated has stippled leaf. This may be a Bryce Bros. version like the pedestaled Dolphin toothpick that also has the stippled leaf and a pedestaled Barrel toothpick. The latter is referred to as "engraved," but may have been mistaken for stippling if seen in a catalog. A dollhouse set is mentioned, but no proof.

Stars and Stripes

Stars and Stripes

(Brilliant): Jenkins Glass Company. Called Brilliant in an 1899 Ward Catalog. Clear, nonflint.

Butter dish	$ 26-32
Creamer (ill.)	27-35
Goblet.	37-42
Pitcher	30-37
Spoonholder.	14-18
Sugar bowl	28-35
Tumbler.	13-18

The States

The States

(Cane and Star Medallion): U.S. Glass Company, 1905. Clear, scarce in emerald green; some pieces gold trimmed, nonflint.

Butter dish, covered	$ 48-56
Celery.	18-25
Compote, 7″, open	25-33
Creamer, table.	18-26
Cup, flared or straight	9-13
Dish, three-handled, round	27-34
Goblet.	30-36
Pitcher, water, gold trimmed (ill.) . . .	54-62
Spoonholder.	20-25
Sugar bowl, covered	37-41
Toothpick, flat, rectangular	45-55
Tumbler.	20-28
Wine	25-32

Emerald green worth 50 percent more.

Stippled Band

(Original name, Frosted; Panelled Stippled Bowl): McKee, 1871. Clear, nonflint.

Butter bowl, covered, 6″	$ 35-42
Celery.	29-35
Compote	
Covered, high (horizontal band)	
6″ (sweetmeat), 7″, 8″, faceted stem .	32-48
Covered, low, 7″, 8″,	
banded stem	30-40
Open	19-25
Creamer, applied handle.	34-40

Egg cup	17-21
Goblet.	18-25
Pitcher, applied handle	50-59
Salt	
Footed.	16-19
Pedestal	20-26
Sauce	
4″, 6″.	6-10
Flat	5-9
Spoonholder, pedestaled.	22-27
Sugar bowl, covered	32-40
Tumbler, footed	21-27
Wine	15-22

Covered pieces have acorn finials. Some pieces also have horizontal clear band. Stemware illustrated in 1871 catalog has no panels, but two other goblets in the literature go well with this pattern as they appear to match the serving pieces.

Stippled Chain

Stippled Chain

Gillinder & Sons, 1870s. Nonflint.

Bowl, oval, 7⅜″	$ 15-22
Butter dish, covered	29-33
Creamer, applied handle (ill.)	24-31
Goblet.	20-26
Salt, footed	17-22
Sauce	4-8
Spoonholder.	19-24
Sugar bowl, covered	30-34

Also see Large Stippled Chain. A sugar bowl exists, which may be another version of this pattern, in which the handles are dogs and the finial is a cat.

Stippled Cherry

Stippled Cherry

Maker unknown. Clear, nonflint.

Bowl, berry, 8″.	$ 18-22
Butter dish	32-40
Creamer.	20-25
Pitcher, water (ill.)	38-48
Plate	
6″ round	16-21
Bread, 9½″ round, no handles,	
"Our Daily Bread".	30-37
Saucedish, 4″	13-19
Spoonholder.	22-26
Sugar bowl, covered	31-38
Tumbler, water	20-28

No goblet.

Stippled Daisy

(continued)

Stippled Daisy

Maker unknown, 1880s. Nonflint.

Butter dish	$ 30-40
Compote, open	26-31
Creamer.	25-31
Dish, oblong.	18-24
Sauce, flat.	8-13
Spoonholder (ill.)	21-28
Sugar bowl	
Covered	34-39
Open	16-24
Goblet?	

Stippled Dart and Balls

Stippled Dart and Balls

Another product of the 1890s. Clear, nonflint.

Butter dish, covered	$ 24-30
Creamer.	15-20
Goblet.	19-22
Pitcher (ill.)	38-44
Sugar bowl, covered	30-37

Stippled Double Loop

Stippled Double Loop

Maker unknown. Clear, nonflint.

Butter dish, covered	$ 20-29
Creamer (ill.)	14-20
Goblet.	22-29
Spoonholder.	13-17
Sugar bowl, covered	19-25

Stippled Fleur-de-Lis

Stippled Fleur-de-Lis

(Frosted Fleur-de-Lis): Maker unknown, c. late 1880s. Clear, amber, blue, green, milk glass; nonflint.

Butter dish, covered	$ 34-44
Cake stand, small or large	29-39
Creamer (ill.)	30-34
Goblet.	27-34
Pitcher	37-43
Sauce	8-12
Spoonholder.	24-31
Sugar bowl, covered	30-41
Tumbler.	16-22
Vase.	14-18
Wine	24-30

Amber, green, milk glass, 40 percent higher; blue, 60 percent higher than clear prices listed.

Stippled Forget-Me-Not

(Original name, Dot): Findlay Flint Glass Company, Ohio, earliest date of production, 1889. Clear, amber, blue, opaque white. Nonflint.

Stippled Forget-Me-Not

Bowl	$ 43-53
Butter dish	53-58
Cake plate on stand, large, small . . .	36-49
Celery	38-44
Compote, covered, 6″, 7″, 8″	48-56
Creamer	34-37
Goblet	32-37
Mug	22-28
Pitcher, water (ill.)	54-59
Plate	
Baby center, 7″, no handles	42-55
Kitten center, 9″ plus handles . . .	40-50
Star (rayed) center, 7″, 9″,	
no handles	26-32
Sauce, flat, footed	13-19
Spoonholder	24-28
Sugar bowl	38-47
Tray, water, flamingo and foliage . .	65-75
Toothpick, hat (rare)	115-132
Tumbler, bar, ½ pt., gill, footed . . .	24-30
Wine	38-44

Amber, blue, opal, 200 percent higher than clear pieces listed. Confirmation of lamp, 6″, and 8″ plates would be appreciated. This pattern was also made without the flower and called Stippled Diamond.

Stippled Fuchsia

Maker unknown, c. 1870s. Clear, nonflint.

Goblet ($25-30) documented. This is not the same as Fuchsia, also called Clear Fuchsia with the stippling added, as the goblet mold is different. See Fuchsia.

Stippled Grape and Festoon

Stippled Grape and Festoon

Doyle & Company, Pittsburgh, 1870. Clear with stippled background. Scarce and more in demand than unstippled versions. Nonflint.

Butter bowl	$ 39-49
Celery	38-46
Compote, covered, low	
standard	49-60
Creamer (ill.)	37-46
Egg cup	30-37
Goblet	30-38
Pitcher, water, applied handle	87-110
Spoonholder	27-32
Sugar	
Covered	40-45
Open	26-32
Wine	38-46

Stippled Leaf and Flower

Stippled Leaf and Flower

(Stippled Leaf and Flower with Moth): Maker unknown, 1870s. Clear, nonflint.

Pitcher, water, 8″ high (ill.) . . . . . . $ 88-94
No proof of other pieces.

Stippled Medallion

Stippled Peppers

Stippled Medallion

Union Glass Company, Somerville, Massachusetts, late 1860s. Clear, usually flint.

Butter bowl, covered.	$ 46-52
Compote, low open	30-36
Creamer, applied handle.	44-50
Egg cup	30-35
Goblet (ill.)	37-45
Sauce, flat.	12-15
Spoonholder.	28-36
Sugar	
Covered	47-56
Open	30-38

Nonflint 40 percent less than flint prices listed.

Stippled Peppers

Sandwich glass, 1870s. Clear, nonflint.

Butter bowl, covered.	$ 30-40
Creamer (ill.)	38-43
Egg cup	25-30
Goblet.	29-36
Salt, footed	24-35
Sauce	7-10
Spoonholder.	27-34
Sugar bowl, covered	37-42
Tumbler, footed	17-23

Stippled Sandbur

Stippled Palm

Stippled Palm

Maker unknown, c. 1865. Clear, nonflint.

Pitcher, applied handle (ill.) . . . . . . $ 62-69

Additional information on other pieces or history appreciated.

Stippled Sandbur

(Stippled Star Variant): Maker unknown, early 1890s. Clear, nonflint. Tends to sun-color to lavender easily.

Bowl	$ 15-23
Butter, covered	22-30
Celery/vase	20-27
Compote, covered	31-37
Creamer (ill.)	18-23
Goblet.	15-25

Sauce, flat.	4-8
Spoonholder.	14-17
Sugar bowl, covered	22-30
Toothpick, has ledge, may be mustard or toy sugar base, 2½″ dia. x 2½″ high	30-40
Wine	15-25

Stippled Star Flower

Stippled Star

Stippled Star

Gillinder & Sons, Greensburg, Pennsylvania, 1870s. Clear, nonflint.

Butter bowl, covered.	$ 36-43
Celery.	35-42
Compote, large, high standard, covered	58-68
Creamer, scarce (ill.).	37-47
Dish, oval, 8″	18-24
Egg cup	28-34
Goblet.	33-37
Pickle dish	14-20
Pitcher, water (ill.)	79-85
Sauce, flat.	10-14
Spoonholder, 5½″ high	23-27
Sugar bowl	
Covered	40-48
Open	18-22
Tumbler.	22-28

Creamer, goblet, salt dip, compote, sugar bowl, and wine reproduced in clear and in new colors. These are heavier and coarser than originals.

Stippled Star Flower

Maker unknown, late 1880s. Clear, nonflint. Three types of goblets are known: Plain rim and lower bowl (Star Flower Band), illustrated; a plain rim, stippled lower bowl version; and a third with a narrow band of stippling above pattern, stippled lower bowl (Stippled Star Flower, Banded).

Value of goblets, $20-25 each. If you know of other pieces or colors, please write.

Stove

Stove

Possibly Bryce Bros., c. 1890s. Clear, amber, blue. A novelty piece with a flatiron finial.

Clear (ill.)	$132-150

Amber or blue, 125 percent higher than clear price listed.

Strawberry

(Fairfax Strawberry): Attributed by early authors to Sandwich, but Bryce patent dates 1870. Clear, opaque white (milk glass); nonflint.

Butter bowl, covered.	$ 47-57
Compote, covered, 8″ dia., low standard.	66-78
Creamer (ill.)	45-54
Egg cup	28-34

 (continued)

Strawberry

Goblet.	28-32
Pickle dish	17-24
Pitcher	
Syrup	64-74
Water	88-115
Salt, footed	30-35
Saucedish, flat.	10-14
Spoonholder.	34-39
Sugar bowl	42-48
Wine (scarce)	27-34

Prices listed are for clear glass. Add 70 percent for opaque. Goblet reproduced.

Strawberry, Falcon

Strawberry, Falcon

Jenkins Glass Company, c. 1915. Clear, nonflint.

Bowl, oval, 10″.	$ 16-21
Butter dish, covered	29-36
Creamer.	20-25
Goblet.	23-30
Mug.	25-30
Pitcher with lid, pint	28-36
Spoonholder.	17-23

Sugar bowl, covered	28-33
Syrup (ill.)	34-41
Toothpick.	40-45

Top or bottom band of concave panels helps distinguish this from other strawberry patterns.

Strigil

Strigil

(Pronounced Stridjl): Maker unknown, late 1880s. Clear, nonflint. Frequently gold trimmed.

Butter dish	$ 30-35
Celery.	17-21
Compote, open	20-25
Creamer.	22-26
Goblet.	23-27
Pitcher (ill.)	32-39
Sauce	4-9
Spoonholder.	14-18
Sugar bowl	30-35
Tumbler.	15-18
Wine	25-33

Strutting Peacock

Strutting Peacock

Possibly Westmoreland Glass Company, late 1880s. Clear, nonflint.

Creamer (ill.) . . . . $ 34-39
Sugar bowl, covered   41-50

Stylized Flower

Stylized Flower

(Panelled Flower; Flower and Panel): Challinor, Taylor & Company, Tarentum, Pennsylvania, 1885, and U. S. Glass Company after 1891. Clear, amber, blue; white, blue, milk glass; mosaic (slag glass).

Butter dish . . . . $ 54-64
Creamer (ill.)   38-45
Pitcher, ½ gal.   52-65
Spoonholder.   29-33
Sugar bowl, covered   48-56

Prices are for milk glass. Water pitcher known in translucent amber; spoonholder known in translucent blue. Both are rare, as few pieces are known in translucent colors. Blue milk glass scarce, add 50 percent; mosaic add 30 percent.

The Summit

(X-Bull's Eye): Thompson Glass Company, Uniontown, Pennsylvania, c. 1895. Clear, ruby stained; nonflint.

Butter dish, covered . . . . $ 30-39
Creamer.   25-31
Salt shaker   19-26
Spoonholder.   20-25
Sugar bowl, covered   30-39

Ruby stain, add 80 percent.

Sunbeam

Sunbeam

McKee & Bros., Jeannette, Pennsylvania, c. 1898-1930. Clear; cobalt or emerald with gold trim; nonflint.

Bowl, berry . . . . $ 30-36
Celery.   19-25
Compote, jelly.   15-19
Creamer.   20-30
Cruet   20-33
Decanter, handled   43-55
Mustard, two handles   20-30
Pitcher   35-45
Plate, 6½" square   14-19
Punch glass, footed (ill.)   17-22
Salt shaker   14-19
Sauce   6-8
Spoonholder.   15-19
Sugar bowl, covered   26-34
Toothpick   27-35
Tumbler.   15-22
Vase, 6"   13-17
Water bottle.   30-38
Whiskey (shot)   11-14
Wine   12-17

Emerald with gold trim, 50 percent higher than clear prices listed. Cobalt 80 percent.

Sunburst

(Squared Sunburst): Jenkins, c. 1905. Clear, nonflint.

Butter dish . . . . $ 18-23
Creamer
  Individual   10-13
  Regular, 4½" high   14-17
Cup   6-10
Pitcher, large (ill.)   22-29
Plate, 6", 7", 11"   27-35
Salt shaker   15-20

(continued)

Sunburst

Spoonholder.	11-13
Sugar bowl	
Individual, open	12-15
Regular, covered	16-20
Tumbler.	8-13

Sunflower

Sunflower

(Lily): Atterbury & Company, Pittsburgh, 1881. Crystal, amber, blue; milk glass, slag.

Butter dish, covered	$ 34-42
Creamer (ill.)	29-34
Spoonholder.	23-28
Sugar bowl	
Covered	30-39
Open	18-25

Amber, 50 percent higher; opaque, 100 percent higher than clear prices listed.

Sunflower Container

Sunflower Container

This is Panelled Sunflower—see for photo of goblet and listing of other pieces.

Sunflower container, neck interior is threaded (ill.)	$ 28-36

Sunk Daisy

Sunk Daisy

(Kirkland): Co-Operative Flint Glass Company, Beaver Falls, Pennsylvania, 1898. Clear, rose, green, and with gold-painted daisies and foliage. Nonflint.

Butter dish, covered	$ 33-37
Carafe.	32-41
Compote, open	20-30
Cracker jar	50-60
Creamer.	22-27
Goblet.	20-30
Pitcher (ill.)	43-51
Salt shaker	20-26
Sauce, flat.	8-11
Spoonholder.	15-20
Sugar bowl, covered	26-35
Wine	19-27

Green or paint, 50 percent higher than clear prices listed.

Sunk Diamond and Lattice

Sunk Diamond and Lattice

Maker unknown, 1885-1890. Clear, non-flint.

Butter dish	$ 23-29
Celery vase	20-25
Compote	
Covered	37-44
Open	20-26
Creamer.	20-23
Pitcher, water (ill.)	30-39
Plate	15-21
Spoonholder.	16-19
Sugar bowl, covered	25-30
Tumbler.	13-17

Sunk Honeycomb

(Corona): This by McKee, 1903-1924, Greensburg, 1890s. Clear as well as with a ruby top, nonflint.

Butter dish	$ 32-41
Cake stand	31-40
Cheese dish, covered.	40-50
Cracker jar	39-47

Sunk Honeycomb

Creamer	
Individual	16-21
Regular	26-32
Cruet with stopper	32-45
Decanter, 12½″ high, original,	
stopper; ruby top	62-71
Goblet.	25-32
Mug	14-20
Pitcher, water, ruby top (ill.).	79-83
Spooner, ruby top	34-39
Sugar, covered.	30-38
Toothpick.	20-30
Tumbler.	16-22
Wine	20-26

Some more refined pieces frequently have polished bases and stuck, rather than pressed handles. Deduct 20 percent for lesser quality.

Sunken Buttons

255

(continued)

Sunken Buttons

(Mitered Diamond): Maker unknown, Ohio, late 1880s. Clear canary, amber, blue; nonflint.

Butter dish, covered	$ 31-40
Compote	
Covered	35-42
Open, low	18-22
Creamer.	21-27
Goblet.	29-38
Pitcher, syrup (ill.)	40-47
Platter	23-29
Salt/Pepper, pr.	24-32
Spoonholder.	13-18
Sugar bowl	
Covered	37-40
Open	15-21
Wine	20-28

Canary, 50 percent higher; amber, blue, 125 percent higher than clear prices listed.

Sunken Primrose

(Florida): Greensburg Glass Co., c. 1893. Clear, clear with frosted panels; clear with ruby stained panels in which the flowers are yellow stained; also with allover gold-bronze background, and with gold leaves and ruby flowers. Not one of the original series, but included in collections of state-named patterns.

Bowl, square (7¾") or round	$ 14-19
Butter, covered	32-39
Cake stand	30-36
Creamer.	21-28
Olive, one handle	13-17
Pitcher, 7½" high	32-37
Sauce, flat, square (4") or round	8-11
Spoonholder.	14-18
Sugar, covered.	30-40
Toothpick.	32-38
Tumbler.	16-19

Frosted, add 30 percent; color stained, add 150-200 percent to clear prices listed. No goblet.

Swag with Brackets

Jefferson Glass Company, Steubenville, Ohio, early 1900s. Clear, blue, green; amethyst, canary; nonflint.

Bowl	$ 20-24
Butter dish, covered	58-67

Swag with Brackets

Celery.	32-41
Creamer.	34-43
Cruet, patterned stopper	30-40
Pitcher, water (ill.)	59-67
Salt shaker	18-22
Sauce	10-14
Spoonholder.	41-51
Sugar bowl, covered	43-53
Toothpick, amethyst	50-60
Tumbler.	28-37

Colors, 90 percent higher than clear prices listed. Toothpick reproduced, but not in opalescent. Novelties made in the original.

Swan

Swan

(Swan with Mesh): Maker unknown, 1880s. Clear, light amber, yellow, deep blue; nonflint.

Butter dish, covered, swan finial . . .	$ 90-122
Creamer.	45-55
Marmalade jar, covered, swan finial	64-72
Pitcher, water (ill.)	74-83
Sauce, footed, round, flat, 4″, 4½″ . .	14-20
Spoonholder.	34-43
Sugar bowl, covered	85-115

Amber, yellow, 45 percent higher; blue, 65 percent higher than clear prices listed.

Swan with Tree

Swan with Tree

U.S. Glass Company, Gas City, Indiana, late 1880s. Clear, nonflint.

Goblet.	$ 100+
Pitcher, water (ill.)	150+

Swirl

(Jersey Swirl): Windsor Glass Company, Pittsburgh, c. 1887. Clear, amber, blue, yellow; nonflint.

Butter dish, covered	$ 32-40
Cake stand	34-41
Celery.	29-33
Compote, covered	40-52
Creamer.	23-30
Goblet	
Buttermilk, large	20-30
Regular	25-34
Pickle caster in frame	100-130
Pitcher, water	50-58
Plate, 6″, 8″, 10″	12-27
Spoonholder.	20-24

Sugar bowl, covered	30-37
Toothpick, cuspidor (rare)	62-75
Tumbler.	17-21

Yellow, 30 percent; amber, blue, 50 percent higher than clear prices listed. Many repros in colored glass and in clear goblet.

Swirl and Cable

Swirl and Cable

Dalzell, c. 1900. Clear, nonflint.

Creamer (ill.)	$ 20-25

Sydney

Sydney

Fostoria Glass Company, 1905. Clear, nonflint.

Bowl, 6″, 8″, 9″	$ 12-18
Butter dish, covered	26-32

(continued)

Celery   22-29
Compote
  Covered   45-53
  Open   31-41
Creamer (ill.)   21-24
Pickle dish, 6″, 8″, 9″   19-27
Pitcher   30-39
Salt shaker, 2 types   13-17
Spoonholder.   14-17
Sugar bowl, covered   25-30
Tumbler.   12-16

Tackle Block

Syrup Jug with Applied Handle

Syrup Jug with Applied Handle

Maker unknown, c. 1865. Bird finial on Britannia lid. Clear, flint.

Syrup jug (ill.). . . . . $ 54-63
Anyone have information on it?

Tackle Block

Maker unknown, probably English, c. 1840s.

Goblet
  Flint (ill.) . . . . $ 38-46
  Nonflint   20-25

Tacoma

(Jewelled Diamond and Fan, Triple X): Greensburg Glass Co., 1894. Model Flint Glass Co., c. 1900. Clear, amber, emerald green; ruby stain. Nonflint.

Banana dish, flat . . . . $ 12-16
Bowl
  Finger, flat rim   10-13
  Punch
    Flat, 12″ or 15″ dia.   35-41
    Footed (pedestal is plain
      6-panel), 12″ or 15″.   78-92
  Round or square, 7″, 8″   13-18
  Salad, oval, squashed, 9″, 10″,.   19-23
Butter, covered   23-30
Cake stand, 9″, 10″   21-29
Celery
  Tray.   12-16
  Vase.   14-18
Compote
  Fruit, shallow, 10″ dia.   17-24
  Jelly, 5″ dia.   10-14
  Round or square, 7″, 8″   14-29
Cracker jar, 5″, 6″ dia.   25-33
Creamer.   16-29
Cruet, 8 oz., faceted stopper   19-23
Cup, custard.   4-8
Decanter, wine, original
  faceted stopper   30-37
Dish, oblong, 7″, 8″   12-17
Goblet.   15-20
Pickle jar, covered, straight sided . . .   28-32
Pitcher
  Jug, ½ gal., squat   23-32
  Tankard, ½ gal.   20-30
Plate, for finger bowl   10-15
Rose bowl, 3½″, 4½″,
  5½″, 6½″   12-24
Salt shaker
  Tapered   10-13
  Straight   10-13
Sauce
  Round, 4″, 4½″, and 5″ ice cream . . .   4-11
  Square, 4″, 4½″   5-10

Spoonholder.	13-17
Sugar, covered.	20-25
Syrup	
Squat	25-31
Tall (molasses can)	28-35
Toothpick.	18-23
Tumbler.	10-14
Vase	
Swung, 8″, 11″ high	17-21
Trumpet, 8″, 10″ high.	14-18
Water bottle.	22-28
Wine	13-17

Goblet is not pictured in the literature. Add 30 percent for amber or green; 50 percent for ruby stain.

Tall Argus

Tall Argus

Maker unknown, 1850s. Clear, flint.

Goblet.	$ 41-49
Pitcher, water (ill.)	117-130

Tape Measure

Tape Measure

(Shields): Portland Glass Company attribution, early 1870s. Clear, nonflint.

Butter dish	$ 40-44
Creamer, applied handle, scarce (ill.). .	39-45
Goblet.	31-38
Pitcher, water (ill.)	55-64
Sauce, flat.	22-28
Spoonholder.	18-22
Sugar	40-44

Teardrop

Teardrop

(Teardrop and Thumbprint): Ripley & Company, Pittsburgh; later, U.S. Glass Company, late 1800s. Plain or engraved; clear ruby stain (scarce); and cobalt, plain or with white enamel decoration.

Bowl, oval	$ 17-22
Butter dish, covered	32-38
Cake stand	33-40
Celery	22-29
Compote, open	34-38
Creamer (ill.)	22-28
Goblet.	16-20
Pitcher, water	50-59
Salt shaker (scarce)	22-30
Sauce	
Flat, 4″.	5-8
Footed.	7-10
Spooner	15-21
Sugar	
Covered	35-41
Open	19-24
Syrup	44-55
Tumbler.	13-17
Wine	14-17

Blue, 100 percent higher than clear prices listed. Ruby stain also made as souvenirs.

Teardrop and Tassel

Teardrop and Tassel

(Original name, Sampson): Indiana Tumbler & Goblet Compay, 1890s. Better known today as Teardrop and Tassel. Clear, green, amber, milk glass, Nile green, chocolate, blue; nonflint.

	Blue	Green	Clear
Butter dish . .	$190-214	$118-135	$46-56
Creamer. . . .	34-42	55-62	36-43
Goblet, rare . .	77-84	97-106	90-100
Pitcher (ill.) . .	226-240	112-118	60-72
Relish tray . .	35-40	38-42	28-35
Spoonholder. .	47-54	67-74	33-39
Sugar bowl . .	67-73	89-107	50-57
Tumbler			
2 types. . . .	47-52	46-52	32-39
Wine (rare) . .	84-93	97-106	67-74

Not all pieces made in all colors.

Bowl	
Pedestal, 8″ dia. x 4″ high	$ 21-24
9″ long x 5″ wide x 2″ dia.	16-20
Butter dish, covered	
(New Martinsville).	35-42
Cake stand	25-29
Celery.	17-26
Compote	28-36
Cracker jar	42-47
Creamer (scarce)	25-35
Cruet (New Martinsville)	22-31
Goblet, 3 types, (ill.)	25-30
Honey, covered, oblong	44-52
Pitcher, water	36-41
Plate, 7″, 9″	16-21
Sauce, round, flat	5-8
Spoonholder.	18-24
Sugar bowl, covered	35-42
Toothpick (scarce).	40-48
Tumbler.	14-19

This pattern represents the teasel plant that was used to comb wool. Confusing pattern is Kentucky, especially in square footed sauces (even Metz listed these under Teasel), probably not made as Teasel. The Kentucky square sauces are frequently seen at shops and shows marked as Teasel. The New Martinsville version, called Long Leaf Teasel, has no fans and arches are equal height. One type of goblet has horizontal "ladders" between the spikes. Spikes and no rim band (Unitt); the other lacks the "ladders" and has the rim band (Metz) and a slightly heavier appearance.

Teasel

Teasel

Bryce Bros., Pittsburgh, 1870s (Lee attribution). New Martinsville.

Tennessee

Tennessee

(Jewel and Crescent): U.S. Glass Company, 1900. One of their States series. Clear, nonflint.

260

Butter dish	$ 47-53
Cake stand, 8½″, 9½″, 10½″	37-42
Creamer.	27-32
Goblet (scarce)	49-55
Pitcher, water (ill.)	41-47
Plate, bread	42-49
Relish, oval	27-35
Spoonholder.	22-27
Sugar bowl, covered	38-47
Tumbler.	24-29
Wine (scarce)	51-59

Tennessee Statehood Mug

Tennessee Statehood Mug

So-called camphor glass, American flag, 16 stars on one side, Cherokee rose on other. Nonflint. Originally painted rose-color with gold.

Mug (ill.) . . . . $ 36-44

Unpainted worth 30 percent less.

Texas

Texas

(Loop with Stippled Panels): U.S. Glass Company, c. 1900, as No. 15,067, and part of the States series. Clear, clear with rose stain, clear with gilded top, crystal, crystal with gilded top, ruby stain, rose stain, nonflint.

Bowl	
Berry	$ 33-39
Covered, 6″, 7″, 8″.	48-65
Butter dish, covered	112-127
Cake stand, footed, 10⅝″	110+
Celery	
Dish.	58-70
Vase.	42-52
Compote, open, 5½″ dia..	38-43
Creamer	
Individual (ill.)	16-22
Regular	48-58
Cruet, pattern inverted	160+
Dish, oval, preserve	36-44
Goblet.	68-79
Horseradish, hole for spoon	44-52
Pitcher	
3 pts., pattern inverted (ill.)	200+
Pattern atypical	300+
Plate, 8¾″.	48-55
Salt shaker	50+
Salt/Pepper, pr., large, small.	100+
Spoonholder.	41-52
Sugar	
Large, covered	90-100
Open.	15-20
Small, covered	60-72
Syrup	260+
Toothpick holder	28-35
Tumbler	
Pattern atypical	36-42
Pattern inverted	33-46
Vase, 6½″, 8″, 9″, 10″	19-39
Wine	59-69

Color stain, add 100-300 percent. Color, gilded top, 150 percent higher than clear prices listed. Vases made straight or cupped.

Thistle

Bryce, McKee & Co., Pat. April 2, 1872. Many authors mistakenly attribute this pattern to Bakewell, Pears who made a pillared flint pattern (Pillar and Bull's Eye) and unrelated candlesticks also called

(continued)

Thistle

Thistle. Known only in clear. Called "early" or "naturalistic" to differentiate it from later thistle patterns.

Bowl, berry, covered	$ 48-56
Butter dish, covered	70-80
Cake stand	55-63
Compote	
Covered, high standard	64-75
Open, low standard, 8″	33-42
Cordial	75+
Creamer (ill.)	63-72
Dish, oval, 9″ x 6″ x 2⅞″	36-43
Egg cup	34-42
Goblet.	41-50
Pickle dish, tapered at one end. . . .	24-29
Pitcher	100+
Plate, 10¾″	31-38
Sauce, flat, 4″	13-19
Spoonholder.	29-37
Sugar bowl, covered	60-67
Tumbler, footed, water	40-47
Wine (scarce)	59-67

Thistleblow

(Panelled Iris, Arcadia): Jenkins No. 514, 1906-1932

Bowl, berry	$ 13-17
Butter, covered	20-30
Celery dish, 10″	13-16
Compote, jelly.	10-12
Creamer	
Berry, stemmed	13-16
Regular, flat	15-19
Goblet.	17-21
Olive, one handle, round	12-16
Pickle dish, 8″	11-14
Punch bowl	59-69
Spoonholder, handled	14-18

Sugar	
Berry, scalloped rim, handled	13-16
Covered: stemmed, handled	20-28
Sundae	
Flat rim	12-14
Scalloped rim	13-15
Vase, 6″	10-14
Wine	14-18

Goblet is not pictured in the literature

Thousand Eye

Thousand Eye

Richards & Hartley, (No. 103), 1875-1893. Their version, listed here, is characterized by scalloped bases. Finials have two rows of the pattern separated by a convex ring. The Adams/U. S. Glass Co. version has three knobs on the finials and under the bowls of pieces like compotes and the celery vase and is worth 25 percent more. New Brighton Glass Co., Pennsylvania, also made the pattern in forms similar to the Richards & Hartley version. Clear, amber, blue, canary, apple green, and clear opalescent only by Richards & Hartley and shown in the literature in the water and milk pitchers, creamer, spooner, celery vase, 8″ low compote, and 4″ footed sauce. Kamm erroneously called this "Daisy," which is really another pattern (Panelled Thousand Eye).

Bowl, 5″, 6″, 8″	$ 16-35
Bread plate, 10″	23-32
Butter dish, pedestal	40-46
Celery vase	22-27
Christmas light, inverted beehive . . .	38-45
Cologne/cruet, pedestal, applied	
handle, original faceted stopper . . .	58-66

Cologne, square, flat, original faceted stopper	35-42
Compote, open, 8″, low	24-30
Creamer	25-31
Goblet	24-30
Hat, toothpick or match	19-25
Ink, patterned lid	33-37
Mug	13-18
Pickle dish	14-19
Pitcher, ¼ gal. (ill.), ½ gal.	42-58
Plate, 6″, 8″, 10″ (bread)	12-32
Salt shaker, straight	17-23
Salt/Pepper, pr. in metal holder	44-56
Sauce, footed, 4″	7-10
Spoonholder	15-19
String holder, beehive shape	49-58
Sugar bowl, covered	32-40
Syrup	66-73
Toothpick, straight	18-20
Tray, oval water	37-45
Tumbler, water (two rows of pattern at base)	14-19

Amber 20 percent higher; yellow, 40 percent higher; apple green, crystal opalescent, blue 60 percent higher than clear prices listed. According to Metz, goblets, mugs, plates were reproduced. The pieces are generally heavier and the colors harsher. The goblet is shown in all the literature with a "doughnut" ring stem similar to those ring stems found on the Adams version of the compotes. The salt shaker shown in Peterson (42C "Thousand Eye, Ringed Center") has "doughnut" typical of the Adams version. Is it possible that only Adams made a goblet in the pattern?

The opaque white and opaque blue low compotes by this name have oval "eyes" and so do not appear to be part of the true Thousand Eye pattern. There are confusing patterns of the period, but the true pattern has diamonds between the eyes, although there are some exceptions such as the oblong honey dish in the Adams version that has no diamonds and has fans on the lid of the piece.

Threading

(Threaded): Possibly Duncan (Kamm), c. late 1880s. Clear, nonflint.

Butter dish, covered	$ 33-39
Compote	
Covered	38-46
Open	23-29
Creamer	22-28
Goblet	17-22

Sauce, footed	5-8
Spoonholder	16-19
Sugar bowl	
Covered	33-39
Open	23-29

This is pressed and of course is heavier than the earlier blown threaded glass made by Sandwich and others. There is a salt shaker and a hat in beaded fine threading, and two hats in a coarse threading.

Three Birds

Three Birds

Dalzell, Gilmore & Leighton Company, Findlay, Ohio, 1880s. Clear, nonflint.

Pitcher, water (ill.) . . . . $ 125+

Three Face

Three Face

(Three Sisters; Three Graces): George A. Duncan & Sons, Pittsburgh, 1878. Clear and crystal with frosted faces. Some pieces transfer etched and copper-wheel engraved. Nonflint.

263 (continued)

Biscuit jar (rare)	$ 900+	Butter dish, covered	$ 33-40
Butter dish	130-157	Cheese dish, covered	39-46
Cake stand, 10″, 11″	114-174	Cracker jar	28-36
Celery		Creamer	22-28
Plain top	77-87	Goblet (ill.)	15-24
Scalloped top	92-100	Spoonholder	13-16
Champagne, saucer (rare)	450+	Sugar bowl	
Claret	150-165	Covered	40-46
Compote		Individual, covered	14-18
Covered, 10″	138-146	Syrup	38-45
Covered, 6″, 7″	47-55	Toothpick	20-26
Open, high standard, 8″, 9″	82-91	Wine	12-15
Creamer, face below spout (ill.)	129-140		
Goblet	88-97		
Lamp, 9″, 10″, 11″	150-200		
Pitcher			
Milk, etched	300+		
Water, ½ gal. (rare)	300+		
Salt dip	36-42		
Salt/Pepper, pr.	62-77		
Sauce, footed, 4″, 4½″	19-25		
Spoonholder	56-65		
Wine	125-150		

Butter dish, cake stand, champagne, 6½″ covered compote, claret, creamer, goblet, lamp, sauce, salt shaker and dips, spoonholder, sugar bowl, wine, reproduced. A toothpick listed in a recent publication is probably a ground down salt shaker. The biscuit jar, salt dips, and champagne reproduced by Metropolitan Museum of Art are embossed "MMA."

Three Leaf Clover

Three Leaf Clover

Maker unknown, c. 1860. Any information on this flint glass spill holder would be appreciated. Value $40-50.

Three-in-One

Three-in-One

(Fancy Diamonds): Imperial Glass Company, Bellaire, Ohio, c. late 1880s. Clear, nonflint. Toothpick in Carnival is reproduction, several colors.

Three Panel

Three Panel

Richards & Hartley, Tarentum, Pennsylvania, 1888. Clear, canary, amber, blue; nonflint.

Bowl, cracker (low foot) 7"; shallow, flared, 8"	$ 29-37
Butter dish, covered	38-47
Celery	
Crimp top	33-41
Straight	27-35
Cologne or cruet, pedestal, applied handle	62-75
Compote, open, 7", 8", straight sides, deep	18-26
Creamer (ill.)	27-32
Goblet	27-32
Mug, large or small	19-26
Pitcher, water, 1 qt., ½ gal.	41-50
Sauce, footed, 4"	10-13
Spoonholder	17-23
Sugar bowl	37-44
Tumbler	20-27

Colors, 40-90 percent higher than clear prices listed. Goblets were reproduced in amber and blue. Misnomer "Thousand Eye Three Panel" is a confusing name found in the literature.

Thumbprint

Thumbprint

(Original name, Argus. Also, Early Thumbprint): Bakewell, Pears & Company, c. 1860. Clear, flint, colors (rare).

Ale glass, 7½"	$120-130
Butter dish	94-103
Celery vase, 2 types	92-115
Champagne	62-76
Claret	115-130
Cordial	62-72

Creamer, applied handle (ill.)	69-78
Decanter, quart	78-87
Goblet, ring stem	51-62
Mug, applied handle	81-91
Sauce, flat, 4"	12-15
Spoonholder	38-42
Sugar bowl, covered	77-82
Tumbler	
Footed	32-39
Bar	62-75
Wine	42-49

Tick-Tack-Toe

Tick-Tack-Toe

Maker unknown, c. late 1880s. Clear, nonflint.

Goblet (ill.) . . . . $ 15-19

Tiebacks

Tiebacks

Boston & Sandwich Glass Company, c. 1850s, opalescent. They were used to hold the window curtains in place. The shanks are pewter.

(continued)

2″ dia., pr. . . . . $ 54-63
3″ dia., pr. (ill.).   58-67
4¼″ dia., pr.   80-85
Reproduced.

Tiny Finecut

U. S. Glass, c. 1900. Clear, ruby stain, emerald green. Found only in wine set that comes in green with silvered leaf decoration, and also with decal semi-nude figures, called "Parisian Wine Set." Original tray is not exact pattern match.

Wine, ruby stain. . . . . $ 30-35
Wine set, decanter, original stopper,
  6 wines, tray
    Clear.   100-125
    Green, plain   150-175
    Green, Parisian set   175-222

Tiny Lion

Tiny Lion

Maker unknown, early 1880s. Clear; clear and frosted; nonflint.

Butter dish, covered . . . . $ 43-49
Celery, 2 handles (ill.)   42-51
Compote   51-61
Creamer.   30-38
Jam jar, handled.   40-47
Pitcher, water   42-51
Spoonholder.   27-36
Sugar bowl
    Covered   38-42
    Open   29-36
No goblet.

Tobin

(Leaf and Star): New Martinsville, c. 1908 and at least into mid-1920s. Clear, usually with gold, with an occasional piece found in cobalt or emerald green. Toothpicks known in orange iridescent, rare ruby stain, or deep amber. Nonflint.

Bowl, 8″, 10″ . . . . $ 13-18
Butter.   24-29
Celery tray, 11″   12-17
Compote, jelly.   10-14
Creamer.   15-21
Goblet, 2 types   18-25
Hair receiver, metal lid with hole . . .   14-20
Humidor, 4″ dia. x 4⅝″ high, metal lid .   35-40
Pitcher
  Ice lip, ½ gal., 8½″ high   25-32
  Regular, ½ gal.   23-30
Relish   9-11
Salt shaker   13-17
Sauce
  Flat, 4¾″   5-9
  Footed, 4½″, 6″ (nut bowl)   5-12
Spoonholder.   12-16
Sugar, covered.   22-26
Toothpick   42-52
Tumbler.   12-17
Vase, tulip, 8¼″   15-21
Wine   20-25

Prices are for good impression and gold in excellent condition. Iridescent add 30 percent; ruby stain add 300-400 percent; other colors add 150-200 percent to clear prices listed.

Torpedo

Torpedo

(Pygmy, Fisheye): Thompson Glass Company, Uniontown, Pennsylvania, 1889. Clear and ruby stained; master salt known in black amethyst.

Bowl

Berry, 8", covered . . . . $ 42-50
Open, 8", 9", flared rim 23-29
Rose, 4" (scarce) 49-56
Waste, scalloped top 27-34
Butter dish, covered 69-78
Cake stand, 9", 10" 53-62
Celery, 6¾" high 31-36
Compote

Covered, 6", 8", 9" 42-65
Covered, jelly, 4" 52-60
Open, jelly, flared rim 27-31
Creamer

Plain underbase, 5¾" 38-43
Torpedo underbase, 6" to spout . . . 42-51
Decanter, 8" 74-84
Goblet 49-54
Salt, individual or master 26-34
Salt/Pepper, pr., 2¼", 3" 62-79
Sauce, 4½", 3½" flat honey 11-14
Spoonholder 29-33
Sugar bowl, covered 52-61
Syrup (ill.) 67-74
Tumbler 27-32
Wine 39-44

Prices are for facets in good condition. Worn pieces are worth less than half.

Tree of Life

Portland Glass Company, Portland, Maine, c. 1867. Clear, amber, blue, purple, canary, green, and etched. Flint and non-flint.

Bowl, flat, 8", oval . . . . $ 33-39
Butter dish 58-66
Celery vase, silver plated frame . . . 62-77
Compote open, 10", "Davis,"
low standard 97-115
Creamer, in plated holder 77-86
Goblet, plain 34-43
Pitcher, water 118-133
Plate, 6" 22-29
Spoonholder 32-37
Sugar bowl, covered 48-55
Tumbler, footed 31-37
Wine 51-60

Flint, add 25 percent. Colors, 50-100 percent higher than clear prices listed. Some pieces came in a silver-plated holder; some pieces signed "P.G. Co. Patent;" others have "Davis" woven in design.

Tree of Life with Hand

Tree of Life with Hand

(Pittsburgh—Tree of Life): George A. Duncan's Sons, 1884. Clear, and listed by Kamm in blue. Nonflint.

Bowl, finger . . . . $ 34-43
Butter dish, covered 78-85
Celery 43-50
Compote, covered 67-73
Creamer (ill.) 52-62
Dish, berry 25-34
Goblet (see below) 39-47
Plate, berry 26-35
Saucedish 18-26
Spoonholder 33-40
Sugar bowl

Covered 53-67
Open 35-43

No goblet made in hand stem, but Millard 2-48 shows a goblet that might be compatible, if indeed it is not this pattern.

Tree of Life with Sprig

(continued)

Tree of Life with Sprig

Maker unknown, pattern has 1870s characteristics. Clear, possibly colors; nonflint.

Butter dish	$ 48-54
Celery.	39-47
Creamer, pressed handle.	38-42
Spoonholder.	33-40
Sugar bowl, covered	45-53
Syrup jug, top missing	
applied handle (ill.)	45-55

Creamer has little wheels below the handle at base. Only the creamer and syrup are documented. More information needed!

Triangular Prism

Triangular Prism

Maker unknown, c. 1850s. Clear, flint, and nonflint.

Bowl, shallow, berry	$ 22-28
Butter dish, covered, bowl type	45-53
Celery.	40-47
Cologne or cruet, pedestal,	
applied handle.	82-97
Compote, open	
Low pedestal (common)	24-29
Tall pedestal.	33-42
Creamer, pedestal, applied handle . . .	40-50
Cup, handled	19-27
Flip glass (huge tumbler)	60-70
Goblet, 2 sizes	49-53
Mug, toy (or whiskey taster),	
pressed handle.	20-30
Salt, master, footed	22-27
Spoonholder, crimped rim	33-37
Sugar bowl, covered, pedestal	46-54

Tumbler, 2 sizes	22-32
Wine (ill.)	26-32

Nonflint, 50 percent less than flint prices listed.

Triple Triangle

Triple Triangle

(Doyle No. 76): Doyle & Company, Pittsburgh, c. 1885, and U. S. Glass Company, probably by Pioneer Glass Company, a decorating firm. Clear and ruby stain, nonflint.

Bowl, 9″	$ 39-46
Bread plate (scarce)	62-75
Butter dish, covered, handled	44-51
Celery dish, oblong	34-39
Creamer.	39-44
Goblet (ill. in clear)	40-46
Mug.	37-45
Pitcher, ½ gal.	79-89
Sauce, 5″.	16-21
Spoonholder, handled	30-35
Sugar bowl, covered, handled	44-52
Tumbler.	32-38
Wine	39-47

Clear, 50 percent less than ruby stain prices listed. Serving pieces scarce in ruby, except for celery dish. This form was made in 8″, 9″, 10″ sizes. Engraving is not common, and a ruby mug is known with leaf engraving.

Troubadour Mug

(Serenade Mug): Now attributed to McKee rather than Indiana Tumbler & Goblet (National) Company, late 1890s.

Troubadour Mug

Amber (ill.)	$150-160
Chocolate	96-125
Clear	44-50
Cobalt.	150-160

Also in clear, green, frosted. Opaque examples other than chocolate are attributed to McKee.

Tulip

Tulip

(Plain Tulip): Attributed to Bryce and Sandwich and other early factories, 1850s. McKee catalog 1859 through 1871, with only the salt pictured continuously. Pieces appearing in that catalog are so indicated. Clear, flint. The butter is known in opaque white.

Butter, flat	$ 68-75
Celery.	24-29
Champagne	71-78
Compote, open, large	47-57
Creamer.	44-52
Goblet.	35-43

Lamp	
Colored base	170-190
High (McKee)	120-140
Plate, 6″	52-65
Salt, pedestal (McKee)	31-38
Spoonholder.	38-43
Sugar bowl	65-72
Sweetmeat, covered (McKee),	
5½″, 7½″	118-145
Syrup (ill.)	40-43
Tumbler.	39-47
Whiskey, handled	40-50
Wine	55-69

Tulip with Sawtooth

Tulip with Sawtooth

(Tulip): Bryce, Richards and Company, Pittsburgh, c. 1854 in flint; later in non-flint.

Butter dish, covered	$ 89-110
Celery vase	63-72
Compote	
High standard	
Covered, large	96-105
Covered, small	77-84
Low standard	
Covered	59-66
Open, 8″	44-49
Creamer (ill.)	89-100
Decanter, quart (handled)	
patterned stopper	155-163
Egg cup, covered.	150+
Goblet, knob stem, 7″ high	54-64
Pitcher	200+
Plate, 6″	60-68
Pomade jar	55-62
Salt	
Master, pedestal, petal rim.	34-40
Master, plain rim	29-33
Spoonholder.	37-44
Sugar bowl, open	48-54
Tumbler, footed or flat, bar	53-62

269

(continued)

Wine   57-62

Wine was reproduced in inferior quality non-flint. Confusing pattern, Small Flowered Tulip, and a later pattern, Richmond. Nonflint worth 50 percent less.

Twin Teardrops

Twin Teardrops

Higbee, c. 1890s. Clear, nonflint.

Bowl, 6" . . . . $ 10-14
Celery   23-28
Compote, open (ill.) 22-26
Cruet   29-38
Dish, banana, flat 20-25
Goblet.   17-21
Plate, 7⅝" square, 9½" round   18-24
Sauce, large   5-10
Sugar, covered.   30-36

Twinkle Star

Twinkle Star

(Frost Flower; Starlight; Utah): U.S. Glass Company, 1901. Clear, clear and frosted. Six-pointed raised stars on *inside* of glass. Nonflint. One of the States series.

Butter dish, covered . . . . $ 35-44
Celery   27-32
Creamer.   30-34
Goblet.   27-32
Pitcher, water, 3 pt. (ill.). 40-46
Salt shaker (scarce) 29-32
Spoonholder.   17-20
Sugar bowl, covered   32-40
Syrup, tin or nickel top   40-48
Tumbler.   14-18

Two Band

Two Band

Maker unknown, c. late 1880s. Clear, nonflint.

Butter dish, covered . . . . $ 39-44
Celery.   24-29
Compote, high, open.   25-35
Creamer (ill.)   31-35
Pitcher   39-45
Plate, handled, large (bread or cake) . . 30-36
Salt shaker   24-30
Spoonholder.   22-27
Sugar bowl, covered   40-47
Toy set
   Butter dish, covered   62-69
   Creamer.   35-40
   Spoonholder.   38-42
   Sugar bowl, covered   55-63
No goblet.

Two Panel

Two Panel

(Daisy in Panel; Daisy in Square): Richards & Hartley Flint Glass Company, Tarentum, Pennsylvania, c. 1880s, and limited production by U. S. Glass. Clear, apple green, amber, blue, canary; nonflint.

Bowls, 7″, 8″, 9″	$ 15-25
Butter dish, covered	36-42
Celery.	24-28
Compote	
Covered, high standard, 9″	42-49
Open, low standard, 9″	31-36
Creamer.	20-25
Goblet (ill.)	24-28
Lamp, tall	60-70
Mug, large or small	23-30
Pickle dish, 9″ x 4″	10-15
Pitcher	30-37
Salt	
Individual	10-13
Master.	18-20
Salt shaker (scarce)	26-32
Sauce	
Flat	6-9
Footed.	8-11
Spoonholder.	17-21
Sugar bowl, covered	32-37
Tray, handles	30-36
Tumbler.	14-19
Wine	20-25

Apple green, 80 percent; canary, 60 percent; amber, blue, 50 percent higher than clear prices listed. Many other pieces. Goblet reproduced in amber and blue. Forms are oval.

Umbilicated Sawtooth

Umbilicated Sawtooth

(Inverted Sawtooth; Inverted Diamond Point): Clear, flint, and nonflint from early 1860s through the transitional period.

Bowl, 8″	$ 35-46
Butter dish, covered, on	
pedestal (sweetmeat) (ill.)	54-62
Champagne	40-49
Egg cup	28-34
Goblet.	34-40
Plate, 6that	29-37
Salt, master, footed, ball rim	22-31
Sauce, ball rim (swirled or	
star center)	9-13
Spill, thumbprint rim and	
bowl collar.	32-38
Tumbler.	29-38
Wine	34-43

Deduct 50 percent for nonflint. Millard's name, Umbilicated Sawtooth, is not accurate because the pattern is diamond points, not sawteeth. Lee calls a similar pattern "Diamond Quilted with Bull's Eye Border" and shows the 6″ plate, and possible Sandwich origin.

Unique

271 (continued)

Unique

Co-Operative Flint Glass Company, 1898. Clear, nonflint.

Butter dish	$ 32-39
Creamer.	35-41
Spoonholder.	14-20
Sugar bowl, covered	30-37
Syrup, metal cap (ill.)	34-42

No goblet or toothpick known. Table set has flat bases; spoonfer and sugar are handleless; butter has plate-type base, probably with inner collar to secure lid.

U.S. Rib

U. S. Daisy

(Erroneously, Lacy Daisy): U. S. Glass, c. 1918. Clear, green; possibly blue, amber. Nonflint.

Bowls
Belled, 9″	$ 13-16
Deep, crimped 9½″	13-16
Salad, cupped, 8½″	13-16
Butter, small	19-23
Creamer (tankard).	13-16

Dishes
Oval, 9½″	10-14
Round, 8″	10-14
Shallow, crimped, 9½″	10-14
Finger bowls, crimped: footed	
or regular	10-14
Jam pot, metal lid	15-19
Mug	8-11

Nappies
Cupped, 8½″.	10-12
Straight sides, 7″.	10-12
Plates, 5½″, 10″	11-15
Puff box, metal lid.	13-16

Rose bowl
Flanged, 4″, 6″	12-16
Regular, 5″.	15-18
Rose jar, 6″	14-16
Salt dip, individual, round	12-15
Salt shaker	13-17
Toothpick, metal holder	35-42

Similar patterns: Nova Scotia Diamond; Cane; some pieces with English registry marks. A kettle toothpick is earlier production.

U.S. Rib

(Rib): U.S. Glass Company, 1900. Green glass with gold rims.

Butter dish	$ 53-62

Creamer, individual, 2½″ (ill.)	32-39
Cruet, original ribbed stopper	72-79
Spoonholder.	26-32
Sugar bowl, covered	40-49
Toothpick.	32-38

Crystal, 50 percent less than green prices listed.

Valentine

Valentine

(Trilby): U.S. Glass Company (Gasport), 1890s. Clear, nonflint.

Butter dish, heart-shaped	$ 75-80
Cologne bottle	
Heart only (no portrait), original	
heart-shaped stopper.	36-42
Creamer.	52-61
Goblet.	79-85
Match holder	57-69
Pitcher, water (ill.)	166-172
Spoonholder.	41-49
Sugar	70-80
Tumbler.	45-51

Scarce.

272

Victoria, Bakewell

Victoria, Bakewell

Bakewell, Pears & Company, early 1860s. Clear, canary, possibly other colors; flint.

Butter saucer (see note)	72-79
Cake stand	
9″	88-98
15″	128-132
Compote	
Covered, 8″, 10″ high	137-142
Open, low, 8″ dia. (ill.)	62-71
Creamer	92-106
Dish, sweetmeat or	
high standard butter	112-122
Sugar bowl (scarce)	172-190

Colors, 200 percent higher than clear prices listed. A Bakewell catalog shows an 8″ footed "butter saucer," lidless that we would call a low cake stand! No goblet.

Victoria, Riverside

(Draped Top; Draped Red Top): Riverside Glass Works, Wellsburg, West Virginia, c. 1894. Clear or with red or amber stain; nonflint. Prices are for ruby stain.

Bowl, 7½″ dia. x 3¼″ high	$ 43-50
Butter dish, covered, 5½″ high . . .	116-128
Cake stand	97-119
Celery	60-72
Compote	
Covered, 6″	89-112
Open, scalloped rim	43-51
Creamer, individual or large	59-68
Cruet, 6″	175-187
Goblet	60-72
Pitcher, water, ½ gal., 8″ high	137-155
Salt/Pepper, pr.	84-97
Sauce, flat, 4½″	18-24
Spoonholder, 4″ high.	52-60
Sugar bowl, covered	42-51

Syrup, 6½″	230-258
Toothpick, 2¾″ high.	172-188
Tumbler, barrel shape, 3½″	40-47

Clear, 60 percent less; amber stain, 30 percent less. Thirty-five pieces were advertised. The toothpick appears to be made from the same mold as the individual creamer Kamm lists and an individual "table set." Could this be a toy set? The typical grated bands are not evident in the original ads. Color stain placement varies.

Waffle

Bryce, Walker & Company, Pittsburgh, 1860s. Also attributed to Sandwich by early authors. Flint crystal, opaque white, colors. Prices are for brilliant flint only.

Butter dish, covered	$ 87-99
Celery, 9″ high	58-70
Champagne goblet	106-112
Claret	96-115
Compote	
Covered, 7″, 9″, high standard . . .	100-150
Open, 6″, low standard	50-58
Creamer, 6¾″ high	118-124
Decanter, pint and quart	87-115
Egg cup	36-42
Goblet, knob stem	51-62
Lamp	
Applied handle	118-130
Tall, all glass.	132-148
Pitcher, water (rare) 9½″ high	300+
Relish, scalloped edge, 4″ x 6″	33-39
Salt	
Covered	112-120
Open, footed	32-39
Sauce, 4″	8-13
Spoonholder or spill	50-60
Sugar bowl, covered	129-141
Tumbler, water, whiskey	64-78
Whiskey, applied handle (mug) . . .	108-120
Wine	55-64

A goblet illustrated in the literature as "Waffle without Thumbprint" is most likely a poorly pressed "Waffle and Thumbprint."

Waffle and Thumbprint

Curling, Robertson & Company, Pittsburgh, c. 1850; New England Glass Company and Sandwich, early; later, Ohio Valley, c. 1850s, 1860s. Clear, flint and nonflint.

Bowl, rectangular,	
5″ x 7″, 6″ x 8″ (ill.)	$ 32-40

(continued)

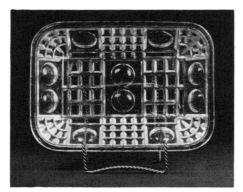

Waffle and Thumbprint

Butter dish, covered	88-106
Celery	68-80
Champagne	64-72
Claret	64-72
Compote, covered, 6″, 7″, 8″ dia. . . .	98-125
Creamer	125-140
Decanter	
Pint	82-90
Quart, original pointed	
panelled stopper	121-131
Goblet	
Knob stem	60-67
Plain stem	49-58
Lamp, finger	89-100
Pitcher, water (rare)	400+
Spillholder or spoonholder	46-53
Sugar bowl, covered	121-130
Tumbler, water, whiskey, footed . . .	70-92
Wine	59-69

Nonflint or dull glass with poor impression, 50 percent less than flint prices listed. Goblet also made with bulb stem that narrows at the base with a stem expanded at the bottom. Also see comment under "Waffle."

Waffle with Fan Top

Maker unknown, c. 1880s. Clear, nonflint.

Goblet (ill.) . . . . $ 17-25

Another member of the Waffle family. A goblet known that is embossed "M. G. Edson & Co."

Washboard

(Original name, Adonis; Pleat and Tuck): McKee & Bros., Pittsburgh, c. 1897. Clear, canary, blue; nonflint.

Waffle with Fan Top

Bowls, 8″, round, oval	$ 16-24
Butter dish, covered	32-41
Cake stand, large	37-47
Celery vase	25-30
Compote, jelly, 4½″ dia.	12-17
Creamer	30-35
Pitcher, qt., ½ gal..	32-41
Plate, 10″	17-21
Salt shaker	17-21
Sauce, flat, 4″, 4½″.	6-10
Spoonholder	22-27
Sugar bowl, covered	35-43
Syrup	48-55
Tumbler	15-19

Colors, 50 percent higher than clear prices listed. No goblet or toothpick.

Washington

Washington

New England Glass Company, Cambridge, Massachusetts, early 1860s. Clear, flint.

Bottle

Bar, blob top.	$ 88-97
Bitters.	66-75
Bowl, oval 6" x 9".	32-38
Butter dish, covered, on pedestal (sweetmeat).	165-178
Celery.	80-90
Champagne	94-112

Compote

Covered, tall, 10".	155-177
Open, low, 9".	58-69
Cordial	136-153
Creamer.	200+
Decanter, qt., patterned stopper	112-125
Egg cup	59-69
Goblet.	64-78
Honey, flat	10-15

Pitcher

Syrup	132-144
Water	300+

Salt

Footed (ill.)	36-42
Individual, flat.	18-24
Master, flat	30-34
Sauce, flat.	10-15
Spoonholder.	43-52
Sugar bowl covered	117-135
Tumbler.	88-95
Wine	100-115

Washington Centennial

Gillinder & Sons, Philadelphia, c. 1876. Clear, nonflint, with a syrup known in opaque white.

Bowl, oval	$ 28-34
Butter dish, covered	84-93
Celery.	50-60
Champagne	67-73
Creamer.	78-85
Goblet.	43-52
Pitcher, 8" to spout top	98-108

Platters

Carpenters Hall	108-114
"The Nation's Birthplace."	112-120
Washington's head.	118-126
Relish, flat, oval, bear paw handles, 9¾" x 5¼", "Centennial 1776-1876"	32-42
Sugar bowl, covered	75-83
Wine	49-57

The George Washington platter comes with the image frosted and is worth 20 percent more.

Washtub Soap Dish

Washtub Soap Dish

Maker and date unknown. A novelty item of the 1860s. Clear glass; also canary, amber, blue. Nonflint.

Washtub, clear	$ 44-58
Washtub, canary or amber.	60-68
Washtub, blue, rare (ill.).	75-88

Water Lily

(Original name, Magnolia; Frosted Magnolia): Dalzell, Gilmore & Leighton Company, Findlay, Ohio, c. 1890. Clear or frosted crystal. Nonflint.

Bowl, 6", 7", 8"	$ 29-42
Butter dish, covered	80-90
Cake stand, large	78-89
Celery vase	59-65
Creamer.	52-62
Goblet.	84-92

Pitcher

Syrup	118-133
Water tankard.	96-112
Salt shaker	41-49
Sauce, flat.	15-20
Spoonholder.	48-54
Sugar bowl, covered	69-74
Tumbler.	30-36

Clear only pieces, 50 percent less.

Waterfall

Maker unknown, 1880s. Clear, light blue, canary; nonflint.

Butter dish	$ 36-41
Celery.	24-32
Compote	47-52
Creamer.	25-31
Pitcher, water, 9" (ill.)	39-46

(continued)

Waterfall

Goblet.	40-47
Pitcher, water	58-69
Plate, 9″, 10″.	34-41
Sauce, 4″, 5″	19-23
Spoonholder.	35-44
Sugar bowl, covered (scarce).	57-62
Tumbler.	22-39

Colors, 100-300 percent higher than clear prices listed. Renditions with more elaborate detailing and additional floral motifs are represented in the Carnival versions, also called simply "Water Lily" or "Cattails and Water Lily" in the earlier literature. No goblet, toothpick, or salt shaker known. A 10⅝″ frosted crystal Fenton (with basketweave) plate is known.

Salt shaker (scarce)	26-33
Spoonholder.	18-23
Sugar bowl, covered	34-40

Colors, 50 percent higher than clear prices listed. Documentation only on pitcher and salt shaker.

Ways Colonial

Waterlily and Cattails

Waterlily and Cattails

Northwood Glass Company in different forms and slight pattern variations. Made only the water set; later pieces by Fenton, after 1900. Clear, frosted crystal, opalescent, and Carnival glass. Fenton version illustrated. Prices are for crystal opalescent.

Bowl, fluted, 10″, 11″, flat rim, 10″	$ 41-49
Butter dish, covered	58-65
Celery vase	27-36
Creamer (ill.)	36-41

Ways Colonial

Curling, Robertson & Company, Pittsburgh, c. 1850, and others. Clear, flint. Extremely rare in opalescent.

Claret	$ 53-60
Goblet.	58-65
Tumbler (ill.)	34-40

Usually, this version is heavy and primitive, characterized by the massive panelled ring under the bowl.

Wedding Bells

Fostoria Glass Company, Moundsville, West Virginia, 1900. Clear, stained rose or green with gold. Nonflint.

Bowl, finger	$ 24-30
Butter dish, covered	55-63
Celery.	29-37
Creamer.	40-44
Compote, covered, high, low foot	47-53

Wedding Bells

Cruet, original patterned stopper . . .	42-50
Cup	12-16
Decanter, qt., original patterned stopper	54-63
Pitcher, half gallon jug (ill.)	72-80
Punch bowl	250+
Salt shaker, 2 types	24-33
Spoonholder.	33-40
Sugar bowl	45-53
Toothpick.	40-46
Tumbler	
Water	22-29
Whiskey (shot)	14-19
Wine	30-35

Color, 60 percent higher than clear prices listed. A wine is shown in the catalog, but no goblet; nor does one appear elsewhere in the literature. Additional pieces are available.

Wedding Lamp

Wedding Lamp

(Marriage Lamp): On June 14, 1870, Daniel C. Ripley patented a mold for producing twin-fountain oil lamps, both by pressing and blowing. Extremely rare today, the one shown here is on display at the Houston Museum, Chattanooga, Tennessee.

Lamp, rare (ill.) . . . . $ 1400+
With blue fonts, add 50 percent.

Wedding Ring

Wedding Ring

(Double Wedding Ring): Maker unknown, 1860s. Clear, flint.

Champagne	$ 79-86
Creamer.	97-112
Decanter, original stopper	110-127
Goblet, regular	62-72
Lamp	
Finger, 5″	59-69
Tall, composite, 10½″	150-162
Pitcher, syrup (ill.)	142-159
Sauce	10-15
Tumbler.	78-83
Wine	54-60

Comes in regular and heavy versions, and a scarce type with an almost square bowl, straight sides, and a faceted, double knob. Single Wedding Ring, a different pattern, is later, lighter, and nonflint. Unitt pictures a "Single Wedding Ring" that is not the goblet he references.

Westmoreland

(Spector Block; Gillinder's Westmoreland): Patented by Thomas W. Mellor, 1889, Gillinder & Sons; U. S. Glass, c. 1891. Clear, nonflint.

Banana dish, flat	$ 18-24
Bowl	
Finger	15-20
Hat shaped, 9″.	19-24
Hexagonal, 9″	19-24
Oval or round, 6″, 7″, 8″, 9″	13-27
Punch, 14″, 15″ flared	250+
Rectangular	17-21
Rose, 3″, 4″, 5″, 6″, 10″.	18-39
Butter	
Individual	50-60
Regular	40-46
Caster bottle	
Mustard	34-39
Oil.	42-48
Shaker.	34-39
Celery	
Tray.	18-24
Vase.	26-32
Champagne	35-42
Cheese, covered	51-59
Cologne bottle, patterned stoppers	
5 sizes, 1 oz. to 12 oz..	18-38
Compote	
Covered, high, 6″, 7″, 8″, 9″	38-69
Open, high, flared, 7″, 8″, 9″, 10″. . .	30-42
Open, high, straight, 7″, 8″, 9″. . . .	30-40
Cracker jar, 5″, 6″, 7″	36-55
Creamer	
Bulbous, ¼ pt., ½ pt.	23-28
Individual berry, 2½″ to side rim. .	13-16
Tankard, ¼ pt., ½ pt., 7½″,	
(called "Pompeian Creamer") . .	30-40
Cruet, patterned stopper	
1 oz., 2 oz..	29-35
4 oz., 6 oz.	25-32
Cup	8-12
Dish	
Oval, 7″, 8″, 9″, 10″, 11″	20-34
Square, 7″, 8″, 9″	24-29
Egg cup	30-35
Goblet.	32-38
Honey, round and deep, with lid . . .	38-43
Ice tub	42-52
Lamp	
Finger lamp, 3½″, one handle,	
no shade	50-60
Tall, with umbrella shade,	
round base, 8½″	134-145
Bell shaped, flat base, 7⅞″.	115-132
Square based, silver filigreed, 10″. .	175-218
Tall, no shade, 9″ to top of collar . .	73-88
Olive, round, one handle.	23-28
Pickle or marmalade jar, straight,	
flat lid	34-39
Pickle jar, bulbous, domed stopper. .	38-45
Pitcher	
Squat, plain rim, qt., ½ gal.	40-50
Tall, scalloped rim, ¼ pt., ½ pt. . .	28-36
Tall, scalloped rim, ¾ gal.	55-62
Plate, 7″, 10½″.	18-25
Salt dip	
Individual	10-14
Master.	13-18
Salt shaker	20-24
Sauce, flat.	10-14
Scent vial, 4 types	14-23
Spoonholder.	17-21
Sugar	
Basket, square or round	41-49
Individual berry with lid	28-34
Regular	37-42
Shaker, heavy pewter top	40-50
Syrup	50-60
Tray	
Pen	13-17
Rectangular, 13″	38-44
Tumbler	
Toy(whiskey or shot)	12-15
Water	22-26
Vase, 10″	18-22
Water bottle.	38-45
Wine	25-30

Confusing patterns: Heisey's Pillows and Bakewell Block, an early flint pattern. A toy set is mentioned, but not pictured in the literature, and may be speculation based on the individual creamer. Discovery of small toothpick (toy spooner) would confirm.

Westmoreland, Westmoreland's

(Late Westmoreland, New Westmoreland): c. 1898. Clear or teal green with gold. Nonflint.

Butter.	$ 36-42
Compote, open, 9¼″ dia. x 7½″ high . .	32-37
Creamer.	29-33
Cruet	30-40
Nappy, oval	13-17
Pitcher	42-48
Salt shaker (scarce)	20-25
Spoonholder.	20-25

Sugar 32-37
Toothpick (rare). 40-50

No goblet. Green add 100 percent to clear prices listed.

Westward Ho!

Westward Ho!

(Pioneer; Tippecanoe): Gillinder & Sons, Philadelphia, about 1879. Clear, frosted; nonflint.

Butter dish, covered
  standard. $174-189
Celery. 109-118
Compote
  Covered, 6″, high standard 169-179
  Covered, 6″, low standard 137-155
  Oval, open, 8″, 9″ 97-110
Creamer (ill.) 89-97
Goblet, frosted 87-96
Jar, jam, covered 162-181
Mug, 2″, 3½″, clear. . . . . 150+
Pitcher
  Milk. 218-224
  Water 208-222
Sauce, 3½″, 4″, footed 26-32
Spoonholder. 90-98
Sugar bowl, covered 152-160
Wine 138-144

Butter dish, 6″ compote, 9″ compote, goblet, water pitcher, sauce, wine reproduced in amethyst, blue green, clear and frosted. Goblets originally in clear or frosted.

Wheat and Barley

(Original name, Duquesne; Hops and Barley; Oats and Barley): Made by Bryce Bros., Pittsburgh, late 1870s, and U.S. Glass, 1890s. Clear, amber, blue, yellow; nonflint.

Wheat and Barley

Butter dish, covered, tab handles . . . $ 24-33
Cake stand, 8″, 9″, 10″ 19-36
Compote
  Covered, 7″, 8″, high standard 34-45
  Open, high standard, jelly, 5″. 14-19
Creamer. 22-27
Goblet. 20-27
Mug. 25-30
Pitcher
  Syrup (scarce) 80-92
  Water (ill.). 40-47
Plate, handled, 7″, 9″. 19-25
Salt/Pepper, pr. 33-40
Sauce, footed, flat, with tab handle, 4″ . 12-17
Spoonholder. 24-32
Sugar bowl, covered 29-34
Tumbler, footed, water 18-26

Canary, amber, 50 percent higher; blue, 65 percent higher than clear prices listed. No toothpick.

Wheat Sheaf

Wheat Sheaf

Maker unknown, late 1870s. Clear. Seldom seen.

279

(continued)

Butter dish	$ 44-55
Celery vase	29-35
Compote, low standard	30-36
Creamer.	34-41
Goblet.	29-38
Pitcher, water (ill.)	55-62
Spoonholder.	27-36
Sugar bowl	39-48
Tumbler.	22-29

The oval bread tray does not appear to be this pattern. Goblet and pitcher are the only pieces documented so far.

Wheel in Band

Wheel in Band

Maker unknown, 1870s. Clear, nonflint.

Butter dish, covered	$ 26-33
Celery.	17-22
Creamer.	18-24
Goblet.	16-22
Jam jar, covered	32-38
Pitcher, water (ill.)	30-36
Spoonholder.	13-19
Sugar bowl, covered	25-30
Wine	16-22

Whirled Sunburst in Circle

Beatty-Brady, c. 1908. Clear, nonflint.

Bowl, 6", 7"	$ 11-16
Butter dish, covered	17-24
Creamer.	14-18
Pitcher, water (ill.)	20-26
Sauce, flat, 4"	4-7
Spoonholder.	10-13
Sugar bowl, covered	15-20
Tumbler.	8-13

Whirled Sunburst in Circle

Wigwam

(Original name, Alhambra; Teepee): Iowa City Glass Company, Iowa City, Iowa, 1880s. Clear, nonflint.

Butter dish, covered, pedestal	$ 175+
Creamer, pedestal, 6½"	125+
Goblet.	150+
Spoonholder, pedestal, flat rim . . .	75+
Sugar bowl, covered	150+

Millard's "goblet," as well as Unitt's, is, in fact, the spoonholder. The goblet is the only piece that has a smaller band of the pattern inverted below the middle belt of diamond points.

Wild Bouquet

(Iris): Northwood & Co., Wheeling, West Virginia, c. 1903. White, blue, canary (rare), green opalescent; custard. Forms are oval, except tumblers and the round tray with four feet that holds the cruet and shakers, and lacks the pattern elements, doubling as the same holder in Chrysanthemum Sprig. Prices are for blue opalescent.

Bowl, berry	$ 89-112
Butter.	389-414
Compote, jelly.	73-96
Creamer.	133-147
Cruet	339-368
Pitcher, water	300+
Salt shaker	150+
Sauce	29-36
Spoonholder.	92-103

Sugar, covered.	179-212
Toothpick.	197-222
Tray, round, footed	129-142
Tumbler.	90-110

The custard version of the butter and sugar was also made without the finial, having instead a solid arch by which to lift the lids. Custard is worth about 400 percent more than white opalescent and the arched versions worth about 25 percent more. Production of canary was limited and values approximate that of custard. White worth about 35 percent, green worth about 25 percent less than blue values given.

Wild Rose and Ladies Lamp

Wild Rose and Ladies Lamp

(Ladies Medallion; Riverside Ladies): Attributed to Riverside Glass Company, Wellsburg, West Virginia. The literature (except for one Northwood attribution) reports that Riverside obtained the molds after Millersburg closed; however, the chronology will not substantiate this claim because Riverside closed in 1907 and Millersburg opened in 1909. It is more probable that the plain honeycomb blank came from Riverside after the 1907 closing, that Millersburg first made the lamp with the ladies and no rose (called simply "Medallion"), retooled it with the wild rose, and then incorporated the two designs into the one ladies lamp, adding the Riverside advertising. That the Riverside advertising for the brass clinch-on collar appears on this lamp can be explained by the fact that these collars appeared in ads up through the 1930s, so even though Riverside glass production stopped, the collar continued to be used on other companies' lamps, such as Albany sewing lamps. It is interesting that none of these lamps has been reported with the clinch-on collars that are patent dated 1882 and 1883.

Lamp, Wild Rose and Ladies,
8½" to top of collar . . . . $ 500+

Original Goofus gold and red paint worth 20 percent more. Colored bases increase value by at least 100 percent. Confirmation of types and colors would be appreciated!

Wild Rose with Bow Knot

Wild Rose with Bow Knot

McKee, National, c. 1901. Clear, colors, frosted (camphor); chocolate (dark as well as pale).

Bowl, 7", 8½"	$ 26-36
Butter dish	47-54
Creamer.	33-42
Cruet	31-38

281

(continued)

Pitcher, clear (ill. in chocolate).	64-72
Salt shaker	18-25
Sauce	9-12
Spoonholder.	28-32
Sugar bowl, covered	42-49
Syrup	60-70
Toothpick (see notes)	40-50
Tray, 10½" x 8"	43-55
Tumbler.	17-22
Vase, 10½"	35-39

Colors, 50 percent higher than clear prices listed. Chocolate, 200-400 percent more. Frosted with painted decoration, add 40 percent to clear prices listed. The toothpick known in a decorated, almost ivory custard is actually a matchholder, made in 1¾" and 2¾" sizes, from a smoke set. Value: $100+, each.

Wild Rose with Scrolling

Wild Rose with Scrolling

(Original name, Sultan): McKee Glass Company, 1915-1925. Clear, frosted crystal, emerald green or frosted green, and chocolate. Stippled background, scarce. Toy set only.

Butter dish, covered, base,	
5⅛" dia. (ill.)	$ 95-112
Creamer, 2¾"	59-65
Spoonholder, 2⅝"	47-55
Sugar bowl, covered, 3" high plus lid .	75-89

The spoonholder is also collected as a toothpick holder. Add 20 percent for frosted; 25 percent for emerald green; 100-300 percent for chocolate.

Wildflower

Wildflower

Adams & Company, Pittsburgh, 1874; U.S. Glass Company, 1891. Clear, canary, amber, blue, apple green, vaseline; nonflint.

Butter dish, flat or footed,	
covered	$ 31-40
Cake stand, large, small	52-61
Celery	26-30
Compote	
High standard	
6", 8", covered	37-47
Open.	32-38
Low standard, 8".	21-25
Creamer	22-28
Goblet.	24-28
Pitcher, water (ill.)	34-39
Salt/Pepper, pr.	37-43
Sauce, flat, round, square	9-12
Spoonholder.	14-19
Sugar bowl, covered	30-34
Tray, water, oval, 11" x 13".	32-42
Tumbler, water	23-29
Wine	32-38

Amber, yellow, blue, 40 percent higher; green, 100 percent higher than clear prices listed. Goblet, 10" plate; round, flat sauce, tumbler, wine reproduced.

Willow Oak

(Oak Leaf; Acorn; Thistle): Bryce Bros., 1880s, called it Wreath. U. S. Glass, 1891. Clear, amber, blue; nonflint.

Bowl, berry, 7", 8"	$ 22-27
Butter bowl, covered, (flanged)	31-38
Cake stand, 8½".	27-35
Celery	33-37
Compote, covered, high standard . . .	38-44
Creamer.	24-29
Goblet.	30-38

Willow Oak

Mug.	37-43
Pitcher, large, (ill.)	33-41
Plate	
Closed handles, 9″	21-27
No handles, 7″	26-32
Salt/Pepper, pr. (scarce)	43-50
Sauce, flat or footed, 4″	9-17
Spoonholder.	18-22
Sugar bowl, covered	38-47
Tray, water	32-38
Tumbler.	28-33

Amber, 40 percent higher; blue, 60 percent higher than clear prices listed.

Wiltec

Wiltec

McKee & Bros., Pittsburgh, c. 1890s. Clear, flint.

Bonbon, cloverleaf.	$ 14-18
Butter dish, covered	20-30
Cigar jar, silver cover	39-46

Creamer.	15-19
Custard cup	8-11
Flower pot, silver lined (scarce)	39-46
Pitcher, ½ gal. jug	30-37
Plate, 6″, 8″, 10″, 11½″	11-22
Punch bowl and foot.	70-83
Spoonholder.	13-18
Sugar bowl, covered (ill.).	20-30
Tumbler.	10-15

Windflower

Windflower

Maker unknown, late 1870s. Clear, non-flint.

Butter dish, flat, covered	$ 54-62
Celery	34-39
Compote, covered, high,	
standard.	66-73
Cordial	40-47
Creamer.	19-27
Egg cup	24-32
Goblet.	49-54
Pitcher, water (ill.)	42-52
Salt, footed, Master	27-32
Sauce, 4″.	10-14
Spoonholder.	22-29
Sugar bowl, covered	34-43
Tumbler, water	28-37
Wine	33-42

Winged Scroll

Winged Scroll

A. H. Heisey Company, Newark, Ohio, 1899. Clear, emerald, vaseline; opaque white (opal), ivorina verde (light custard), frequently decorated with gold.

Bowl, round	$ 99-115
Butter dish, covered	149-162
Celery (scarce).	250-268
Creamer.	95-106
Cruet	200-225
Pitcher, tankard.	169-194
Spoonholder.	70-89
Sugar bowl, covered (ill.).	110-122
Toothpick	
Bulbous	100-127
Straight (match).	189-223

Prices are for custard with good gold.

Wooden Pail

Wooden Pail

(Oaken Bucket): Bryce Bros., 1880s. Clear, amber, blue, canary. Probably a container for candy, mustard, baking powder, coffee. Bryce Bros. called it their Bucket

Set. Made in miniature and full size. Amethyst, rare; nonflint.

Butter dish, covered	$ 64-71
Creamer.	52-57
Pitcher (ill.)	54-63
Spoonholder.	32-41
Sugar bowl	
Covered	47-56
Open	34-42

Miniature same price as large. Yellow, amber, 60 percent higher; blue, 85 percent higher; amethyst, 275 percent higher than clear prices listed.

Woodflower

Sandwich, 1870s. Clear and stippled.

Creamer.	$ 68-74
Goblet.	66-73
Sugar bowl, covered	84-92

Wreath and Shell

Wreath and Shell

Albany, Indiana, Glass Company. late 1880s. Opaque colors.

Butter dish, covered	$ 87-94
Rose bowl (ill.)	67-74
Tumbler.	77-86

Wyoming

(Enigma): U.S. Glass Company, Gas City, Indiana, 1907. Crystal, colored glass, including mosaic glass; nonflint.

Butter dish, covered	$ 47-54
Cake stand, 9″	74-83

Wyoming

Creamer.	35-44
Goblet.	34-41
Pitcher, milk, water (ill.).	39-47
Spoonholder.	31-38
Sugar bowl	
Covered	37-45
Open	32-40
Tumbler.	29-37
Wine	47-54

X-Log

X-Log

(Prism Arc): Maker unknown, c. mid-1880s. Clear, nonflint.

Bowl, vegetable, oval (ill.)	$ 24-32
Butter dish, covered	38-47
Cake stand	48-55
Creamer.	39-47
Goblet.	32-41
Mug.	29-38
Spoonholder.	34-42
Sugar bowl, covered	39-46
Wine	32-41

Yale

Yale

(Crow-Foot): McKee Glass Company, Jeannette, Pennsylvania, 1894. Clear, nonflint.

Butter dish, covered	$ 29-36
Cake stand	50-57
Celery.	28-32
Compote, covered	34-39
Cordial	16-20
Creamer, regular.	24-29
Goblet.	28-34
Pitcher	
Syrup	32-38
Water (ill.).	37-46
Plate	24-32
Salt/Pepper, pr.	42-51
Saucedish, 4", 6"	19-27
Spoonholder.	29-36
Sugar bowl, covered	38-44
Tumbler.	23-32

Yoked Loop

(continued)

Yoked Loop

(Scalloped Loop): Maker unknown, c. 1860s. Clear, flint.

Goblet.	$ 39-46
Sugar bowl	
Covered	57-64
Open (ill.)	40-48

York Colonial

York Colonial

Possibly Sandwich, c. 1850s, clear, flint; also opalescent, amethyst, blue. Later, Central Glass Company, c. 1870s, clear, nonflint.

Ale, footed.	$ 56-64
Celery.	108-119
Compote, covered	109-120
Creamer.	117-124
Goblet.	80-87
Sugar bowl (base ill.)	65-75
Tumbler.	45-54

Colors (rare), 200 percent higher than clear prices listed. Central Glass pieces, 50 percent lower than Sandwich prices listed.

York Herringbone

Maker unknown, late 1880s. Clear; clear with ruby stain; nonflint. Souvenir pieces sold at 1893 World's Fair.

Celery.	$ 37-44
Creamer, green, individual	
(ill.)	57-62
Spoonholder.	45-53

York Herringbone

Yuma Loop

Yuma Loop

O'Hara Glass Company, late 1850s or early 1860s. Clear, flint. Contemporary of Loop (O'Hara). Same values.

Zanesville

(Erroneously, Esther, a case of mistaken identity in the literature): Robinson Glass Co., No. 122, c. 1895. Clear; clear with frosting, usually enameled with blue forget-me-nots; ruby stain, souvenir. Nonflint.

Butter.	$ 25-32
Carafe.	22-28
Creamer.	19-24
Cruet	
Individual, 3½″ (4 oz.)	15-20
Regular	20-25
Salt shaker (rare)	20-25
Spoonholder.	14-18
Sugar, covered.	23-29
Toothpick.	21-24

Frosted with enameled flowers add 30 percent, ruby stain add 50 percent to clear prices listed. Confusing pattern, Esther.

Zipper

Celery.	19-27
Cheese dish	49-60
Compote	
Covered	35-45
Open	24-32
Creamer, high or low foot	20-25
Dish, oblong, 9⅜″ x 6″	17-21
Goblet.	20-25
Jar, jam, covered	29-37
Pickle dish	11-16
Pitcher, water, qt., ½ gal.	38-45
Salt shaker	20-25
Sauce	5-10
Spoonholder.	15-21
Sugar bowl	
Open	18-24
Covered	33-39
Tumbler.	12-16

Zigzag Band

Zigzag Band

Maker unknown, 1880s. Clear, nonflint.

Creamer (ill.)	$ 17-23

Information needed on other pieces. Only creamer is documented.

Zipper

(Original name, Cobb): Richards & Hartley Glass Company, Tarentum, Pennsylvania, c. 1880s. Clear, nonflint.

Butter dish, covered	$ 34-39

Zipper Slash

Zipper Slash

George A. Duncan & Sons, Washington, Pennsylvania, 1893. Stained ruby or yellow above pattern; some are souvenirs. Nonflint.

287

(continued)

Banana dish.	$ 19-24
Bowls	13-25
Butter dish, covered	36-42
Celery vase	28-34
Champagne	25-32
Compote, covered, 6″, 7″, 8″.	40-65
Creamer (ill.)	25-30
Individual	14-20
Cruet	33-39
Cup	10-14
Goblet.	25-30
Pitcher, water	36-43
Sauce, footed	6-9
Sherbet	12-14
Spoonholder.	17-23
Sugar bowl	30-35
Toothpick.	22-27
Tumbler.	14-17
Wine	19-26

Ruby, yellow, 50 percent higher. "Pan American" 1901 souvenir pieces known.

If you have information concerning *any* pattern, please let us hear from you. If you don't agree with the prices quoted, please let us hear from you. If you think the piece illustrated is a spoonholder rather than a celery (etc.), please let us hear from you. Constructive criticism is *always* welcome.

Glass Companies

An asterisk indicates firms which exhibited their wares at the Centennial Exhibition in Philadelphia, Pennsylvania, in 1876.

* Adams & Company, Pittsburgh, 1861; joined U.S. Glass Company in 1891 as Factory A.

Aetna Glass & Manufacturing Company, Bellaire, Ohio, 1880.

American Glass Company, Anderson, Indiana, 1889.

Anchor-Hocking Glass Company (see Ohio Flint Glass Company).

* Atterbury & Company, Pittsburgh, about 1858.

Bakewell & Company (also called Bakewell & Page), 1809.

Bakewell & Ensell, Pittsburgh, 1807.

Bakewell, Page & Bakewell, 1824.

* Bakewell, Pears & Company, 1836.

Bay State Glass Company, Cambridge, Massachusetts, about 1849.

Beatty, Alexander J. & Sons, Steubenville, Ohio, about 1850. Moved to Tiffin, Ohio, in 1890.

Beatty-Brady Glass Company, Steubenville, then to Dunkirk, Indiana, in 1898. Both taken over by the U.S. Glass Company; Factory S at Steubenville and Factory T at Tiffin.

Beaumont Glass Company, Martins Ferry, Ohio, 1895. Sold to Hocking Glass in 1905.

Beaver Falls Co-Operative Glass Company, Beaver Falls, Pennsylvania, 1879.

Beaver Falls Glass Company, Beaver Falls, Pennsylvania, 1887.

Bellaire Goblet Company, Bellaire & Findlay, Ohio, 1878; merged with U.S. Glass Company in 1891. Both plants were moved to Tiffin, Ohio, under the name Factory M.

Belmont Glass Company, Bellaire, Ohio, 1866.

* Boston & Sandwich Glass Company, Sandwich, Massachusetts, 1825.

Boston Silver-Glass Company, East Cambridge, Massachusetts, 1857.

Brilliant Glass Works, Brilliant, Ohio (originally called Novelty Glass Company), 1880.

Bryce, McKee & Company, Pittsburgh, 1850.

Bryce, Richards & Company, Pittsburgh, 1854.

Bryce, Walker & Company, Pittsburgh, 1865.

Bryce Bros., Pittsburgh, 1882. Taken over by U.S. Glass Company around 1889 and named Factory B.

Bryce Bros. again entered the business Hammondsville, Pennsylvania, 1896.

Bryce, Higbee & Company (also known as Homestead Glass Works), Pittsburgh, 1879.

J. B. Higbee Glass Company, Bridgeville, Pennsylvania, 1900.

* Excelsior Glass Works, Wheeling, West Virginia; moved to Martins Ferry, Ohio, in 1879 under the name Buckeye Glass Company.

Campbell, Jones & Company, Pittsburgh, 1865.

Canton Glass Company, Canton, Ohio, 1883; factory moved to Marion, Indiana, in 1894. In 1899 it joined with National Glass Company. In 1903 the factory site changed to Cambridge, Ohio. Another Canton Glass Company was founded in Marion, Indiana, in 1904.

Jones, Cavitt & Company, Ltd., Pittsburgh, 1886.

*Central Glass Company, Wheeling, West Virginia, 1863. (Famous for their Coin pattern.) Joined U.S. Glass Company in 1891 as Factory O.

Challinor, Taylor, Ltd., Tarentum, Pennsylvania, 1884-1894.

Columbia Glass Company, Findlay, Ohio, 1886; incorporated into U.S. Glass Company in 1891 as Factory J.

Consolidated Lamp & Glass Company, Pittsburgh and Coraopolis, Pennsylvania, 1894.

Co-Operative Flint Glass Company, Beaver Falls, Pennsylvania, 1889.

*Crystal Glass Company, Pittsburgh, 1868; later moved to Bridgeport, Ohio, in 1882.

Craig & Ritchie, Wheeling, West Virginia, 1824 or 1826—said to be the first plant in the U.S. for pressing glass. Before Sandwich on Cape Cod.

R. B. Curling & Sons (originally called Curling, Price & Company), Pittsburgh, 1827.

Dalzell, Gilmore & Leighton Company, Findlay, Ohio, 1888.

Diders, McGee, Brilliant, Ohio, date unknown.

Dithridge & Company, Pittsburgh, 1860s; also a factory at Martins Ferry, Ohio.

Doyle & Company, Pittsburgh, 1866; purchased by Phoenix Glass Company, Phillipsburgh, New Jersey, in the early 1880s. In 1891, firm was purchased by U.S. Glass Company, known as Factory P.

Dugan Class Company, Indiana, Pennsylvania, in 1892 (originally known as Indiana Glass Company).

*George Duncan & Sons, Pittsburgh, 1874; George A. Duncan & Sons, Washington, Pennsylvania, 1894; Duncan & Heisey Company, 1886-1889, Pittsburgh; Duncan & Miller Glass Company, Washington, Pennsylvania, 1870s—U.S. Glass Company's Factory D.

East Liverpool Glass Company, East Liverpool, Ohio, 1882.

Elson Glass Company, Martins Ferry, Ohio, 1882.

Enterprise Glass Works, Ravenna, Ohio, 1878.

Fenton Art Glass Company, Martins Ferry, Ohio, 1906; factory moved to present location in Williamstown, West Virginia, in 1906. The firm is still in business.

Findlay Flint Glass Company, Findlay, Ohio, 1888.

Fort Pitt Glass Works—better known as Dithridge & Company.

Fostoria Glass Company, Fostoria, Ohio, 1887; the factory was moved to Moundsville, West Virginia, in 1891, and is still in operation today.

Franklin Flint Glass Company, Philadelphia, 1861.

Gillinder & Bennett, Philadelphia, 1863.

*Gillinder & Sons, Philadelphia, 1867; later sold to U.S. Glass Company and named Factory G.

Graham Glass Works, Brilliant, Ohio, 1895.

Greensburg Glass Company, Greensburg, Pennsylvania, 1889 (previously operated as Brilliant Glass Works, Brilliant, Ohio).

A. H. Heisey Glass Company, Newark, Ohio, 1895.

Hemingray Glass Company, Cincinnati, Ohio, and Covington, Kentucky, founded in Cincinnati around 1848.

Hipkins Novelty Mold Shop, Martins Ferry, Ohio, 1884.

*Hobbs, Brockunier & Company, Wheeling, West Virginia, 1863; factory known as J. H Hobbs Glass Company. Taken over by U.S. Glass Company in 1891, calling their new acquisition Factory H.

Homestead Glass Works, Pittsburgh, 1879.

Huntington Glass Company, Huntington, West Virginia, 1891. Originally called Central City until incorporated as Huntington in 1909.

C. Ihmsen & Company, Pittsburgh, 1850s.

Imperial Glass Company, Bellaire, Ohio, 1901. Still in business today.

Indiana Glass Company, Dunkirk, Indiana, 1897. Joined National Glass Company merger in 1899.

Indiana Tumbler & Goblet Company, Greentown, Indiana, 1894. In 1899, firm merged with nineteen other factories to become National Glass Company.

Jefferson Glass Company, Steubenville, Ohio, 1901; moved to Follansbee, West Virginia, in 1907.

Jenkins Glass Company, Greentown, Indiana, 1894.

Jersey Glass Company, Jersey City, New Jersey, 1825.

Jones, Cavitt & Company, Pittsburgh, 1884.

*Keystone Tumbler Works, Rochester, Pennsylvania, 1897.

King Glass Company, Pittsburgh, 1880. This firm was absorbed into the U.S. Glass Company in 1891, thereafter known as Factory K.

King, Son & Company, Pittsburgh, 1869.

Kokomo Glass Company, Kokomo, Indiana, 1899. It was destroyed by fire but rebuilt in 1906 as the D. C. Jenkins Glass Company.

*LaBelle Glass Company, Bridgeport, Ohio, 1872.

Lancaster Glass Company, Lancaster, Ohio, 1915.

McKee & Brothers Glass Works, Pittsburgh, 1853-1888. Moved to Jeannette, Pennsylvania; known as McKee-Jeannette Glass Works, 1889-1908. Called McKee Glass Company from 1908-1951, when purchased by Thatcher Glass Manufacturing Company. Now owned by Jeannette Glass Company.

Model Flint Glass Company, Findlay, Ohio, 1888.

Mosaic Glass Company, Fostoria, Ohio, 1887.

Muhleman Glass Works, LaBelle, Ohio, 1888.

National Glass Company, Bellaire, Ohio, 1877. Not bthe aNational Glass Company.

National Glass Company, Cambridge, Ohio, 1901 (also called Cambridge Glass Company).

New Brighton Glass Company, New Brighton, Pennsylvania, 1884. Originally known as American Ferroline Company.

*New England Glass Company, Cambridge, Massachusetts, early 1800s. Later New England Glass Works.

Nickel Plate Glass Company, Fostoria, Ohio, 1888. Joined the U.S. Glass Company in 1891, becoming their Factory N.

Northwood: Union Glass Works, Martins Ferry, Ohio, 1887; Elwood City, Pennsylvania, 1890; Indiana, Pennyslvania, 1895; Wheeling, West Virginia, 1901 (this factory is probably where he made most of his Carnival Glass.)

Novelty Glass Company, LaGrange, Ohio, 1880; later became U.S. Glass Company's Factory T.

* O'Hara Glass Company, 1848. Joined U.S. Glass Company in 1891 as Factory L.

Ohio Flint Glass Company, Lancaster, Ohio, 1899. Soon merged with the National Glass Company—out of these combines emerged today's giant Anchor-Hocking Glass Company.

Oriental Glass Company, Pittsburgh, early 1890s.

Phoenix Glass Company, Monaca, Pennsylvania, 1880.

Pioneer Glass Company, Pittsburgh, 1891.

Portland Glass Company, Portland, Maine, 1864.

* Richards & Hartley Glass Company, Tarentum, Pennsylvania, 1884-1893.

* Ripley & Company, Pittsburgh, 1866; joined U.S. Glass Company in 1891 as Factory F.

Riverside Glass Company, Wellsburgh, West Virginia, 1879.

Robinson Glass Company, Zanesville, Ohio, 1893.

* Rochester Tumbler Company, Rochester, Pennsylvania, 1872.

Steiner Glass Company, Buckhannon, West Virginia, 1870s.

Tarentum Glass Company, Tarentum, Pennsylvania, 1894-1918.

Thompson Glass Company, Uniontown, Pennsylvania, 1889.

* Union Glass Company, Somerville, Massachusetts, 1851.

United States Glass Company, 1891 (see Factories A-T).

Specialty Glass Company, East Liverpool, Ohio, 1889.

West Virginia Glass Company, Martins Ferry, Ohio, 1861.

Westmoreland Glass Company, during World War I.

Westmoreland Specialty Company, early 1890s.

Windsor Glass Company, Pittsburgh, 1887.

Whitla Glass Company, Beaver Falls, Pennsylvania, 1887. In 1890 the company reorganized as Valley Glass Company.

NOTE: There were probably many other glass companies, but as some stayed in business less than a year. Since many never published a catalog or advertised their products in newspapers, etc., the above list gives a fairly comprehensive list of the "better known" producers of pressed glass in the United States from 1824 until the early 1900s.

Index